European Art and the Wider World
1350–1550

European Art and the Wider World 1350–1550

Edited by Kathleen Christian and Leah R. Clark

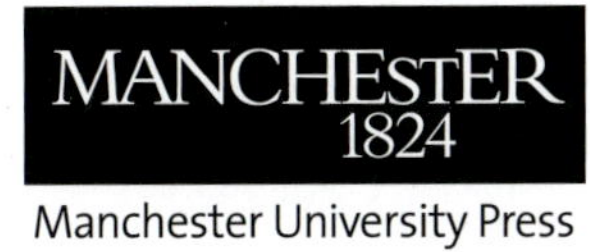

Manchester University Press

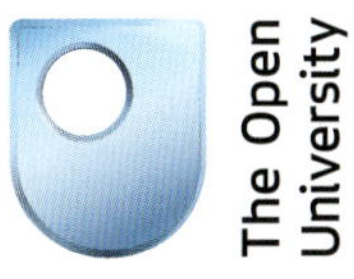

The Open University

Published by Manchester University Press
Altrincham Street, Manchester M1 7JA
www.manchesteruniversitypress.co.uk

in association with

The Open University, Walton Hall, Milton Keynes MK7 6AA
www.open.ac.uk

First published 2017

This publication forms part of the Open University module *Art and its global histories*
(A344). Details of this and other Open University modules can be obtained from
Student Recruitment, The Open University, PO Box 197, Milton Keynes MK7 6BJ,
United Kingdom (tel. +44 (0)300 303 5303; email general-enquiries@open.ac.uk).

Edited and designed by The Open University
Typeset by The Open University

Printed in the United Kingdom by The Westdale Press Limited, Cardiff.

British Library Cataloguing-in-Publication Data
A catalogue record for this book is available from the British Library

Library of Congress Cataloging-in-Publication Data applied for

ISBN 978 1 5261 2290 2 (paperback)
ISBN 978 1 5261 2291 9 (ebook)

Contents

Preface

This is the first of four books in the series *Art and its Global Histories*, which together form the main texts of an Open University Level 3 module of the same name. Each book is also designed to be read independently by the general reader. The series as a whole offers an accessible introduction to the ways in which the history of Western art from the fourteenth century to the present day has been bound up with cross-cultural exchanges and global forces.

Each book in the series explores a distinct period of this long history, apart from the third, which focuses on the art and visual culture of the British Empire, with particular reference to India. The present book, *European Art and the Wider World 1350–1550*, examines European art and material culture in the 'age of exploration' through the lens of expanding global connections and conflicts. Chapter 4 is a revised and updated version of Paul Wood, 'Art in fifteenth-century Venice: an aesthetic of diversity', from the book *Locating Renaissance Art* produced for the Open University module *Renaissance art reconsidered* (AA315).

All of the books in the series include teaching elements. To encourage the reader to reflect on the material presented, each chapter contains short exercises in the form of questions printed in bold type. They are followed by discursive sections, the end of which is marked by ❧.

The four books in the series are:

> *European Art and the Wider World 1350–1550*, edited by Kathleen Christian and Leah R. Clark

> *Art, Commerce and Colonialism 1600–1800*, edited by Emma Barker

> *Empire and Art: British India*, edited by Renate Dohmen

> *Art after Empire: From Colonialism to Globalisation*, edited by Warren Carter.

There is also a companion reader:

> *Art and its Global Histories: A Reader*, edited by Diana Newall.

Introduction

Kathleen Christian and Leah R. Clark

This book examines select examples of European art and visual culture made between *c.*1350 and 1550, asking how art and objects from this period can be read as the products of global connections. It is concerned with the ties that joined Europe to the wider world at a time when commodities, ideas, designs and technologies circulated over long distances, crossed boundaries and travelled between cultures, with significant consequences for the visual arts. This period in European history is traditionally understood as 'the Renaissance', which is often celebrated as a high point in the European tradition, and associated with new inventions inspired by the revival of an indigenous classical past. Recently, however, the Renaissance has become globalised, as alternative readings of the art of the period take into account the interdependencies that bound Europe with the rest of the world.

It has long been recognised that the Renaissance was a time of remarkable transformation, when many genres and conventions that would come to define European art were invented or re-energised. Looking at the engraving of *Adam and Eve* by the German artist Albrecht Dürer (Plate 0.1), the artistic priorities characteristic of this era become apparent: attention to the idealised human body and the natural world, for example, or the meticulous use of shading to create the illusion of volume. Dürer's image is a print on paper made from an engraved copper plate, a technique developed in the fifteenth century which first made it possible for artists to disseminate their visual inventions widely. From Jan van Eyck's mastery of the oil painting technique, to Filippo Brunelleschi's or Leon Battista Alberti's inventive reinterpretation of antique architecture, to the landscapes of Albrecht Altdorfer in Germany, to painting on canvas and the rise of portraiture and self-portraiture, the Renaissance established new techniques and modes of visual representation that would endure for centuries.

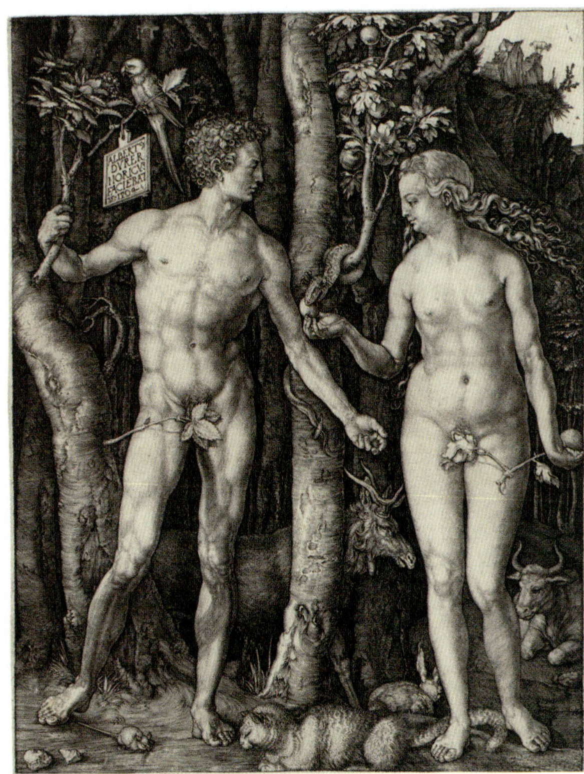

Plate 0.1 Albrecht Dürer, *Adam and Eve*, 1504, engraving, 25 × 19 cm. Rijksmuseum, Amsterdam, object number RP-P-OB-1155.

European Renaissance art favoured realism, an emphasis on the human figure, naturalism and the perspectival or illusionistic representation of pictorial space. On the surface, one might therefore have the impression that the arts of Renaissance Europe are fundamentally different and separate from contemporary visual traditions in other parts of the world. It is often mistakenly asserted, for example, that European Renaissance art is figural while Islamic art is iconoclastic or shuns all form of figural representation, when in fact there is a rich tradition of figurative representation in the Islamic secular arts. Rather than focusing on oppositions and one-to-one comparisons, however, the approach of global art history is instead to search for commonalities, interdependencies, overlaps and dialogues between Europe and the wider world. Such approaches are transforming the study of the Renaissance by recasting a period long positioned at the centre of a European canon as culturally diverse and intertwined.

On the whole, the importation of non-European art did not bring about fundamental shifts in the dominant modes of representation prevailing in Europe during this period. What did deeply affect European art, however, was the vast movement of materials, objects, ideas and technologies which circulated globally in this era. This was a time when Chinese porcelain dishes could be found in merchants' houses in Florence or on the Swahili coast of Africa;[1] when the edges of garments worn by figures of Christian saints in Italian Renaissance paintings were decorated with an imitation Arabic script (Chapter 1, Plate 1.10); and when the leading Venetian artist Gentile Bellini worked as a court painter for the Ottoman sultan Mehmed II the Conqueror (r.1444–46 and 1451–81) in Constantinople (Chapter 4, Plate 4.8). As will be explored in Chapter 2 of this book, more than 700 years of Muslim rule established a lasting tradition of Islamic crafts, art and architecture on the Iberian peninsula. These select examples underline the extent to which European visual culture is the product of multiple traditions and perspectives, to a greater degree than has been recognised in the history of art.

Throughout this period, world powers exchanged valuable goods as diplomatic gifts and Europeans imported objects from around the globe: textiles from different, sometimes very distant parts of Asia;

ivories carved in Africa for Portuguese traders; Mamluk brassware from Syria and Egypt; and featherwork from Meso-America.[2] In the Renaissance the high aesthetic and cultural value accorded to refined imported or gifted goods represents the continuation of a long-lived hierarchy, whereby many of the most prized things known in Europe were imported from Asia.[3] For Europeans the 'East' had been – since the ancient origins of the long-distance trade networks later known as the Silk Road – a source of colourful, glittering, aromatic things: silk, spices such as pepper and saffron, porcelain, jewels, ointments, perfumes and pigments.[4] Desire for these luxuries only increased in the Renaissance, and access to them was a coup that, at different points in time, gave Venice, Lisbon, Antwerp or other places vast cultural and economic advantages (Plate 0.2). Goods, technologies and ideas arrived from elsewhere, even if Europeans usually had only a vague awareness of where they had originated or how they had travelled. Significantly, what have been called the 'four great inventions' – gunpowder, paper, movable type used in printing and the compass – originated in China and passed directly to Europe through contact with the Mongols or indirectly via Islamic cultures that had adopted and developed them (Plate 0.3).[5]

Taking a global perspective on this period entails re-examining the circumstances that gave rise to the period known as the Renaissance. After the end of the ancient Roman Empire, western Europe was a loose conglomeration of different political authorities. On the periphery of the Eurasian continent, it was cut off from the vibrant, wealthy cities of the Byzantine Empire or western and central Asia, which were connected to the silk roads. Around the twelfth to the fifteenth centuries, however, Europe was catching up with those, more prosperous parts of the world. First, during what has been called the 'commercial revolution' which began in the twelfth century, there were improvements in trade, infrastructure and banking systems, as well as in industry and crafts.[6] Artisans developed an aptitude for imitating imported goods and using them as a basis for local products that could compete with the originals.[7] Then the fifteenth century brought new prosperity and further innovation in the arts and sciences, with the invention of the printing press (1440s) as well as expanded participation in global trade.[8] By the

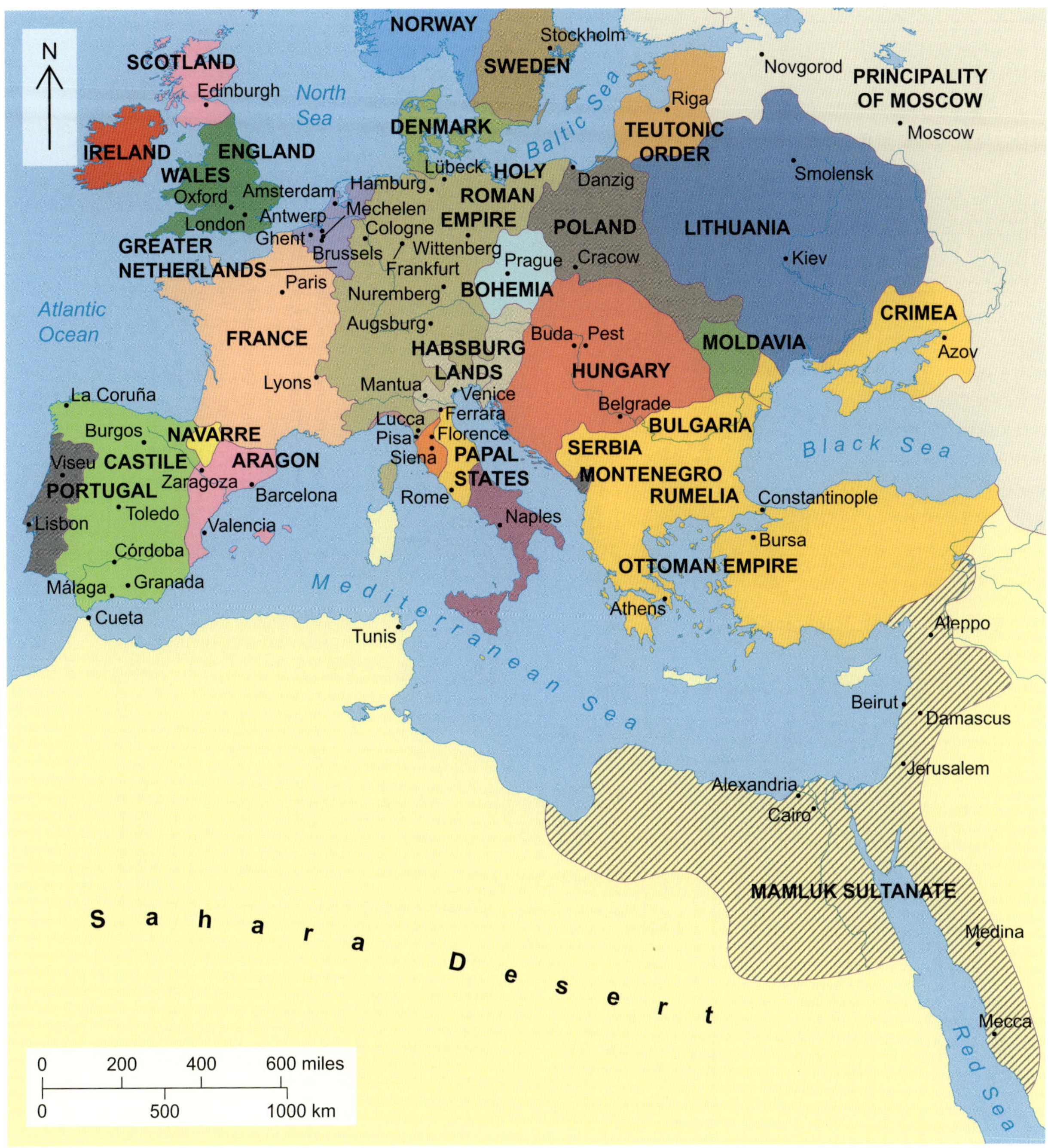

Plate 0.2 Europe *c*.1500.

end of the fifteenth century, Iberian powers claimed major victories in the global competition to control the highly profitable spice trade by navigating new overseas routes. At a time when the Mamluks and the Ottoman Empire dominated much of the Mediterranean, the Portuguese reached Asia by sailing around Africa. By 1511 they had established outposts across the west and east coasts of Africa and in Brazil, Hormuz in the Persian Gulf, Goa on the west coast of India and Malacca on the Malay Peninsula. In 1492, Columbus sailed west on behalf of Isabella I of Castile and Ferdinand II of Aragon (r.1474/75–1504) in the hopes of finding a new passage to Asia but, as was understood only later, reached a previously

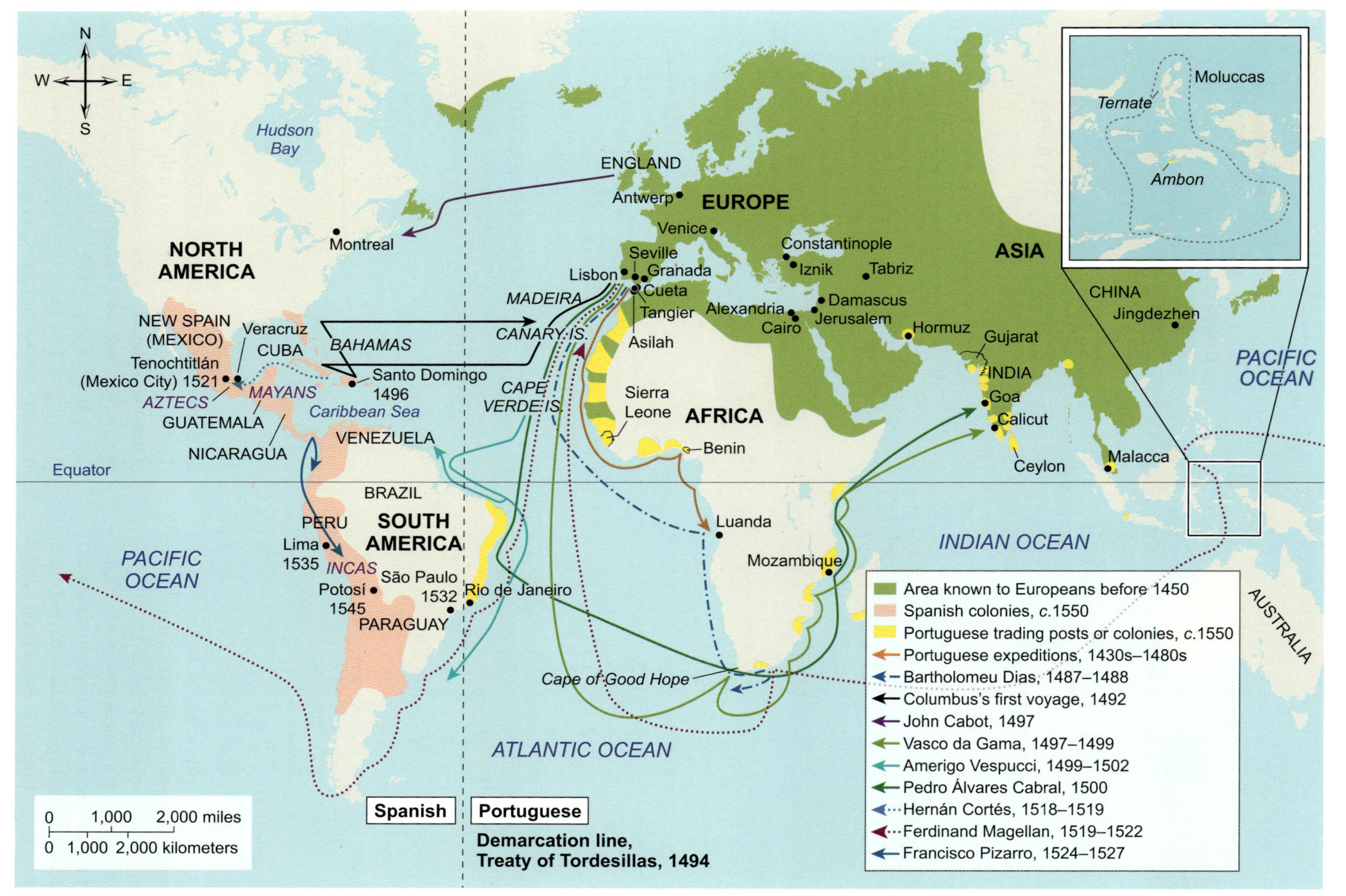

Plate 0.3 Navigation routes and areas of Spanish and Portuguese trade and colonisation c.1430–1550.

unknown continent. By skilful navigation and cartography, by means of military force, slavery and religious conversion, Europe entered into entangled relationships with the wider world. Still, Europe was not dominant on a global scale; this would only occur after *c*.1800 when western Europe became industrialised. In an earlier era, European kingdoms and states competed with many intertwined global powers, which rose and fell in rivalry for access to the same goods and resources.

Traditionally, the Renaissance has not been seen in terms of global connections, but as an isolated and uniquely European phenomenon born of a self-sustaining revival of an indigenous classical past. A concept of rebirth was already present in sixteenth-century European, particularly Italian rhetoric, as when the artist and biographer Giorgio Vasari referred to a *rinascita* (rebirth) of the arts. Yet it was only in the 1800s that the Swiss historian Jacob Burckhardt first used the term Renaissance to denote the rebirth of classical culture in Italy and the rise of individualism which, he believed, opened up new possibilities for human creativity.[9] It is important in this context to remember that the nineteenth century was a time when many European nations were colonial powers and when Europe was conceived as the most 'modern' and 'advanced' part of the globe. It post-dates what has been termed the 'great divergence', the process of division between the seventeenth and nineteenth centuries that separated western Europe from the rest of Eurasia, in terms of its industrialisation, wealth, colonial possessions and military might.[10] In the nineteenth century, the Renaissance was imagined as the highly creative, inspired period that initiated innovations in the arts and sciences, leading Europe towards global hegemony. To tell the story of the rise of the West, antiquity, Renaissance and modernity were imagined as stepping stones in a progressive path. Karl Marx closely associated the Renaissance with the birth of capitalism in western Europe, while arguing that 'Oriental despotism' supposedly kept Asia stagnant and blocked it from further advance.[11]

The nineteenth century – when the field of art history took shape – was a time of nationalism, when efforts were being made to define and celebrate national (Italian, French, Spanish, German) cultures. Art history played a significant role in this task. From the outset it conceived of separate, national artistic traditions which could influence one another or be compared side by side, yet were inherently coherent and distinct.[12] Art history established a normative point of reference – the western European nation – which gave shape to the discipline's vocabulary, institutions, canons and periodisation. Eurocentrism, colonialism and nationalism became embedded into art-historical research, museum displays, textbooks and university courses. Traditionally non-European visual culture or objects that exist between different cultures, or across cultures, fit awkwardly, at best, into this system.[13] Consider, for example, the usually strict separation of objects in museums into galleries devoted to European national schools (such as Italian, or Netherlandish), on the one hand, and the whole of Asian art or Islamic art on the other, setting up vast asymmetries and making connections very difficult to imagine.

There are many complex historical, economic and cultural factors that have kept Renaissance art isolated from a global and intercultural context. Increasingly vocal critiques have, however, questioned past assumptions, for example the classic opposition between West and East, which unreasonably balances a relatively small West against an exceedingly large and diverse East. While some art historians had been selectively engaged with dialogues between Europe and the wider world,[14] a pronounced shift occurred in the 1990s, when the 500th anniversary of Columbus's first voyage to America helped inspire a rethinking of the 'age of exploration'.[15] An important book edited by Claire Farago in 1995 broke a general silence among Renaissance art historians on 'the contribution of non-European cultures to Western aesthetics'.[16] Since then art history and other disciplines have often looked back to methods pioneered in the 1940s by the French historian and founder of the Annales School, Fernand Braudel. Braudel wrote a monumental study of the Mediterranean, which envisioned the Christian and Islamic cultures bordering it as part of a single history, given their common geography and economic codependence.[17] He followed this up with a global history of trade and commerce.[18] His work presents a model of a global, 'total history' that has offered an appealing alternative to national history. More recently post-colonial studies have expanded and added nuance to what have been called connected, crossed, braided or transcultural concepts of history. Borrowing from colonial terms used to denote racial mixing, historians and art historians have at times invoked the idea of mestizo, creole or hybrid cultures, as an alternative model to supposedly 'pure' national cultures.[19]

These discussions and methodological debates have also inspired the question of whether the Renaissance in Europe was an exceptional or unique historical event.[20] The anthropologist Jack Goody has asked in a recent book whether there were Renaissances (meaning, for him, a revival of the past that leads to cultural advance) in other parts of the world, for example in China under the Song dynasty (960–1279).[21] This book will not be concerned, however, with comparisons between European and other cultures. Instead, it will focus on the arts of Europe (western Europe as distinguished from eastern Europe and Byzantium) through the selective exploration of two themes. One is the interdependency of the world brought about by global trade during the Renaissance, allowing economic, technical and artistic achievements to emerge in Europe from crossed cultures and vivid connections. The second is the insight which images, particularly in the form of visual representations of 'the Other', offer into European cultural perceptions in this era. Europeans developed complex attitudes towards non-Christians and non-Europeans in places of coexisting cultures and religions – in the Iberian peninsula and the Mediterranean, for example – or through images and texts related to direct contacts brought about by expanded trade and exploration. The first contacts made between Europe and other parts of the globe in this era are of almost unimaginable significance. While Norsemen had explored the North Atlantic from the tenth century, European voyages to the Americas in the fifteenth ushered in a new era of interconnection between two biospheres previously separated by a great ocean. People, places and a great diversity of cultures, objects and ideas came together for the first time. In Europe, the vast majority of new encounters were not direct, but filtered through imaginative texts and images; direct and indirect knowledge of the wider world continued to be mediated by a vast inheritance of stereotypes and prejudices, myths and religious beliefs.

The four chapters that follow will consider the histories of canonical European works of art and of objects which crossed the borders of Europe, Asia, Africa and America. The topic of discussion remains the art of Europe in a book written by specialists in this field; as such its outlook on global connections in the period has its clear limitations. Interactions between Europe and the wider world were certainly not one-sided, and history can be seen from many different perspectives; historians of European art risk appropriating, even recolonising other cultures, if their terminology, methods and aesthetic canons are imposed upon other, distinctive visual traditions.[22] Aware of these challenges, the goal here has been to re-examine the subject traditionally defined as 'Art of Renaissance Europe', testing its assumptions, rediscovering the significance of the non-European and non-Christian within it, and expanding its scope. To this end, Chapter 1 focuses on the altarpiece, a major genre of Renaissance art which developed in connection with the wider world, rather than in isolation. Chapter 2 considers art in the encounter between the diverse cultures and religions of Spain – al-Andalus (the Islamic territories of what is now Spain) and the Christian kingdoms of Castile and Aragon – and between the Christian Spanish and the indigenous peoples of the New World. Chapter 3 examines European collections of non-European objects as wide ranging as Meso-American featherwork and Turkish costume to Chinese porcelain and Afro-Portuguese ivories. Chapter 4 explores Venice as the crossroads of Europe, Asia and Africa. This Italian republic was until the sixteenth century the principal European gateway for global goods, whose cultural connections can be read in the work of local painters. While Chapters 1 and 3 consider the relationship between European visual culture and imported objects – rarities and luxuries from distant parts of the globe – Chapters 2 and 4 are focused more specifically on works of art made in the contact zones of the Iberian peninsula and Venice, where diverse religions and cultures came together. Artistic encounters discussed in Chapters 1 and 3 are generally indirect, while those in Chapters 2 and 4 emerge out of situations involving cohabitation and competition or a more directly shared material and visual culture.

I Questions and debates

The topics and case studies selected for inclusion in this book emerge out of lively debates that have accelerated since the 1990s and 2000s, when numerous publications, conferences and exhibitions addressed the 'global' dimensions of European Renaissance art. The shift occurred within a time which has seen the rise of global political and economic powers outside Europe, as well as a sharpening of public debate around issues of trade, consumption and globalisation.

A significant increase of interest in 'material culture', as well, has opened up the study of objects and images that in the past were overlooked in favour of 'fine art' (painting, sculpture and architecture) and were infrequently studied in their own right.[23] Material culture in its broadest sense includes any physical traces of the past, but in this book it will generally refer to the so-called decorative arts: ceramics, textiles and objects. Refined examples of foreign craftsmanship were greatly prized and seamlessly integrated with fine art in this period. And it is in this realm that one can most clearly read the direct impact of imports from Asia, Africa and America on many different artistic, technical and commercial aspects of the European Renaissance. Objects and goods imported from around the world – or which arrived via diplomatic gift-giving – inspired admiration, imitation and creative response among European artists and craftsmen. This phenomenon has been studied particularly in the context of Italy, the most important European port of entry for global goods in the fifteenth century.[24] Of late, however, the scope of interest in Europe's globalised material culture has broadened to other parts of Europe, for example to Antwerp, which grew into a major hub of global trade in the first half of the sixteenth century, or to Portugal and particularly Lisbon, which from the end of the fifteenth century rapidly emerged as the centre of a vast commercial empire and colonial enterprise.[25]

Numerous museum exhibitions have begun to showcase objects and works of art which speak of the interconnected relationships that bound Europe together with the wider world.[26] The exhibition *Bellini and the East* (2005–06), for example, joined a number of groundbreaking studies on the relationship between the Ottoman Empire and Venice.[27] Within the field of

Italian Renaissance art history, Venice – given its close political and economic ties with the Mamluk Sultanate and Ottoman Empire – was the first point of departure for discussions about cultural exchange. The topic was brought to the fore in Deborah Howard's book, *Venice and the East* (2000), on the impact of the Islamic world on Venetian architecture.[28] Since then historians and art historians have continued to focus attention on the relationship between the Ottoman Empire and Europe, arguing for example that the Ottomans should be considered not as an entity posited against Europe, but as an integral part of Renaissance history and art history.[29] Others have stressed the common cultural heritage of the Mediterranean and the ethnic, linguistic, religious and political diversity that constitutes its very identity.[30] It has become increasingly clear, however, that Europe's global connections stretched far beyond the Mediterranean, and attention has also turned to other networks and nodes of trade such as the Indian Ocean, the Baltic Sea and the Persian Gulf.

While recent approaches are by no means singular or congruent, all of them have sought alternatives to the histories of nations or monolithic, isolated cultures. Attention is given instead to the complexity of cultural relationships, as well as to the inequalities built into these relationships, which in some cases make terms such as 'cultural encounter' or 'cultural exchange' seem too neutral, simple or benign. Among the concepts that are now widely used, though still much debated, are 'cultural transfer' and 'hybridity'.

Cultural transfer was a concept developed in the 1980s to break down the rigid separation of national histories and the historical model of comparing cultures one to one, stressing instead cross-cultural communication and shared ideas, travel and a sense of mutual curiosity.[31] It describes something more than the simple movement of objects, ideas or technologies from one place to another, but instead focuses on how, why and under what conditions cultural goods cross boundaries and acquire new identities.[32] To take an example, paper was invented in China, likely by the second century BCE. After it was adopted and perfected by Islamic cultures in central Asia, it reached Islamic North Africa and Spain, where artists began to use it to make patterns, draw sketches or create illustrated books. During the eleventh and twelfth centuries, paper was transferred from Islamic to Christian Europe. It then brought about revolutionary cultural change when in the 1450s Johannes Gutenberg first began to print books on paper with his printing press.[33] It became, furthermore, an important agent of artistic innovation, as reproductive images printed on paper vastly increased the movement of visual ideas around the world. It was also only by means of extensive drawing on paper that Leonardo da Vinci developed scientific inventions and devised carefully planned, harmonious compositions out of interlocking ideal geometric shapes.

These examples illustrate one of the themes that will be explored throughout this book: as technologies, ideas and images travelled from place to place, they underwent change, cultural transfer and repurposing, often leading to innovation and creative insight. This was the case when objects – textiles, glass, ceramics and metalwork – moved from one place to another, often across great distances, acquiring complex histories of reception and imitation in multiple contexts.[34] For instance, European altarpieces (Chapter 1, Plate 1.14) often included images of oriental carpets at the foot of the Virgin Mary's throne. Although Western artists painted these objects realistically, after closely observing imported rugs, 'the oriental rug' did not simply move intact from one culture to another. Instead, each step along the way brought about shifts in meaning and purpose. In this case, European artists, who probably would not have known exactly where oriental carpets came from, responded to them imaginatively; they depicted them in paint using European artistic techniques of illusionism, perspective and realism, inserting them into a framework of Christian symbolism that was meaningful in a new context, but entirely alien to their culture of origin.

Another concept employed in this book is hybridity, a term developed in post-colonial studies to describe the mixed nature of global relationships. Originally used in biology to describe the combination of two species of plants or animals to produce a new specimen, it was then employed in a derogatory sense during the colonial period to refer to miscegenation or the mixing of the white races (the coloniser) with the dark-skinned (the colonised). It was then famously used in the work of Homi Bhabha to reflect the interdependence of coloniser and colonised and to underline that there is no 'pure' racial or national identity.[35] More recently, it has been applied to cultural artefacts, from texts to works of art. For instance, Meso-Americans were asked by Spanish missionaries attempting to convert them to Christianity to use their indigenous art of featherwork to portray Christian subjects.[36] A famous example of featherwork depicts the Christian subject of the *Mass of Saint Gregory* and was made for Pope Paul III (r.1534–49) (Chapter 2, Plate 2.23). The quality and skill of the work was even used by Europeans as a gauge of the 'humanity' of the craftsmen who had made it. These hybrid objects thus emerge out of a process whereby two artistic traditions conjoin, emerging out of an interdependent, though starkly unequal, relationship between coloniser and the colonised.

The discussion above has only briefly and selectively introduced new challenges to the field of Renaissance art history. Even the question of how to refer to or define the chronological boundaries of this period remains unresolved, and 'early modern' is sometimes used to avoid the outmoded concepts that the term 'Renaissance' still carries with it. Jerry Brotton has employed the term 'global Renaissance', preserving the traditional term for the period as a point of entry to challenge its precepts and expand its scope.[37] Others have questioned the timespan usually associated with the Renaissance, *c.*1400–1600: from a global perspective, on the one hand, *c.*1400 seems too late, since it excludes the very long history of global exchange that came before it. On the other hand, the term 'first global age' has been used to refer to a longer period, *c.*1400–1800, when exploration gave way to large-scale global interaction. This book begins in the fourteenth century to recognise the impact of Eurasian trade at that time. It does not use the word Renaissance since the focus is not on unpacking the concept, but on the two themes introduced above, which will now be discussed in more detail: global connections brought about by travel and trade, and the visual arts of Christian Europe as a mediator of imagined ideas about the wider world.

2 Trade and travelling objects

The connected world of the fifteenth and sixteenth centuries was, as has been mentioned, very long in the making. Since antiquity, silks, spices and other goods had travelled from different parts of the Asian continent into Europe.[38] Their demand and supply intensified with the emergence of prosperous and sophisticated cites in Islamic western and central Asia: long-distance trade supplied these global entrepôts with desirable commodities from sub-Saharan Africa, India, Indonesia and China. Thus in the ninth century, Europeans could only envy the splendour of Abbasid Baghdad when its caliph, Harun al-Rashid (r.786–809), sent stunning diplomatic gifts to the Holy Roman Emperor Charlemagne (r.768–814), including silk textiles, spices, medicines, balsams, perfumes, monkeys and even an elephant.[39]

This list of gifts epitomises the wealth and sophistication of urban capitals in Asia at a time when Europe remained, by comparison, barren and provincial. A powerful and enduring European fantasy image of 'the East' – a vaguely understood, ill-defined geographic expanse that was considered a place of luxury and wealth – developed out of this disparity. Europe's access to these riches improved, however, from the time of the Crusades in the eleventh century, when rival European trading powers – notably, the merchant mariner cites of Pisa, Genoa and Venice – fought competitively among one another to claim their share of the East and its wealth. During the Crusades, Europe entered the eastern Mediterranean, establishing an important model for the future of overseas colonisation and ushering in a new era of prosperity and cultural revival.[40]

In the thirteenth and fourteenth centuries a temporary period of unity across the Eurasian continent facilitated European participation in global trade. In the early thirteenth century, the descendants of Genghis Khan (r.1206–27) took control of China, and within decades almost all of Asia was brought together under loosely allied khanates – kingdoms ruled by Genghis's descendants – creating what is called the 'Pax Mongolica'.[41] Over the next century the khanates opened up trade and diplomacy with foreigners and promoted cross-cultural fertilisation in the craft industries across Asia, bringing about rapid

innovations through the movement of luxury goods from place to place, notably textiles.[42] During this time, European travellers and merchants were able to cross all of Asia; a journey from Venice to China in the 1260s is famously described by the Venetian Marco Polo, even if his account is largely, if not wholly, fictitious.[43] His traveller's tale evokes bustling hubs of trade such as Tabriz, the glittering capital of the Il-Khanid dynasty and a 'market for merchandise from India and Baghdad, from Mosul and Hormuz ... [where] Latin merchants come'.[44]

The Pax Mongolica began to collapse in the mid-fourteenth century, and direct travel and trade between Europe and Asia were further curtailed by the rise of the Ottoman Empire and its expansion westward. Sultan Mehmed II brought about the final conquest of the former Byzantine Empire and, in 1453, its capital Constantinople. In the aftermath of this momentous event, trade formerly conducted through Byzantium and the Black Sea was all but blocked to Europeans. By the end of the fifteenth century, Mamluk Alexandria in Egypt had emerged as a fulcrum between Venice and India, a key trading partner of the Mamluks and a source of goods from China and the rest of Asia.[45] Iberian monarchs, however, mounted a direct challenge to the Venetian–Mamluk trading axis. The kings of Portugal initiated a new era of overseas expansion and colonisation in 1415, when they captured Ceuta on the north coast of Morocco. Then, under the sponsorship of Prince Henry the Navigator (1394–1460), further raids, conquests and commercial alliances extended Portugal's influence on the west coast of Africa, where they traded in gold and African slaves.[46] Eventually, Vasco da Gama navigated the Cape of Good Hope, reaching the Persian Gulf and finally Calicut in 1498, causing panic among Portugal's rivals in the Mediterranean.[47]

It was probably by accident, on his way to India in 1500, that the Portuguese explorer Pedro Álvares Cabral landed in Brazil. He could claim it for the Portuguese since it lay to the east of an imaginary line established by the Treaty of Tordesillas, negotiated between the rival kingdoms of Castile and Portugal in 1494 to divide new discoveries between them. This line is shown in the Cantino Planisphere of 1502 (Plate 0.4), which

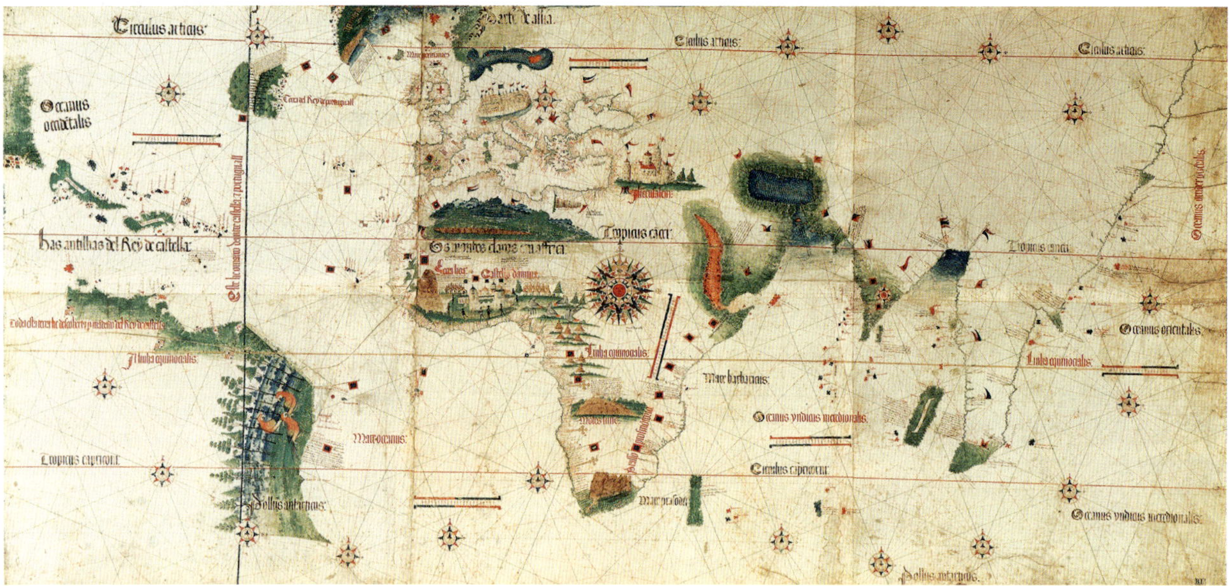

Plate 0.4 Cantino Planisphere, showing the line of the Treaty of Tordesillas and explorations to Central America, Newfoundland, India and Brazil, 1502. Biblioteca Estense, Modena. Photo: © DEA PICTURE LIBRARY/age fotostock.

an Italian duke covertly obtained from a Portuguese cartographer at a time when navigational knowledge was a valuable state secret. Here the coastlines of Brazil, Africa and Asia, even Ceylon (Sri Lanka), which the Portuguese reached only in 1506, are shown emerging into European consciousness. Captions on the map give details of international trade networks, noting for example the cloves, sandalwood, ivory, precious stones, pearls and porcelain available on the Malay Peninsula. By 1511, the Portuguese were already trading there; by the 1520s they were in China and by 1543 in Japan.[48]

Portugal's rivals, the Catholic Monarchs of Castile and Aragon, attempted to reach Asia by sailing west, with the voyages of the Italian Christopher Columbus they sponsored from 1492; in the sixteenth century the era of the conquistadores saw the Spanish conquest of the Aztec Empire in Mexico (from 1517) and the Inca Empire in Peru (from 1532). The dramatic coming together of Europe and the Americas set in motion the 'Columbian exchange', the back and forth movement of people, technology, agriculture and diseases that transformed the history of the globe, vastly expanded African slavery and, ultimately, decimated the population of the Americas.

Around the time of the Pax Mongolica, European centres – in dialogue with and in imitation of the sort of goods that had been imported via long-distance trade – improved their own production of commodities, luxuries and crafts. In the process, Europe began to compete more successfully in global markets. By the fourteenth century, Flemish textiles made with English wool were being exported to Syria,[49] while the Venetians were producing enamelled glasswork using techniques that had originated in the Islamic world. Spanish and Italian potters imitated Islamic lustreware (ceramics with an iridescent glaze), and in the sixteenth century the Genoese became successful producers of blue-and-white maiolica, a less expensive alternative to Chinese porcelain.[50] Whereas previously, luxury textiles had been overwhelmingly imported from Asia, by the sixteenth century, European fabrics were in demand in Ottoman markets: at that time, Ottoman kaftans could be made from European cloth, such as one possibly made for the sultan which is still preserved in the Topkapı Palace (Plate 0.5).[51] The kaftan can be compared to what seems its twin, the sumptuous silk, velvet and gold dress worn by the Duchess of Florence Eleonora di Toledo in her portrait with her son Giovanni, painted by Bronzino (Plate 0.6).[52]

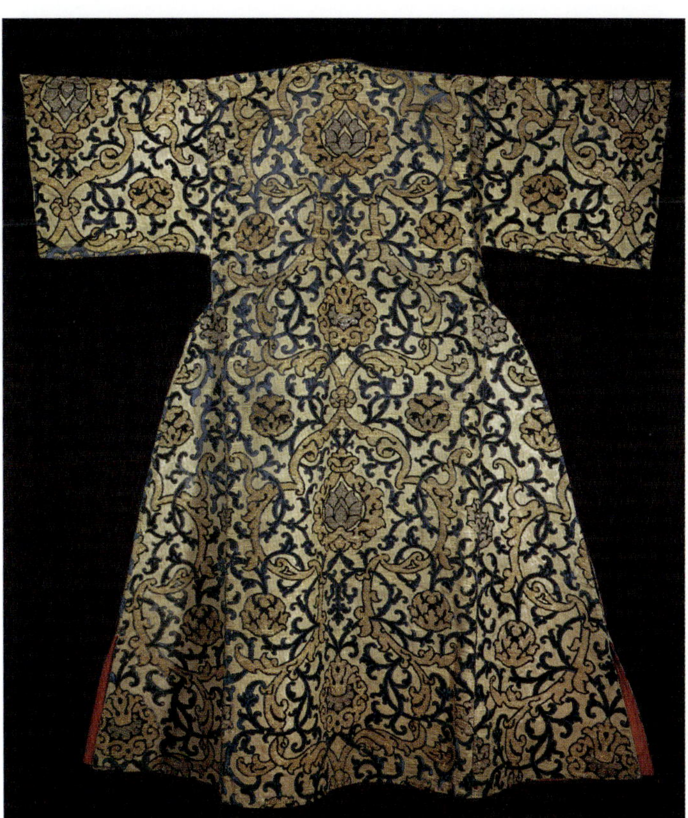

Plate 0.5 Ottoman kaftan made of European cloth, seventeenth century, velvet stitches on gold cloth with blue velvet decoration and stylised lotus pattern. Topkapı Palace, Istanbul, inv. 12/360 vs. Photo: Banri Namikawa.

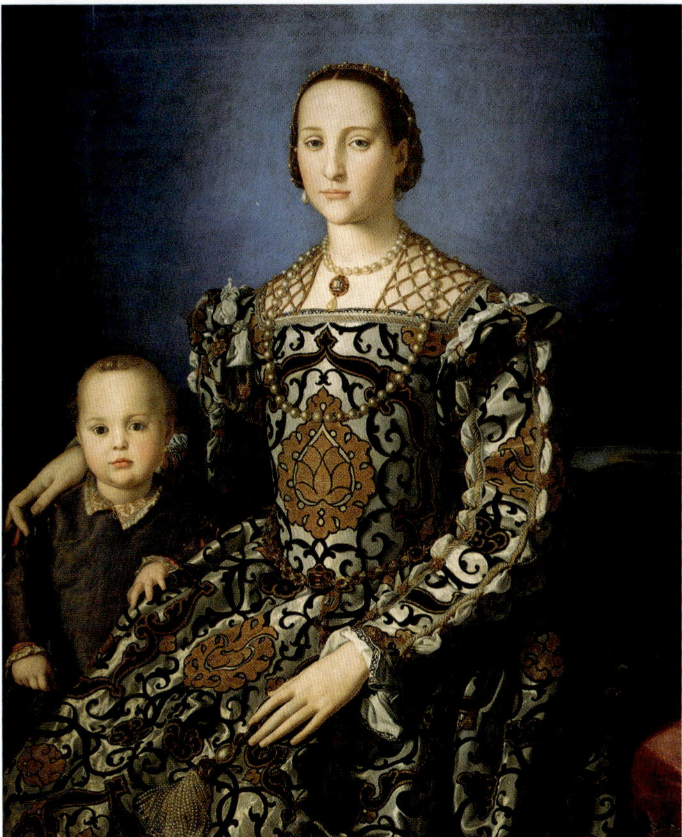

Plate 0.6 Agnolo Bronzino, *Portrait of Eleanor of Toledo and her Son Giovanni de Medici*, c.1545, oil on panel, 115 × 96 cm. Uffizi Gallery, Florence. © 2017. Photo: Scala, Florence – courtesy of the Ministero dei Beni e delle Attività Culturali.

3 Imagining the world

Looking back on this period from the present, the profit motives that drove global trade or consumers' desire for objects of great beauty and rarity seem easy enough to grasp. Much more difficult to access are attitudes, perceptions, hostilities and stereotypes that connected and divided cultures and religions in this era. The close analysis of images, however, offers one of the most significant and expressive points of entry into such issues. It is important to remember that in Europe and elsewhere this was not a time of tolerance, cultural relativism or secularism. Violence and deep-set mistrust of the Other were long ingrained in European culture and extended into the wider world as well. Travel and direct encounter were rare and, as was mentioned, popular perceptions drew imaginatively upon convention, misinformation, biblical or classical history, or details from highly embellished 'travel' literature.

Europeans' understanding of the world's geography was also culturally conditioned. Europe and Asia were not naturally separated by any geographic boundary. Yet, according to a classical tradition articulated by the Greek historian Herodotus, they were two of three separate regions of the globe – Europe, Asia and Africa – all encircled by a great ocean. Such a conception continued in the medieval Christian era, as seen in so-called T-O maps: the T is formed by the waters of the Mediterranean, Nile and the Don (a river in Russia that the ancient Greeks understood as the border between Europe and Asia), while the O is the Ocean surrounding them. Asia occupies one half of the world, Europe and Africa the other half and Jerusalem, Christianity's spiritual home, is usually positioned at the centre of the T.[53] One splendid example comes from a fifteenth-century history of the world presented to the Duke of Burgundy (Plate 0.7). While Asia is shown as twice the size of the other regions, there is little sense in this image that any one place or people is superior to the others, and the parts of the world appear harmonious and unified.

The borders of Asia, Africa and Europe were porous in classical and early medieval perception. Alexander the Great's empire had spread far into Asia, and the Roman Empire had brought together western and eastern Europe, North Africa and the Middle East. After Christianity was adopted in the Roman Empire from the

fourth century CE, it was not only a European religion.[54] Instead, it was spread throughout the world and its origins and spiritual centre were located in the Levant, rather than Europe. It was only with the birth of Islam in the seventh century and its rapid spread into the Middle East, North Africa, Spain and Sicily, that Christianity became more specifically European.

In its early history, Islam spread not only by means of military conquest, but also through alliances and policies that encouraged religious tolerance.[55] It came into more direct conflict and opposition with Christianity, however, between the eleventh and the fifteenth centuries, when Europeans launched a series of Crusades to try to win back Jerusalem and the Holy Land. With the failure of the Crusades, Christianity was overwhelmingly centred in Europe and disconnected from the Christian communities remaining in Asia and Africa. The conflict with Islam brought a greater sense of coherency and unity to Christian Europe and its conception of the wider world: having been pushed back, the Church developed a universalist approach aimed at spreading Christianity to all of Europe, to the Holy Land and to the rest of humanity.[56] In the fifteenth century, the discovery of America seemed to confirm the necessity of expanding both the Christian religion and European civilisation in all directions; it also seemed to put Europe at the centre of the world rather than its western edge.

In the T-O map examined earlier, the three continents are associated with Ham, Japheth and Shem, the three sons of Noah. According to the Book of Genesis, after the Great Flood wiped away the rest of humanity, only Noah and his sons were left to repopulate the earth. Ham, according to the passage, shamed his father, and Noah cursed Ham's son Canaan, condemning him to be the servant of Japheth and Shem.[57] In the T-O map, the three continents are each associated with a different son: Ham was thought to have populated Africa, Japheth Europe and Shem Asia. There is little sense that Ham and his descendants are inferior to Japheth or Shem, despite the curse described in Genesis. The image reflects the belief that all descendants of Noah – Christians, Jews and Muslims – share a common ancestry. It was thought that the sons of Noah, all followers of Abrahamic religions and all monotheistic, could be collectively termed 'people of the book', in recognition that all of

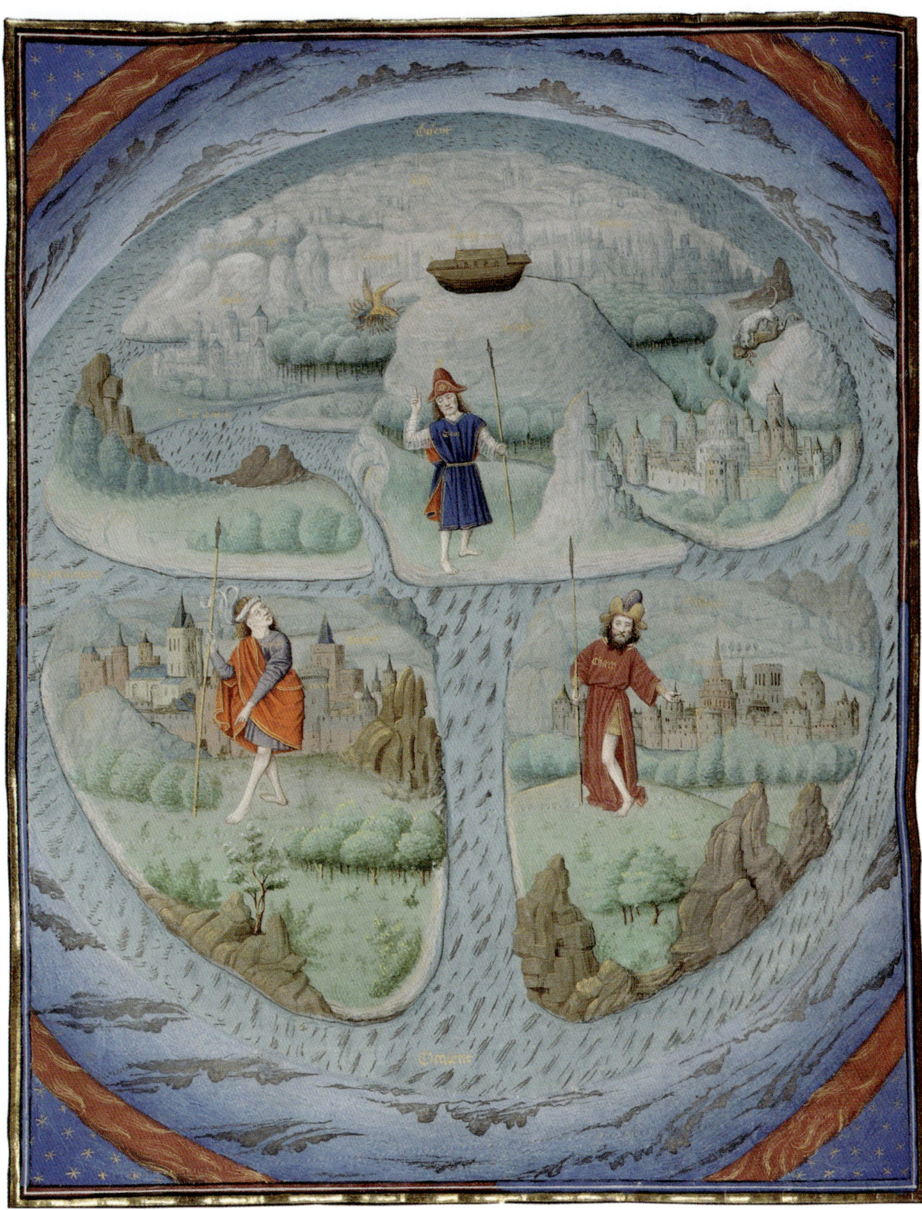

Plate 0.7 Master of Mansel, T-O map with Shem in Asia (top), Japheth in Europe (bottom left) and Ham in Africa (bottom right), in Jean Mansel, *La fleur des histoires*, c.1459–63. Royal Library of Belgium, Brussels, Ms 9231 f° 281v° figure 6. Used with permission.

these religions were in possession of a sacred scripture, and that these scriptures shared certain commonalities.

While to some extent a sense of common heritage gave these religions a shared identity, it also fostered the sense among Christians that Judaism and Islam were distortions and betrayals of the one, 'true' faith. Non-Christians in Europe and beyond were widely vilified and demonised: the thirteenth century has been identified as a turning point in this regard, when heresy and blasphemy were stamped out in dramatic campaigns and restrictions imposed against Jews, including the forced wearing of badges.[58] A distancing of the Other can be traced in European images of the time, as a range of visual stereotypes emerged to express degrees of difference from a European norm, measured in terms of physical oddities and deformities, or darker skin colour.[59] Slavery had been a long-standing practice in Europe, yet the fifteenth-century trade in African slaves could rely upon European perceptions of dark skin which were largely negative. Writers at the time began to 'justify' the slave trade in Africa with reference to the writings of Aristotle, as well, now, to the notion that Canaan's descendants had been cursed and therefore condemned to servitude.[60]

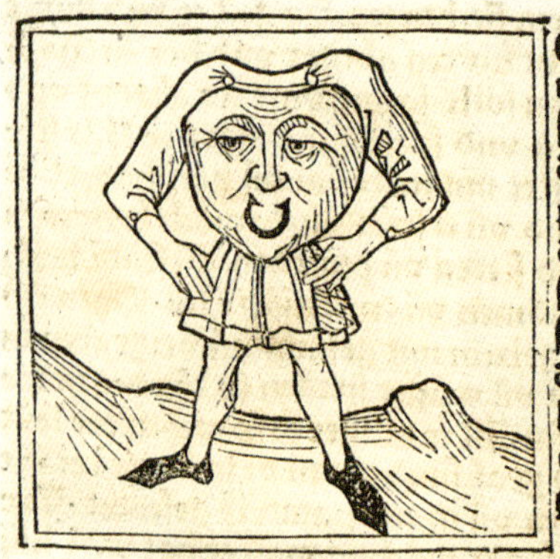

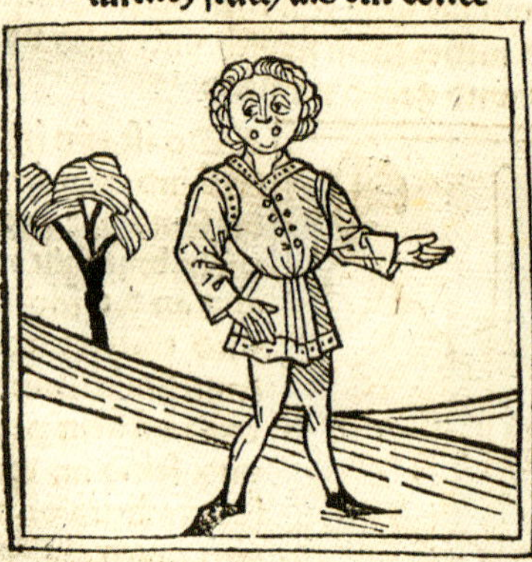

Plate 0.8 Headless man and man without mouth, in John Mandeville, *Das buch des ritters herr hannsen von monte villa*, translation by Michel Velser, Augsburg, 1482. Bayerische Staatsbibliothek München, 2 Inc.c.a. 1083, fol. 69r.

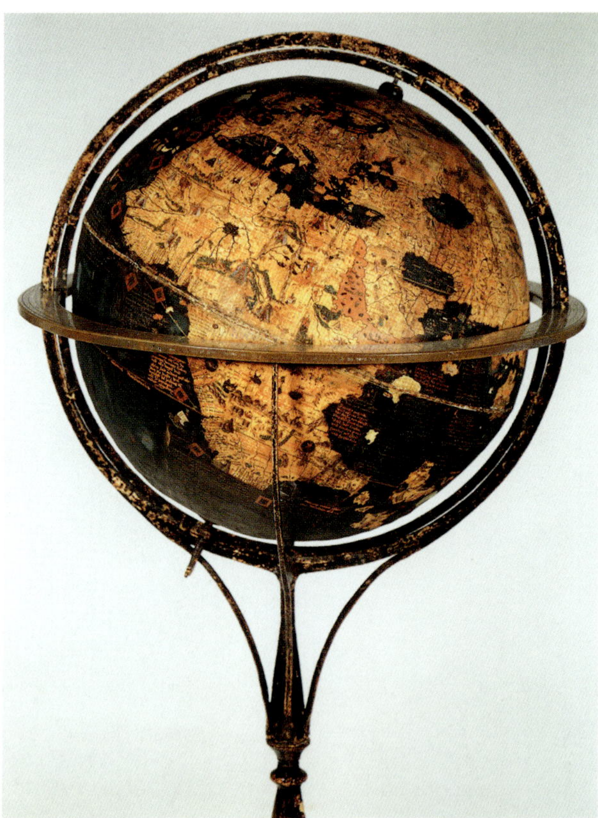

Plate 0.9 Martin Behaim, with Georg Glockendon, Erdapfel (Africa), 1492–94. Germanisches Nationalmuseum, Nuremberg, Inv.No.: 1826 WI. Photo: © Germanisches Nationalmuseum.

European aggression and conquest in the 'age of exploration' were closely bound up with conversion: 1492 was the year when Columbus reached America and also, on the Iberian peninsula, the year when the last Muslim stronghold was defeated and an edict issued mandating the conversion or expulsion of all Jews. The conversion of Muslims and other non-Christians, many believed, was necessary to bring about the Apocalypse, or the second coming of Christ, which was widely expected to happen in the year 1500.

Another important aspect of the European concept of the Other was an antique belief, carried over without cessation to the Renaissance, in 'monstrous' peoples: it was thought that climate had an effect on physical appearance and moral character[61] and that monstrous, grotesque beings such as satyrs, one-eyed cyclopes or men with the heads of dogs inhabited the harshest, most extreme parts of the world.[62] This vivid visual and textual tradition fed into an imagery of deformed or monstrous Others, whether Muslims, Jews or peoples in distant parts of the world.[63] Marco Polo's diary, and the popular *Travels of Sir John Mandeville*, a fourteenth-century text by an author whose identity is still contested, report on the discovery of grotesque beings in different parts of Asia. Illustrations to Mandeville's text popularised the imagery of these bizarre people in distant places, as seen in woodcuts depicting the beings who inhabited certain unnamed islands in the East (Plate 0.8).[64] Even the earliest surviving terrestrial globe, Martin Behaim's Erdapfel made in Nuremberg in 1492–94 for a group of southern German merchants tempted by the commercial potential of overseas trade (Plate 0.9), is annotated throughout with notes on the monstrous peoples of the world. Belief in their existence was so ingrained that when Columbus was in the Caribbean islands, he expected to find

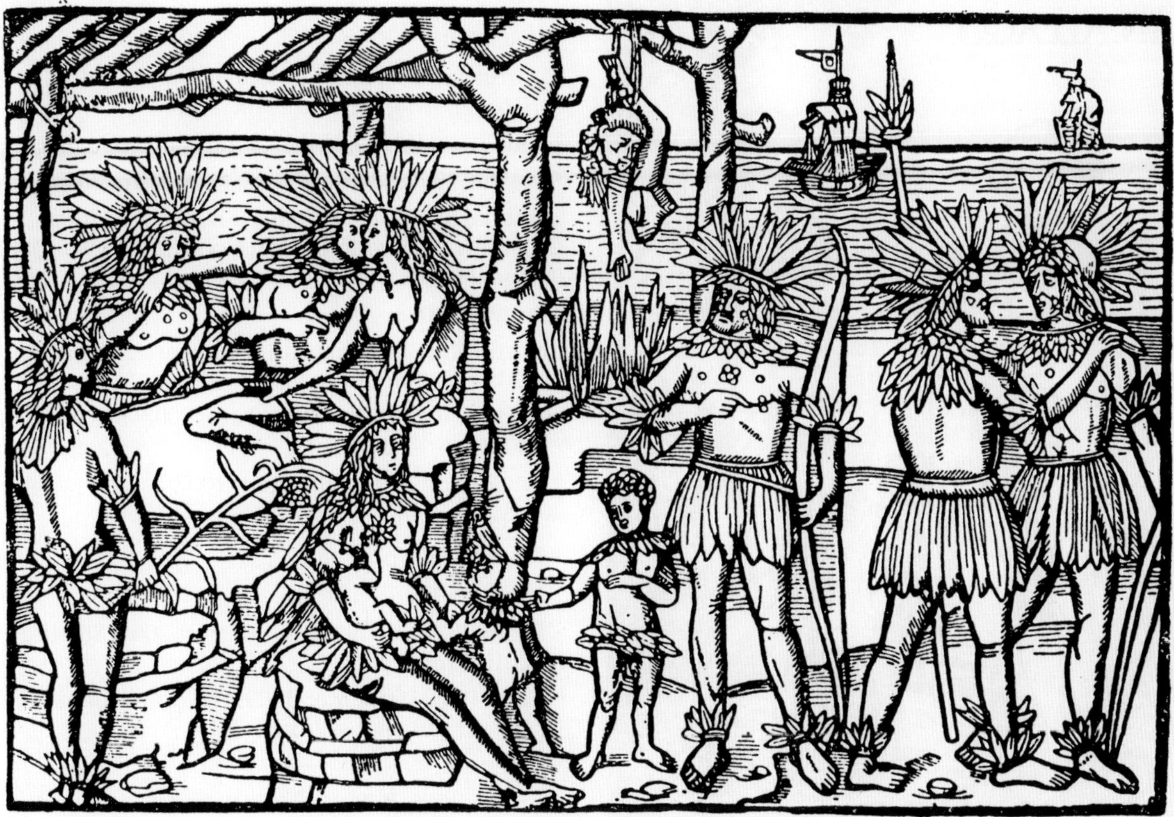

Plate 0.10 Johann Froschauer, *Cannibals*, c.1505, woodcut. Based on a description of Brazilian Tupinambá in a German translation of a letter by Amerigo Vespucci. Photo: © akg-images.

them and showed drawings of dog-headed men to those he encountered in the hopes of locating such creatures.[65] The Erdapfel also serves as a reminder that ancient scientific opinion that the world was spherical had never been lost, despite a myth invented in the nineteenth century that Columbus's voyages had disproven widespread belief in a flat earth.

The European perception that the peoples encountered in America and sub-Saharan Africa lived in what to Europeans seemed an uncivilised state – without monotheism or written scripture, without monumental architecture, naked or dressed in skins – usually meant they were cast as brutish and savage. Such notions were not universal, however, and became more difficult to sustain after Europeans encountered the highly sophisticated Aztec and Inca Empires. The first known European image of the indigenous peoples of the Americas, a German woodcut of c.1505, is based on a widely read letter by the explorer Amerigo Vespucci (after whom the Americas were later named) describing South Americans, probably the Tupinambá of coastal

Brazil (Plate 0.10).[66] They are shown semi-naked, wearing costumes of feather skirts and headdresses that the artist has invented, and eating human flesh. The alien and exotic appearance of Tupinambá in this print can be contrasted with another from a few years later representing the peoples of Africa: a woodcut by Hans Burgkmair labelled 'in Allago', in reference to Algoa Bay at the south-east tip of Africa (Plate 0.11). Burgkmair represents a man, woman and child with reference to the iconography of Adam and Eve, borrowing from Dürer's engraving of the subject (Plate 0.1) and classical sculpture, while drawing upon a strand of thought that considered pagans to be innocents, living in an ideal state of nature that protected them from the moral corruption that was thought to plague Europe. The print combines idealised bodies with details of costume based in part on the observation of African artefacts in European collections. It points to the European impulse to organise and classify the diverse peoples of the world,[67] drawing upon fact and fantasy to map out differences largely in terms of dress.

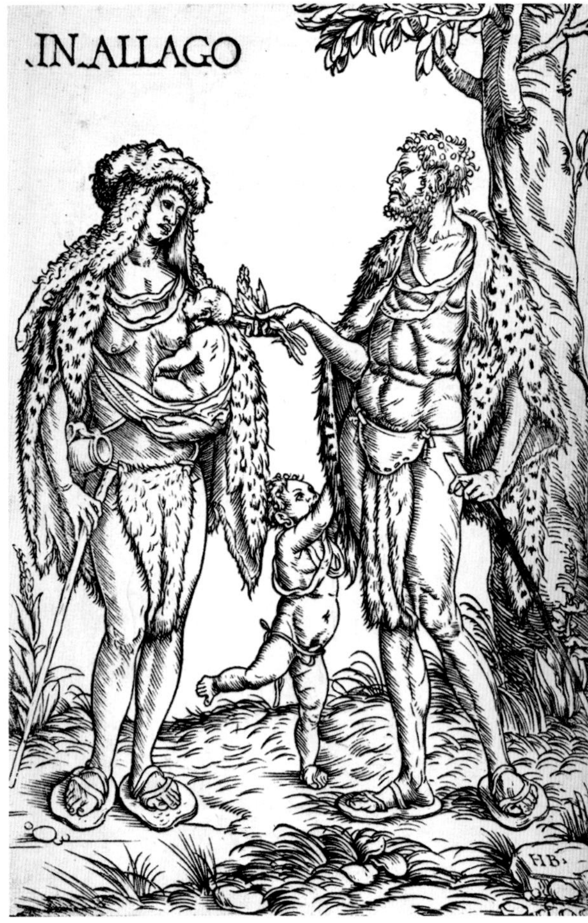

Plate 0.11 Hans Burgkmair, *In Allago*, 1508, woodcut. Photo: © Bridgeman Images.

This and the other themes briefly introduced here will be examined further in the chapters to follow. They will trace overarching motifs such as the fluid combination of the religious and commercial in European engagement with the world and the pronounced sense of confusion, or deliberate distortion, seen in European representations of the Other. Select examples of visual culture will be examined for the insight they offer into trade, contact, movement and cultural transfers. Pointed case studies will be aimed at repositioning the visual culture of this period in the context of global networks, breaking down boundaries and binaries set up by nationalism and colonialism that have made the Renaissance seem an isolated, strictly European phenomenon.

Notes

1 Meier, 2015.

2 Martin and Bleichmar, 2015; Burghartz, Burkart and Göttler, 2016; Um and Clark, 2016.

3 Abu-Lughod, 1989; North, 2010; Frankopan, 2015.

4 Shalem, 1996; Massing, 2007; Frankopan, 2015.

5 Abu-Lughod, 1989; Bloom, 2001; Brotton, 2003; Jardine and Brotton, 2005; Goody, 2007; Van Dalen and Burnett, 2011.

6 Spufford, 2003.

7 Martin and Bleichmar, 2015; Burghartz, Burkart and Göttler, 2016; Um and Clark, 2016.

8 Goldthwaite, 1993; Belozerskaya, 2002; Belozerskaya, 2005.

9 Burckhardt, 2002; Kallendorf, 2007.

10 Pomeranz, 2000.

11 Goody, 1996, pp. 1–10.

12 Powers, 1995.

13 Elkins, 2006; Kesner, 2007; Carrier, 2008; Sheriff, 2010; Wood, 2014.

14 Lach, 1965; Wittkower, 1989; DaCosta Kaufmann, Dossin and Joyeux-Prunel, 2015.

15 Levenson, 1991.

16 Farago, 1995, p. 1.

17 Braudel, 1992.

18 Braudel, 1981–84.

19 Subrahmanyam, 1997b; Gruzinski, 2002; Werner and Zimmermann, 2006; DaCosta Kaufmann, Dossin and Joyeux-Prunel, 2015.

20 Abu-Lughod, 1989; Farago, 1995; Frank, 1998; Jardine and Brotton, 2000; Hobson, 2004; Goody, 1996; Goody, 2007; Frankopan, 2015.

21 Goody, 2010. Extract reproduced in Newall, 2017, pp. 102–12.

22 Peterson, 2008; Shalem, 2012. Extract reproduced in Newall, 2017, pp. 80–92.

23 Jardine, 1996; Ajmar-Wollheim and Molà, 2011, Extract reproduced in Newall, 2017, pp. 92–102; Farago, 2012; Findlen, 2013; Riello and Gerritsen, 2016; Richardson, Hamling and Gaimster, 2017.

24 Contadini, 1999; Mack, 2002; Ajmar-Wollheim and Molà, 2011; Contadini, 2013.

25 Levenson, 2007; Jordan Gschwend and Lowe, 2015.

26 Levenson, 1991; Jackson and Jaffer, 2004; Campbell and Chong, 2005; Carboni, 2007; Levenson, 2007; Peck, 2013.

27 Campbell and Chong, 2005.

28 Howard, 2000, Avcıoğlu and Sherman, 2015.

29 Goffman, 2002; Jardine and Brotton, 2005; Goffman, 2007; Harper, 2011; Aksan and Goffman, 2007; Norton, Contadini and Norton, 2013.

30 Horden and Purcell, 2000; Abulafia, 2003; Abulafia, 2005.

31 Espagne and Werner, 1988.

32 Schmale, 2003; Burke, 2009; Espagne, 2015; Burghartz, Burkart and Göttler, 2016.

33 Bloom, 2001.

34 Levi, 2012.

35 Bhabha, 1994.

36 Dean and Leibsohn, 2003.

37 Brotton, 2003; Joselit, Wood and Flood, 2010.

38 Frankopan, 2015.

39 Shalem, 1996.

40 Jacoby, 2005.

41 Abu-Lughod, 1989.

42 Allsen, 1997; Rossabi, 2002.

43 Wood, 1995.

44 Abulafia, 1987, p. 460; Abu-Lughod, 1989, p. 165.

45 Abu-Lughod, 1989, pp. 148–9.

46 Russell, 1995.

47 Subrahmanyam, 1997a.

48 Bethencourt, 2007; Levenson, 2007.

49 Abu-Lughod, 1989, p. 84.

50 Abulafia, 1987, p. 408; Ajmar-Wollheim and Molà, 2011; Jacoby, 2010.

51 Atil, 1987, pp. 177–98; Rogers, 2002.

52 Contadini, 2013, pp. 46–7; Monnas, 2008, p. 191.

53 Brotton, 2004, pp. 29–30.

54 Hay, 1966.

55 Frankopan, 2015, pp. 79–101.

56 Hay, 1966; Jones, 1971; Pagden, 2002; Wintle, 2009.

57 Braude, 1997; Pagden, 2013.

58 Hannaford, 1996, pp. 87–126.

59 Hahn, 2001; Heng, 2011a and 2011b; Strickland, 2012; Patton, 2012.

60 Whitford, 2009; Spicer, 2012.

61 Bartlett, 2001.

62 Wittkower, 1942; Lach, 1965; Friedman, 1981; Mittman and Dendle, 2012.

63 Strickland, 2012.

64 Silver, 2010, p. 219.

65 Pagden, 1993; Braham, 2012; Patton, 2015.

66 Sturtevant, 1976, p. 420; Markham, 2010, pp. 42–52.

67 Massing, 2007; Leitch, 2009.

Bibliography

Abulafia, D. (1987) 'Asia, Africa and the trade of medieval Europe', in Miller, E., Postan, C. and Postan, M. M. (eds) *The Cambridge Economic History of Europe from the Decline of the Roman Empire*, 2nd edn, Cambridge, Cambridge University Press, vol. 2, pp. 402–73.

Abulafia, D. (ed.) (2003) *The Mediterranean in History*, Los Angeles, CA, J. Paul Getty Museum.

Abulafia, D. (2005) 'Mediterraneans', in Harris, W. V. (ed.) *Rethinking the Mediterranean*, Oxford, Oxford University Press, pp. 64–93.

Abu-Lughod, J. L. (1989) *Before European Hegemony: The World System A.D. 1250–1350*, Oxford, Oxford University Press.

Ajmar-Wollheim, M. and Molà, L. (2011) 'The global Renaissance: cross-cultural objects in the early modern period', in Adamson, G., Riello, G. and Teasley, S. (eds) *Global Design History*, London and New York, Routledge, pp. 11–20.

Aksan, V. H. and Goffman, D. (eds) (2007) *The Early Modern Ottomans: Remapping the Empire*, Cambridge, Cambridge University Press.

Allsen, T. (1997) *Commodity and Exchange in the Mongol Empire: A Cultural History of Islamic Textiles*, Cambridge, Cambridge University Press.

Atil, E. (1987) *The Age of Sultan Süleyman the Magnificent*, Washington, DC, National Gallery of Art; New York, H. Abrams.

Avcıoğlu, N. and Sherman, A. (2015) *Artistic Practices and Cultural Transfer in Early Modern Italy: Essays in Honour of Deborah Howard*, Farnham, Ashgate Publishing.

Bartlett, R. (2001) 'Medieval and modern concepts of race and ethnicity', *Journal of Medieval and Early Modern Studies*, vol. 31, no. 1, pp. 39–56.

Belozerskaya, M. (2002) *Rethinking the Renaissance: Burgundian Arts across Europe*, Cambridge, Cambridge University Press.

Belozerskaya, M. (2005) *Luxury Arts of the Renaissance*, London, Thames & Hudson.

Bethencourt, F. (2007) *Portuguese Oceanic Expansion, 1400–1800*, Cambridge, Cambridge University Press.

Bhabha, H. (1994) *The Location of Culture*, London and New York, Routledge.

Bloom, J. (2001) *Paper before Print: The History and Impact of Paper in the Islamic World*, New Haven, CT and London, Yale University Press.

Braham, P. (2012) 'The monstrous Caribbean', in Mittman, A. S. and Dendle, P. J. (eds) *The Ashgate Research Companion to Monsters and the Monstrous*, Farnham and Burlington, VT, Ashgate Publishing, pp. 17–47.

Braude, B. (1997) 'The sons of Noah and the construction of ethnic and geographical identities in the medieval and early modern periods', *The William and Mary Quarterly*, vol. 54, no. 1, pp. 103–42.

Braudel, F. (1981–84) *Civilization and Capitalism, 15th–18th Century*, 3 vols (ed. S. Reynolds, trans. M. Kochan), New York, HarperCollins.

Braudel, F. (1992) *The Mediterranean and the Mediterranean World in the Age of Philip II*, London, HarperCollins (originally published in French in 1972).

Brotton, J. (2003) *The Renaissance Bazaar from the Silk Road to Michelangelo*, Oxford, Oxford University Press.

Brotton, J. (2004) *Trading Territories: Mapping the Early Modern World*, London, Reaktion Books.

Burckhardt, J. (2002) *The Civilization of the Renaissance in Italy* (trans. S. G. C. Middlemore), New York, Modern Library (originally published in German in 1860).

Burghartz, S., Burkart, L. and Göttler, C. (eds) (2016) *Sites of Mediation: Connected Histories of Places, Processes, and Objects in Europe and Beyond, 1450–1650*, Leiden, Brill.

Burke, P. (2009) 'Translating knowledge, translating cultures', in North, M. (ed.) *Kultureller Austausch: Bilanz und Perspektiven der Frühneuzeitforschung*, Cologne, Böhlau Verlag, pp. 69–80.

Campbell, C. and Chong, A. (eds) (2005) *Bellini and the East*, New Haven, CT and London, Yale University Press; London, National Gallery.

Carboni, S. (ed.) (2007) *Venice and the Islamic World, 828–1797*, New Haven, CT and London, Yale University Press; New York, Metropolitan Museum of Art.

Carrier, D. (2008) *A World Art History and its Objects*, University Park, PA, Pennsylvania State University Press.

Contadini, A. (1999) 'Artistic contacts: current scholarship and future tasks', in Burnett, C. and Contadini, A. (eds) *Islam and the Italian Renaissance*, London, The Warburg Institute, pp. 1–60.

Contadini, A. (2013) 'Sharing a taste? Material acquisitions and intellectual curiosity around the Mediterranean, from the eleventh to the sixteenth century', in Contadini, A. and Norton, C. (eds) *The Renaissance and the Ottoman World*, Farnham and Burlington, VT, Ashgate Publishing, pp. 23–61.

DaCosta Kaufmann, T., Dossin, C. and Joyeux-Prunel, B. (2015) 'Introduction. Reintroducing circulations: historiography and the project of global art history', in DaCosta Kaufmann, T., Dossin, C., Joyeux-Prunel, B. and Woodfield, R. (eds) *Circulations in the Global History of Art*, Farnham and Burlington, VT, Ashgate Publishing, pp. 1–22.

Dean, C. and Leibsohn, D. (2003) 'Hybridity and its discontents: considering visual culture in colonial Spanish America', *Colonial Latin American Review*, vol. 12, pp. 5–35.

Elkins, J. (2006) *Is Art History Global?*, London and New York, Routledge; New York, Taylor & Francis Group.

Espagne, M. (2015) 'Cultural transfers in art history', in DaCosta Kaufmann, T., Dossin, C., Joyeux-Prunel, B. and Woodfield, R. (eds) *Circulations in the Global History of Art*, Farnham and Burlington, VT, Ashgate Publishing, pp. 97–112.

Espagne, M. and Werner, M. (eds) (1988) *Transferts: les relations interculturelles dans l'espace franco-allemand (XVIIIe et XIXe siècle)*, Paris, Editions Recherche sur les civilisations.

Farago, C. (2012) 'On the peripatetic life of objects in the era of globalization', in Sheriff, M. D. (ed.) *Cultural Contact and the Making of European Art since the Age of Exploration*, Chapel Hill, NC, University of North Carolina Press, pp. 17–43.

Farago, C. (ed.) (1995) *Reframing the Renaissance: Visual Culture in Europe and Latin America 1450–1650*, New Haven, CT and London, Yale University Press.

Findlen, P. (ed.) (2013) *Early Modern Things: Objects and their Histories, 1500–1800*, Abingdon and New York, Routledge.

Frank, A. G. (1998) *ReORIENT: Global Economy in the Asian Age*, Berkeley, CA, University of California Press.

Frankopan, P. (2015) *The Silk Roads: A New History of the World*, London, Bloomsbury.

Friedman, J. B. (1981) *The Monstrous Races in Medieval Art and Thought*, Cambridge, MA, Harvard University Press.

Goffman, D. (2002) *The Ottoman Empire and Early Modern Europe*, Cambridge, Cambridge University Press.

Goffman, D. (2007) 'Negotiating with the Renaissance state: the Ottoman Empire and the new diplomacy', in Aksan, V. H. and Goffman, D. (eds) *The Early Modern Ottomans: Remapping the Empire*, Cambridge, Cambridge University Press, pp. 61–74.

Goldthwaite, R. A. (1993) *Wealth and the Demand for Art in Italy 1300–1600,* Baltimore, MD and London, Johns Hopkins University Press.

Goody, J. (1996) *The East in the West*, Cambridge, Cambridge University Press.

Goody, J. (2007) *The Theft of History*, Cambridge, Cambridge University Press.

Goody, J. (2010) *Renaissances: The One or the Many?*, Cambridge, Cambridge University Press.

Gruzinski, S. (2002) *The Mestizo Mind: The Intellectual Dynamics of Colonization and Globalization*, London and New York, Routledge.

Hahn, T. (2001) 'The difference the middle ages makes: color and race before the modern world', *Journal of Medieval and Early Modern Studies*, vol. 31, no. 1, pp. 1–37.

Hannaford, I. (1996) *Race: The History of an Idea in the West*, Baltimore, MD, Johns Hopkins University Press.

Harper, J. G. (ed.) (2011) *The Turk and Islam in the Western Eye, 1450–1750*, Burlington, VT, Ashgate Publishing.

Hay, D. (1966) *Europe: The Emergence of an Idea*, New York, Harper Torchbooks.

Heng, G. (2011a) 'The invention of race in the European Middle Ages I: race studies, modernity, and the Middle Ages', *Literature Compass*, vol. 8, no. 5, pp. 315–31.

Heng, G. (2011b) 'The invention of race in the European Middle Ages II: locations of medieval race', *Literature Compass*, vol. 8, no. 5, pp. 332–50.

Hobson, J. M. (2004) *The Eastern Origins of Western Civilisation*, Cambridge, Cambridge University Press.

Horden, P. and Purcell, N. (2000) *The Corrupting Sea: A Study of Mediterranean History*, Malden, MA, Blackwell.

Howard, D. (2000) *Venice and the East: The Impact of the Islamic World on Venetian Architecture, 1100–1500*, New Haven, CT and London, Yale University Press.

Jackson, A. and Jaffer, A. (eds) (2004) *Encounters: The Meeting of Asia and Europe, 1500–1800*, London, Victoria and Albert Museum.

Jacoby, D. (2005) *Commercial Exchange across the Mediterranean: Byzantium, the Crusader Levant, Egypt, and Italy*, London, Variorum.

Jacoby, D. (2010) 'Oriental silks go West: a declining trade in the later Middle Ages', in Schmidt Arcangeli, C. and Wolf, G. (eds) *Islamic Artefacts in the Mediterranean World: Trade, Gift Exchange and Artistic Transfer*, Venice, Marsilio, pp. 71–88.

Jardine, L. (1996) *Worldly Goods: A New History of the Renaissance*, London, Papermac.

Jardine, L. and Brotton, J. (2000) *Global Interests: Renaissance Art between East and West*, London, Reaktion Books.

Jones, W. R. (1971) 'The image of the barbarian in medieval Europe', *Comparative Studies in Society and History*, vol. 13, no. 4, pp. 376–407.

Jordan Gschwend, A. and Lowe, K. (2015) *The Global City: On the Streets of Renaissance Lisbon*, London, Paul Holberton Publishing.

Joselit, D., Wood, C., Flood, F. B., Yiengpruksawan, M., Russo, A., Wang, E. and Nagel, A. (2010) 'Roundtable: the global before globalization', *October*, vol. 133 (summer), pp. 3–19.

Kallendorf, C. W. (2007) 'Renaissance', in Kallendorf, C. W. (ed.) *A Companion to the Classical Tradition*, Malden, MA, Blackwell Publishing, pp. 30–43.

Kesner, L. (2007) 'Is a truly global art history possible?', in Elkins, J. (ed.) *Is Art History Global?*, London and New York, Routledge; New York, Taylor & Francis Group, pp. 81–111.

Lach, D. F. (1965) *Asia in the Making of Europe Vol. 1: The Century of Discovery*, Chicago, IL and London, University of Chicago Press.

Leitch, S. (2009) 'Burgkmair's peoples of Africa and India (1508) and the origins of ethnography in print', *The Art Bulletin*, vol. 91, no. 2, pp. 134–59.

Levenson, J. A. (ed.) (1991) *Circa 1492: Art in the Age of Exploration*, Washington, DC, National Gallery of Art, London and New Haven, CT, Yale University Press.

Levenson, J. A. (ed.) (2007) *Encompassing the Globe: Portugal and the World in the 16th and 17th Centuries*, Washington, DC, Smithsonian.

Levi, S. C. (2012) 'Objects in motion', in Northrop, D. (ed.) *A Companion to World History*, Malden, MA, Wiley-Blackwell, pp. 321–38.

Mack, R. (2002) *Bazaar to Piazza: Islamic Trade and Italian Art*, Berkeley, CA, University of California.

Markham, C. R. (ed.) (2010) *The Letters of Amerigo Vespucci and Other Documents Illustrative of His Career*, Farnham and Burlington, VT, Ashgate Publishing.

Martin, M. and Bleichmar, D. (eds) (2015) 'Introduction', *Objects in Motion in the Early Modern World, Art History*, vol. 38, no. 4, special issue, pp. 604–19.

Massing, J. M. (2007) 'Hans Burgkmair's depiction of native Africans', *Studies in Imagery, Vol. II: The World Discovered*, London, The Pindar Press, pp. 114–40.

Meier, S. P. (2015) 'Chinese porcelain and Muslim port cities: mercantile materiality in coastal East Africa', *Art History*, vol. 38, no. 4, pp. 702–17.

Mittman, A. S. and Dendle, P. J. (eds) (2012) *The Ashgate Research Companion to Monsters and the Monstrous*, Farnham and Burlington, VT, Ashgate Publishing.

Monnas, L. (2008) *Merchants, Princes and Painters: Silk Fabrics in Italian and Northern Paintings, 1300–1550*, New Haven, CT and London, Yale University Press.

Newall, D. (ed.) (2017) *Art and its Global Histories: A Reader*, Manchester and Milton Keynes, Manchester University Press in association with The Open University.

North, M. (2010) 'Introduction – artistic and cultural exchanges between Europe and Asia, 1400–1900: rethinking markets, workshops and collections', in North, M. (ed.) *Artistic and Cultural Exchanges between Europe and Asia, 1400–1900*, Farnham and Burlington, VT, Ashgate Publishing, pp. 1–8.

Norton, C., Contadini, A. and Norton, C. D. (eds) (2013) *The Renaissance and the Ottoman World*, Farnham and Burlington, VT, Ashgate Publishing.

Pagden, A. (1993) *European Encounters with the New World*, New Haven, CT and London, Yale University Press.

Pagden, A. (2002) 'Europe: conceptualizing a continent', in Pagden, A. (ed.) *The Idea of Europe: From Antiquity to the European Union*, Cambridge, Cambridge University Press; Washington, DC, Woodrow Wilson Center Press, pp. 33–55.

Pagden, A. (2013) 'The peopling of the New World: ethnos, race and empire in the early-modern world', in Eliav-Feldon, M., Isaac, B. and Ziegler, J. (eds) *The Origins of Racism in the West*, Cambridge, Cambridge University Press, pp. 292–312.

Patton, P. A. (2012) *Art of Estrangement: Redefining Jews in Reconquest Spain*, University Park, PA, Pennsylvania State University Press.

Patton, P. A. (2015) 'Introduction: race, color and the visual in Iberia and Latin America', in Patton, P. A. (ed.) *Envisioning Others: Race, Color, and the Visual in Iberia and Latin America*, Leiden, Brill, pp. 1–17.

Peck, A. (ed.) (2013) *Interwoven Globe: The Worldwide Textile Trade, 1500–1800*, New York, Metropolitan Museum of Art.

Peterson, J. F. (2008) 'Renaissance: a kaleidoscopic view from the Spanish Americas', in Elkins, J. and Williams, R. (eds) *Renaissance Theory*, London and New York, Routledge; New York, Taylor & Francis Group, pp. 321–32.

Pomeranz, K. (2000) *The Great Divergence: China, Europe, and the Making of the Modern World Economy*, Princeton, NJ, Princeton University Press.

Powers, M. J. (1995) 'Art and history: exploring the counterchange condition', *Art Bulletin*, vol. 77, no. 3, pp. 382–7.

Richardson, C., Hamling, T and Gaimster, D. (eds) (2017) *The Routledge Handbook of Material Culture in Early Modern Europe*, Abingdon and New York, Routledge.

Riello, G. and Gerritsen, A. (eds) (2016) *The Global Lives of Things: The Material Culture of Connections in the First Global Age*, London and New York, Routledge.

Rogers, J. M. (2002) 'Europe and the Ottoman arts: foreign demand and Ottoman consumption', in Bernardini, M. (ed.) *Europa e Islam tra secoli XIV–XVI*, 2 vols, Naples, Istituto universitario Orientale, vol. 2, pp. 709–36.

Rossabi, M. (2002) 'The Mongols and their legacy', in Komaroff, L. and Carboni, S. (eds) *The Legacy of Genghis Khan: Courtly Art and Culture in Western Asia, 1256–1353*, New York, Metropolitan Museum of Art; New Haven, CT and London, Yale University Press, pp. 12–35.

Russell, P. E. (1995) *Portugal, Spain and the African Atlantic, 1343–1490: Chivalry and Crusade from John of Gaunt to Henry the Navigator*, Aldershot, Variorum.

Schmale, W. (ed.) (2003) *Kulturtransfer: Kulturelle Praxis im 16. Jahrhundert*, Innsbruck, StudienVerlag.

Shalem, A. (1996) *Islam Christianized: Islamic Portable Objects in the Medieval Church Treasuries of the Latin West, Ars faciendi*, vol. 7, Bern, Peter Lang.

Shalem, A. (2012) 'Dangerous claims: on the "othering" of Islamic art history and how it operates within global art history', in Bruhn, M., Juneja, M. and Werner, E. A. (eds), theme issue, *Universalität der Kunstgeschichte?, kritische berichte: Zeitschrift für Kunst- und Kulturwissenschaften*, vol. 40, no. 2, pp. 69–86.

Sheriff, M. D. (2010) 'Cultural contact and the making of European art, 1492–1930', in Sheriff, M. D. (ed.) *Cultural Contact and the Making of European Art since the Age of Exploration*, Chapel Hill, NC, University of North Carolina Press, pp. 1–16.

Silver, L. (2010) 'India ink: imagery of the subcontinent in early modern Europe', in Saurma-Jeltsch, L. E. and Eisenbeiß, A. (eds) *The Power of Things and the Flow of Cultural Transformations: Art and Culture between Europe and Asia*, Berlin, Deutscher Kunstverlag, pp. 217–37.

Spicer, J. (2012) 'European perceptions of blackness as reflected in the visual arts', in Spicer, J. (ed.) *Revealing the African Presence in Renaissance Europe*, Baltimore, MD, Walters Art Museum, pp. 35–59.

Spufford, P. (2003) *Power and Profit: The Merchant in Medieval Europe*, London, Thames & Hudson.

Strickland, D. H. (2012) 'Monstrosity and race in the late Middle Ages', in Mittman, A. S. and Dendle, P. J. (eds) *The Ashgate Research Companion to Monsters and the Monstrous*, Farnham and Burlington, VT, Ashgate Publishing, pp. 365–86.

Sturtevant, W. C. (1976) 'First visual images of native America', in Chiapelli, F. (ed.) *First Images of America: The Impact of the New World on the Old*, Berkeley, CA, University of California Press, vol. 1, pp. 417–54.

Subrahmanyam, S. (1997a) *The Career and Legend of Vasco da Gama*, Cambridge, Cambridge University Press.

Subrahmanyam, S. (1997b) 'Connected histories: notes towards a reconfiguration of early modern Eurasia', *Modern Asian Studies*, vol. 31, pp. 735–62.

Um, N. and Clark, L. (2016) 'The art of embassy: situating objects and images in the early modern diplomatic encounter', *Journal of Early Modern History*, vol. 20, no. 1, pp. 3–18.

Van Dalen, B. and Burnett, C. (eds) (2011) 'Between Orient and Occident: transformation of knowledge', *Annals of Science*, vol. 68, no. 4, special issue, pp. 445–51.

Werner, M. and Zimmermann, B. (2006) 'Beyond comparison: histoire croisée and the challenge of reflexivity', *History and Theory*, vol. 45, pp. 30–50.

Whitford, D. M. (2009) *The Curse of Ham in the Early Modern Era: The Bible and the Justifications for Slavery*, Farnham and Burlington, VT, Ashgate Publishing.

Wintle, M. (2009) *The Image of Europe: Visualizing Europe in Cartography and Iconography throughout the Ages*, Cambridge, Cambridge University Press.

Wittkower, R. (1942) 'Marvels of the East: a study in the history of monsters', *Journal of the Warburg and Courtauld Institutes*, vol. 5, pp. 159–97.

Wittkower, R. (1989) *Selected Lectures of Rudolf Wittkower: The Impact of Non-European Civilizations on the Art of the West*, Reynolds, D. M. (ed.), Cambridge, Cambridge University Press.

Wood, F. (1995) *Did Marco Polo Go to China?*, London, Secker & Warburg.

Wood, P. (2014) *Western Art and the Wider World*, Malden, MA, Oxford and Chichester, John Wiley & Sons.

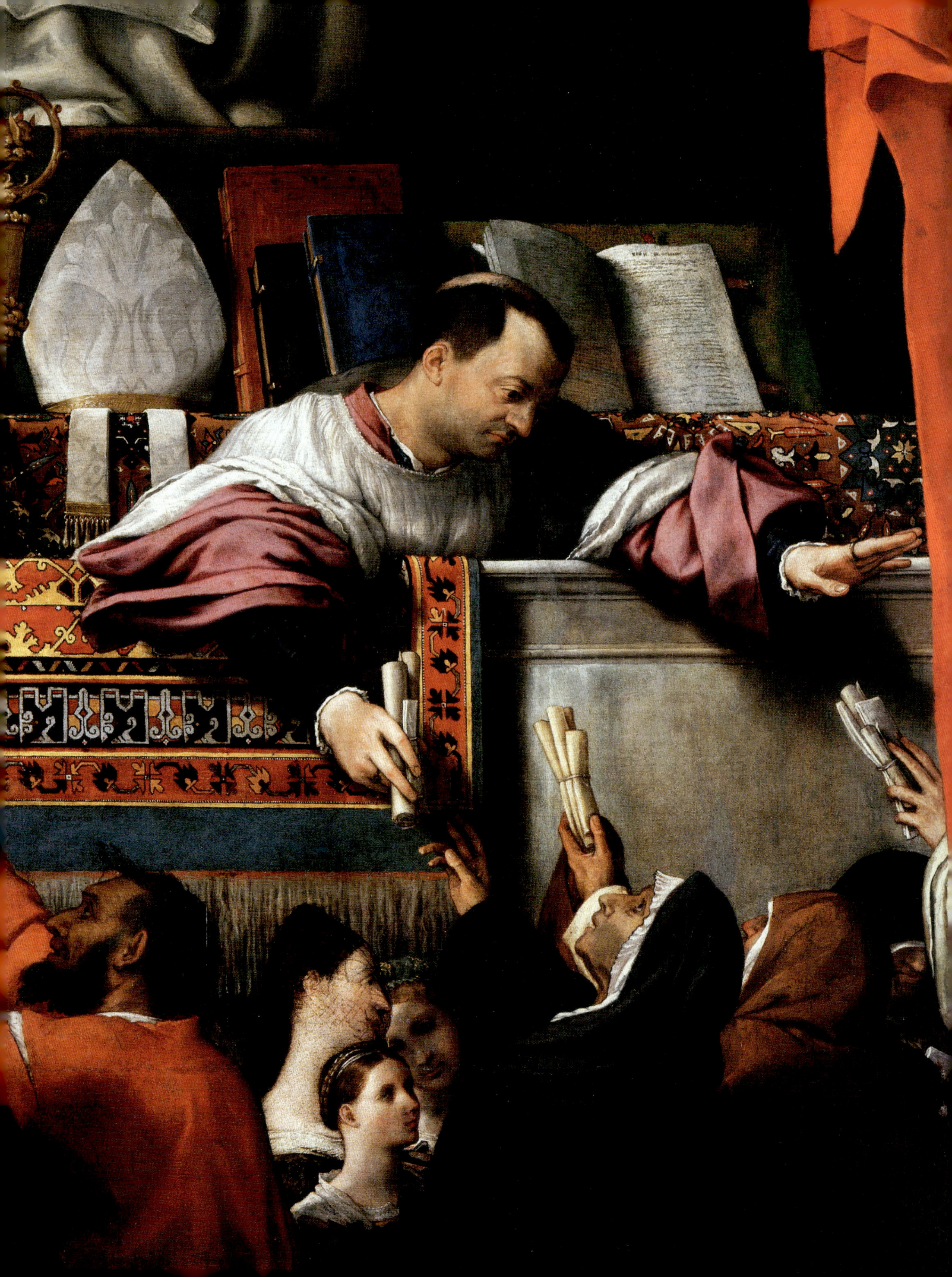

Chapter 1

Renaissance altarpieces: the far in the near

Kathleen Christian

Introduction

The altarpiece, a type of devotional image that has long been considered a paragon of European and Christian art, features prominently in Renaissance art history. In museums, altarpieces are the star attractions of Renaissance galleries, where they usually appear grouped together according to national schools (Italian, Spanish, Netherlandish, etc.). A large body of art-historical literature has analysed shifts in the style and format of altarpieces, or explored issues of patronage and liturgical use. Numerous studies and exhibitions have shed light on the development of altarpieces in particular regions of Europe, or considered artistic cross-currents within Europe, for example the influence of Netherlandish altarpieces on Italian ones.[1]

A notable number of altarpieces, however, reference multiple cultural identities, mixing and combining European and non-European. To take an example, the altarpiece of *Saint Michael Enthroned*, by the Italian artist Angelo Puccinelli (Plate 1.2), represents Saint Michael wearing an Asian-style silk cloak decorated with dragons, echoing the defeated dragon underneath his feet. The cloth is painted as if woven in gold and shimmering purple silk. A detail of this painted textile (Plate 1.3) can be compared to examples of real patterned silks made in Asia, such as a gold and silk cloth showing makaras – mythical combinations of aquatic and terrestrial animals – chasing winged phoenixes against a background of leaves and lotus flowers (Plate 1.4). This particular example, a type of luxury cloth called lampas, was originally bright red and gold and was woven either in a central Asian workshop or in the Mongol capital of Dadu (now Beijing). It brings together Chinese phoenixes and lotuses with makaras, Hindu motifs adopted into Chinese textile design.[2] Puccinelli's painted textile might not rely, however, on authentically Asian examples such as this one, but instead on Italian imitations of such fabrics; the artist could easily have known examples made in his hometown of Lucca, which was between the twelfth and fourteenth centuries a leading European centre for the production of silks styled upon Asian imports. Puccinelli has painted Saint Michael's cloth a deep purple, a reflection of the Byzantine practice of allowing only emperors and members of the imperial family to wear this colour. A consideration of the diversity of cultures 'woven' together in the Saint Michael altarpiece offers a new perspective, one which is supported by a growing body of research linking Renaissance art with global consumption and trade, the diplomatic exchange of gifts between distant powers and the desirability in Europe of objects imported from afar.[3]

Plate 1.1 (Facing page) Lorenzo Lotto, *The Alms of Saint Anthony* (detail from Plate 1.15). Photo: © 2017. Cameraphoto/Scala, Florence.

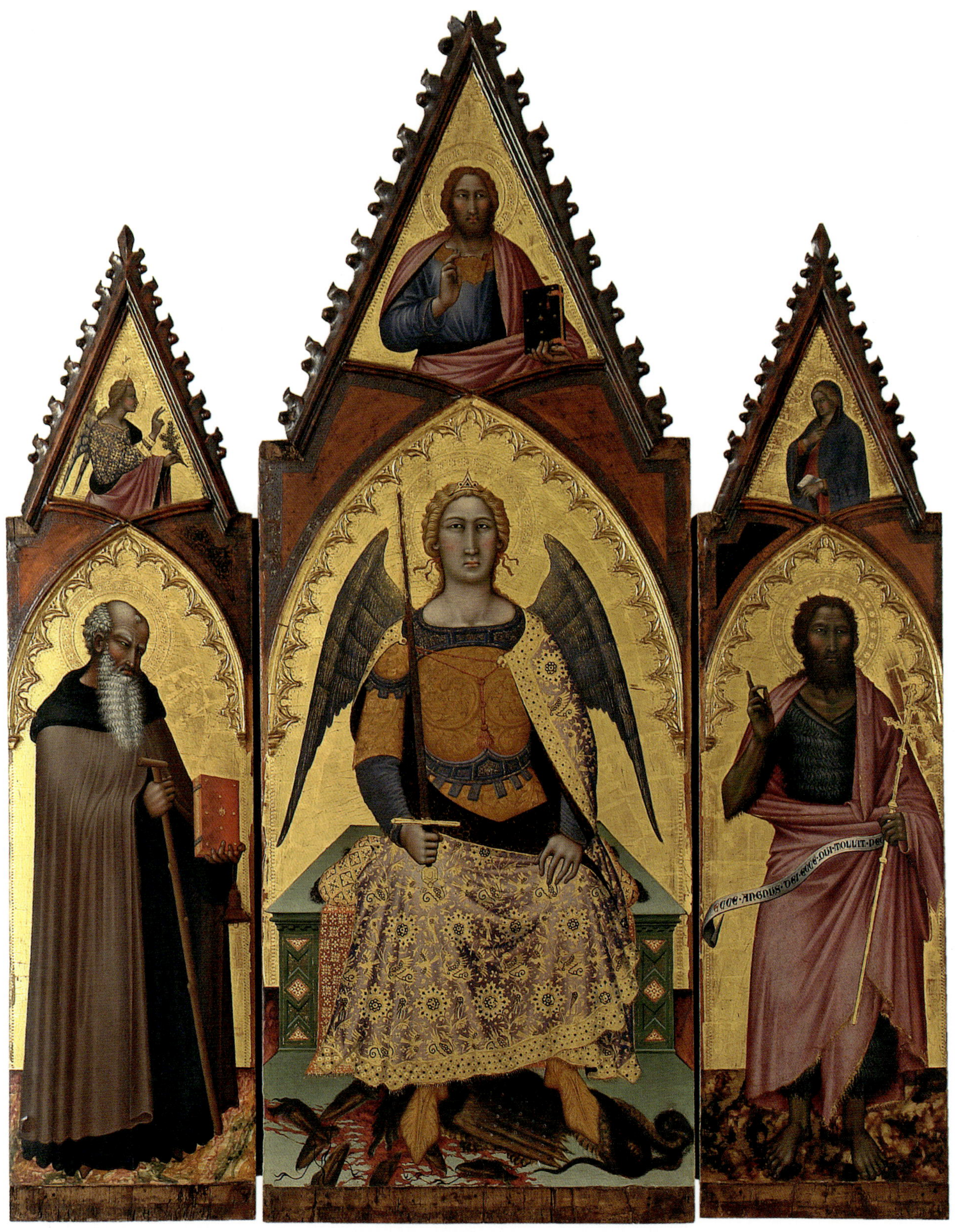

Plate 1.2 Angelo Puccinelli, *Saint Michael Enthroned with Saints Anthony Abbot and John the Baptist*, formerly in the church of San Pellegrino in Siena, *c.*1360–65, tempera on panel, 182 × 154 cm. Pinacoteca Nazionale, Siena. Photo: By permission of the Ministero dei Beni e delle Attività Culturali e del Turismo, Museums of Tuscany, Pinacoteca Nazionale di Siena.

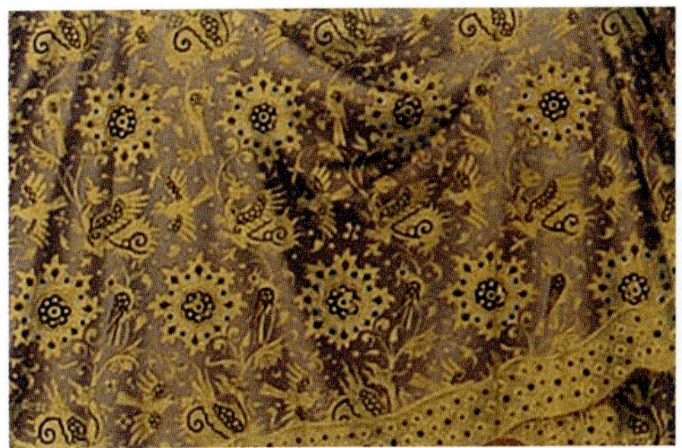

Plate 1.3 Angelo Puccinelli, detail from *Saint Michael Enthroned with Saints Anthony Abbot and John the Baptist* (detail from Plate 1.2). Photo: ART Collection/Alamy.

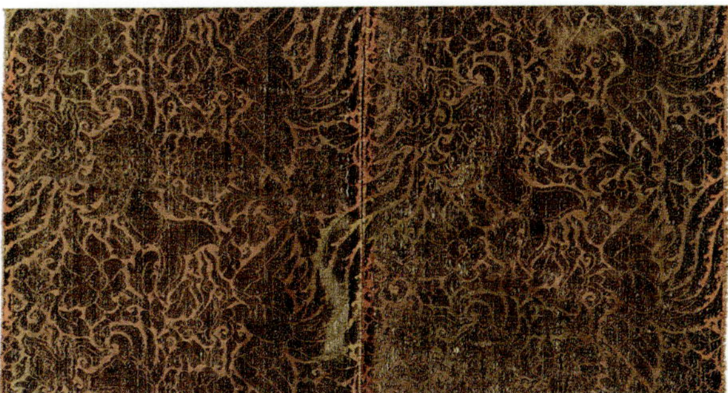

Plate 1.4 Lampas cloth from central Asia or Dadu, thirteenth century, gold and silk. The David Collection, Copenhagen, inv. no. 46a-b/1992. Photo: Pernille Klemp.

To explore these topics further, this chapter will consider Renaissance altarpieces from four different perspectives: first, their reference to highly prized objects imported from distant places; second, their commentary on Europe's place in the world and Christian perceptions of the Other; third, their use of non-European materials and techniques; and fourth, their export abroad as part of the effort to convert non-Christians. It will ask how Mongol, Indian, East Asian, Persian, Arab and Turkic (Islamic) and African cultures potentially informed the richly imaginative visual expressions of Renaissance altarpieces, with reference to Italian, Netherlandish, German and Portuguese examples. Consideration will be given to shifts that occur in this period, in particular the accelerated collecting and consumption of luxury objects – many imported from the Islamic world – among wealthy European elites, the European expansion into Africa, America and Asia from the 1400s, and the significant growth and increasingly intertwined cultural complexity of global commerce and trade from the mid-fifteenth century onwards. Varying ways in which altarpieces express the Church's universalist ambitions for the conversion of non-believers will also be explored.

Before tackling these topics, it is useful to review briefly the functions and formats of these works. Although altarpieces could be portable objects, most were made to stand on top of altar tables, where they provided a backdrop for the mass and represented awe-inspiring visions of the divine to the faithful with great material and visual splendour. Their usual setting was either on the high altars of churches or the altars of family chapels that were paid for and maintained by private

donors. Altarpieces varied greatly in their form and subject matter, so as to identify the dedication of an altar (to the Virgin, Christ or saints) or to represent other holy figures of relevance to the church, monastic order or wealthy donor responsible for it. They also varied significantly: from paintings to sculptures in wood, stone or precious metals, to a combination of painted panels, statues and shrines.

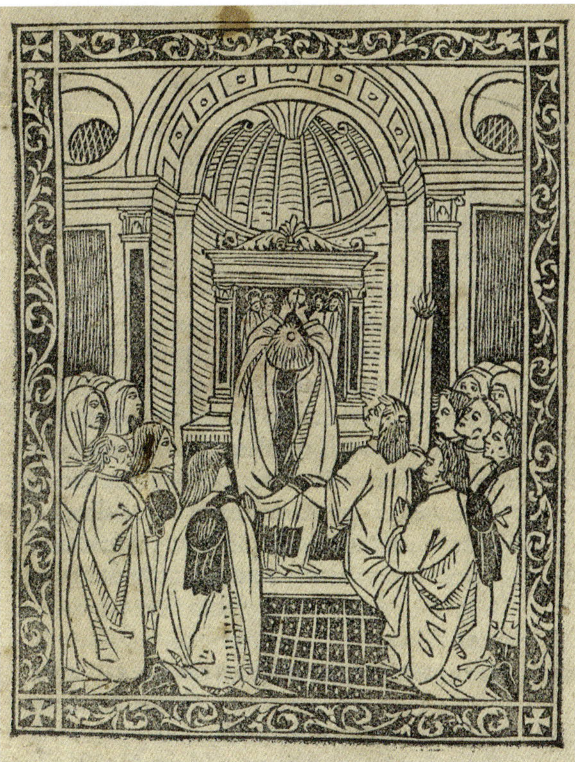

Plate 1.5 Unknown artist, 'Elevation of the host', woodcut in Girolamo Savonarola, *Tractato del sacramento & de mysterii della messa*, c.1493. The British Library, London, shelfmark IA.27498 Photo: © The British Library Board.

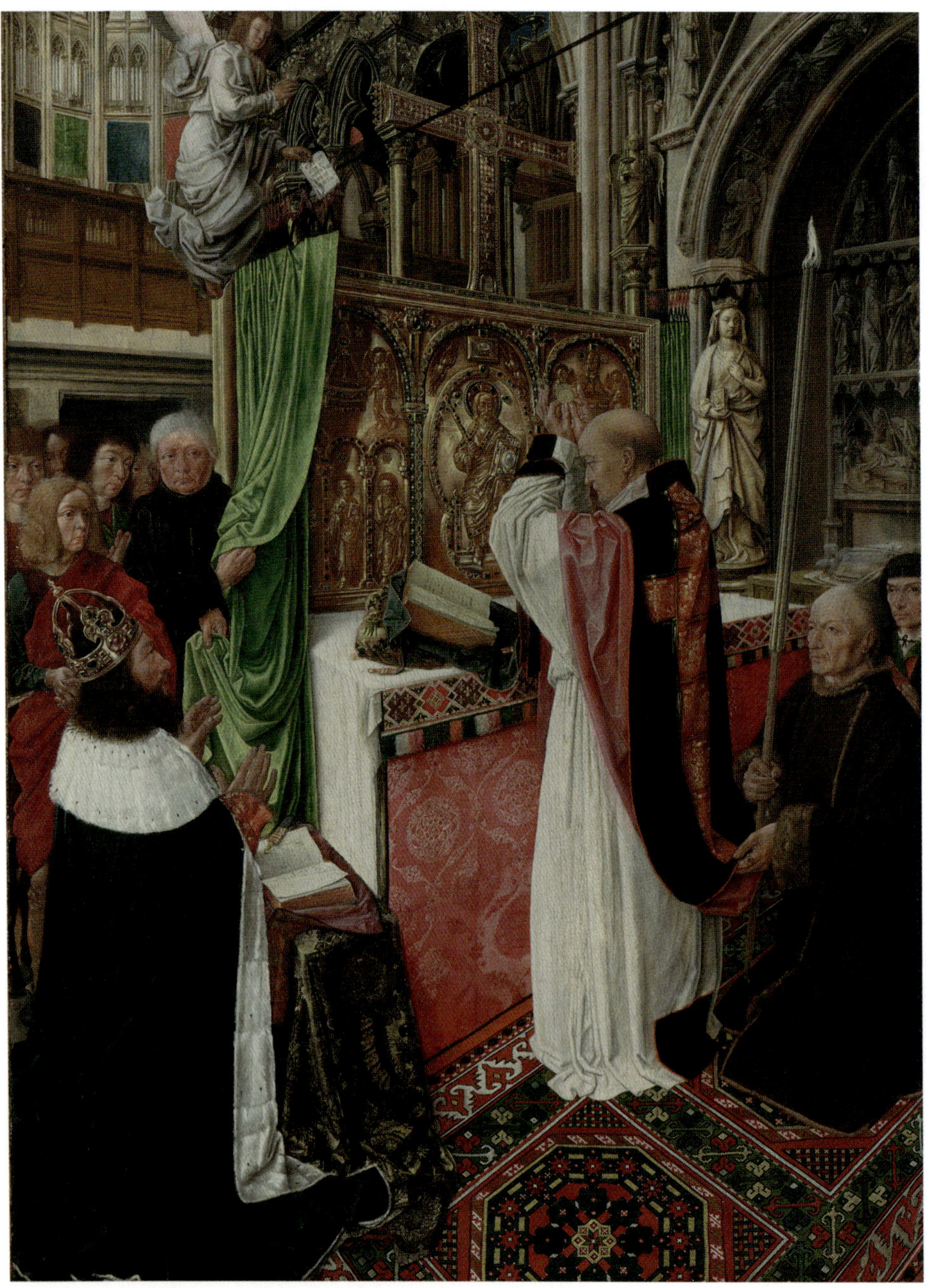

Plate 1.6 Master of Saint Giles, *The Mass of Saint Giles*, c.1500, oil on panel, 62 × 46 cm. National Gallery, London. Photo: National Gallery.

After the Fourth Lateran Council of 1215, priests more uniformly adopted the practice of holding up the host, the bread wafer representing the body of Christ, during mass so the congregation could see it. When the priest's back was turned towards them, as was usual, worshippers would witness the host raised in front of the altarpiece, as is shown in a fifteenth-century Italian woodcut (Plate 1.5). *The Mass of Saint Giles* (Plate 1.6), one panel of a multipart, double-sided altarpiece by an anonymous artist, shows the

elevation of the host in front of an altarpiece in the church of Saint Denis, the royal burial church of the French kings. Here the celebrant elevates the host for the eyes of King Charles Martel (r.718–41), who prays for the forgiveness of a sin, which an angel above delivers to him. A curtain is drawn back to allow the king to receive the spiritual benefits that come from the privileged sight. Seeing the host was a significant event, especially considering that it was only on special occasions that the congregation received the host in edible form (for most, only at Easter). The altarpiece inspired awe and devotion as a visually splendid complement to this holy sight.

There are distinct regional differences in the shapes, materials and styles of European altarpieces. Italian altarpieces were complex structures painted on separate panels joined together with elaborate frames (polyptychs) until the beginning of the fifteenth century, when they began to take the form of unified scenes painted on a single panel, or pala. By contrast, Netherlandish painted altarpieces often consisted of a central panel with hinged outer wings which were usually kept folded inwards to conceal the central image, but could be opened up for the mass. In southern Europe curtains were often used to hide altarpieces until the celebration of the mass, when they were revealed to the eyes of viewers.[4] Today many Renaissance altarpieces have been disassembled, removed from their original settings and cut into individual panels which are divided between various museums. Yet in their original, full splendour and in their intended settings, altarpieces were elaborate assemblages. Seen by flickering candlelight, they were mysterious and holy objects that occupied a place of great ritual and aesthetic importance in the culture of European Christendom.

Altarpieces were often monumental works custom-made for specific settings, to inspire the devotion of a particular congregation and identify the dedications of altars and churches. In this sense they were site-specific and thoroughly grounded in their local contexts, which were undoubtedly the centre of viewers' attention and concern. However, especially in places with links to global trade, significant aspects of local identities, channelled by the appearance, materials and symbolism of the altarpiece, were inseparably connected with the wider world.

1 Imported objects

As representations of saints, holy figures and biblical scenes, altarpieces were visual repositories for the most refined and heavenly things on earth. Their symbolic language drew upon objects of foreign origin, in part because the world beyond had been – for many centuries – the source of transportable luxury items: 'spices' including sugar, pepper and saffron, enamelled glass, silk, metalwork, exotic animals, jewels and porcelain. These were things of unusual rarity, antiquity, craftsmanship and cost, valued for their colour, texture, scent or sheen. The evocation of such magnificent objects imparted to altarpieces an aura of other-worldly splendour that enhanced their religious function. In many, if not most cases, Europeans did not know where these imported objects came from, much less their intended meaning or purpose. Adapted into new settings, their origins were confused or forgotten, as their forms, aesthetic or material qualities were repurposed, creatively reinvented or translated into a new symbolic language.[5]

Textiles

As we have seen in the Saint Michael altarpiece (Plate 1.2), Asian textiles or imitations of them were closely mimicked in altarpieces, particularly those produced in the commercial hubs of Europe. During the Pax Mongolica (thirteenth to fourteenth centuries), the opening up and promotion of the silk industries in China and west and central Asia brought textiles to Europe as luxury goods or diplomatic gifts. Textiles imported from across Asia into Europe, where they were sometimes used in Christian clerical vestments and burial shrouds, were known as 'tartar' cloths.[6] In Europe the term 'Tartars' originally referred to the Mongols, Turkic peoples and others united by Genghis Khan (r.1206–27) and derives from the word 'Tartarus', or the underworld, in reference to fears of their advance westward.[7] Although the Tartars were often regarded as savage, or even cannibalistic, Marco Polo's accounts had stressed the wealth and luxury of the Mongol court of Genghis Khan's grandson Kublai Khan (r.1260–95) in China, and the import of silk and gold textiles only seemed to confirm his descriptions. One of these textiles is imitated, for example, in the sumptuous cloth-of-gold cloak worn by the angel Gabriel in Simone Martini and Lippo Memmi's *Annunciation* painted for the Cathedral of Siena in 1333 (Plates 1.7 and 1.8).[8] Artists likely need not have travelled far to see such fabrics up close, since surviving Italian church inventories from the time, such as that of the basilica of San Francesco in Assisi, list numerous examples of tartar silks.[9]

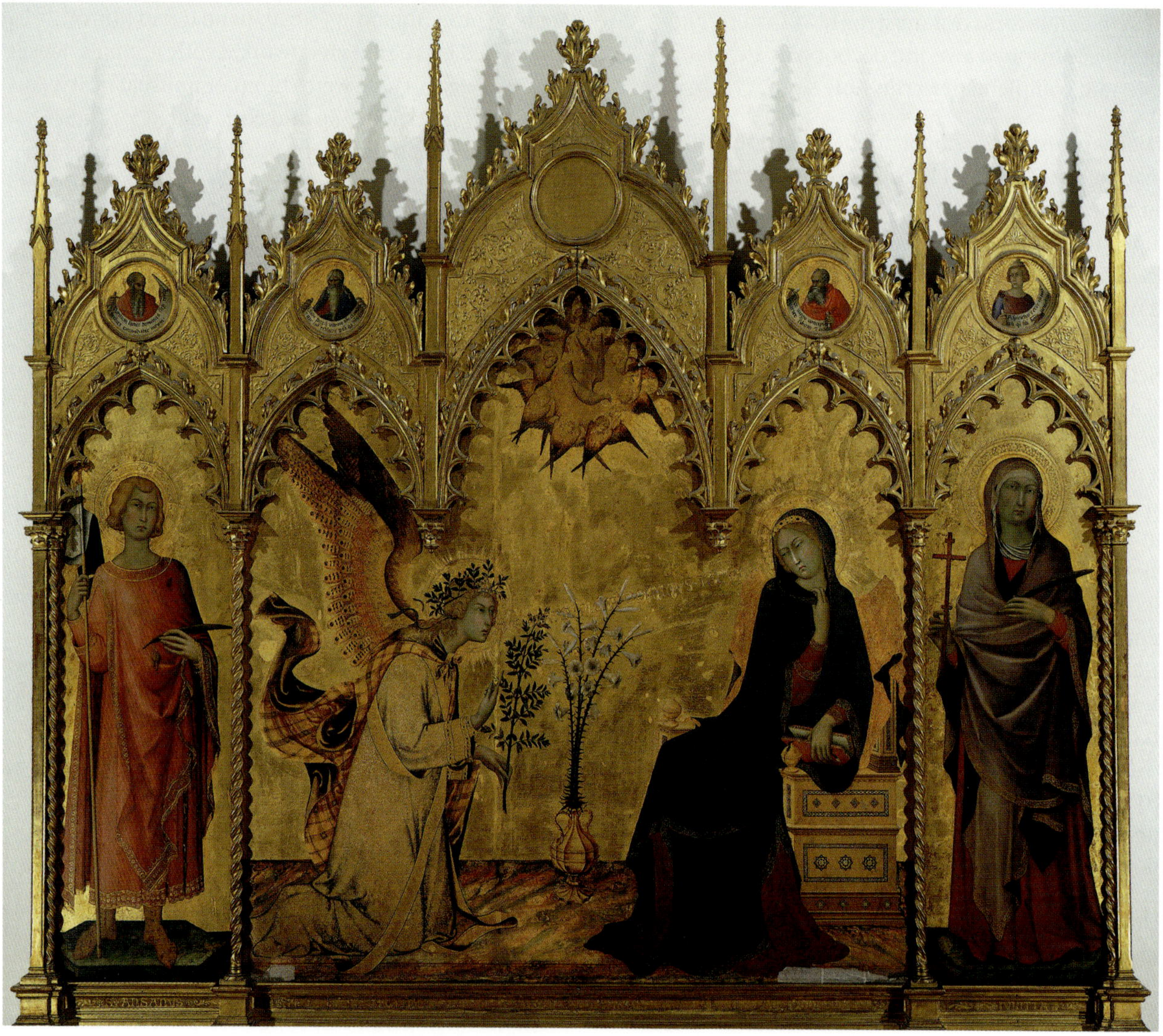

Plate 1.7 Simone Martini and Lippo Memmi, *Annunciation with Saints Margaret and Ansanus*, 1333, tempera and gold leaf on panel, 265 × 305 cm. Uffizi Gallery, Florence. Photo: Getty.

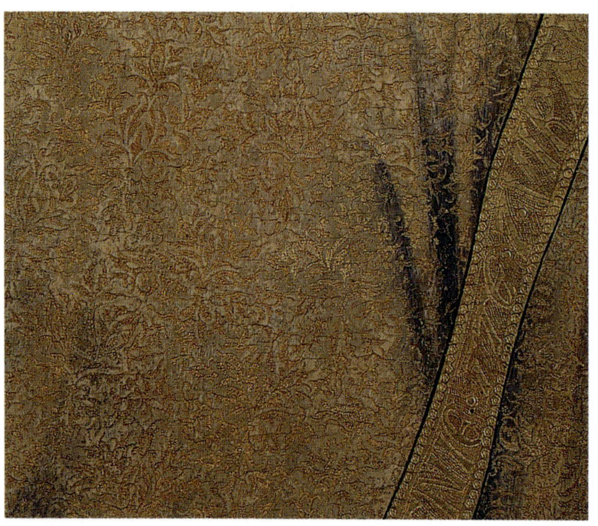

Today, textiles are a marginalised topic and are rarely discussed in relation to the history of art. Part of the problem is that so few from this period have survived, and when they do it is often difficult to know their place of origin, precisely because of their cross-cultural identity. It is nevertheless important to recognise the role of luxury textiles in the transmission of visual ideas. Textiles, made to be sturdy and transportable, were ideal diplomatic gifts. Prized across Eurasia and Africa, they functioned like a form of currency in the early modern world, moving easily between cultures

Plate 1.8 Simone Martini and Lippo Memmi, *Annunciation with Saints Margaret and Ansanus* (detail from Plate 1.7).

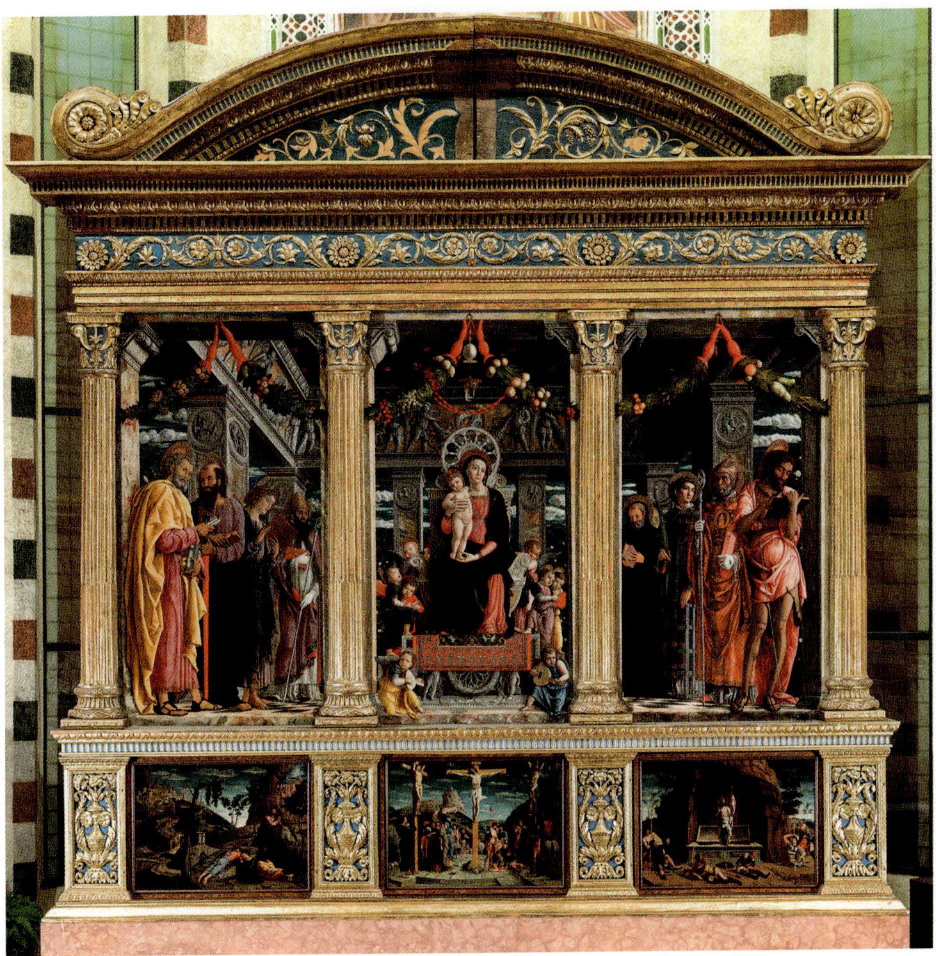

Plate 1.9 Andrea Mantegna, San Zeno altarpiece, *c.*1457–60. Basilica di San Zeno, Verona. Photo: © 2017 Scala, Florence.

and over great distances.[10] Textiles carried designs far and wide, inspiring imitation and cross-cultural invention in many different artistic environments. They were also universally recognisable status symbols and markers of prestige. In European altarpieces, artists and patrons paid careful attention to painted textiles as a way of conferring honour on holy figures and on themselves, through association with the most valuable and desirable textiles from the global market.

Pseudo-Arabic

Another motif found in altarpieces is known as 'pseudo-Arabic', an ornamental type of writing that imitates Arabic scripts, but is not in any way legible or meaningful.[11] Examples can be seen in the haloes and the borders of garments in Mantegna's San Zeno altarpiece (Plates 1.9–1.10) and Gentile da Fabriano's *Adoration of the Magi* (Plates 1.11–1.12). In a Christian

context it is already seen in Byzantine art of the ninth to tenth centuries, appearing in Crete soon after the Arab conquest of the island.[12] Later, in much of Europe from the thirteenth to the sixteenth centuries, one finds examples of pseudo-Arabic script in panel painting, glass painting, manuscript illumination and other art forms. It is above all, however, in Italy – a major port of entry for Islamic textiles, ceramics and other imported goods – that pseudo-Arabic took hold. In early Renaissance Italian altarpieces Mary, Christ and the saints are often shown wearing cloaks with pseudo-Arabic inscribed on sleeves and hems, or reading books written in pseudo-Arabic script. Although pseudo-Arabic was the most widespread form of imitation script, others such as pseudo-Hebrew (for example in the letters on the textile behind Mary in Plate 1.25) and pseudo-'Phags-pa (a Mongolian script) were also used, at a time when the expansion of global trade was fostering greater awareness of and interest in other languages.[13]

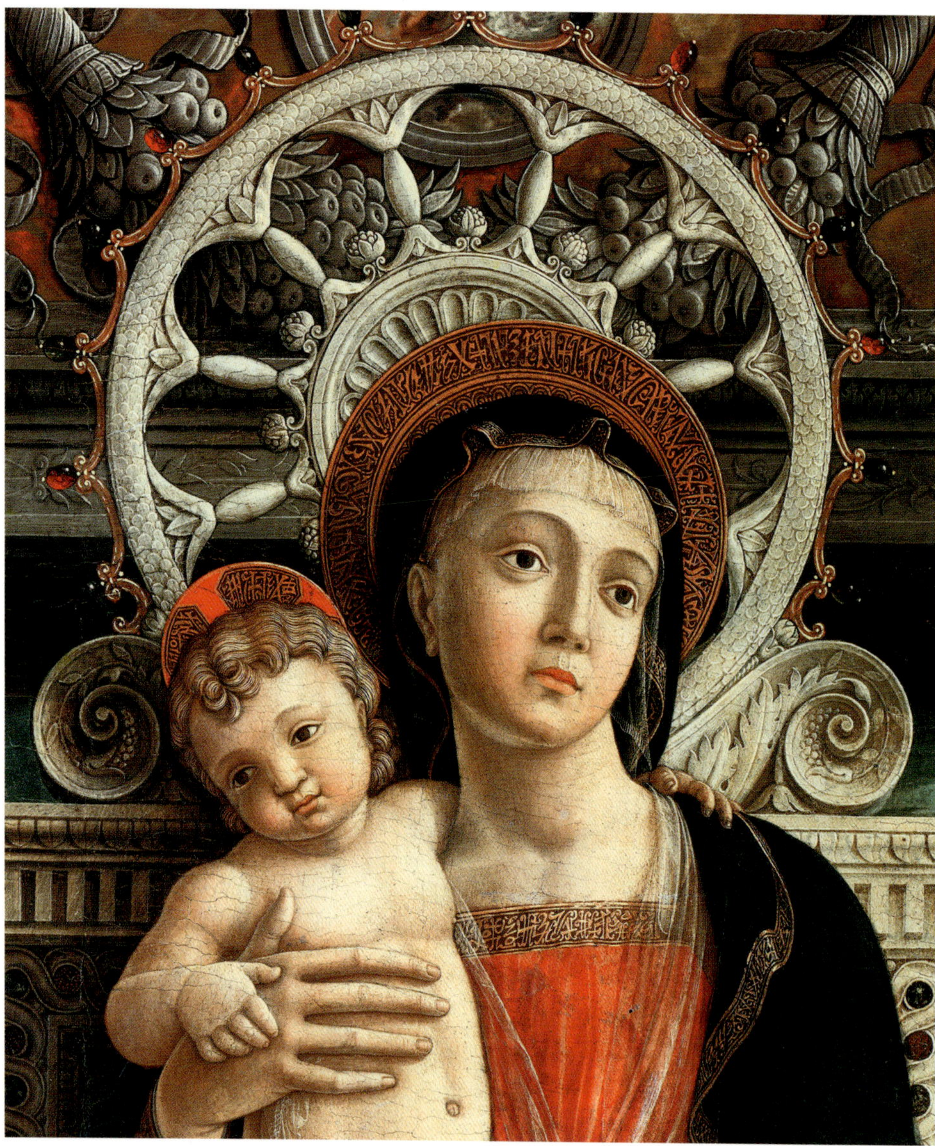

Plate 1.10 Andrea Mantegna, San Zeno altarpiece (detail from Plate 1.9).

The processes of transmission and transformation that connect Arabic calligraphy with the pseudo-Arabic in altarpieces are complex and sometimes involved 'mediators', like the pseudo-Arabic inscriptions that were a common feature of Byzantine icons and churches.[14] Certainly, however, the import of Islamic objects into Europe was a key impetus in the popularity of pseudo-Arabic, whose appearance in Christian art is a direct response to the ubiquity and aesthetic beauty of Arabic script in Islamic visual culture. As has often been noted, the pseudo-Arabic on the borders of textiles worn by holy figures in altarpieces borrows from a type of honorific robe produced in the Islamic world from around the seventh to the fourteenth centuries. These robes featured embroidered Arabic inscriptions, usually on their borders, recording the names of rulers, the year and place the textile was produced, as well as the *shahāda* or Islamic declaration of faith. Such textiles, as well as the embroidery itself, are referred to as tiraz. To add to its aesthetic value, the Arabic script used in tiraz was highly stylised and decorative, at times even to the point of being illegible, and this decorative quality was prized and retained in European pseudo-Arabic. Since tiraz was long sought after in Europe and was often given as a prestigious diplomatic gift, examples would have been available for artists to observe and imitate.

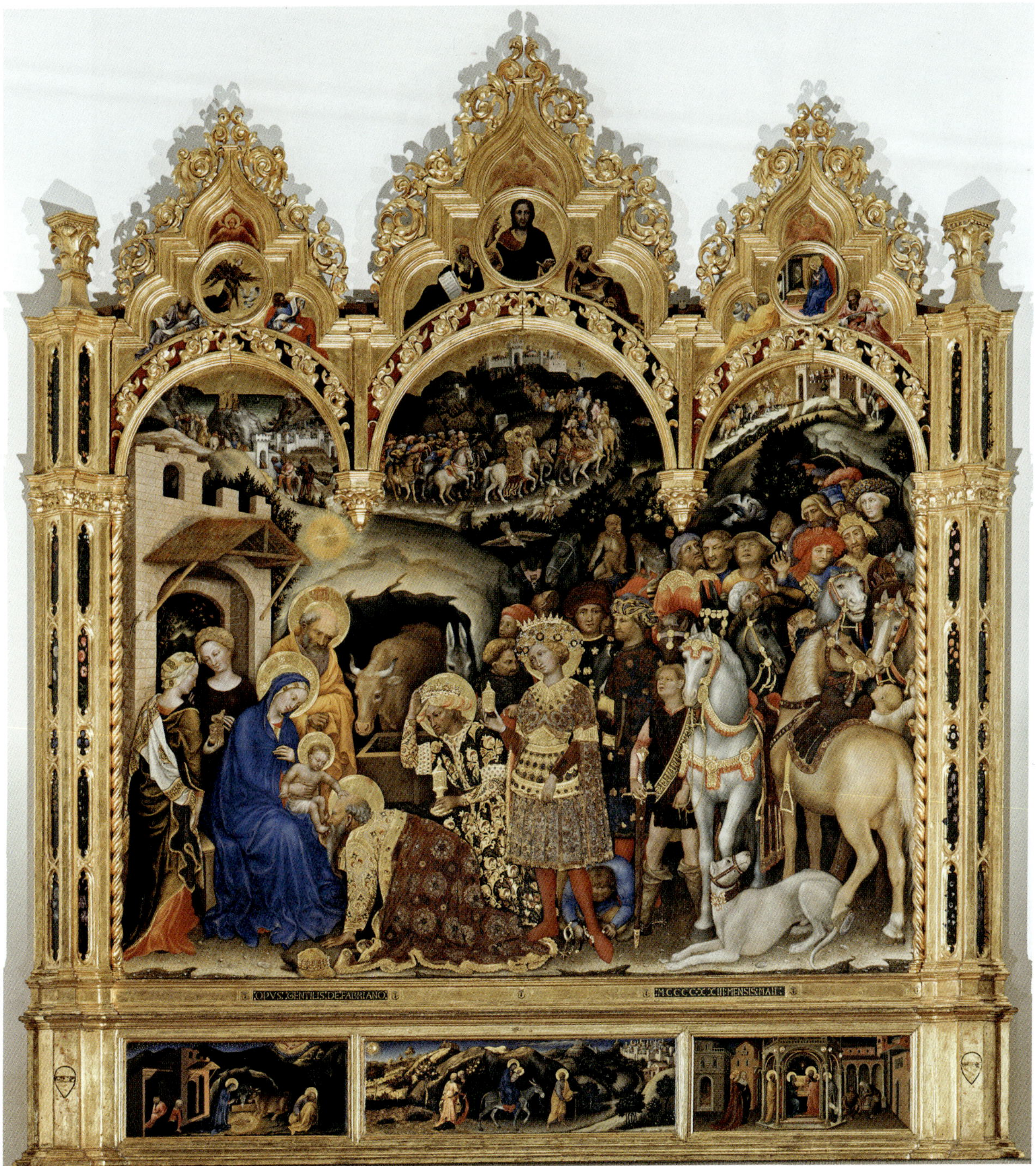

Plate 1.11 Gentile da Fabriano, *Adoration of the Magi*, 1423, tempera on panel, 203 × 282 cm. Uffizi Gallery, Florence. Photo: Bridgeman Images.

Arabic writing was also known through the import of ceramics,[15] enamelled glass or metalwork that arrived in Europe via similar channels.[16] Brass bowls with inlaid Arabic inscriptions, created in Mamluk Egypt and greatly valued in Italy (Plate 1.13), almost certainly inspired the representation in Italian altarpieces of haloes inscribed with pseudo-Arabic.

Comparisons have been made, for example, between inlaid Mamluk brass bowls and the haloes in Gentile's

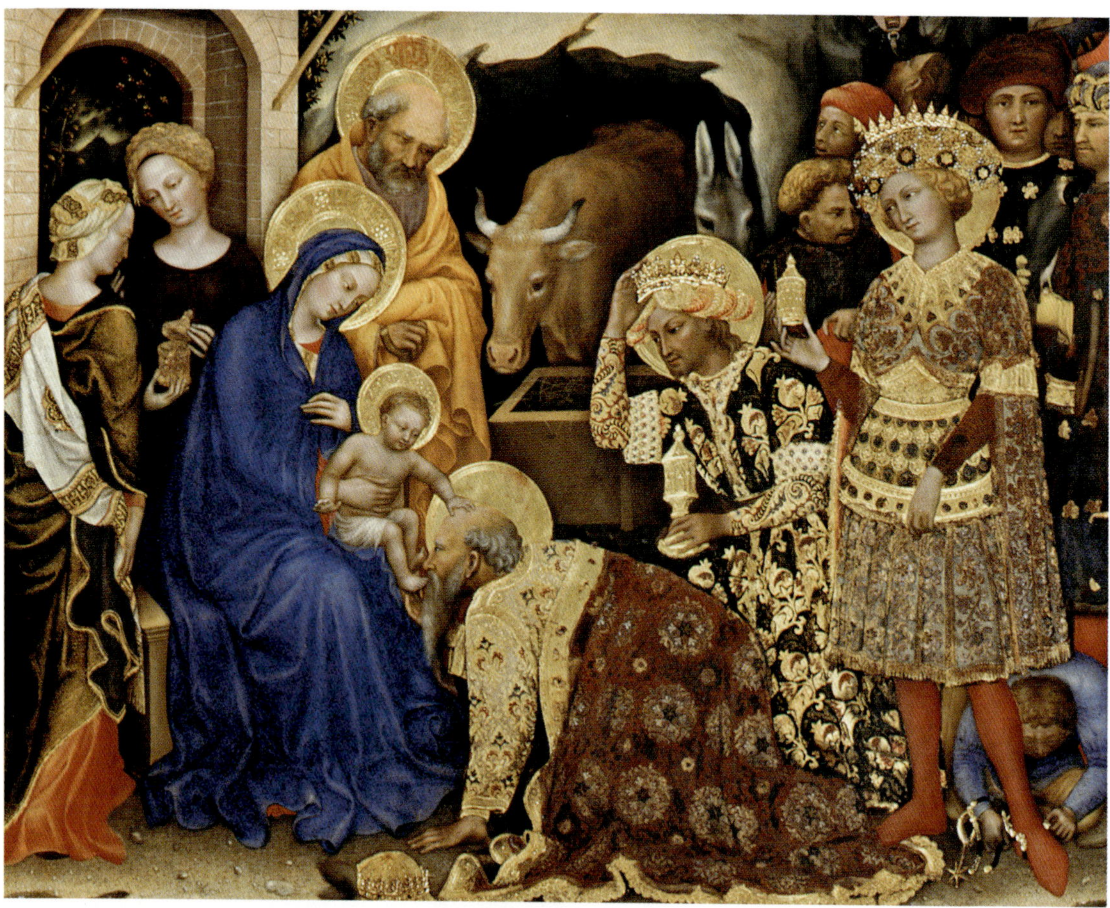

Plate 1.12 Gentile da Fabriano, *Adoration of the Magi* (detail from Plate 1.11).

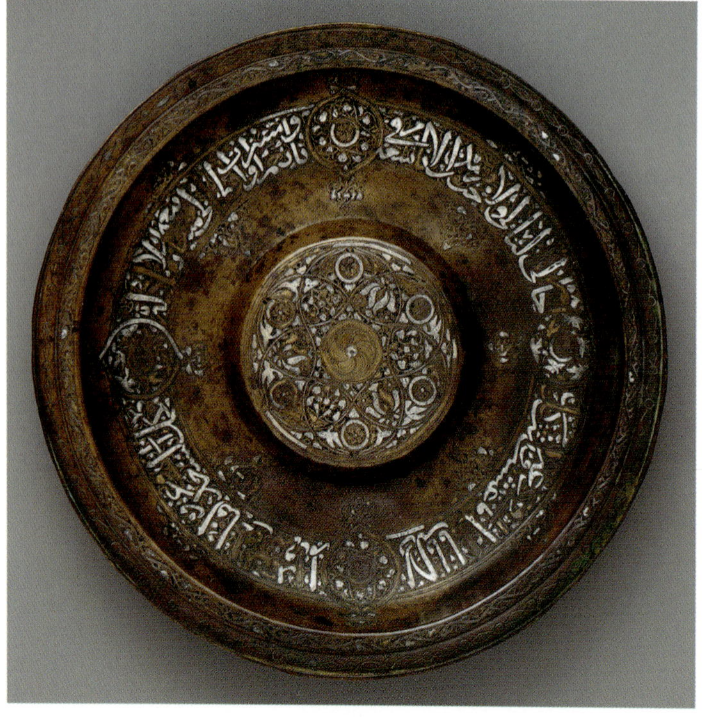

Plate 1.13 Islamic Mamluk bowl, *c.*1345–60, brass inlaid with silver and gold, diameter 29 cm. Metropolitan Museum of Art, New York, purchase, James and Diane Burke Gift, in honor of Dr Marilyn Jenkins-Madina, 2014. Photo: © 2016 The Metropolitan Museum of Art/Art Resource/Scala, Florence.

Adoration of the Magi, commissioned by the wealthy Florentine banker Palla Strozzi in 1423 for his family chapel in Santa Trinita (Plates 1.11–1.12). The haloes of Mary and Joseph (Plate 1.12) bear pseudo-Arabic inscriptions and are divided into four sections separated by rosettes: in these aspects, they recall the design of a fourteenth-century brass bowl from Mamluk Egypt, inlaid with an Arabic inscription divided into four sections.[17] Such formal similarities leave little doubt that the artist was directly inspired by the close observation of Mamluk metalwork. It is an example of the artistic and material exchange between Italians and Mamluks that increased after Florence's acquisition of the major sea ports of Pisa (1406) and Livorno (1421), which strengthened commercial and diplomatic ties and accelerated gift-giving between the two powers.[18]

While Christian and Islamic cultures shared common aesthetic interests, exchanging artistic objects as part of deeply rooted commercial and diplomatic relationships, members of each religion nevertheless regarded the other side as 'infidels'. Why, then, was pseudo-Arabic popular in sacred Christian images? While the significance of the motif no doubt depended upon the eye of the beholder, art historians have proposed several explanations. One is that artists wished to mimic Islamic objects decorated with Arabic writing, such as ceramics, metal vessels and textiles, which Christians had brought back from the Crusades (eleventh to thirteenth centuries) in the Holy Land.[19] Many such objects had been donated to church treasuries and were prized as relics: for example, a tiraz cloth made in Fatimid Egypt revered as the 'veil of Saint Anne' after its donation to the Cathedral of Apt in Provence. It seems that artists who used pseudo-Arabic in altarpieces wanted to imitate relics inscribed with Arabic writing, like the veil of Saint Anne, in order to impart a sacred aura to devotional images. Many of the narratives depicted in altarpieces are set in Palestine, yet in the Renaissance this Holy Land was Islamic, ruled by the Mamluk sultans from the thirteenth century and then, after 1517, by the Ottomans. While Islam did not, of course, exist at the time of Christ, in the fourteenth and fifteenth centuries, allusion to prized objects of Islamic material culture – which had been so eagerly acquired during the Crusades – may have invoked the Holy Land for viewers. Thus, in the same way that a tiraz cloth could be understood as a relic of Saint Anne, pseudo-Arabic may have been a means, however confused, of instilling a sense of sacredness in altarpieces.[20]

The fact that Christianity's Holy Land lay in Muslim hands reminds us of the origins of the Christian religion in the Middle East, outside of Europe. Altarpieces originated in the Catholic Church, which was administered from Rome. Yet this Church's spiritual homeland was Jerusalem, and its most sacred scripture was originally written not in Latin, but in Greek, Aramaic and Hebrew.[21] All of these aspects factor into what has been called the 'orientation' of early Italian altarpieces, that is, the gravitational pull that the East, however vaguely defined, exerts upon their imagery.[22] Reference to the East in fourteenth- and fifteenth-century altarpieces reflects Europe's profound sense of loss with regard to Jerusalem – still the most important site of Christian pilgrimage – and to frequent calls in Europe for a new crusade. For Christians in Europe, the East was sacred: it was thought to be the direction not only of the Holy Land, but also of the earthly Paradise from which Adam and Eve were expelled. It was the primary direction of Christian prayer and until the sixteenth century the apses and altars of most Christian churches faced east.[23]

Oriental carpets

The Christian religious significance of the Orient overlapped, as well, with a sense of the commercial and aesthetic value of goods from Asia and the desire of viewers to handle, view or own luxury objects imported from afar. The blurring of sacred and secular became more pronounced in the fifteenth century, as a result of a vast expansion in consumer culture in Renaissance Europe. From the 1300s to the 1500s one finds a sharp escalation in luxury consumption among wealthy elites.[24] During this time, imports from outside Europe increased, as did the market for European-made manufactured goods and luxury items which borrowed from or imitated non-European imports. By the fifteenth century, the industrial regions of the Netherlands, Flanders, Italy and southern Germany in particular were producing a dazzling array of objects, such as glass, wool and silk textiles, tapestries, woodwork, metalwork and ceramics, many of them responding to highly desirable imported goods.[25]

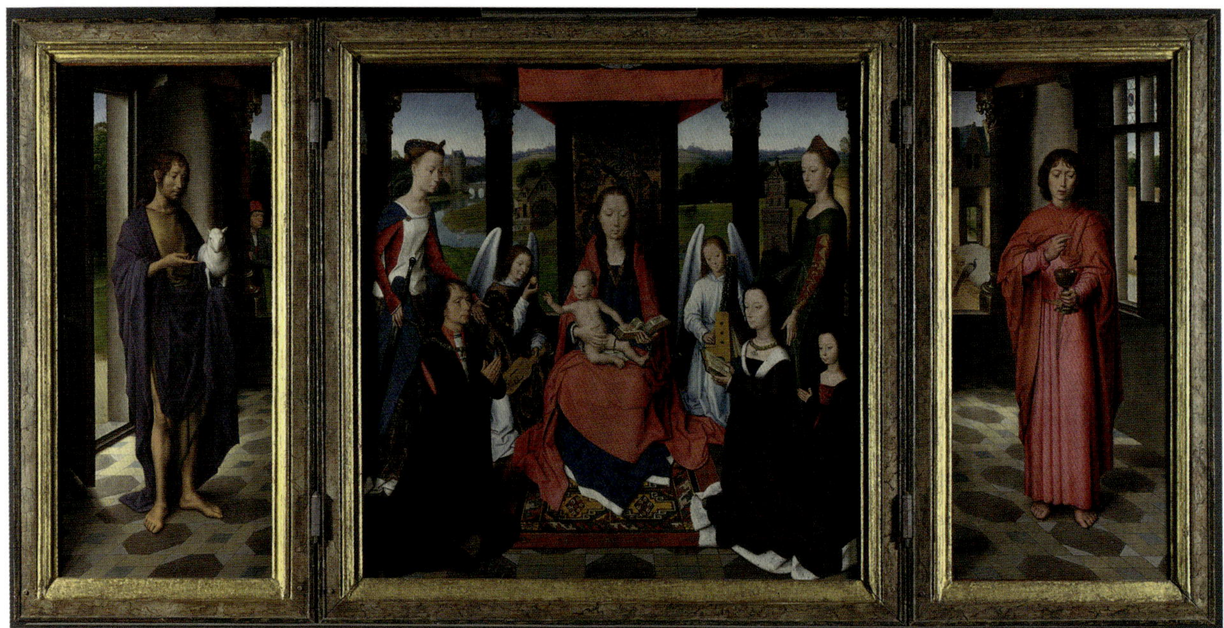

Plate 1.14 Hans Memling, Donne Triptych, c.1478, oil on oak panel, 142 × 70 cm. National Gallery, London. Photo: National Gallery.

In the fifteenth century, wealthy, urban elites were also more often commissioning altarpieces in the interest of conspicuous consumption and social prestige. The ownership of altars in private chapels expanded and new altarpieces were commissioned for them, many including prominent portraits of donors dressed in sumptuous clothing. Altarpieces more openly celebrated the diffuse array of belongings displayed in elite homes, in a way that, as Lisa Jardine has written, 'transmutes the spiritual awe of beholding the mother of God into a secular frisson of desire at the lavishness of her surroundings'.[26] They relish the newness and intense visual interest of what has been called a Renaissance 'empire of things'.[27] With the expansion of private wealth and consumption of luxuries in the fifteenth century, artists carried over into altarpieces the sense of costliness, refined materials and splendour valued in personal effects and domestic settings.

This phenomenon is exemplified by the rise in popularity of the oriental rug, one of the visually stunning imports that became much in demand in elite domestic, civic and ecclesiastical settings, while also assuming a prominent place in altarpiece design. These carpets were produced exclusively in the Islamic world and were not taken up, like other valuable goods were, as a type to be imitated and produced locally in Europe.[28] In the fifteenth century their popularity

exploded. This was a time when dealers could even provide European customers with made-to-order rugs, for example with a family's coat of arms woven into them.[29] In Islamic cultures, carpets were most often laid on the floor. In Europe, however, they were usually draped over tables, writing desks, chests or other domestic furnishings, or adorned churches, or functioned as luxurious outdoor or indoor hangings, particularly during diplomatic receptions or civic processions. They covered the ground only in very special circumstances, such as when they were laid in front of altars or thrones. Thus their appearance in altarpieces and devotional paintings at the feet of the Virgin marks the grandeur and holiness of the setting, acknowledging the Virgin's status as Queen of Heaven.

Oriental carpets first appeared in altarpieces in the fourteenth century in Italy, the centre of the European carpet trade, but featured in altarpieces throughout Europe by the fifteenth century. At that time, Netherlandish painters used techniques that had been pioneered in northern Europe – pigments mixed with translucent oils and applied with minuscule brushstrokes – to represent the vibrant colours of carpets in stunningly realistic style. In the 1430s for example, in the domain of the Dukes of Burgundy, Jan van Eyck incorporated them into his work, while Hans Memling stands out for his use of the motif of painted

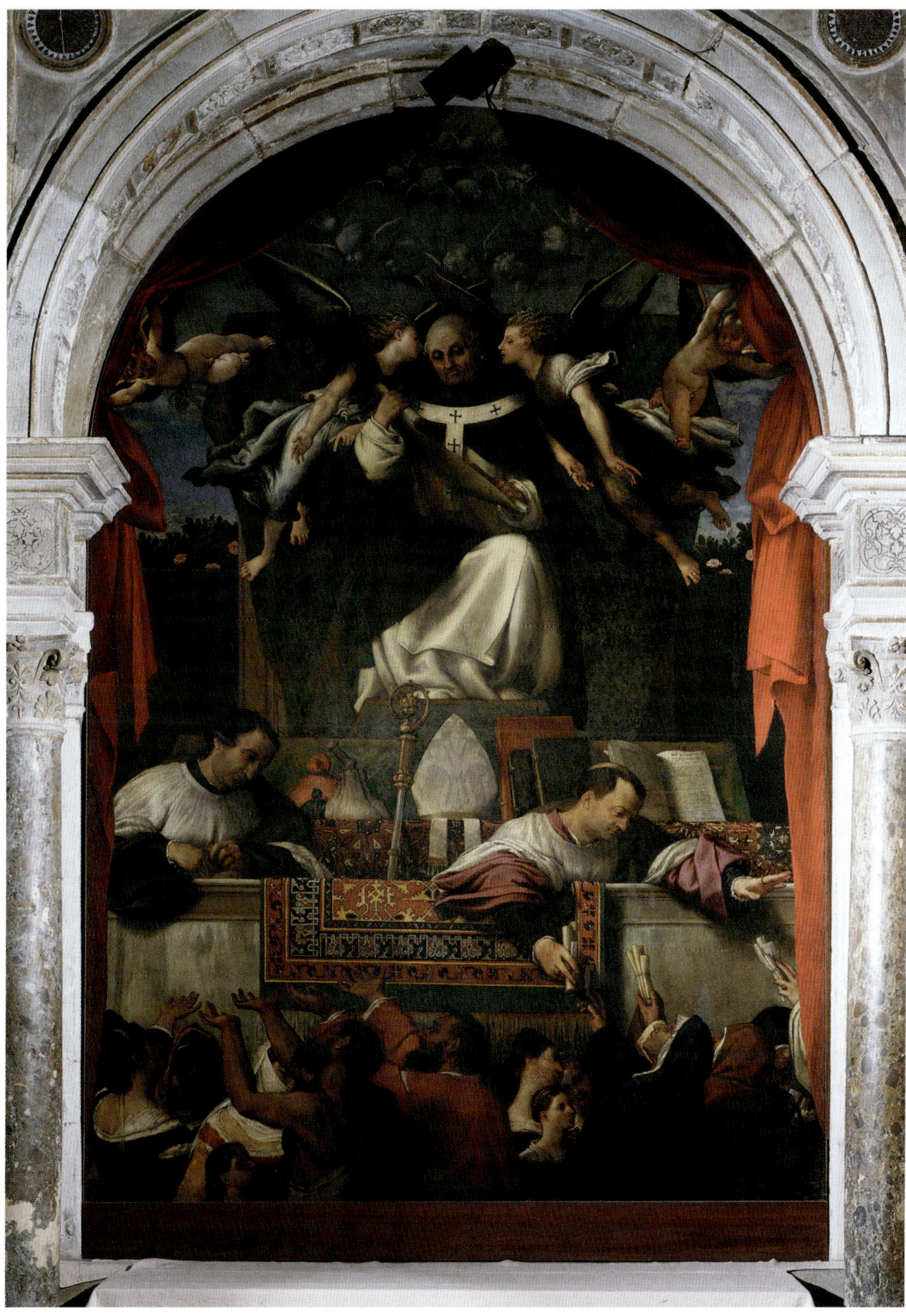

Plate 1.15 Lorenzo Lotto, *The Alms of Saint Anthony*, 1542, oil on panel, 332 × 235 cm. Basilica dei Santi Giovanni e Paolo, Venice. Photo: © 2017 Scala, Florence.

carpets underneath the Madonna's throne. A carpet probably inspired by Turkish models lies at the foot of the Virgin in Memling's Donne Triptych (Plate 1.14). This was a small altarpiece painted for Sir John Donne, a Welsh diplomat for the House of York who probably commissioned it on a visit to Bruges. Donne, his wife and daughter kneel before the Virgin. Their patron saints, Catherine (with a sword) and Barbara (with a tower), intercede between the Donne family and the Virgin. The carpet provides a suitable honorific covering for the floor where the Virgin is seated, establishing a barrier of sacredness and authority around her, while the patrons' sumptuous clothing is allowed to touch its outer corners. It also references the patrons' cosmopolitan taste and privileged access to imported goods.

Through the depiction of rugs in altarpieces from the fifteenth century one can gauge patrons' appreciation for and access to finely crafted objects, as well as the desirable colours, textures and materials of imported goods. Patrons and viewers were also keenly interested in artists' abilities to capture these qualities in paint, in a way which showcased their creativity and skill. In this sense the 'cultural transfer' of non-European objects involved not only their movement from their place of origin to new contexts, but also their representation in art using European artistic techniques, such as realism and illusionism. Indeed, the increasing importance of the commercial trade in novelties and exotic objects has been linked to a rising interest in visual observation and naturalistic visual description in the Renaissance, as seemingly lifelike, faithful artistic representations (of a rhinoceros, an oriental carpet or a Turk) became a means of comprehending the strangeness and newness of the outside world.[30]

The illusionistic representation of oriental carpets is stressed in the Venetian artist Lorenzo Lotto's *The Alms of Saint Anthony* altarpiece (Plate 1.15) commissioned by the Dominicans of Santi Giovanni e Paolo in Venice, begun in 1525 or 1526 but delivered only in 1542. Here Lotto foregrounds the depiction of a rug – a type made in western Anatolia that has since become known as a 'Lotto carpet' – laid over a balustrade, reflecting the practice of using oriental rugs as hangings during ceremonial and festive occasions.[31] Placed front and centre, it dazzles with its vibrant colours. Above, Saint Anthony, who was known for his devotion to charity, reads petitions collected from the crowd below and – aided by the counsel of angels – directs the distribution of alms to those he has deemed worthy. He is seated in a throne above an altar table laid out with liturgical objects, books, his bishop's mitre and crosier, and another large oriental carpet, with reference to the Venetian practice of covering altars with oriental rugs. Venice was the European centre for the import of such carpets, which provided a powerful creative stimulus for Lotto. He adopted them as favoured compositional and colouristic devices, in this instance using them to separate out the three hierarchical tiers of the altarpiece and to draw the viewer in with their realism and intense visual interest.[32]

Exercise

Look carefully at Gentile da Fabriano's *Adoration of the Magi* (Plates 1.11–1.12). How are global trade and diplomacy reflected in its appearance?

Discussion

The altarpiece shows the arrival of the three magi in Bethlehem. As the lavish procession winds its way from the back to the front of the painting, the kings are shown several times, at different moments of the narrative, with a large retinue accompanying them. As will be discussed in the next section, the magi were understood as foreign kings; to evoke their distant origins, the second magus wears a turban, as do members of the magi's train.

The painting is overloaded with detailed depictions of costly textiles and accessories, many of the sort that were accessible in Italy only via global trade and available to the Strozzi family only because of their vast wealth and diplomatic connections. The haloes inscribed in pseudo-Arabic are, as discussed earlier, an imaginative artistic response to Islamic metalwork, textiles and other objects, which were at the time greatly admired in Florence and other commercial centres of Italy. The clothing of the figures makes reference to the patterned silks and gold brocade velvets which were traded across cultures. The white shawl of an attendant, who examines the gift of the first magus (Plate 1.12), is decorated with pseudo-Arabic and resembles an Islamic robe of honour embroidered with tiraz. Exotic animals in the train of the magi – one can see two monkeys riding on a camel near the centre of the panel and, to the right, the heads of a lion and a leopard – serve as a reminder that Asian and African animals were much sought-after in Europe as collectables and diplomatic gifts.

2 Outsiders in the altarpiece

The Pfullendorf altarpiece

In altarpieces, depictions of Muslims and other non-Christian people often claim Christianity's status as a global, universal religion, focusing attention on the idea that the rest of the world should rightfully convert to the one, 'true' faith. An interesting example of the depiction of non-Christians can be found in an anonymous southern German altarpiece likely made in Ulm, *c*.1500, for a church in Pfullendorf near Lake Constance. The Pfullendorf altarpiece was originally painted on both front and back, though now only scant traces of the decoration of the exterior survive. The sculpted figures that were once incorporated into the large altarpiece have also unfortunately been lost, and what remains are sixteen panels divided between different museums. Eight illustrate scenes from the life of the Virgin, and another eight show prophets, half-length figures leaning outside of open windows. Originally, the prophets held long, curling scrolls. As is shown in the reconstructions here (Plates 1.16–1.17), the prophets were originally positioned next to principal narrative scenes of the life of the Virgin, as if they were looking onto these events through arched windows.

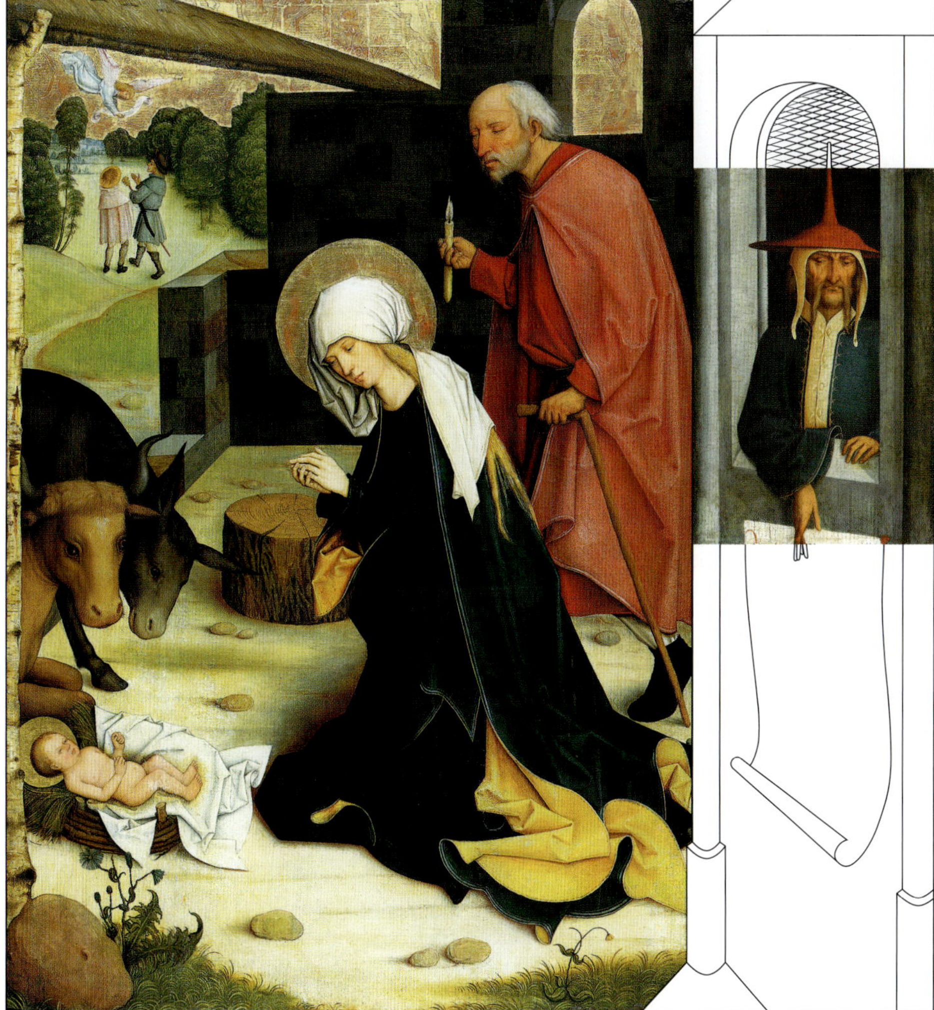

Plate 1.16 Reconstruction of a section of the Pfullendorf altarpiece, *The Birth of Christ and Prophet*. Panels: *The Birth of Christ*, Städel Museum, Frankfurt and *Prophet*, Staatsgalerie, Stuttgart. Photos: Städel Museum/Artothek and BPK/Staatsgalerie Stuttgart.

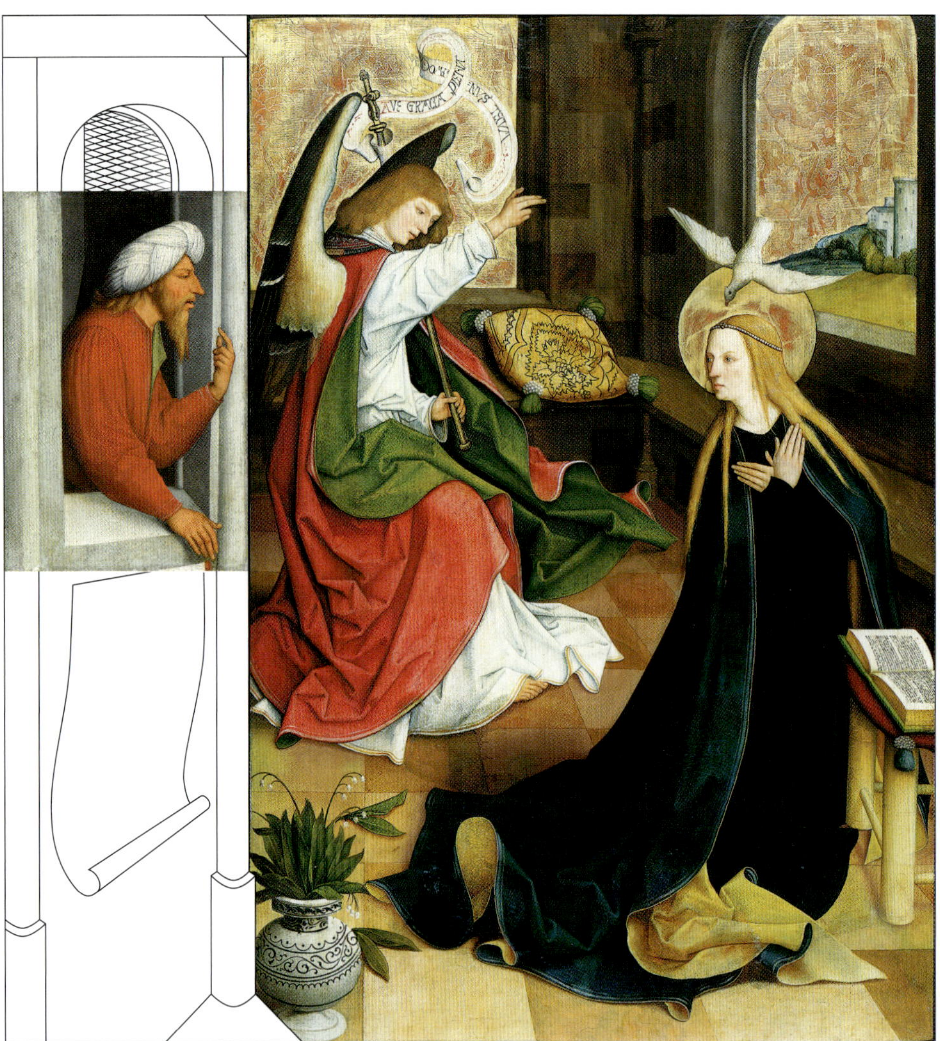

Plate 1.17 Reconstruction of a section of the Pfullendorf altarpiece, *Annunciation and Prophet*. Panels: *Annunciation*, Städel Museum, Frankfurt and *Prophet*, Staatsgalerie, Stuttgart. Photos: Städel Museum/Artothek and BPK/Staatsgalerie Stuttgart.

These prophets are figures who lived before the time of Christ, yet are able to see into the future and foretell the events of Christ's life. They represent enlightened wise men who lived in the distant past, and their scrolls are meant to be divinely inspired writings which predict the events illustrated in the main panels. With its representation of prophets in niches, the Pfullendorf altarpiece looks to the design of the *Biblia pauperum* (Plate 1.18), a printed book illustrating biblical scenes. In the *Biblia pauperum*, Hebrew prophets with scrolls bearing writings – to be understood as prophecies of Christ's coming – are shown above and below, while at the centre of each page is a narrative from the Christian New Testament (here, Christ's entry into Jerusalem), with parallel narratives from the Old Testament to either side (here, David received in triumph after his victory over Goliath, and Elijah received in Jericho).

Following the notion of typological correspondence, Old Testament stories are presented as a prefiguration of the events narrated in the Christian gospel. Such beliefs underpin the Christian approach to Hebrew scripture, which was understood as a divinely inspired prophecy of the future Christian era. While in the *Biblia pauperum* prophets are represented as Hebrew patriarchs, the Pfullendorf altarpiece uses a grab bag of conventions to represent not only Hebrew, but also vaguely Muslim and Asian wise men. Some wear Islamic-style turbans (Plate 1.17). Another, with a forked beard and a blue and white costume (Plate 1.16), is seemingly meant to be Mongol or Turkic, like figures of similar physiognomy and dress which appear in Italian art in the fourteenth century.[33] This prophet's red, pointed hat, however, conjures up the image of the Jewish hat or *pileum cornutum*, usually yellow or

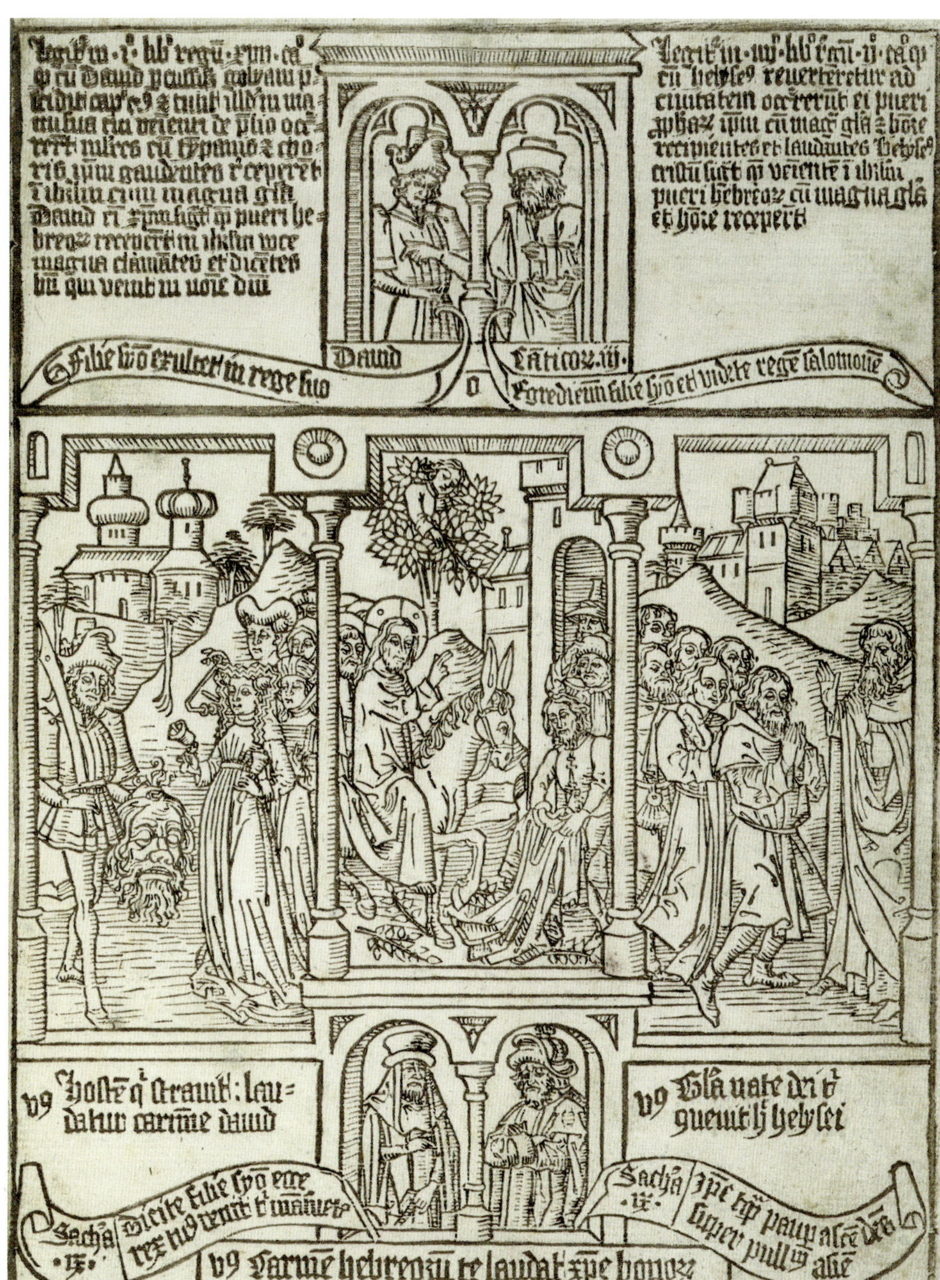

Plate 1.18 French School, David received in triumph after his victory over Goliath, the entrance of Christ into Jerusalem and Elijah received at the gates of Jericho by the sons of the prophets, in *Biblia pauperum*, early fifteenth century, xylograph. Photo: Musée Condé, Chantilly, France/Bridgeman Images.

white, that was part of the prescribed dress imposed upon Jews in many parts of Europe.[34]

These figures are marked by signs of difference and are housed in niches that separate them from the main scenes of the Virgin's life. At the same time, as prophets, they are granted an honourable role in the altarpiece, a conundrum characteristic of Christian Europe's relationship with the non-Christian world. For example, in recognition of their wisdom, in his

Divine Comedy (*c.*1308–20) the Italian poet Dante placed the Muslim philosophers Avicenna and Averroes, and Saladin, the sultan who had defeated the crusaders and captured most of the Christian Holy Land, together with virtuous pagans – Greek and Roman philosophers, poets and statesmen – in the first circle of hell, that is, in a comfortable place of limbo rather than the realm of torture and agony to which Mohammed is condemned.[35] Yet the superficial inclusion granted to select non-Christians by Dante and the Pfullendorf altarpiece is hardly a sign of tolerance. Famous representatives of other religions and cultures might be deemed admirable, or elements of non-Christian cultures adopted in the service of Christian interests, but they are presented as if they have no legitimacy or authenticity of their own.

There are clear commonalities between Judaism, Islam and Christianity, the three religions 'of the book'; all are in possession of a holy scripture, all are monotheistic, and all share common beliefs, such as the status of Abraham or Moses as prophets. In the Renaissance, this did not go unnoticed and on a certain level encouraged cultural and intellectual exchange.[36] However, even if influences or ideas were brought in, Christianity remained, in Edward Said's words, a 'closed system' which made Judaism and Islam permanent outsiders.[37] In the Pfullendorf altarpiece, Christianity's prophets are represented as Jewish or Muslim or Asian as if to sweep the non-Christian world back in time, to an era before Christ since they (like the ancient Greeks) live in ignorance, having not yet accepted the one, 'true' faith. Their conversion seemed to Christians a logical step forward, since adherents of the religions of the book were already on the path towards the Christian religion, having adopted some fragmentary parts of its truth. In this sense, the image bolsters the Church's and Europe's position in the world, and carries out the essential functions of the altarpiece: that is, to make didactic statements of religious authority and to serve as a guide to the values and beliefs of worshippers.

The Adoration of the Magi

Altarpieces offer insight into processes of assimilation, conversion and appropriation that fit non-Christian religions into a Christian world-view, history and theology. This sometimes operates through the representation in altarpieces of Others who are marked by signs of difference. 'Exotic' figures are featured prominently, for example, in images of the adoration of the magi. Between the mid-fifteenth century and c.1530 the subject of the three kings offering gifts to Christ at his birth became enormously popular. Particularly in northern Europe, one or more of the kings was typically depicted with reference to Asian/Islamic or African stereotypes. The Gospel of Matthew (2: 1–12) states that at the time of Christ's

birth magi 'from the East' followed a star to the infant and gave him gifts of gold, frankincense and myrrh, using the Greek word *magos*, a term derived from the Persian *magush* referring to Persian priests or wise men. Over the centuries, however, more specific imagery of these Eastern kings emerged: there were three kings of different ages, one old, one middle-aged and one young. Psalm 71, verse 11 mentions kings of Arabia and 'Sheba' who came to be identified with the magi, and although Sheba was likely meant to refer to Saba in Arabia, it was eventually understood as a place in Africa. Around the eleventh or twelfth centuries, writers asserted that one of the three magi was dark-skinned and that the three as a group stood in for the three continents of Asia, Africa and Europe, and thus the whole world.[38] By the twelfth century the magi had acquired names and, although these were not always assigned consistently, the name Balthasar was usually given to the youngest, Caspar to the middle-aged and Melchior to the eldest. In the fifteenth century the subject was widely adopted in art, in part because depictions of the magi's lavish dress and royal accoutrements appealed to aristocratic patrons. Artists even flattered high-status patrons by including their portraits in these scenes, painting them in the guise of the kings.

Scenes of the three magi directly reference Europe's sense of its place in the world, registering European global ambitions and the effects of increased contact with other parts of the world. Often one can detect a parallel between the three kings and the three regions of classical and medieval tradition, Asia, Africa and Europe. The eldest or middle-aged king was sometimes shown as Islamic or Asian, using referents such as a turban or Semitic features, while the third, youngest magus was often depicted, particularly in northern Europe, as African. These images could thus visualise a sense of a hierarchy of the regions of the world that put Europe and Asia above Africa, while also imagining a time when the globe would one day be united under a universal Christian Church. They read as visions of a moment when the kings of all peoples would express devotion and obedience to Christ.

In Europe it was known that there were Christian communities in distant parts of Asia and Africa, and during the 'age of exploration' hopes were high that contact could be made with them: if these were large or wealthy Christian kingdoms, it was thought, they would ally with Europe in a crusade against Islam waged on multiple fronts. The imagery of the three magi speaks to these aspirations which were focused on a figure known as Prester John. By the twelfth century a popular belief had emerged about the existence of this fictitious Christian king, who was thought to be a direct descendent of the magi. Prester John was said to rule over a vastly wealthy kingdom somewhere in Asia, particularly India, or in Africa. If only contact could be made with him, he would use his great wealth to help expel the Muslims from the Holy Land.[39]

Interest in Prester John focused more specifically on Africa after accounts reached Europe of the wealth of Musa Keita I, the Islamic ruler of Mali (r.?1312–37),

who spent unheard-of quantities of gold during a pilgrimage to Mecca in 1324–25. Europeans often referred to him as 'Mansa Musa'. A detail from the Catalan Atlas of 1375, a map (Plate 1.19) made for King Charles V of France (r.1364–80) by the Jewish cartographer Abraham Cresques of Majorca, shows 'Musse Melli' enthroned, holding a golden orb, and described as a rich and noble lord 'on account of the abundance of gold gathered in his kingdom'.[40] Amid these developments, the motif of the 'black magus' emerged in the fourteenth century in central Europe and Germany (relics of the magi were splendidly enshrined in Cologne Cathedral) and it continued predominantly in northern Europe.[41] It seems to have appeared first in the Netherlands in Hans Memling's influential *Adoration of the Magi* (Plate 1.20), inspired by the central panel of Rogier van der Weyden's Saint Columba altarpiece. Here enduring visual

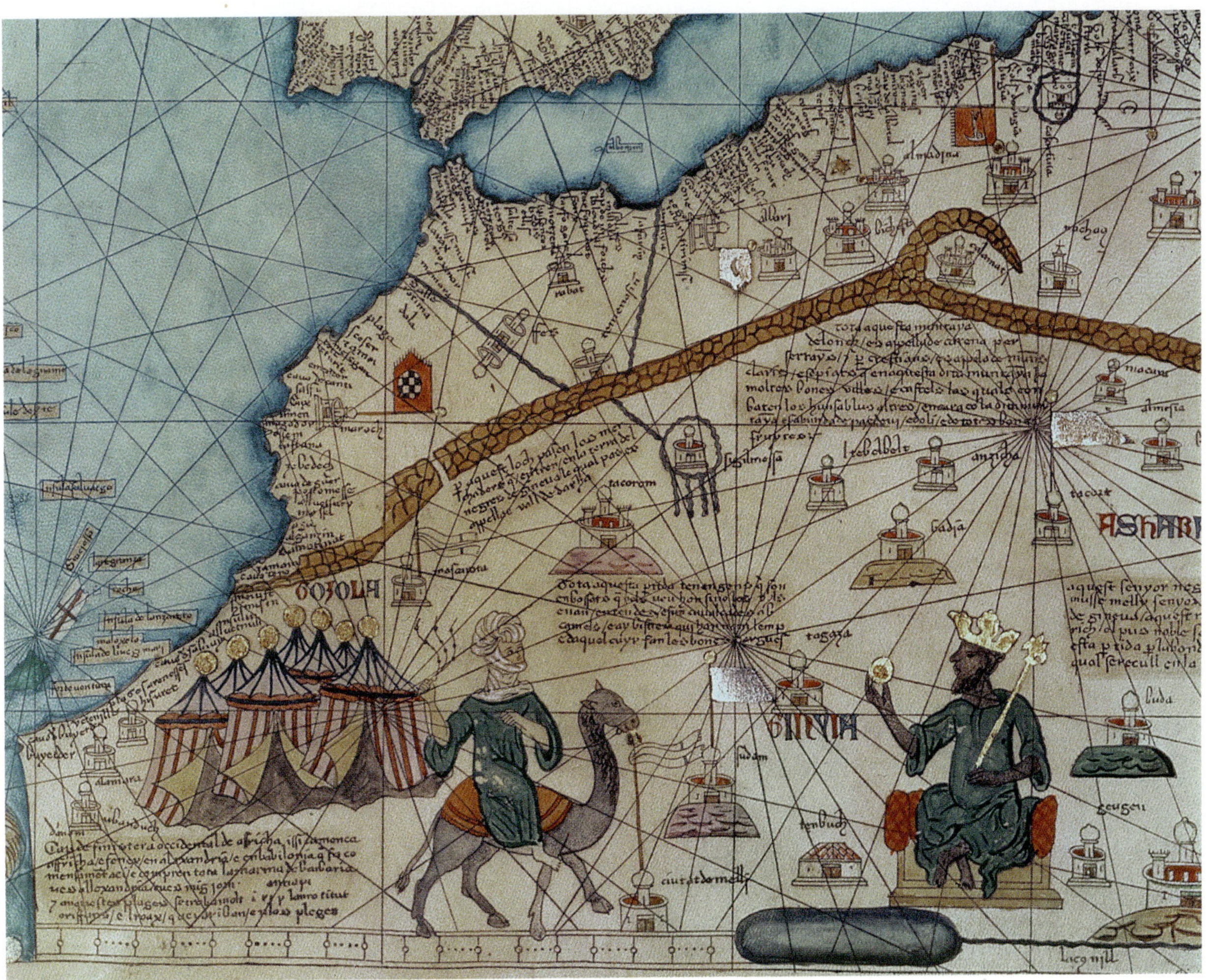

Plate 1.19 Abraham Cresques, Catalan Atlas, 1375, parchment. Bibliothèque Nationale, Paris. Photo: Bridgeman Images.

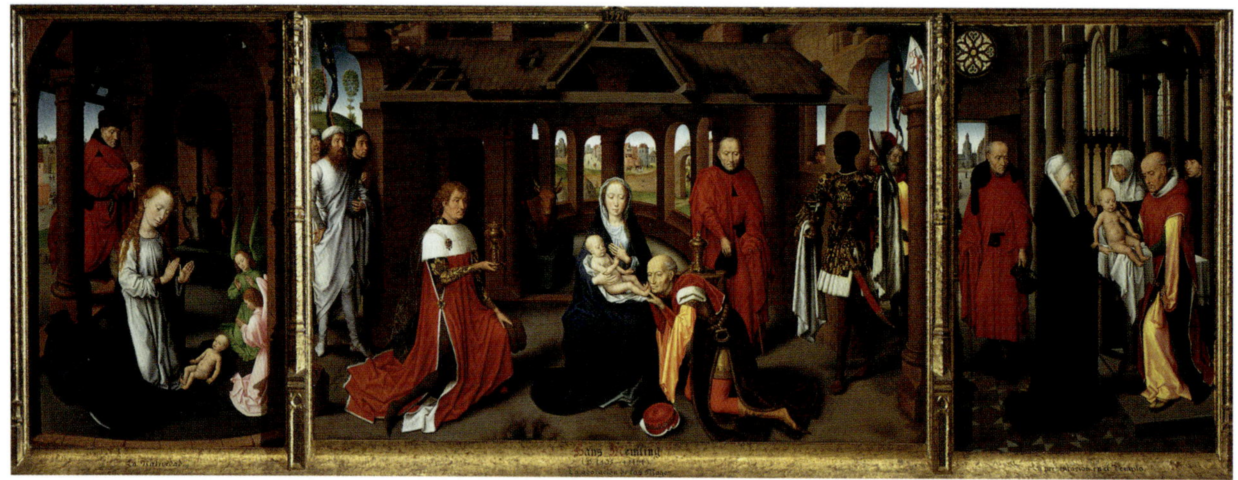

Plate 1.20 Hans Memling, *Adoration of the Magi*, 1470–72, oil on panel, 95 × 271 cm. Prado, Madrid. Photo: Getty.

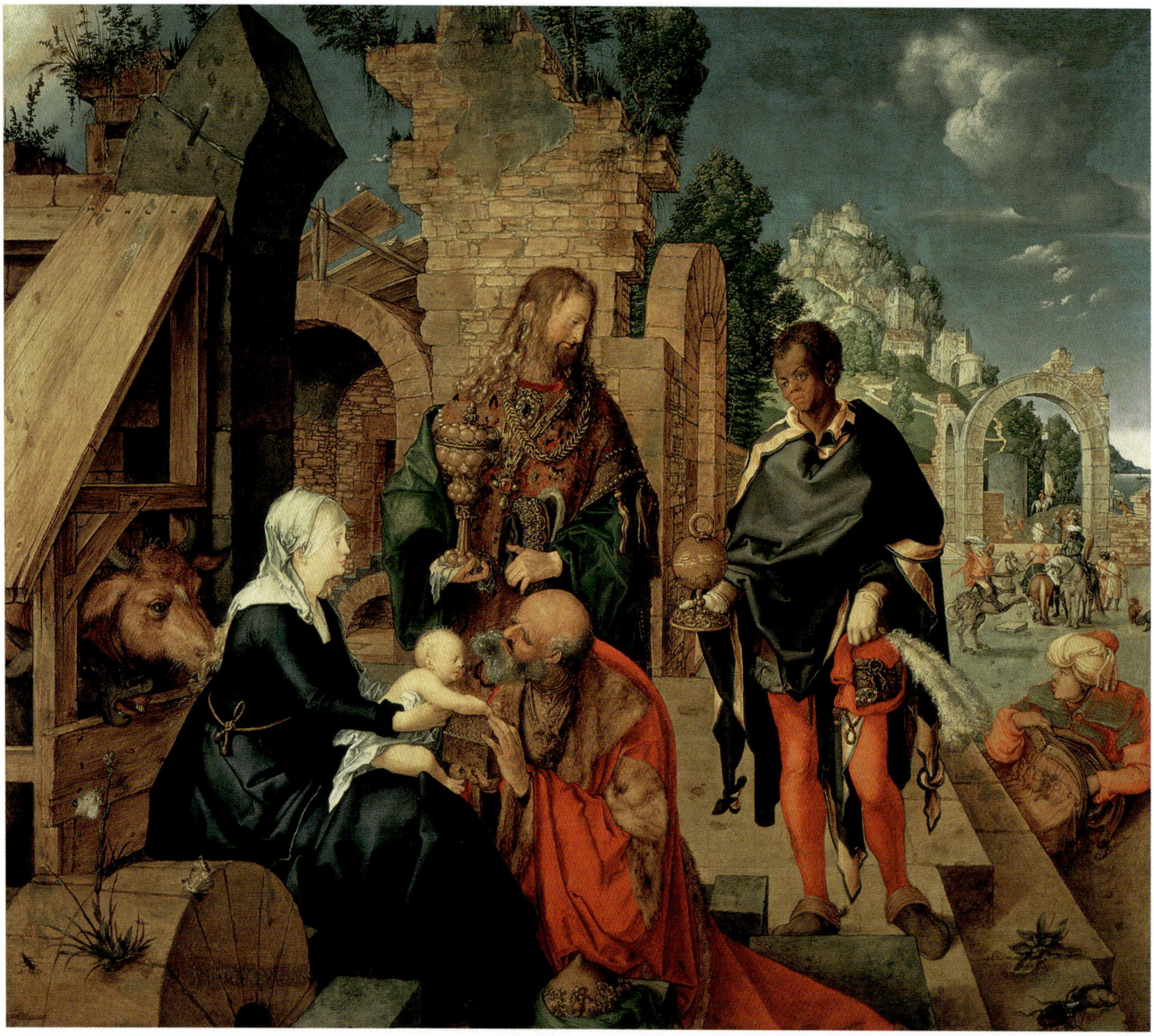

Plate 1.21 Albrecht Dürer, *Adoration of the Magi*, 1504, oil on panel, 100 × 114 cm. Uffizi Gallery, Florence. Photo: Bridgeman Images.

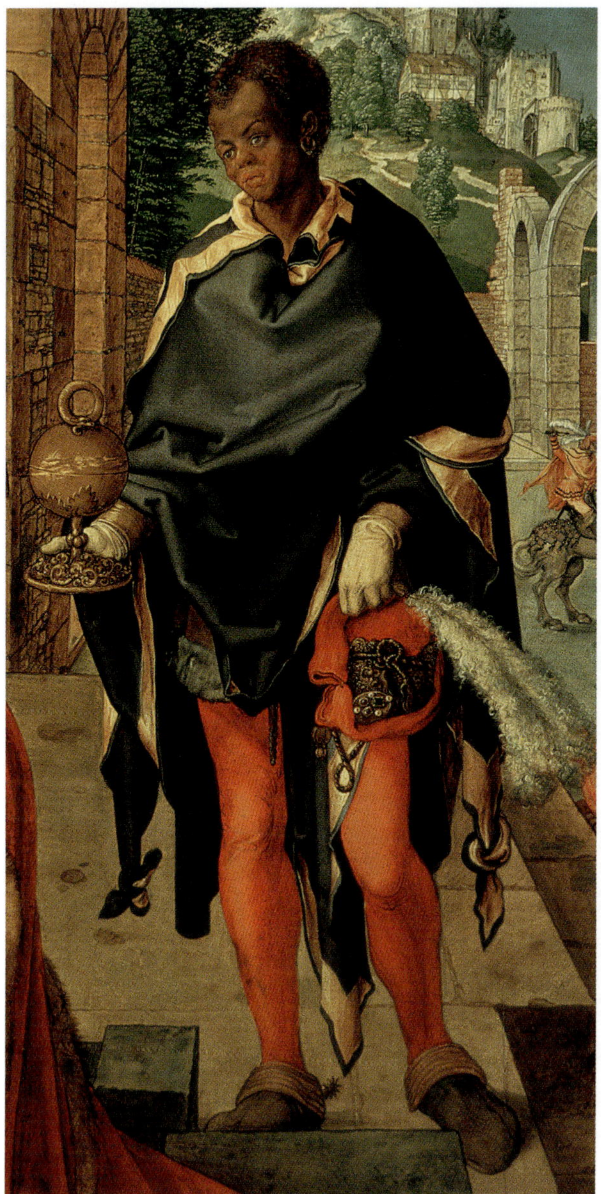

Plate 1.22 Albrecht Dürer, *Adoration of the Magi* (detail from Plate 1.21).

conventions for the African magus are already present. He is the youngest (Balthasar) and the furthest away from Christ,[42] set apart by the colour of his skin and his single earring. The earring is a symbolic stand-in for African gold and a sign of difference, which would be reserved exclusively for this exotic 'third' king who could combine African with Asian stereotypes. The African king was, in the fifteenth and sixteenth centuries, sometimes shown wearing a turban or dressed in exuberant, colourful dress, sometimes

with feminised or sexualised overtones. These representations are not highly degrading, and the African king is always shown as a noble and regal figure, evoking the legendary Prester John. At the same time, he is branded as an outsider and an unfamiliar spectacle who is clearly positioned at the bottom of the hierarchy of kings.[43]

Portuguese expeditions on the West African coast during the fifteenth century had initiated the Atlantic slave trade that brought Africans into Spain and Portugal and from there to the rest of Europe. A paradoxical situation arose which saw an increased interest in the imagery of African kings at a time when African slavery was expanding.[44] The German artist Albrecht Dürer drew remarkable charcoal portraits of Africans he encountered in Europe, one of them a slave or servant named Katharina, whom he drew in the house of a Portuguese factor in the Netherlands, and another an anonymous African man, probably also a slave or servant in a noble home, whom he might have considered a model for a king.[45] While Dürer's drawings capture his subjects with sensitivity, the artist likely regarded them as curiosities, at a time when African servants could be purchased as status symbols or given as gifts.[46] In 1504, Dürer painted an altarpiece of the three magi for Frederick III the Wise, Elector of Saxony, who commissioned it along with other artistic treasures for the church he built for his castle in Wittenberg (Plates 1.21 and 1.22).[47] Dürer took the opportunity to include his own self-portrait in his altarpiece, as the middle-aged magus standing close to Christ and the Virgin. He followed the usual practice of representing the black magus as the furthest away, on the outside edge of the scene, although in a much nobler guise than the caricatured, turbaned 'Turk' next to him, who seems to be reaching for gifts.

Dürer's Turk shows how adorations offered patrons and artists an excuse to marvel not only at the magi themselves, but also at an array of 'exotic' people, luxury goods, animals and servants in their train. Such details played into the appeal of these topics among wealthy patrons drawn to the opulence and pageantry of royal processions, as well as to the world of trade, commerce and global commodities evoked by the magi and their entourage. The Asian and African attributes of the magi assimilate them to the rare gifts that they are shown offering to Christ. These are the presents of gold and costly ointments they brought with them from

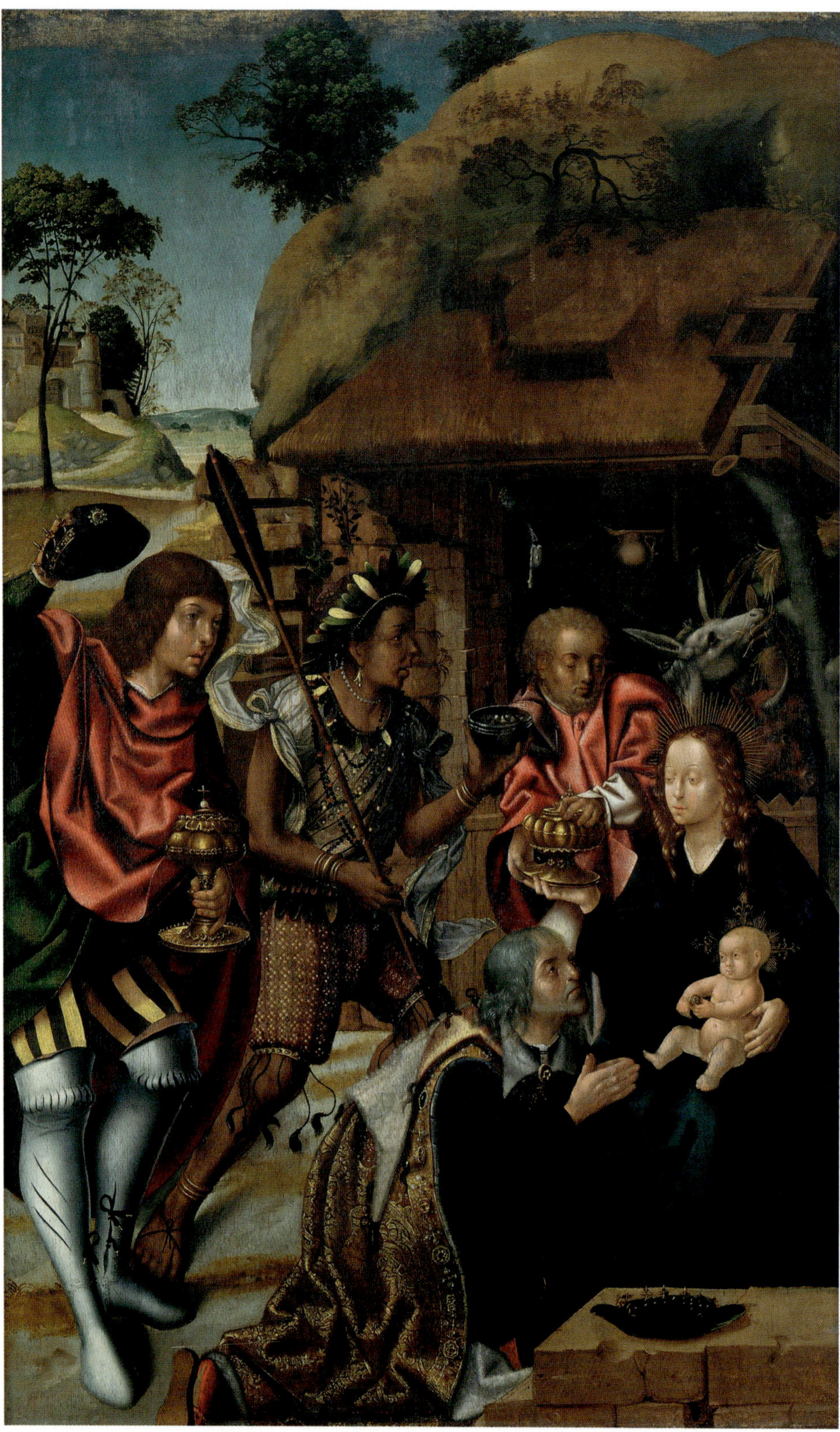

Plate 1.23 Attributed to Vasco Fernandes, *Adoration of the Magi*, 1501–06, oil on panel, 132 × 79 cm. Vasco Museum, Viseu. Photo: Direção-Geral do Património Cultural/ Arquivo e Documentação Fotográfica.

some adorations, artists chose to depict the magi's gifts with reference to the global trade in luxuries, as is seen in the porcelain cup that the senior magus offers to Christ in Mantegna's *Adoration* (Chapter 3, Plate 3.4). Their crossover with the topics of expansionism and trade helped to make adoration scenes a runaway success in Lisbon and Antwerp, two major hubs of commerce; in the sixteenth century Antwerp became a veritable factory for the production of these scenes, which were popular locally and also exported widely in Europe and beyond.[49]

A unique and surprising representation of the youngest king is found in an adoration attributed to the Portuguese painter Vasco Fernandes, also known as Grão Vasco or Great Vasco. It was commissioned from Vasco and a team of other artists by the Bishop of Viseu in northern Portugal as part of a large, multi-panelled high altar of the Cathedral of Viseu, which was the artist's birthplace.[50] The altarpiece illustrates scenes from the life of Christ, including the adoration of the magi (Plates 1.23 and 1.24). At the moment of its creation, the Portuguese could claim major victories under Manuel I (r.1495–1521), namely Vasco da Gama's voyage to India in 1497–99 and the arrival of Pedro Álvares Cabral in 1500 in what would later be known as Brazil. In recognition of Cabral's discovery, Vasco's altarpiece replaces Balthasar, elsewhere shown as African, with an American or Asian magus; it was not yet clear whether Brazil was a previously unknown part of Asia or on a new continent. The tribute was fitting given that Cabral had personal ties to Viseu, where his noble family owned property. Indeed, the oldest magus kneeling before Christ, offering a gift of gold coin stamped with the Portuguese royal insignia to the Virgin, has been thought to be a portrait of Cabral. Cabral was only in his mid-thirties at the time, yet is likely shown as the elderly Melchior in the altarpiece in deference to his status.

The youngest magus at the centre wears a European shirt and breeches decorated with feathers, yet the rest of his body is notably exposed, alluding to the nudity of the Tupinambá – the native population of coastal Brazil – that both shocked and titillated Europeans. The magus wears a feather headdress and holds a feathered arrow; as Jean Michel Massing has pointed out, these objects and the magus's featherwork are

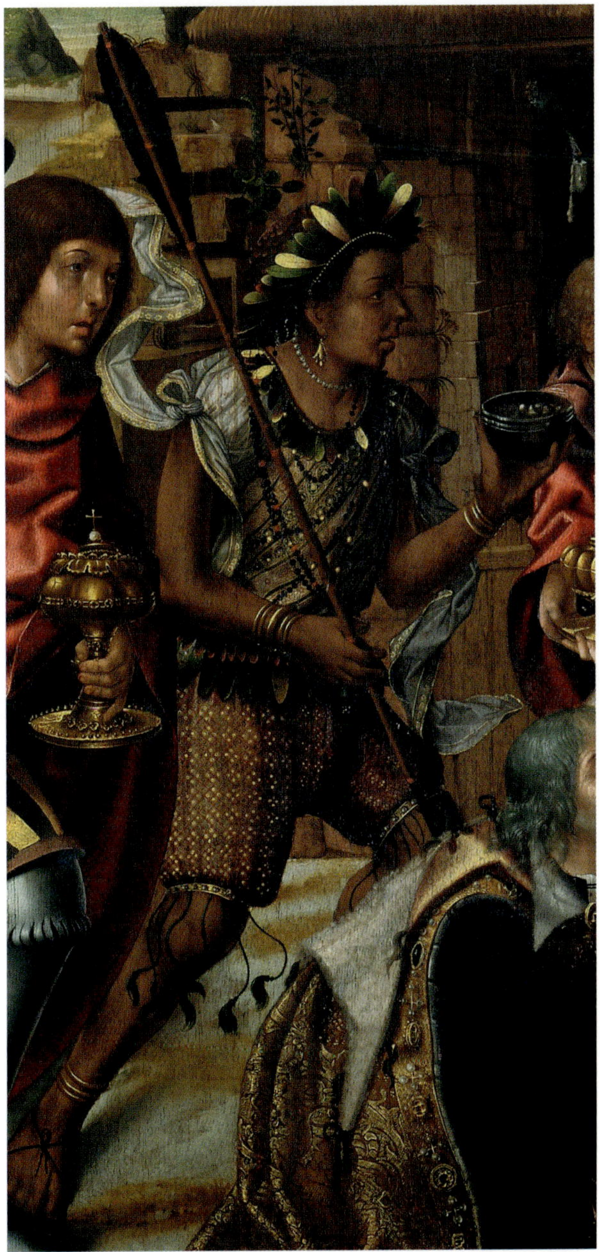

Plate 1.24 Attributed to Vasco Fernandes, *Adoration of the Magi* (detail from Plate 1.23).

afar, implicitly associating them with phenomena such as diplomatic tributes, the global trade in gold (Melchior's gift), and the merchants who imported precious fragrant oils from the Levant. The containers the magi carry – lidded chalices, or caskets decorated with jewels – are often inspired by real containers that had long been imported from the Islamic world.[48] In the first known full-colour, realistic and ethnographic representations of artefacts and costumes from the New World.[51] Their realism suggests that some elements of his dress may have been modelled on drawings of Tupinambá made in Brazil, or on the Tupinambá that Cabral may have brought back with him to Portugal. What is certainly exaggerated, however, is his jewellery, including his prominent earring, the pearls and beads around his neck, his gold bracelets and ankle bracelets, notable signs of the wealth Portugal hoped to derive from newly discovered territories. The magus runs towards Christ, draperies and feathers flying in the air, delivering coins in a silver-mounted coconut shell, as if to show how quickly this wealth will come and how enthusiastically the New World will embrace the Christian faith. This and other adoration altarpieces offer to their audience of worshippers a celebration of Christianity's universalist mission, as well as a sense of certainty about the willing conversion of non-Christians.

3 Pigments, materials and techniques

Global trade brought a constant influx of materials and technical knowledge into Europe, with major consequences for the visual arts. In the pre-industrial world, all forms of manufacturing and medicine relied upon a rather limited list of raw materials, some of which were sourced only with great difficulty via long-distance trade networks. Discovering new plants and minerals or new supplies of essential resources were key motivating factors in global trade and overseas exploration. When new territories were reached, botanists were among the first off the ship to scout for potential finds.[52] The discovery of new pigments was an important catalyst in global trade, particularly because of their commercial value as dyes in the textile industries, and new colours became available to artists as a result. This section will consider the significance of the trade in materials for the appearance and symbolic meaning of altarpieces, then turn briefly to the movement of technical and scientific knowledge around the world and its relevance for the visual arts. Pigments and materials of different origins could communicate particular associations – economic, cultural, geographic – to viewers.[53] Even though these are easily lost upon a modern-day audience and

difficult to recover, they were an important part of the meaning of works of art in this era: artists' guild regulations and contracts for altarpieces often made exacting demands regarding the type and expense of the materials artists could use.

Pigments, the substances that gave paint its colour when mixed with a binder (in Europe in this period, either linseed or walnut oil to make oil paint, or egg yolk to make tempera), were made from natural materials. Some were easily available locally, while other particularly valuable ones were imported from distant lands.[54] Among the most expensive was a deep blue pigment known as ultramarine. It was extracted from lapis lazuli, a stone quarried with great difficulty from the mountains of what is now Afghanistan. Ultramarine had been used since antiquity, but in the thirteenth century the Pax Mongolica made it more easily accessible. As a result, in the fourteenth century, stunning ultramarine blues from Afghanistan became a hallmark of European altarpieces and other works of art, where they were a distinctive marker of opulence, as recognisable and as costly as gold.[55] In the Ghent altarpiece (Plate 1.25), the artist first painted the robe of the Madonna with base layers of azurite, a less expensive blue pigment, but topped these with layers of ultramarine, then with transparent glazes mixed with ultramarine to create rich, shimmering blues, whose original effects have since been dulled by layers of varnish.[56]

Conceptually, pigments belonged to the same category as the medicines and spices brought to Europe from the distant corners of the world: one need only think of a substance such as bright yellow turmeric, which is used for its flavour, colour and medicinal properties, to understand how these categories overlap. In southern Europe, pigments were most often dispensed by apothecaries, who were traders in drugs and other varieties of precious substances and spices, while in northern Europe, grocers often traded in both pigments and spices.[57] The trade in pigments had long stimulated cultural exchange and innovations in art and design. For example, Persian traders in the fourteenth century supplied China with cobalt, leading to the invention of a distinctive, visually striking and commercially successful blue-and-white porcelain ware.

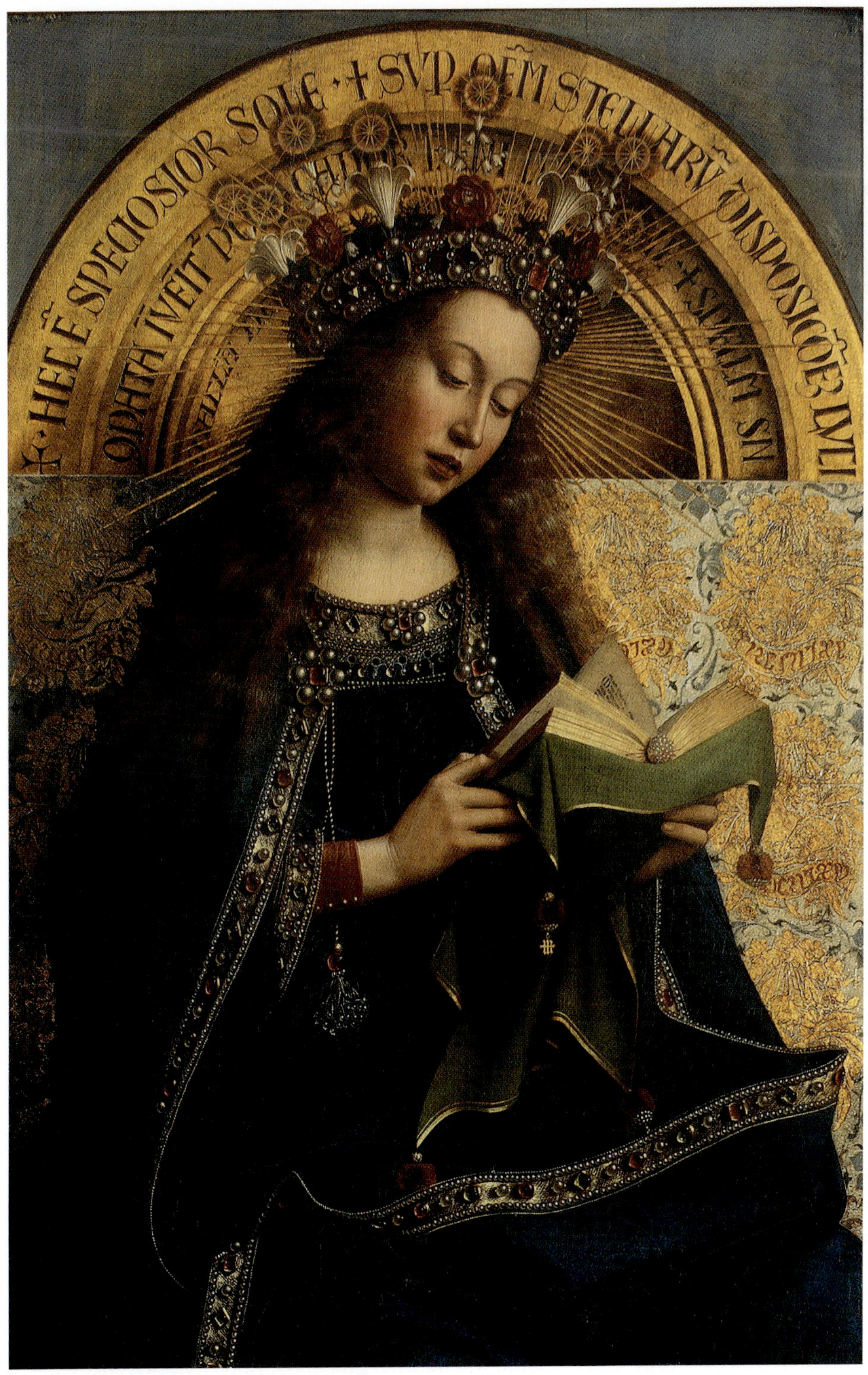

Plate 1.25 Hubert and Jan van Eyck, detail of the Virgin Mary from the Ghent altarpiece, 1430–32, oil on panel. Saint Bavo Cathedral, Ghent. Photo: Bridgeman Images.

Like blues, red pigments hit the eye instantly and the discovery of new shades could bring significant profits in the craft and textile industries. Overseas voyages and new finds added to the European repertoire of reds, with significant consequences in the commercial sphere and the arts. European red pigments were most often made from the mineral ore cinnabar, or from leftover strips of cloth that had been dyed with kermes, a red colour created from the secretion of a type of insect harvested in different parts of Europe.

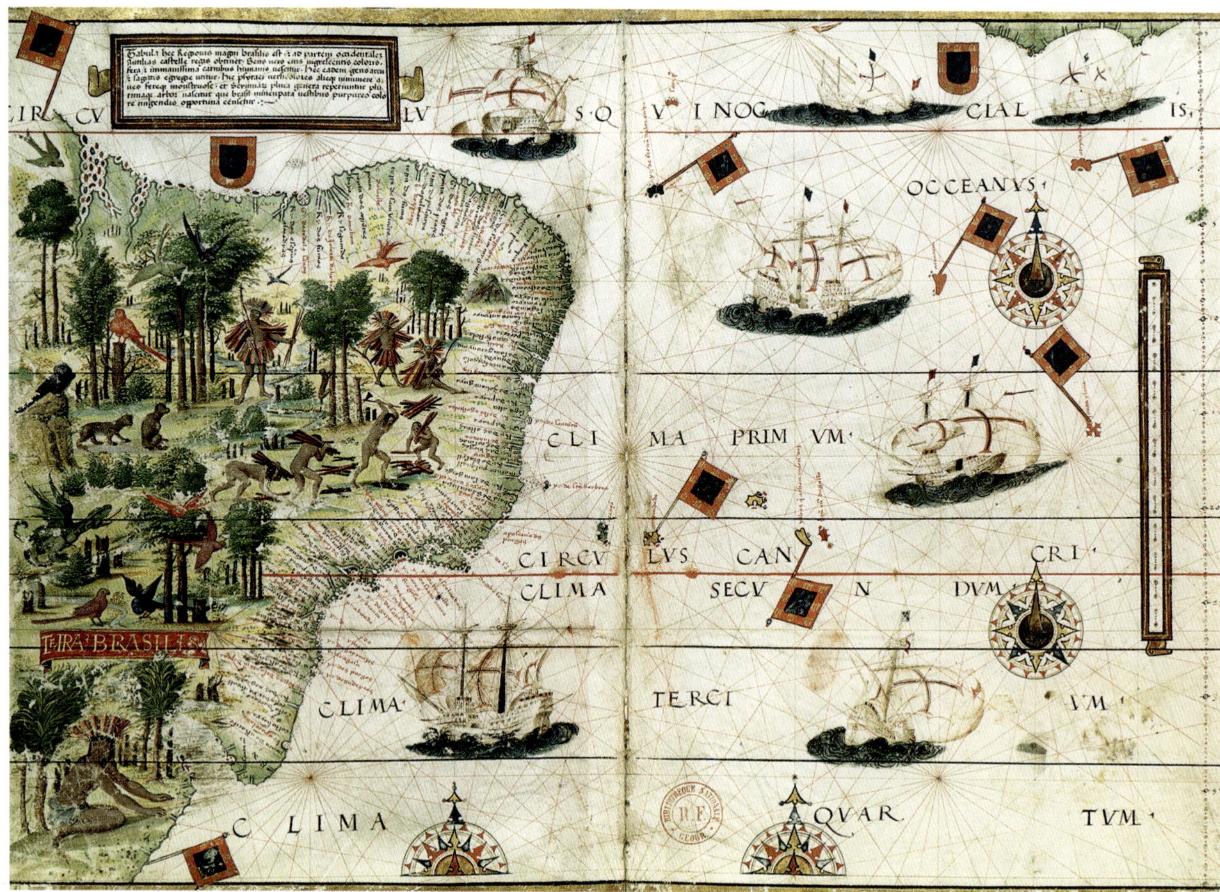

Plate 1.26 Cartography attributed to Lopo Homem, Pedro Reinel and Jorge Reinel, illustrated by miniaturist António de Holanda, *Terra Brasilis*, in the Miller Atlas, *c.*1525. Bibliothèque Nationale, Paris. Photo: Bridgeman Images.

Other types of reds, however, were imported from abroad, for example stick lac, the secretion of an insect harvested in India and South-East Asia, and dyes derived from sappanwood, an Asian tree. Sappanwood was known in Portuguese as *pau-brasil*, since the red colour recalled that of burning embers, or *brasa*. Soon after Cabral landed in Brazil in 1500, the Portuguese discovered trees of the same genus as *pau-brasil*; these trees and their pigment were so important to the Portuguese that they named this land 'Brasil'.[58] The labour-intensive harvest of the wood was carried out by indigenous Tupinambá, who received tools and other goods in exchange. An extraordinary map of the north-west coast of Brazil, made *c.*1525 (Plate 1.26), shows Portuguese ships ferrying their precious cargo across the Atlantic. It reflects a detailed knowledge of the coastline, yet a dim perception of the interior as a land of exotic animals and of naked workers cutting and carrying logs, goaded on by men in colourful feather costumes. Around the same time, the Spanish conquest of Mexico brought knowledge of cochineal, an Aztec dye derived from insects which could produce a deep red very similar to kermes.[59] After it was introduced in Europe in the sixteenth century, it was soon highly prized as both an artistic pigment and a textile dye, and eventually became, after silver, the most valuable European export from the Americas.[60]

Gold was another global commodity essential in altarpiece production, especially between the thirteenth and fifteenth centuries when it was often used in the backgrounds and frames of altarpieces. It gave altarpieces a holy aura and made them shine like mirrors, reflecting candlelight from the altar table and casting a brilliant light into their surroundings. Such effects were only possible because of facilitated trade with the gold-rich West African coast, particularly during the twelfth to thirteenth centuries, when camel caravans transported gold mined in the western Sudan (what is now Ghana), across the Sahara, to the Mediterranean ports in North Africa where it could be accessed by European merchants. Although Europe's first major gold mine opened in Serbia in 1252, African gold carried by Muslim traders continued to dominate the European markets. In the fifteenth century, the Portuguese could claim a major victory when they established direct trade with the gold-producing kingdoms of sub-Saharan Africa.[61]

Glittering emeralds and balas rubies originated primarily in India and travelled into Europe over the silk roads, via Persia and Egypt. The global supply of pearls came principally from India, Ceylon and Persia. Thus the jewels and pearls that were such an integral part of the European visual language of magnificence were imported by the thousands from Asia.[62] India's abundance of gems fuelled speculation that it was home to the earthly Paradise, and its mystique contributed to the European image of the East as a place of other-worldly luxury and wealth.[63] Altarpieces often evoke the colour and luminosity of gems. The costliest altarpieces could include real jewels, while others incorporated imitation gems made of glass or paste. Artists strove to replicate their brilliance in paint, as is seen in the gems and pearls adorning the crown and cloak of the Madonna in Hubert and Jan van Eyck's Ghent altarpiece (Plate 1.25), where the oil technique is used to mimic their radiance and translucence.

The search for pigments, gems and other precious materials is just one example of the ways in which global networks impacted on Renaissance art. Another is the corpus of scientific knowledge circulating around the world, which was also a vital stimulus for artists in this era. An illustration can be found in Fra Angelico's San Marco altarpiece (Plate 1.27), painted for the Dominican monastery of San Marco in Florence, c.1440. The work is widely celebrated as an early example of the transition in Italy from the multi-panelled polyptych to the single pala, whose frame could be imagined as a window

onto the world. In Fra Angelico's altarpiece, the Virgin and Child are shown enthroned and flanked by angels and saints. In the foreground, saints Cosmas and Damian, patron saints of the Medici family (who donated the altarpiece), kneel upon an Anatolian-style carpet, its border decorated with red balls in reference to those in the Medici coat of arms.

The San Marco altarpiece is an early example of a type painted on a unified, single panel that presents an illusionistic view into a three-dimensional world. It is notable for its exacting use of linear perspective, a technique for constructing space perfected by central Italian artists in the early fifteenth century. Fra Angelico exploits the geometric pattern in the rug to set up lines that seem to recede into the painting and converge at a single, 'vanishing' point, symbolically positioned at Mary's womb. Artists in fifteenth-century Italy, particularly in Florence, touted linear perspective as a hallmark achievement of their profession that allied them with the illustrious science of geometry. Perspective has been seen as a fundamental invention of the Italian Renaissance and of European art generally. Yet, as Hans Belting and others have pointed out, the Islamic science of optics played a critical role in the development of linear perspective.[64] The science of perspective, as it was laid out by the Florentine architect and humanist Leon Battista Alberti in his treatise *On Painting* (Italian edition 1435, Latin edition 1439–41), originated in the study of optics and the mechanics of human vision. At that time in Europe, these fields relied heavily upon treatises by Arab and Persian scholars composed between the ninth and eleventh centuries and subsequently translated into Latin. The work of thinkers known in Europe as al-Kindi (c.801–73), Avicenna (c.980–1037) and Alhacen (c.965–c.1040) was critical for the study of optics, and when Alberti composed his book on perspective he relied upon a treatise called *Perspectiva* written by Alhacen, a scientist and polymath who had worked in Fatimid Cairo.

In the Renaissance, new discoveries were often inspired by cross-fertilisation from Islamic science. During the first two to three centuries of the Abbasid caliphate in Baghdad (eighth to tenth centuries CE), Arab scholars had avidly compiled and translated philosophical and scientific writings from the Persian,

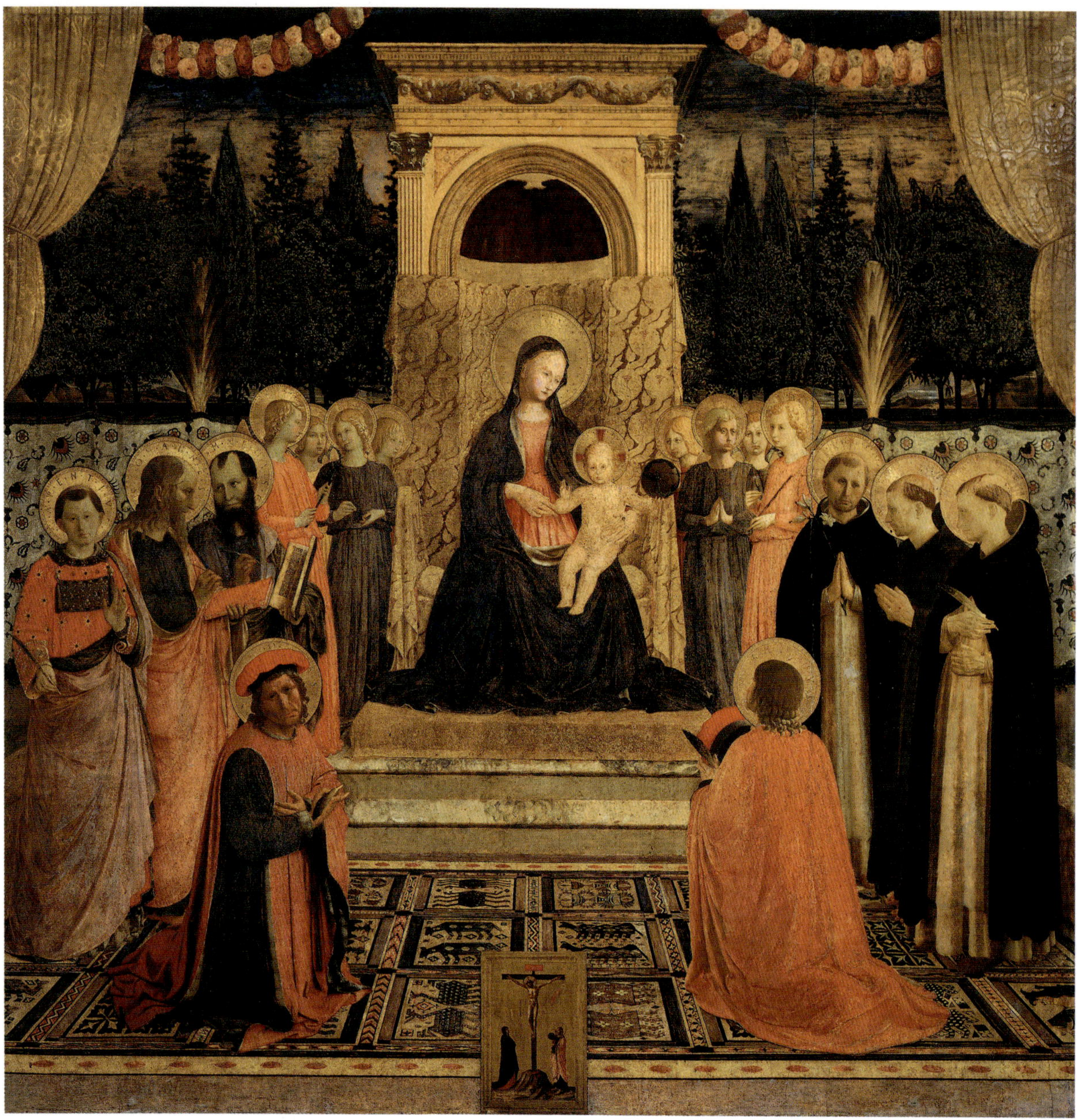

Plate 1.27 Giovanni da Fiesole (Fra Angelico), main panel from the San Marco altarpiece, c.1440, tempera on wood, 220 × 227 cm. Pala di San Marco, Florence. Photo: Getty.

Indian and Greek traditions. This is seen as the beginning of what has been called an Islamic Golden Age in the arts and sciences that lasted until the thirteenth century. In Christian Europe, particularly in the contact zones of Spain and Sicily, Arabic texts and commentaries were a critical stimulus to science, philosophy and medicine. They often mediated and transmitted ancient Greek knowledge that had been forgotten in western Europe.[65] While the concept of the Renaissance stresses innovations brought about by the revival of an indigenous, classical tradition via the rediscovery of ancient Greek and Roman knowledge, Islamic science and philosophy played a significant role in the process, offering a constant, if under-recognised source of ideas, as well as access to classical antiquity.

Exercise

Look again at the detail of the Van Eyck brothers' Ghent altarpiece (Plate 1.25). What meanings might the gold, blue and painted gems have evoked for viewers? How might the movement of goods and materials around the world have informed their understanding of the altarpiece?

Discussion

In the pre-industrial world, most viewers would have had some knowledge of the properties of natural materials, for example wood, textiles or metals; it is quite possible that many would have been highly attentive to the quality and rarity of pigments, especially if they had any experience in buying textiles. Each viewer would have had a different perspective on, and a different reaction to the material splendour of the altarpiece, since gold, gems and pearls could convey a wide variety of moral, religious and symbolic meanings. Yet viewers may well have been sensitive to the symbolic and physical properties of 'exotic' materials they had never seen before, or could only rarely glimpse. The religious significance of altarpieces can thus be connected to artistic materials and to the real or imagined place of origin of these materials. Viewers' understanding or misconception of the origins of materials may have evoked particular associations; perhaps viewers would have connected gold with Africa and ultramarine with central Asia. Thoughts of distant places may have conjured up the image of Prester John, or the wealth of foreign kingdoms to the East, or, perhaps, the image of India and the lost Eden that some believed could be found there.

4 The Saint Catherine altarpiece in Goa

All of the examples discussed above were displayed in European contexts and served as aids to Christian devotion. How did the meaning of altarpieces change, however, when they were displayed in the churches of overseas colonies? Portable altarpieces were likely stocked in ships as part of the liturgical equipment needed for new settlements. Others were made in Europe for export to the colonies, although over time altarpieces were more often made by local artisans, who had converted to Christianity and learned European artistic techniques. While very few colonial altarpieces survive from the early sixteenth century, several were made in Portugal for export to Goa and Cochin during the first decades after the Portuguese arrived in India.[66] One exceptional surviving example is the altar of Saint Catherine painted for the church of Saint Catherine in Goa, which will be the focus of this discussion.

When Vasco da Gama first landed in Calicut (Kozhikode) in 1498, sources state that he sent off the ship a *degredado*, a term used to refer to a convict or a recent convert to Christianity, to make contact with the local population. Finding a group of Tunisian merchants who had some knowledge of Spanish and Italian, this representative reportedly told them, 'we come in search of Christians and spices'.[67] The statement reveals Portugal's commercial motivations in India, which had Islam in particular as its target: direct access to spices and other Asian goods would divert profits from Muslim middlemen. Setting up trading stations and fortresses around the coast of Africa, the Persian Gulf and India, then Ceylon in 1505 and Malacca in 1511, Portugal would indeed establish a lucrative 'pepper empire' that brought it vast quantities of spices, porcelain, jewels, textiles and other luxury goods.[68] Papal bulls issued in the fifteenth century, as well as the Treaty of Tordesillas, had granted the Portuguese royal house the right to conquer and rule non-Christian territories in Africa and Asia. The papacy also granted the Portuguese the benefits of Padroado Real (Royal Patronage), a system that offered them certain freedoms to administer the Church in the Orient.[69] Portugal would understand these favours as a divine mandate to conquer Islam and convert pagans overseas.

The *degredado*'s statement also reveals that when the Portuguese arrived in India they expected to find it populated with Christians. Da Gama believed this since previous contact had been made between Europeans and the Saint Thomas Christians, who had long roots in southern India and who believed Saint Thomas the Apostle had travelled there to spread the Gospel and had died there (although now most historians believe that Christianity was brought to India by traders from the Persian Gulf around the seventh century CE). Da Gama was so convinced he would find Christians in India that during the entire three months of his stay in Calicut he sustained the belief that Hinduism was actually a form of Christianity, and that the temples he encountered were churches decorated with unusual images of the saints. The misconception was soon corrected, certainly by 1500, when Cabral first made contact with the Saint Thomas Christians in Kerala.[70]

In 1510, on the feast day of Saint Catherine, the governor of Portuguese India, Afonso de Albuquerque, captured Goa from the Islamic sultans of Bijapur. Goa had long been a merchants' colony and important harbour and became an ideal base from which to send back spices and other precious cargo to Portugal: one shipment brought the rhinoceros which inspired Dürer's famous woodcut (see Chapter 3, Plate 3.23).

It would also become the religious centre of the Portuguese overseas empire. In 1511, soon after the conquest of Goa and in thanks for his victory, Albuquerque founded a church of Saint Catherine. At first it was a temporary structure made of mud bricks and palm leaves, with a painted altarpiece of Saint Catherine. In 1514, money was found for a new church, which was completed by 1532.[71] By 1530, Goa had been made the capital of the Estado da Índia (the Portuguese overseas empire) and in 1534, Pope Paul III elevated it to Episcopal See, with authority over a vast territory stretching from the Cape of Good Hope to the 'islands of China'. The church of Saint Catherine was at that time elevated to the status of cathedral.[72] In recognition of these events, a multi-panelled, monumental altarpiece (Plate 1.28), was commissioned in Portugal for Saint Catherine sometime in the 1530s, perhaps by King João III (r.1521–57) as a personal donation. It was painted for export by the leading Portuguese artist Garcia

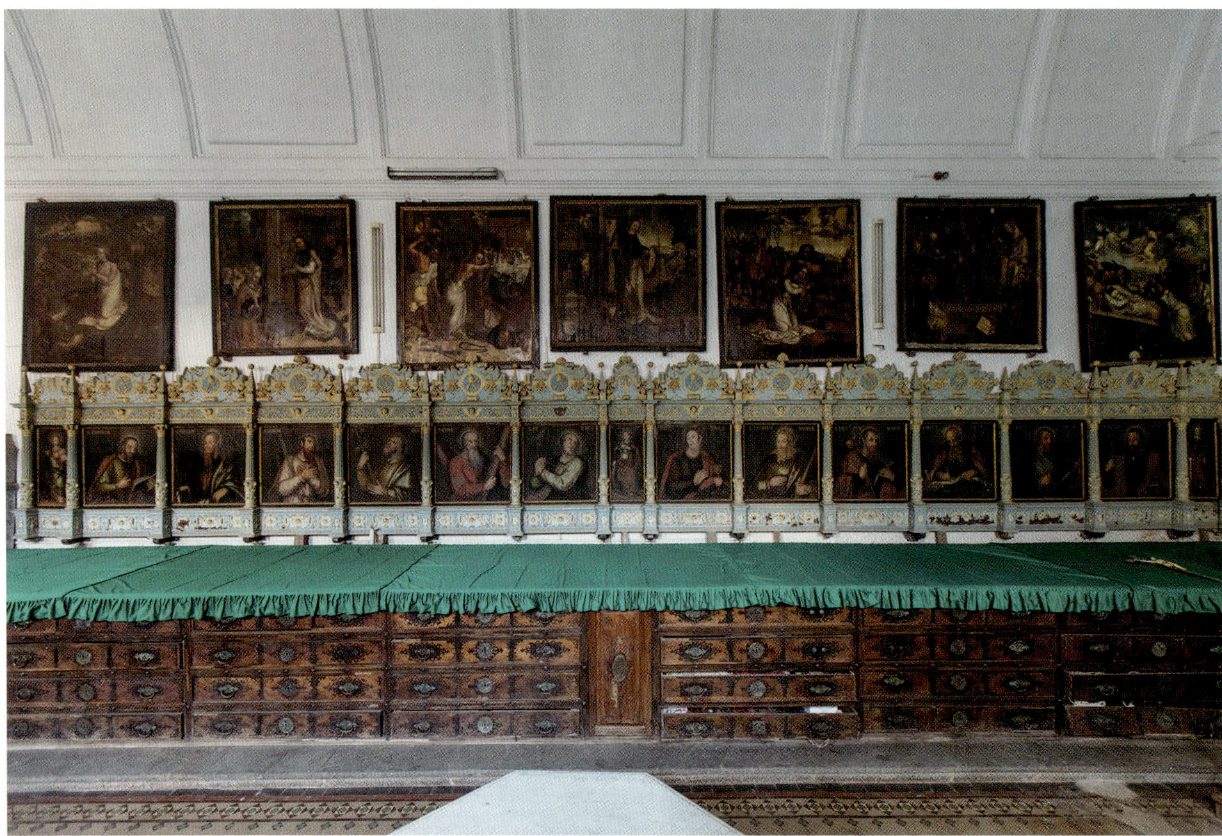

Plate 1.28 Garcia Fernandes, seven detached panels from the Saint Catherine altarpiece (at top), with unrelated images of saints underneath, c.1538, oil on panel. Sacristy, Se Cathedral, Old Goa. Photo: The Open University.

Fernandes and may have arrived in 1539 on the ship that brought Goa its first bishop.[73] This large European altarpiece for Goa's new cathedral would bolster a sense of permanence, identity and authority for the Portuguese in India. They saw India as a battleground against Islam and a land that was rightfully and historically Christian, even if the locals continued to regard them as outsiders from an obscure kingdom of 'the Franks'.[74]

Seven large, detached panels from the altarpiece survive, in rather poor condition, and are now on display in the sacristy of the massive cathedral built in 1562–1631 to replace that of 1514–32. In Plate 1.28 the seven panels are shown lined up along the top of the wall, while the images of saints visible underneath are unrelated and were not part of the altarpiece.

Each panel illustrates a different event from the life of the popular fourth-century saint as it was narrated in the *Golden Legend* (a thirteenth-century compilation of saints' lives). According to this account, Saint Catherine was born to noble parents in Alexandria, Egypt, when it was part of the pagan Roman Empire. She was inspired to convert from paganism to Christianity as a teenager and became an eloquent spokesperson for her new religion, converting many hundreds. The *Golden Legend* relates that the Roman Emperor Maxentius (r.306–12) pitted her against 50 of the greatest pagan philosophers and orators to debate the relative merits of paganism and Christianity. Catherine won, converting her opponents in the process, and later she would even convert Maxentius's wife, the empress. Maxentius was not persuaded, however, and after a first attempt at her execution on a breaking wheel failed, he had Catherine beheaded.

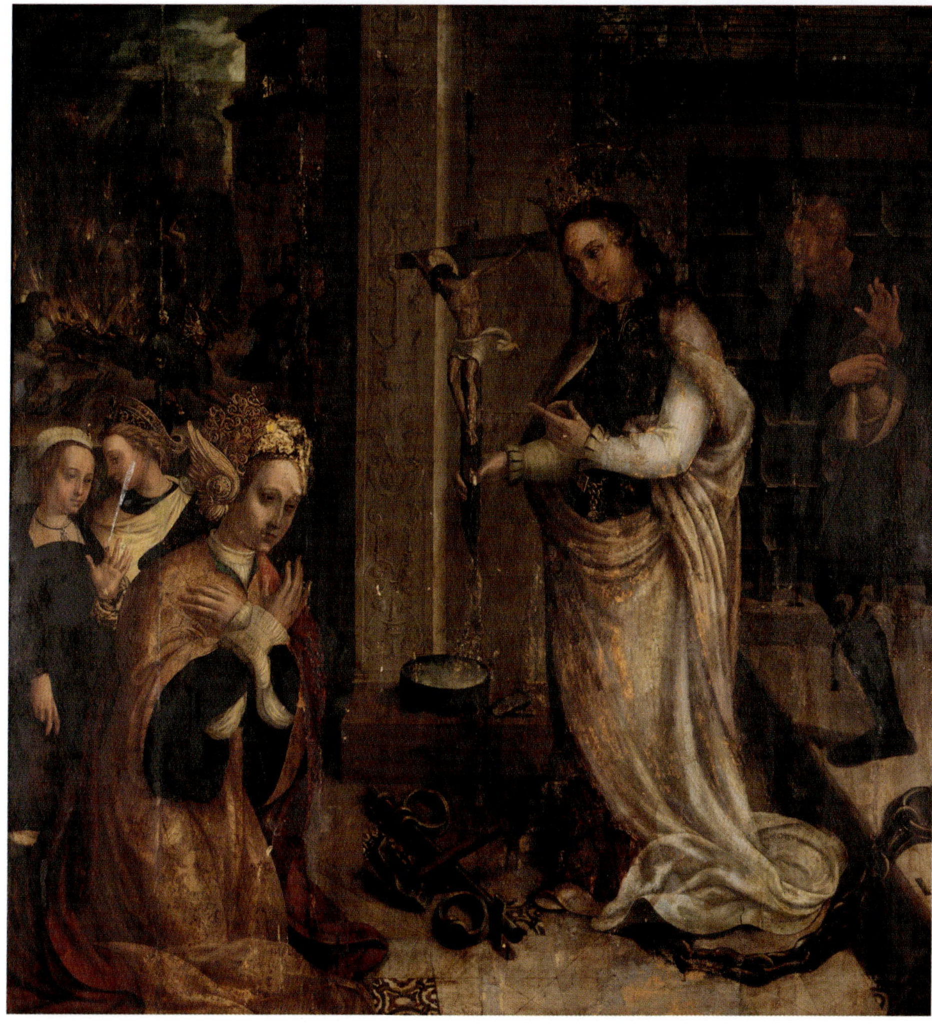

Plate 1.29 Garcia Fernandes, *Saint Catherine Converting the Empress of Rome*, c.1538, oil on panel. Se Cathedral, Old Goa. Photo: The Open University.

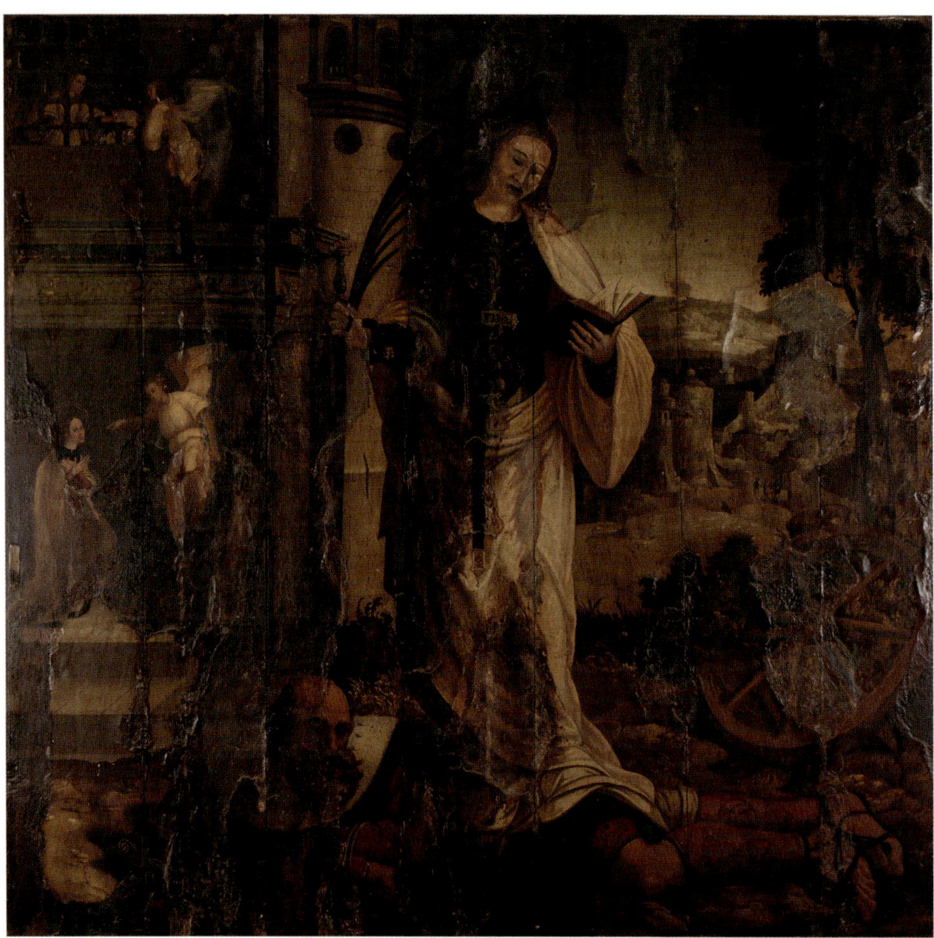

Plate 1.30 Garcia Fernandes, *Saint Catherine Crushing Paganism*, c.1538, oil on panel. Se Cathedral, Old Goa. Photo: The Open University.

The panels of Fernandes' large-scale altarpiece illustrate these events from Catherine's life and martyrdom in a clear, didactic style. In scenes of *Saint Catherine Preaching among the Doctors*, *Saint Catherine Converting the Empress of Rome* (Plate 1.29) and *Saint Catherine Crushing Paganism* (Plate 1.30), Catherine is depicted as a monumental, classicising and sculptural figure, on the model of Italian art of the time. Style and content come together in a direct and forceful statement of Portuguese intentions for the conversion of the Indies to Christianity. Indeed, *Saint Catherine Converts the Empress of Rome* and *Saint Catherine Crushing Paganism* were not subjects usually included in European altarpieces illustrating the story of Saint Catherine, but are present here because of their evangelising themes. The altarpiece captures the sentiments of the 1530s when the Church in Goa was moving towards a more militant approach to conversion and when harsher measures were being taken, including the accelerated destruction of Hindu and Muslim places of worship.[75] It would have vividly put the life of Saint Catherine – patron of preachers – before the eyes of Goa's new bishop, offering him an example of steadfast faith and a reminder of the eloquence and determination needed to convert vast numbers of non-believers. For potential converts, its didactic visual narrative and large scale may have been effective tools of persuasion.

Conclusion

The altarpieces examined in this chapter developed in a global context, through interdependencies and interests that bound Europe to the rest of the world. A closer look at the type has revealed aspects of what might be called the 'far within the near', that is, symbolic, aesthetic and material aspects that arose from the global interconnectivities of this era. These connections were examined in terms of Europeans' consistent engagement with Islamic objects and other imports, in part to evoke a sense of splendour, sacredness and magnificence suited to this elevated genre of devotional imagery. In the fifteenth and sixteenth centuries, with the expansion of trade, altarpieces referenced the array of global goods displayed in elite homes, appealing to the patrons who commissioned them. Given the didactic role of altarpieces, they often made targeted statements of belief about Christianity's place in the wider world; for example, as expressions of nostalgia for the lost Holy Land, anxieties about the prospect of Christianity's further contraction or faith in the prospect of worldwide conversion. As was seen, they subtly articulate fantastic and imaginary ideas about other religions and cultures, appropriating what was deemed useful and filtering it through local values, systems of belief and methods of representation. The conversion of Jews and Muslims had long been a theme of Christian religious art, but as was seen in the popular subject of the three magi, hopes for the Christianisation of Africans and the peoples of the New World also found expression. Taking these perspectives into account, one can see the significant effects of travel and global trade on the subjects, materials and techniques of this major genre of European art.

Notes

[1] E.g. Humfrey and Kemp, 1990; Humfrey, 1993; Borsook and Superbi Gioffredi, 1994; Nethersole, 2011; Jacobs, 2011.

[2] Watt and Wardwell, 1997, no. 41.

[3] Goldthwaite, 1993; Jardine, 1996; Ajmar-Wollheim and Molà, 2011; Findlen, 2012; Martin and Bleichmar, 2015; Gerritsen and Riello, 2016; Um and Clark, 2016.

[4] Nethersole, 2011, p. 22.

[5] Shalem, 1996; Massing, 2007c; Contadini, 2010; Wolf and Schmidt Arcangeli, 2010; Contadini, 2013.

[6] Rossabi, 1997; Von Fircks, 2014.

[7] Strickland, 2003.

[8] Mack, 2002, pp. 35–7; Monnas, 2008, pp. 63–76.

[9] Monnas, 2008, p. 63; Prazniak, 2010.

[10] Rossabi, 1997; Monnas, 2008; Contadini, 2013, pp. 40–53: Contadini, 2016.

[11] Mack, 2002, pp. 51–71; Contadini, 1999, pp. 4–5; Contadini, 2013, pp. 40–3; Nagel, 2011; Schulz, 2016.

[12] Aanavi, 1969, pp. 28–35.

[13] Mack, 2002, p. 52; Schultz, 2016.

[14] Fontana, 1999.

[15] Spallanzani, 1978, pp. 98–102.

[16] Mack, 2002, pp. 139–47; Pixley, 2003; Spallanzani, 2010.

[17] Leemhuis, 2000, pp. 292–3; Mack, 2002, pp. 65–6; Contadini, 2013, p. 42; Schultz, 2016, p. 63.

[18] Behrens-Abouseif, 2004; Behrens-Abouseif, 2014, pp. 112–15.

[19] Shalem 1996; Contadini, 1999, p. 4; Mack, 2002, pp. 4–5, 52–3, 59.

[20] Shalem, 2002.

[21] Frankopan, 2015, p. 35.

[22] Nagel, 2013.

[23] Dölger, 1925; Lang, 2004.

[24] Goldthwaite, 1993; Jardine, 1996; Belozerskaya, 2002; Welch, 2005; Ajmar and Dennis, 2006.

[25] Goldthwaite, 1993; Belozerskaya, 2002; Spufford, 2003; Contadini, 2006.

[26] Jardine, 1996, pp. 11–12.

[27] Goldthwaite, 1987; Myers, 2001.

[28] King and Sylvester, 1983; Contadini, 1999, pp. 6–7; Mack, 2002, pp. 73–93; Curatola, 2004; Spallanzani, 2007; Monnas, 2008, pp. 242–5; Contadini, 2013, pp. 37–40; Kim, 2016.

[29] Spallanzani, 2007, p. 105.

[30] Smith and Findlen, 2002.

[31] Mack, 2002, p. 88.

[32] Kim, 2016.

[33] Lach, 1965, pp. 72–3; Wittkower, 1989.

[34] Schreckenberg, 1996, p. 15.

[35] Said, 1978, pp. 69–70.

[36] Bisaha, 2004, pp. 143–56; Dalrymple, 2005; Dimmock and Hadfield, 2008.

[37] Said, 1978, pp. 67–73.

[38] Kaplan, 1985, pp. 20–34; Trexler, 1997, pp. 124–57; Massing, 2011, p. 267; Strickland, 2016, pp. 23–53.

[39] Kaplan, 1985, pp. 43–62.

[40] Zorach and Phillips, 2016, p. 271.

41 Kaplan, 1985, pp. 71–84; Trexler, 1997, p. 102; Wintle, 2009, pp. 191–216; Kaplan, 2010; Massing, 2011, pp. 276–7.

42 Koerner, 2010, pp. 36–9.

43 Pinson, 1996; Trexler, 1997, pp. 104–18; Lowe, 2005, p. 24; Koerner, 2010.

44 Earle and Lowe, 2005; Kaplan, 2010, p. 111; Lowe, 2012.

45 Massing, 2007b, pp. 366–7.

46 Kaplan, 2005; Lowe, 2005; Lowe, 2012.

47 Devisse and Mollat, 2010, pp. 195–6; Koerner, 2010, pp. 89–92.

48 Shalem, 2002.

49 Massing 2008, pp. 36–7; Devisse and Mollat, 2010, pp. 206–9; Koerner, 2010, pp. 47–63; Massing, 2011, p. 270.

50 Teixeira, 1991; Rodrigues, 1992; Koerner, 2010, pp. 7–17; Nagel, 2013, pp. 25–7.

51 Massing, 2007a, p. 105.

52 De Vos, 2014; Bruquetas, 2014.

53 Feeser, Daly Goggin and Fowkes Tobin, 2012.

54 Kirby, Nash and Cannon, 2010; Phipps, 2013.

55 Dunlop, 2009; Plesters, 2012; Dunlop, 2015.

56 Brinkman et al., 1988–89.

57 Kirby, Nash and Cannon, 2010; De Vos, 2014.

58 Phipps, 2013, pp. 128–30.

59 Anderson, 2014.

60 Molà, 2000, pp. 107–37.

61 Curtin, 1983; Abulafia, 1987, pp. 462–70; Dunlop, 2009; Dunlop, 2015; Passeri, 2015; Zorach and Phillips, 2016, pp. 27–30.

62 Lightbown, 1992, pp. 26–8; Belozerskaya, 2005, pp. 47–83; Spieß, 2010; Buettner, 2015; Crespo, 2015.

63 Welch, 1991; Silver, 2010.

64 Edgerton, 1975, pp. 72–4; Belting, 2011.

65 Gutas, 1998; Saliba, 2007; Van Dalen and Burnett, 2011; Frankopan, 2015, pp. 96–9.

66 Rodrigues, 1999, p. 372.

67 Turner, 2007.

68 Schwartz, 2007.

69 Lach, 1965, pp. 229–45.

70 Mundadan, 1984; Mundadan, 1999; Gillman and Klimkeit, 1999, pp. 155–202; Moffett, 1992, pp. 266–71.

71 Pereira, 2005, pp. 80–1.

72 Lach, 1965, p. 235; Pereira, 2005, pp. 80–1.

73 Caetano, 1998, pp. 62–5; Rodrigues, 1999, pp. 376–8; Lopes, 2011, pp. 115–18.

74 Subrahmanyam, 2008.

75 Kamat, 1999; Osswald, 2013, pp. 115–86.

Bibliography

Aanavi, D. (1969) *Islamic Pseudo Inscriptions*, PhD thesis, Ann Arbor, MI, University Microfilms.

Abulafia, D. (1987) 'Asia, Africa and the trade of medieval Europe', in Miller, E., Postan, C. and Postan, M. M. (eds) *The Cambridge Economic History of Europe from the Decline of the Roman Empire, Volume 2: Trade and Industry in the Middle Ages*, 2nd edn, Cambridge, Cambridge University Press, pp. 402–73.

Ajmar, M. and Dennis, F. (eds) (2006) *At Home in Renaissance Italy*, London, Victoria and Albert Museum.

Ajmar-Wollheim, M. and Molà, L. (2011) 'The global Renaissance: cross-cultural objects in the early modern period', in Adamson, G., Riello, G. and Teasley, S. (eds) *Global Design History*, London and New York, Routledge, pp. 11–20.

Anderson, B. C. (2014) 'Evidence of cochineal's use in painting', *Journal of Interdisciplinary History*, vol. 45, no. 3, pp. 337–66.

Behrens-Abouseif, D. (2004) 'European arts and crafts at the Mamluk court', *Muqarnas*, vol. 21, Essays in Honor of J. M. Rogers, pp. 45–54.

Behrens-Abouseif, D. (2014) *Practising Diplomacy in the Mamluk Sultanate: Gifts and Material Culture in the Medieval Islamic World*, London, I.B. Tauris.

Belozerskaya, M. (2002) *Rethinking the Renaissance: Burgundian Arts across Europe*, Cambridge, Cambridge University Press.

Belozerskaya, M. (2005) *Luxury Arts of the Renaissance*, London, Thames & Hudson.

Belting, H. (2011) *Florence and Baghdad: Renaissance Art and Arab Science*, Cambridge, MA, Harvard University Press.

Bisaha, N. (2004) *Creating East and West: Renaissance Humanists and the Ottoman Turks*, Philadelphia, PA, University of Pennsylvania Press.

Borsook, E. and Superbi Gioffredi, F. (eds) (1994) *Italian Altarpieces 1250–1550: Function and Design*, Oxford, Clarendon.

Brinkman, P. W. F., Kockaert, L., Maes, L., Thielen, E. and Wouters, J. (1988–89) 'Het Lam Godsretabel van van Eyck: een heronderzoek naar de materialen en schildermethoden. 2. De hoofdkleuren blauw, groen, geel en rood', *Bulletin de l'Institut Royal du Patrimoine Artistique*, vol. 22, pp. 26–49.

Bruquetas, R. (2014) 'The search for the perfect color: pigments, tints, and binders in the scientific expeditions to the Americas', *Journal of Interdisciplinary History*, vol. 45, no. 3, pp. 367–87.

Buettner, B. (2015) 'Precious stones, mineral beings: performative materiality in fifteenth-century Northern art', in Anderson, C., Dunlop, A. and Smith, P. H. (eds) *The Matter of Art: Materials, Practices, Cultural Logics, c.1250–1750*, Manchester, Manchester University Press, pp. 205–22.

Caetano, J. O. (1998) 'Garcia Fernandes: uma exposição à procura de um pintor', in Caetano, J. O. (ed.) *Garcia Fernandes: um pintor do Renascimento, eleitor da misericórdia de Lisboa*, Lisbon, Museu de São Roque, pp. 11–77.

Contadini, A. (1999) 'Artistic contacts: current scholarship and future tasks', in Burnett, C. and Contadini, A. (eds) *Islam and the Italian Renaissance*, London, The Warburg Institute, pp. 1–60.

Contadini, A. (2006) 'Middle-Eastern objects', in Ajmar, M. and Dennis, F. (eds) *At Home in Renaissance Italy*, London, Victoria and Albert Museum, pp. 308–21.

Contadini, A. (2010) 'Translocation and transformation: some Middle Eastern objects in Europe', in Saurma-Jeltsch, L. E. and Eisenbeiß, A. (eds) *The Power of Things and the Flow of Cultural Transformations: Art and Culture between Europe and Asia*, Berlin, Deutscher Kunstverlag, pp. 42–64.

Contadini, A. (2013) 'Sharing a taste? Material acquisitions and intellectual curiosity around the Mediterranean, from the eleventh to the sixteenth century', in Contadini, A. and Norton, C. (eds) *The Renaissance and the Ottoman World*, Farnham and Burlington, VT, Ashgate Publishing, pp. 23–61.

Contadini, A. (2016) 'Threads of ornament in the style world of the fifteenth and sixteenth centuries', in Payne, A. and Necipoğlu, G. (eds) *Histories of Ornament: From Global to Local*, Princeton, NJ and Oxford, Princeton University Press, pp. 290–305.

Crespo, H. (2015) *Jewels from the India Run*, Lisbon, Fundação Oriente.

Curatola, G. (2004) 'A sixteenth-century quarrel about carpets', *Muqarnas*, vol. 21, Essays in Honor of J. M. Rogers, pp. 129–37.

Curtin, P. D. (1983) 'Africa and the wider monetary world 1250–1850', in Richards, J. F. (ed.) *Precious Metals in the Late Medieval and Early Modern Worlds*, Durham, NC, Carolina Academic Press, pp. 231–68.

Dalrymple, W. (2005) 'Foreword: the porous frontiers of Islam and Christiandom: a clash or fusion of civilisations?', in MacLean, G. (ed.) *Re-Orienting the Renaissance: Cultural Exchanges with the East*, Basingstoke and New York, Palgrave Macmillan, pp. ix–xxiii.

De Vos, P. (2014) 'Apothecaries, artists, and artisans: early industrial material culture in the biological old regime', *Journal of Interdisciplinary History*, vol. 45, no. 3, pp. 277–366.

Devisse, J. and Mollat, M. (2010) 'The African transposed', in Bindman, D. and Gates, H. L. (eds) *Image of the Black in Western Art, Volume II: From the Early Christian Era to the 'Age of Discovery', Part 2: Africans in the Christian Ordinance of the World*, Cambridge, MA and London, Belknap Press of Harvard University Press, pp. 185–279 (Originally published 1979).

Dimmock, M. and Hadfield, A. (2008) *The Religions of the Book: Christian Perceptions, 1400–1660*, Basingstoke and New York, Palgrave Macmillan.

Dölger, F. J. (1925) *Sol salutis: Gebet und Gesang im christlichen Altertum, mit besonderer Rücksicht auf die Ostung in Gebet und Liturgie*, Münster, Verlag der Aschendorffschen Verlagsbuchhandlung.

Dunlop, A. (2009) 'Materials, origins, and the nature of early Italian painting', in Anderson, J. (ed.) *Crossing Cultures: Conflict, Migration and Convergence*, Melboune, Miegunyah Press at Melbourne University Press, pp. 472–6.

Dunlop, A. (2015) 'On the origins of European painting materials, real and imagined', in Anderson, C., Dunlop, A. and Smith, P. H. (eds) *The Matter of Art: Materials, Practices, Cultural Logics, c.1250–1750*, Manchester, Manchester University Press, pp. 68–96.

Earle, T. F. and Lowe, K. J. P. (eds) (2005) *Black Africans in Renaissance Europe*, Cambridge, Cambridge University Press.

Edgerton, S. Y. (1975) *The Renaissance Rediscovery of Linear Perspective*, New York, Basic Books.

Feeser, A., Daly Goggin, M. and Fowkes Tobin, B. (2012) 'Introduction: the value of color', in Feeser, A., Daly Goggin, M. and Fowkes Tobin, B. (eds) *The Materiality of Color: The Production, Circulation, and Application of Dyes and Pigments, 1400–1800*, Aldershot and Burlington, VT, Ashgate Publishing, pp. 1–10.

Findlen, P. (2012) *Early Modern Things: Objects and their Histories, 1500–1800*, London and New York, Routledge.

Fontana, M. V. (1999) 'Byzantine mediation of epigraphic characters of Islamic derivation in the wall paintings of some churches in southern Italy', in Burnett, C. and Contadini, A. (eds) *Islam and the Italian Renaissance*, London, The Warburg Institute, pp. 61–7.

Frankopan, P. (2015) *The Silk Roads: A New History of the World*, London, Bloomsbury.

Gerritsen, A. and Riello, G. (eds) (2016) *The Global Lives of Things: The Material Culture of Connections in the Early Modern World*, London and New York, Routledge.

Gillman, I. and Klimkeit, H.-J. (1999) *Christians in Asia before 1500*, Richmond, Curzon.

Goldthwaite, R. A. (1987) 'The empire of things: consumer demand in Renaissance Italy', in Kent, F. W. and Simons, P. with Eade, J.C. (eds) *Patronage, Art and Society in Renaissance Italy*, Oxford, Oxford University Press, pp. 153–75.

Goldthwaite, R. A. (1993) *Wealth and the Demand for Art in Italy, 1300–1600*, Baltimore, MD, Johns Hopkins University Press.

Gutas, D. (1998) *Greek Thought, Arabic Culture: the Graeco–Arabic Translation Movement in Baghdad and Early 'Abbāsid Society' (2nd–4th/8th–10th Centuries)*, London and New York, Routledge.

Humfrey, P. (1993) *The Altarpiece in Renaissance Venice*, New Haven, CT, and London, Yale University Press.

Humfrey, P. and Kemp, M. (eds) (1990) *The Altarpiece in the Renaissance*, Cambridge, Cambridge University Press.

Jacobs, L. F. (2011) *Opening Doors: The Early Netherlandish Triptych Reinterpreted*, University Park, PA, Pennsylvania State University Press.

Jardine, L. (1996) *Worldly Goods: A New History of the Renaissance*, London, Papermac.

Kamat, P. (1999) 'The politics of conversion and collaboration of the Estado da Índia and the Hindus of Goa: 1510–1789', *Vasco da Gama e a Índia*, Lisbon, Fundação Calouste Gulbekian, vol. 2, pp. 179–202.

Kaplan, P. H. D. (1985) *The Rise of the Black Magus in Western Art*, Ann Arbor, MI, UMI Research Press.

Kaplan, P. H. D. (2005) 'Isabella d'Este and black African women', in Earle, T. F. and Lowe, K. J. P. (eds) *Black Africans in Renaissance Europe*, Cambridge, Cambridge University Press, pp. 125–54.

Kaplan, P. H. D. (2010) 'Italy, 1490–1700', in Bindman, D. and Gates, H. L. (eds) *Image of the Black in Western Art, Vol. III: From the 'Age of Discovery' to the Age of Abolition, Part I: Artists of the Renaissance and Baroque*, Cambridge, MA and London, Belknap Press of Harvard University Press, pp. 92–189.

Kim, D. Y. (2016) 'Lotto's carpets: materiality, textiles, and composition in Renaissance painting', *The Art Bulletin*, vol. 98, no. 2, pp. 181–212.

King, D. and Sylvester, D. (1983) *The Eastern Carpet in the Western World from the 15th to the 17th Century*, London, Arts Council.

Kirby, J., Nash, S. and Cannon, J. (2010) *Trade in Artists' Materials: Markets and Commerce in Europe to 1700*, London, Archetype.

Koerner, J. L. (2010) 'The epiphany of the black magus circa 1500', in Bindman, D. and Gates, H. L. (eds) *Image of the Black in Western Art, Vol. III: From the 'Age of Discovery' to the Age of Abolition, Part I: Artists of the Renaissance and Baroque*, Cambridge, MA and London, Belknap Press of Harvard University Press, pp. 7–92.

Lach, D. F. (1965) *Asia in the Making of Europe, Vol. 1: The Century of Discovery*, Book 1, Chicago, IL and London, University of Chicago Press.

Lang, U. M. (2004) *Turning towards the Lord: Orientation in Liturgical Prayer*, San Francisco, CA, Ignatius Press.

Leemhuis, F. (2000) 'Heiligenscheine fremder Herkunft: Arabische Schriftzeichen in Aureolen der italienischen Malerei des frühen fünfzehnten Jahrhunderts', *Der Islam*, vol. 72, pp. 286–306.

Lightbown, R. W. (1992) *Mediaeval European Jewellery, with a Catalogue of the Collection in the Victoria & Albert Museum*, London, Victoria and Albert Museum.

Lopes, R. O. (2011) *Confluências da Arte Cristã na Índia, na China e no Japão, séc. XVI a XVIII*, PhD thesis, Lisbon, University of Lisbon.

Lowe, K. (2005) 'The stereotyping of black Africans in Renaissance Europe', in Earle, T. F. and Lowe, K. J. P. (eds) *Black Africans in Renaissance Europe*, Cambridge, Cambridge University Press, pp. 17–47.

Lowe, K. (2012) 'The lives of African slaves and people of African descent in Renaissance Europe', in Spicer, J. (ed.) *Revealing the African Presence in Renaissance Europe*, Baltimore, MD, The Walters Art Museum, pp. 13–33.

Mack, R. (2002) *Bazaar to Piazza: Islamic Trade and Italian Art*, Berkeley, CA, University of California.

Martin, M. and Bleichmar, D. (eds) (2015) 'Introduction', *Objects in Motion in the Early Modern World, Art History*, vol. 38, no. 4, special issue, pp. 604–19.

Massing, J. M. (2007a) 'Early European images of America: the ethnographic approach', *Studies in Imagery, Vol. II: The World Discovered*, London, Pindar Press, pp. 94–113.

Massing, J. M. (2007b) 'The quest for the exotic: Albrecht Dürer in the Netherlands', *Studies in Imagery, Vol. II: The World Discovered*, London, Pindar Press, pp. 376–405.

Massing, J. M. (2007c) 'From Marco Polo to King Manuel I of Portugal: the early European fascination with Chinese porcelain', *Studies in Imagery, Vol. II: The World Discovered*, London, Pindar Press, pp. 376–405.

Massing, J. M. (2008) 'The black magus in the Netherlands from Memling to Rubens', in Schreuder, E. and Kolfin, E. (eds) *Black is Beautiful: Rubens to Dumas,* Zwolle, Waanders, pp. 32–50.

Massing, J. M. (2011) *Image of the Black in Western Art, Vol. III: From the 'Age of Discovery' to the Age of Abolition, Part 2: Europe and the World Beyond*, Cambridge, MA and London, Belknap Press of Harvard University Press.

Moffett, S. H. (1992) *A History of Christianity in Asia, Volume 1: Beginnings to 1500*, San Francisco, CA, HarperCollins.

Molà, L. (2000) *The Silk Industry of Renaissance Venice*, Baltimore, MD, Johns Hopkins University Press.

Monnas, L. (2008) *Merchants, Princes and Painters: Silk Fabrics in Italian and Northern Paintings, 1300–1550*, New Haven, CT and London, Yale University Press.

Mundadan, A. M. (1984) *History of Christianity in India, Vol. 1: From the Beginning up to the Middle of the Sixteenth Century (up to 1542)*, Bangalore, Theological Publications in India.

Mundadan, A. M. (1999) 'The St. Thomas Christians and the Portuguese', *Vasco da Gama e a Índia*, Lisbon, Fundação Calouste Gulbekian, vol. 3, pp. 7–19.

Myers, F. R. (2001) *The Empire of Things: Regimes of Value and Material Culture*, Santa Fe, NM, SAR Press.

Nagel, A. (2011) 'Twenty-five notes on pseudoscript in Italian art', *Res*, vol. 59/60, spring/autumn, pp. 228–48.

Nagel, A. (2013) *Some Discoveries of 1492: Eastern Antiquities and Renaissance Europe*, Groningen, University of Groningen and The Gerson Lectures Foundation.

Nethersole, S. (2011) *Devotion by Design: Italian Altarpieces before 1500*, London and New Haven, CT, Yale University Press; London, National Gallery.

Osswald, C. (2013) *Written in Stone: Jesuit Buildings in Goa and their Artistic and Architectural Features*, Goa, Goa 1556 and Golden Heart Emporium Book Shop.

Passeri, I. (2015) 'Gold coins and gold leaf in early Italian paintings', in Anderson, C., Dunlop, A. and Smith, P. H. (eds) *The Matter of Art: Materials, Practices, Cultural Logics, c. 1250–1750*, Manchester, Manchester University Press, pp. 97–115.

Pereira, A. N. (2005) *A arquitectura religiosa cristã de Velha Goa, segunda metade do século XVI-primeiras décadas do século XVII*, Lisbon, Fundação oriente.

Phipps, E. (2013) 'Global colors: dyes and the dye trade', in Peck, A. (ed.) *Interwoven Globe: The Worldwide Textile Trade, 1500–1800*, New York, Metropolitan Museum of Art, pp. 120–35.

Pinson, Y. (1996) 'Connotations of sin and heresy in the figure of the black king in some northern Renaissance adorations', *Artibus et Historiae*, vol. 17, no. 34, pp. 159–75.

Pixley, M. L. (2003) 'Islamic artifacts and cultural currents in the art of Carpaccio', *Apollo*, vol. 158, no. 501, pp. 9–18.

Plesters, J. (2012) 'Ultramarine', in Roy, A. (ed.) *Artists' Pigments: A Handbook of their Characteristics, Vol. 2*, new edition, Washington, DC, National Gallery of Art and London, Archetype, pp. 37–65.

Prazniak, R. (2010) 'Siena on the silk roads: Ambrogio Lorenzetti and the Mongol global century, 1250–1350', *Journal of World History*, vol. 21, no. 2, pp. 177–217.

Rodrigues, D. (1992) 'Adoração dos magos', *Grão Vasco e a pintura europeia do Renascimento*, Portugal, Comissão Nacional para as Comemorações dos Descobrimentos Portugueses, pp. 91–2.

Rodrigues, D. (1999) 'A pintura na antiga Índia portuguesa', *Vasco da Gama e a Índia*, Lisbon, Fundação Calouste Gulbekian, vol. 3, pp. 369–94.

Rossabi, M. (1997) 'The silk trade in China and central Asia', in Watt, J. C. Y. and Wardwell, A. E. (eds) *When Silk was Gold: Central Asian and Chinese Textiles*, New York, Metropolitan Museum of Art, pp. 7–19.

Said, E. W. (1978) *Orientalism*, London and Henley, Routledge & Kegan Paul.

Saliba, G. (2007) *Islamic Science and the Making of the European Renaissance*, Cambridge, MA, MIT Press.

Schreckenberg, H. (1996) *The Jews in Christian Art: An Illustrated History* (trans. J. Bowden), New York, Continuum.

Schulz, V.-S. (2016) 'Intricate letters and the reification of light: prolegomena on the pseudo-inscribed haloes in Giotto's Madonna di San Giorgio alla Costa and Masaccio's San Giovenale Triptych', *Mitteilungen des Kunsthistorisches Institutes in Florenz*, vol. 58, no. 1, pp. 59–93.

Schwartz, S. B. (2007) 'The economy of the Portuguese Empire', in Bethencourt, F. and Curto, D. R. (eds) *Portuguese Oceanic Expansion, 1400–1800*, Cambridge, Cambridge University Press, pp. 19–48.

Shalem, A. (1996) *Islam Christianized: Islamic Portable Objects in the Medieval Church Treasuries of the Latin West, Ars faciendi*, vol. 7, Bern, Peter Lang.

Shalem, A. (2002) 'The portraiture of objects: a note on representations of Islamic objects in European paintings of the 14th–16th centuries', in Bernardini, M., Borrelli, C., Cerbo, A. and Sánchez García, E. (eds) *Europa e Islam tra secoli XIV–XVI*, Naples, Istituto universitario Orientale, vol. 1, pp. 497–521.

Silver, L. (2010) 'India ink: imagery of the subcontinent in early modern Europe', in Saurma-Jeltsch, L. E. and Eisenbeiß, A. (eds) *The Power of Things and the Flow of Cultural Transformations: Art and Culture between Europe and Asia*, Berlin, Deutscher Kunstverlag, pp. 217–37.

Smith, P. H. and Findlen, P. (2002) 'Introduction: commerce and the representation of nature in art and science', in Smith, P. H. and Findlen, P. (eds) *Merchants and Marvels: Commerce, Science, and Art in Early Modern Europe*, London and New York, Routledge, pp. 1–25.

Spallanzani, M. (1978) *Ceramiche orientali a Firenze nel Rinascimento*, Florence, Cassa di Risparmio di Firenze.

Spallanzani, M. (2007) *Oriental Rugs in Renaissance Florence*, Florence, S.P.E.S.

Spallanzani, M. (2010) *Metalli islamici a Firenze nel Rinascimento*, Florence, S.P.E.S.

Spieß, K.-H. (2010) 'Asian objects and Western European court culture in the middle ages', in North, M. (ed.) *Artistic and Cultural Exchanges between Europe and Asia, 1400–1900: Rethinking Markets, Workshops and Collections*, Farnham and Burlington, VT, Ashgate Publishing, pp. 9–28.

Spufford, P. (2003) *Power and Profit: The Merchant in Medieval Europe*, London, Thames & Hudson.

Strickland, D. H. (2003) *Saracens, Demons & Jews: Making Monsters in Medieval Art*, Princeton, NJ and Oxford, Princeton University Press.

Strickland, D. H. (2016) *The Epiphany of Hieronymus Bosch: Imagining Antichrist and Others from the Middle Ages to the Reformation*, London, Harvey Miller Publishers.

Subrahmanyam, S. (2008) 'On the hat wearers, their toilet practices, and other curious usages', in Chatterjee, K. and Hawes, C. (eds) *Europe Observed: Multiple Gazes in Early Modern Encounters*, Lewisburg, PA, Bucknell University Press, pp. 45–81.

Teixeira, J. (1991) 'Adoration of the magi', in Levenson, J. A. (ed.) *Circa 1492: Art in the Age of Exploration*, Washington, DC, National Gallery of Art; New Haven, CT and London, Yale University Press, pp. 152–3.

Turner, J. (2007) 'Spices and Christians', in Levenson, J. A. (ed.) *Encompassing the Globe: Portugal and the World in the 16th and 17th Centuries*, Washington, DC, Smithsonian Institution, pp. 45–53.

Trexler, R. C. (1997) *The Journey of the Magi: Meanings in History of a Christian Story*, Princeton, NJ, Princeton University Press.

Um, N. and Clark, L. (2016) 'The art of embassy: situating objects and images in the early modern diplomatic encounter', *Journal of Early Modern History*, vol. 20, no. 1, pp. 3–18.

Van Dalen, B. and Burnett, C. (eds) (2011) 'Between Orient and Occident: transformation of knowledge', *Annals of Science*, vol. 68, no. 4, special issue, pp. 445–51.

Von Fircks, J. (2014) 'Panni Tartarici: splendid cloths from the Mongol Empire in European contexts', *Orientations*, vol. 45, no. 7, pp. 72–81.

Watt, J. C. Y. and Wardwell, A. E. (eds) (1997) *When Silk was Gold: Central Asian and Chinese Textiles*, New York, Metropolitan Museum of Art.

Welch, E. (2005) *Shopping in the Renaissance: Consumer Cultures in Italy 1400–1600*, New Haven, CT and London, Yale University Press.

Welch, S. C. (1991) 'Encounters with India: land of gold, spices, and matters spiritual', in Levenson, J. A. (ed.) *Circa 1492: Art in the Age of Exploration*, Washington, DC, National Gallery of Art; New Haven, CT and London, Yale University Press, pp. 363–6.

Wintle, M. (2009) *The Image of Europe: Visualizing Europe in Cartography and Iconography throughout the Ages*, Cambridge, Cambridge University Press.

Wittkower, R. (1989) 'China and Europe I: early connections', in Reynolds, D. M. and Wittkower, M. (eds) *The Impact of Non-European Civilizations on the Art of the West*, Cambridge, Cambridge University Press, pp. 145–60.

Wolf, G. and Schmidt Arcangeli, C. (eds) (2010) *Islamic Artefacts in the Mediterranean World: Trade, Gift Exchange and Artistic Transfer*, Venice, Marsilio.

Zorach, R. and Phillips Jr., M. W. (2016) *Gold*, London, Reaktion Books.

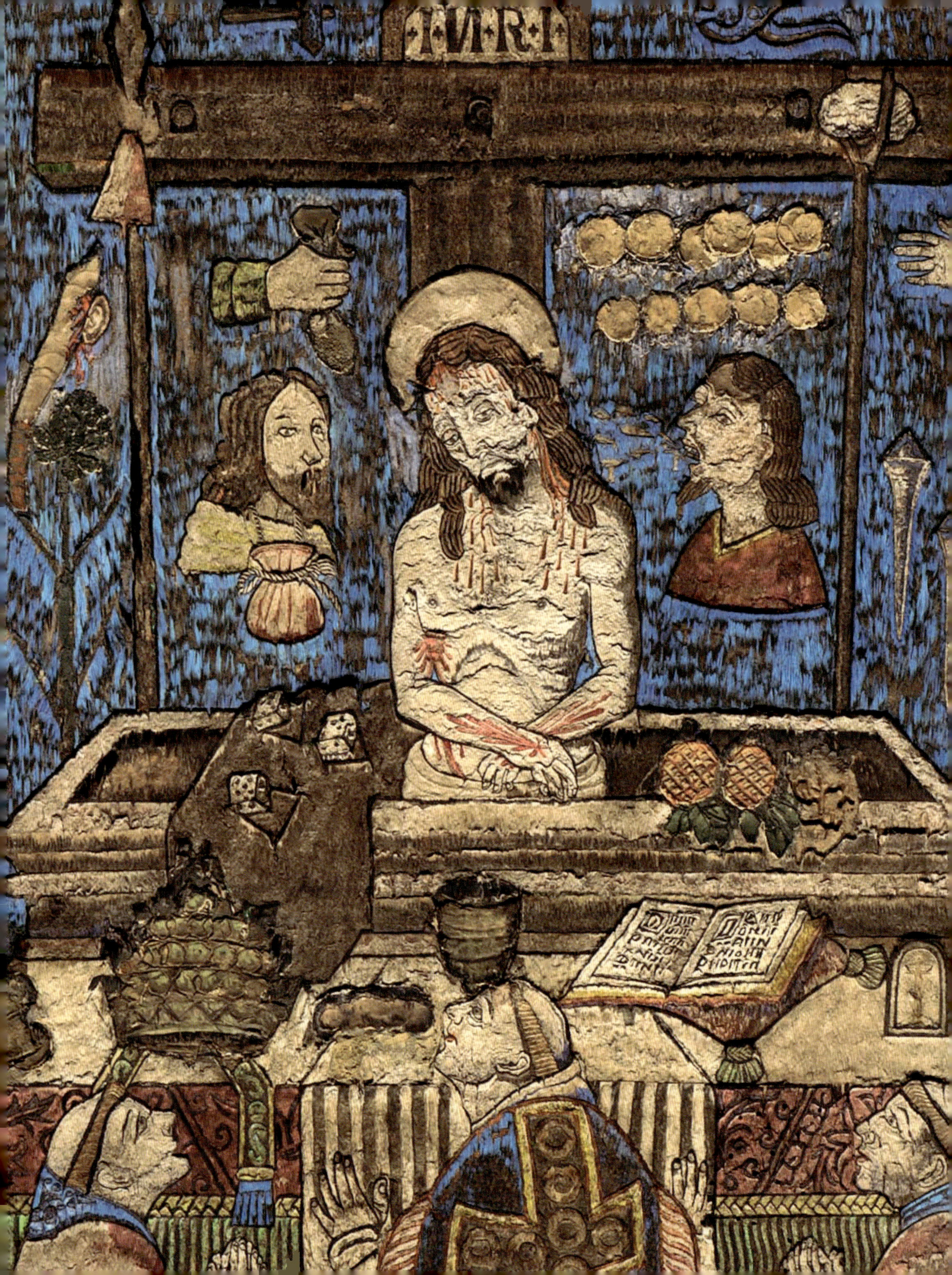
I · N · R · I

Chapter 2

Cultural crossings in Spain and the New World 1350–1550

Kim Woods

Introduction

In 1526, Charles V, ruler of Spain (1516–56) and from 1519 Holy Roman Emperor, visited the historic town of Córdoba in southern Spain. Córdoba had been the capital of al-Andalus, or Islamic Spain, and had fallen to Christian armies nearly 300 years earlier in 1236. Its grand mosque was 'cleansed' and converted to Christian use as a cathedral with only limited modifications to its architecture.[1] In 1523, however, planning began on a new and intrusive Renaissance choir, to be inserted into the middle of the historic building, which Charles himself authorised. He visited the cathedral three years later and legend has it was appalled by what he saw, saying: 'had I known what was here I would never have dared touch the old structure. You have destroyed something that was unique in the world and added something one can see anywhere!'[2] It is doubtful whether Charles actually uttered this famous speech, but in opposing the new scheme the town council of Córdoba did indeed declare the mosque to be 'unique in the world'.[3] The fact that it was built as a Muslim rather than as a Christian place of worship was not an issue: the mosque had long since become a source of civic pride. This famous, and infamous, episode serves to introduce the cross-cultural heritage of medieval and Renaissance Spain, and two of the competing forces that shaped it: Christianity and Islam.

The size and splendour of the Córdoba mosque testify to the historic importance of Córdoba as the ancient capital of Islamic al-Andalus – a term that signified not modern-day Andalusia but all Iberian territories under Muslim rule. Spain as we know it today did not exist as a politically unified country until after the conquest of Granada in 1492 by the so-called Catholic rulers Queen Isabella of Castile (r.1476–1504) and her husband King Ferdinand of Aragon (r.1479–1516). Up to that point and indeed beyond it, the history of Spain was one of immigration and cultural diversity. Muslim Arabs conquered most of the Iberian peninsula from 711, overrunning the previous settlers, the Visigoths. These Iberian Muslims were often known in Christian Europe as 'Moors', which historically has been a somewhat pejorative term, though the term 'Moorish' arguably has more positive cultural resonances today. Christian territories were concentrated in the north of the peninsula and were bolstered by immigration from Europe. The substantial Jewish population in both Islamic and Christian territories constituted a significant third culture. After 1492, Christian Spanish explorers and conquerors, or conquistadores, also encountered indigenous cultures of the New World of Central and South America. Arguably, the art and visual culture of no other country in Europe testify to such a long,

Plate 2.1 (Facing page) *Mass of Saint Gregory* (detail from Plate 2.23).

complex and contested history of cultural encounter as Spain. It is impossible to speak in terms of a national culture, still less a national art. Al-Andalus and Christian Spain were frontier societies on the very edge of Islamic North Africa, Christian Europe and latterly the New World. As such they were crossing points for cultures, artists and luxury goods and often sites of creative invention.

Art and visual culture, far from serving an innocent aesthetic purpose or as a neutral means of recording different cultures or new lands, were deeply implicated in all of these cultural encounters. Islamic visual culture permeated Christian Spain long after the conquest of Muslim territories by Christian forces, though the reasons for its longevity remain contested. Christian imagery was used not only for liturgical and devotional purposes but also as a means of conveying the Christian message in efforts to convert those of other faiths, whether within Spain or in the New World. Art also became a test case for conversion to Christianity: although both Judaism and Islam sometimes tolerated painting in a secular setting, both strictly forbade the use of imagery in a religious context. One Arabic account of the compulsory conversion to Christianity of the conquered Muslims of Granada in 1498 reveals the horror with which Muslims 'saw their sons and their daughters worshipping crosses and bowing down before idols'.[4] It is clear that using Christian images was a crucial sign of this conversion.

The varied heritage, cultural diversity and connections of the Hispanic world up to 1550 are powerful reasons for choosing to explore it in this chapter. Another reason is that the art and visual culture of Spain and the New World are still relatively little-studied in comparison with the art of Renaissance Italy or late medieval and Renaissance northern Europe. Once a frontier territory, Spain remains something of a frontier subject in late medieval and Renaissance art history today.

I Córdoba mosque

Córdoba fell to the Christian ruler of Castile Ferdinand III (r.1217–52) in 1236 and the great mosque was adapted for Christian worship, as was the custom.[5] Renamed the church of Santa Maria, it was restored under Alfonso X (r.1252–84), who legislated in 1263

that Muslim craftsmen must offer two unpaid days' work on it a year.[6] By the time the new Catholic cathedral was built in the sixteenth century, Islamic rule was a distant memory, but the mosque bore witness to Córdoba's past importance and seems to have been a source of civic pride. In 1523, when plans for the new Catholic cathedral were drawn up, legend has it that there was much opposition in the city and that workers even refused to obey orders to damage the structure of the mosque.

This mosque, one of the largest in the world and extended three times, was begun in 785, around 150 years after the death of Mohammed in 632 (Plate 2.2). The vast mosque reads as a forest of columns forming 19 aisles which run north to south toward the *mihrab* – the niche in the south wall that theoretically indicates the direction of Mecca. Each aisle is defined by black or red marble columns supporting two sets of arches, one above the other. Both sets of arches are built in blocks of alternating colour; the upper arches are rounded while the lower arches are a distinctive horseshoe shape. The mosque would have been brightly lit by the courtyard to the north, domed skylights and lamps; with its original intricately coloured carpets, it would have been truly breathtaking. The courtyard at Córdoba mosque was also as imposing, about 120 metres in length, surrounded by arcades and with basins for ritual washing to either end. The original mosque garden had 'aisles' of trees that echoed the mosque's architectural aisles, and may have been the first of its kind.[7]

Around the *mihrab* is the decorative stucco work distinctive of Islamic architecture, with mosaic inscriptions from the Quran in gold and blue (Plate 2.3). However, even in this landmark mosque, the network of other cultures may be traced. A chronicler writing at the end of the thirteenth century claimed that in 964, when the *mihrab* and the cupola, or small dome, above it were completed, envoys of the caliph were sent to recruit craftsmen skilled in the art of mosaic; the caliph ensured that there would be others learned in this art to continue alone once the craftsmen returned home.[8] The result is a hybrid combination of aniconic (non-figurative) forms associated with both Byzantium and the Muslim Umayyad caliphate.

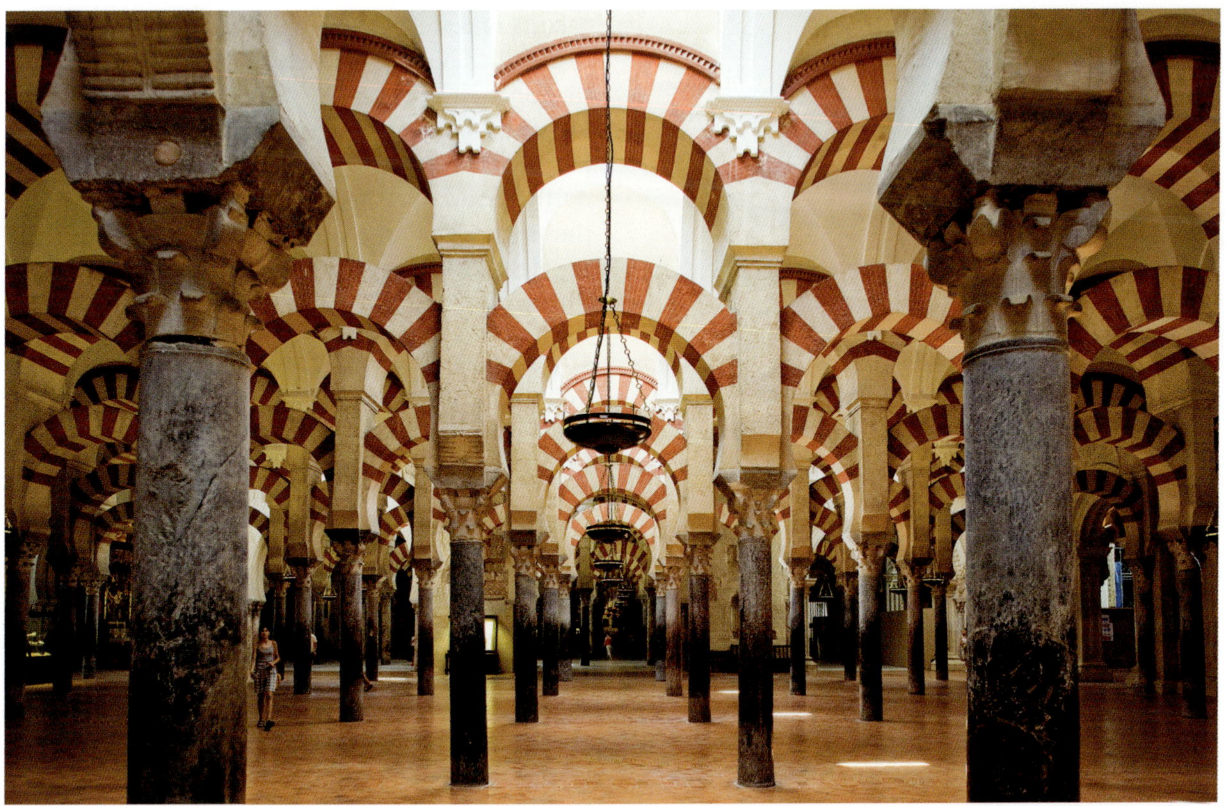

Plate 2.2 Interior of Córdoba mosque. Photo: © akg-images/Bildarchiv Steffens.

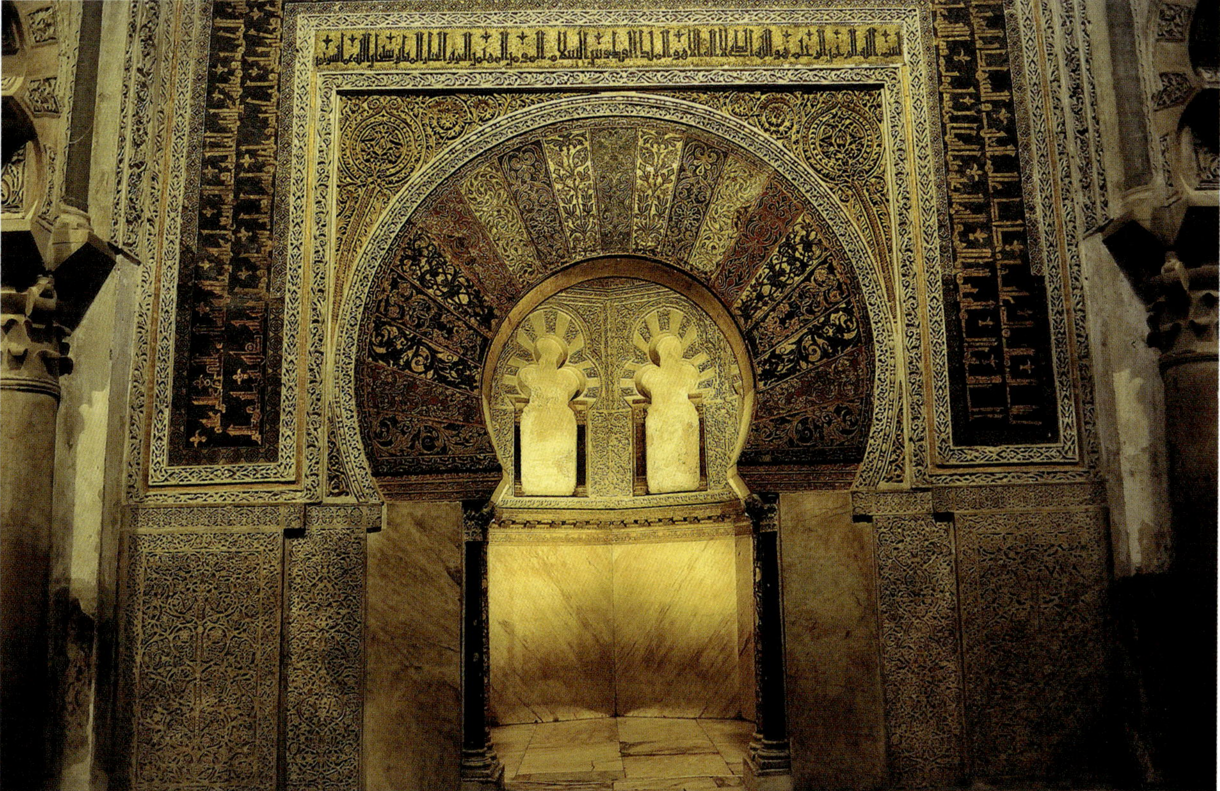

Plate 2.3 *Mihrab* wall, Córdoba mosque. Photo: © Arturo Cano Miño/age fotostock.

Exercise

Look carefully at the photographs of the Córdoba mosque and *mihrab* wall (Plates 2.2 and 2.3). From your own observation and from the brief discussion above, which features do you think might be characteristic ingredients of Islamic architecture?

Discussion

The horseshoe-shaped arches are distinctive; they differ from the round-headed or pointed arches found in European late medieval buildings, for example. The decorative plaster work on the *mihrab* is also characteristic. The Arabic inscriptions are another feature. Vernacular dedicatory inscriptions are found on other buildings, but not integrated into plaster decoration as they are here. The different coloured stone blocks in the arches (known as banded arches) are also noteworthy.

It is sometimes possible to associate artistic forms, features or techniques strongly with a particular visual culture. Visual cultures can also be 'entangled', so that it is very difficult to trace or interpret the connections or even decide where a feature first appeared. The horseshoe arch so distinctive of Islamic art is arguably an 'entangled' feature. These arches are also found in Visigothic churches in the far north of Spain – churches that date from between the conversion of the Visigothic rulers of Iberia in 589 and the Islamic conquest of 711. Horseshoe arches were also reintroduced to the Christian north of the country by Christian refugees from the Islamic south.[9] The banded arches associated with Islamic buildings are also found in Roman buildings predating Islamic architecture; this feature also recurs in early medieval European buildings, whether appropriated from Islam or as a survival of the Roman past.[10]

2 Historical outline

The conquest and reconquest of the Iberian peninsula are key to understanding its complex culture. Invading Muslim forces arrived in 711 via North Africa, defeating the Christian Visigoths in almost all of the peninsula apart from the north-west and establishing the sophisticated Umayyad regime (756–1031). The balance of power shifted very slowly from Islamic to Christian dominance. Almost immediately after the conquest, the north-western Christian kingdom of Asturias began to regain ground. The Christian kingdom of Navarre based around Pamplona in the north-east also emerged in the eighth century, while the kingdoms of Aragon and Castile were formed in the eleventh century. Portugal also became a separate Christian kingdom in 1139.

The Umayyad caliphate of al-Andalus disintegrated into a series of rival statelets or *taifas* during the first half of the eleventh century. This disunity led ultimately to the loss of the key Muslim city of Toledo in 1085 to Alfonso VI of Leon and Castile (r.1065–1109). The shock of this defeat prompted the incursion of the Almoravids from North Africa, in turn superseded from 1146 by the Almohads. These regimes differed from their Umayyad predecessors in both their Berber, North African ethnicity and culture and their missionary zeal. In 1212 the legendary victory of Las Navas de Tolosa against the Almohads was won by the Castilian ruler Alfonso VIII (r.1158–1214) with the combined forces of Castile, Navarre, Aragon and France. Córdoba fell in 1236 to Ferdinand III of Castile and Seville in 1248. Meanwhile, James I of Aragon (r.1213–76), known as the Conqueror, conquered Valencia and the Balearic Islands.

Islamic al-Andalus was eventually confined to the southern territory of Granada, with a new, stable ruling dynasty – the Nasrids. The first Nasrid ruler, Muhammad I (r.1232–72), acknowledged Castilian overlordship in 1246, securing his Nasrid dynasty from further erosion. This cultured regime coexisted alongside its neighbour Castile with relative stability until the fifteenth century, when Castile made a determined move to conquer the remaining Islamic territories. This impulse was subsequently described as the *reconquista* or reconquest of the whole of Iberia for Christianity. The last Nasrid ruler, Muhammad XII (r.1482–92), known to the Christians as Boabdil, recognised Castilian overlordship in 1485, but this was not enough to halt the invaders.

The conquest of the last Islamic stronghold of Granada in 1492 was the first of three crucial events in that year which marked a fundamental shift in Spanish politics and culture. The second was Christopher Columbus's famous voyage to discover a western passage to Asia, which instead proved the first step in exploring and conquering the New World of the Americas. Although Italian by birth, he was sponsored by Ferdinand and Isabella, and it was they who reaped the territorial and material benefits of his voyage and the subsequent conquests of Mexico and Peru. Third, in 1492 the Jewish population of Castile and Aragon was offered the choice of expulsion or conversion. During the sixteenth century the same ruthless choice was gradually extended to the Muslim population also: Granada Muslims in 1501, Muslims in the rest of Castile in 1502 and Muslims in Aragon in 1526. On the death of Ferdinand of Aragon in 1516, the newly unified kingdom of Spain along with its territories in the New World was inherited by his young grandson Charles, also ruler of the Low Countries and future Holy Roman Emperor. Charles's reign lasted until 1556, when he officially ceded power to his son Philip II. By then, the Spanish Empire also included extensive areas of the New World.

3 Convivencia

Although the history of Spain was one of religious and territorial conflict, it was also one in which heterogeneous and diverse populations coexisted. The term used to describe this is 'convivencia', which means, literally, living together. Under the Umayyads of al-Andalus both Judaism and Christianity were respected as 'religions of the book' – religions claiming to be derived from divinely inspired scripture, as was Islam. Jews and existing Mozarabic, or Arab-speaking Christians, living in Umayyad al-Andalus were 'dhimmis': protected people with legal status. As Christians progressively conquered al-Andalus from the north, local Muslims were not routinely evicted, not least because Muslim agricultural skills were badly needed.[11] Jewish communities were also numerous, both in old Christian territories such as Galicia and in more recently conquered territories such as Andalucia. The Christian kingdoms of Castile and Aragon also adopted legal frameworks to safeguard Muslim and Jewish communities in return for paying higher taxes or tributes.

There is much debate about whether this legal convivencia corresponded with any real spirit of cultural or religious tolerance at local level. The fundamental religious differences between Muslim, Jew and Christian always had the potential to erupt

into trouble and there were certainly serious lapses: for example, the repressive policies of the Almoravids and Almohads in al-Andalus and the 1391 pogrom against Jews in Christian Castile and Aragon. Nevertheless, this was a fundamentally pluralist society, in which cultures were inevitably on some level porous and, despite significant religious barriers, were susceptible to 'acculturation' – permeability to influence from the outside.[12]

The fifteenth century saw a hardening of attitudes in Christian Spain, however, and, under Ferdinand and Isabella, the feasibility and certainly the desirability of governing a heterogeneous population with such varying cultures and beliefs was called into question.[13] The fifteenth century also saw a shift in the visual arts, as elite artistic projects were increasingly given to imported craftsmen, particularly from the Netherlands. By the mid-sixteenth century royal, aristocratic and elite clerical patronage was dominated by Italianate tastes and traditions. The cultural and religious landscape of unified Christian Spain looked very different by the time Philip II assumed power in 1556.

4 Heritage, hybridity and appropriation

Luxury goods from the Islamic kingdom of al-Andalus were much in demand, both in the Islamic 'homeland' of North Africa and in Christian Europe. Ceramic lustreware was a distinctively Islamic craft developed in the ninth century, for example. Traditionally, it involved gold-coloured designs traced in metal oxide on an opaque white lead-glazed base, though in Spanish lustreware the traditional gold is supplemented by blue decoration. The craft was adopted in al-Andalus under the Almoravids and Almohads, and Málaga became the most famous centre of production under the Nasrids. The craft was also established in Christian-ruled Manises and Paterna on opposite banks of the river Turia, just outside the port of Valencia. Manises trade was promoted by Christian overlord Pedro Boil after a trip to Granada in 1308–09, a very telling example of a Christian deliberately adopting and exploiting an Islamic craft.[14] Here, at least by the fifteenth century, the Muslim workforce was probably supplemented by Christians who had learned to master the technique. It is often very difficult to tell Manises lustreware made in Christian Valencia from Málaga lustreware made in Islamic al-Andalus.

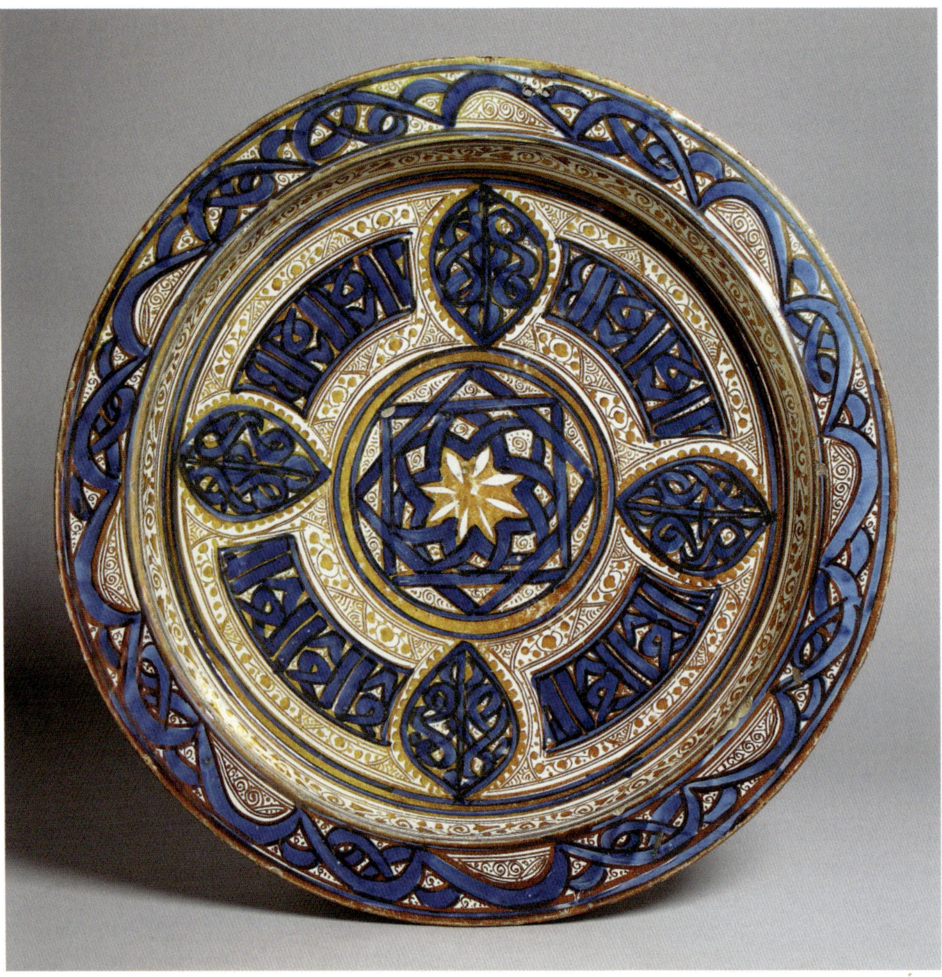

Plate 2.4 Bowl, 1420–30, tin-glazed earthenware, diameter 46 cm (Manises, Valencia?). The Metropolitan Museum of Art, New York, The Cloisters collection, 56.171.127. © 2017. Image copyright The Metropolitan Museum of Art/Art Resource/Scala, Florence.

The densely patterned large lustreware bowl in the Metropolitan Museum of Art (Plate 2.4) is judged to have been made in Manises in the early years of the fifteenth century, but follows traditional Islamic formulas. On its interior it has a motif characteristic of Islamic visual culture – the eight-pointed star made of two superimposed squares. Within it is a second eight-pointed star made of interlocking, curving lines.[15] The decoration around the stars recalls Arabic letter forms. On the underside of the bowl (Plate 2.5) there is a bull painted in the more traditional gold on white and distributed to fit the circular shape as if moving around the rim in a clockwise direction, a strategy again typical of Islamic lustreware.[16]

During the fifteenth century in particular, Manises produced 'hybrid' ceramics, combining features from different cultures. Hybridity here meant preserving the sought-after metallic look of Islamic lustreware, but customising it for a Christian market. A plate surviving from a lavish set commissioned in 1454 by Maria of Castile, wife of the Aragonese King Alfonso V (r.1416–58), now in the Victoria and Albert Museum, is painted in the traditional white and gold lustre but with the patron's coat of arms in the middle.[17] Other plates from Manises include the IHS monogram of Christ and even Christian inscriptions such as 'Ave Maria' around the rim.

Far from being considered tainted by their associations with the 'infidel' or the 'enemy', Islamic ceramics were a luxury item highly in demand in Christian Spain, Spanish Naples and further afield. There is a great deal of debate about why this should have been so, but the allure and sophistication of the Nasrid court of Granada and its legendary Alhambra may go some way to explain it.

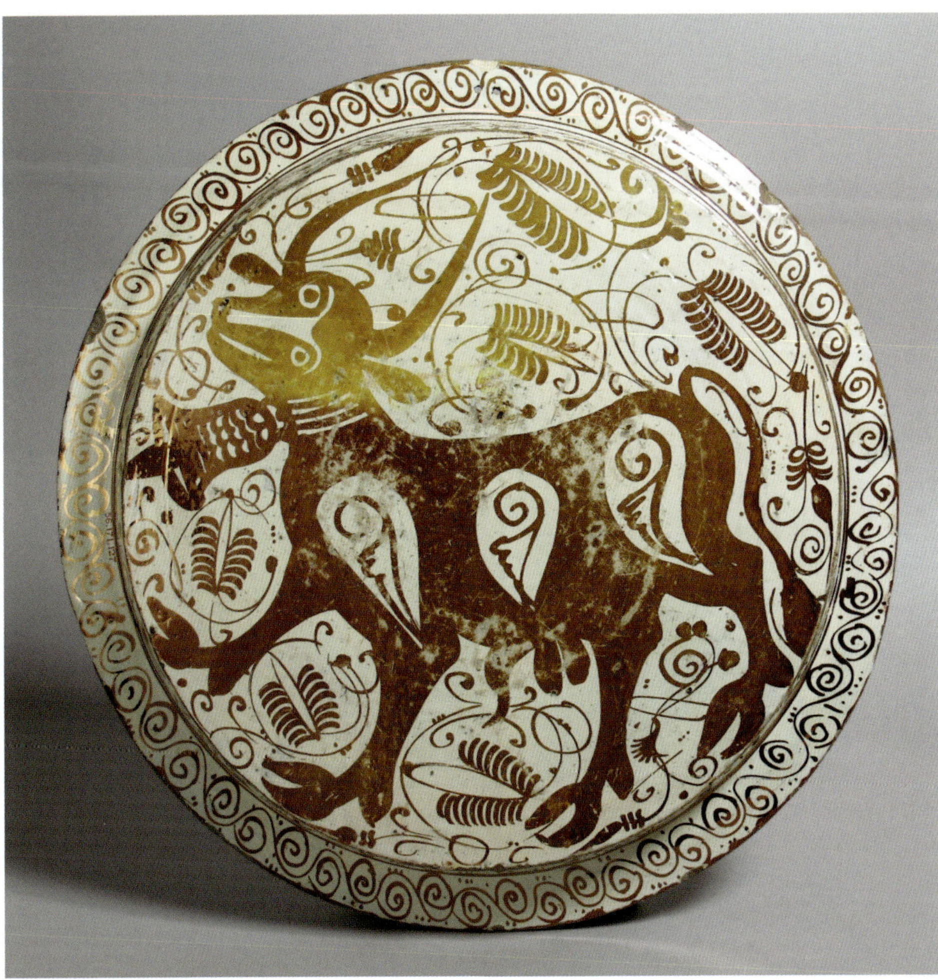

Plate 2.5 Reverse of bowl, 1420–30, tin-glazed earthenware, diameter 46 cm (Manises, Valencia?). The Metropolitan Museum of Art, New York, The Cloisters collection, 56.171.127. © 2017. Image copyright The Metropolitan Museum of Art/Art Resource/Scala, Florence.

5 The Alhambra

The Alhambra is the most celebrated Islamic palace in Spain and the epitome of Nasrid architectural culture. After the defeat of Granada in 1492, Ferdinand and Isabella took it over as a royal palace and made a point of preserving it, perhaps as an appropriated landmark that bore witness to the triumph of Christianity over Islam, but perhaps also out of admiration.[18] Charles V inserted a Renaissance-style palace into the precincts but, unlike the mosque at Córdoba, most of the Islamic structure was left undisturbed.

The Alhambra was an enclosed royal palace complex set above and looking down on the vast Nasrid capital city of Granada. It was built largely under Nasrid rulers Yusuf I (r.1333–54) and Muhammad V (r.1354–59 and 1362–91). An inscription in the Sala de la Barca at the north end of the Court of the Myrtles (see below) refers to the capture of the key port of Algeciras near the Strait of Gibraltar from Castile in 1369, and this,

together with other inscriptions referring to power and victory, suggest that parts of the palace at least were built after this date.[19]

Entering from the west through the older zones of the complex, the visitor moves through to the two newer and probably more private palaces with more limited access: the Comares Palace, with its Court of the Myrtles running north–south (Plate 2.6); and the Palace of the Lions, with its famous courtyard running east–west.[20] Around each courtyard is a series of rooms, and each zone is connected by indirect passageways that lend an air of secrecy to the whole complex.[21] Little of the history or function of the two palaces is known – the suggestion that the Palace of the Lions might have been a madrasa, or Islamic school, like the one Yusuf had founded in Granada itself, seems not to have won general consensus.[22] Islamic tradition, archaeology and the poetic or Quranic inscriptions

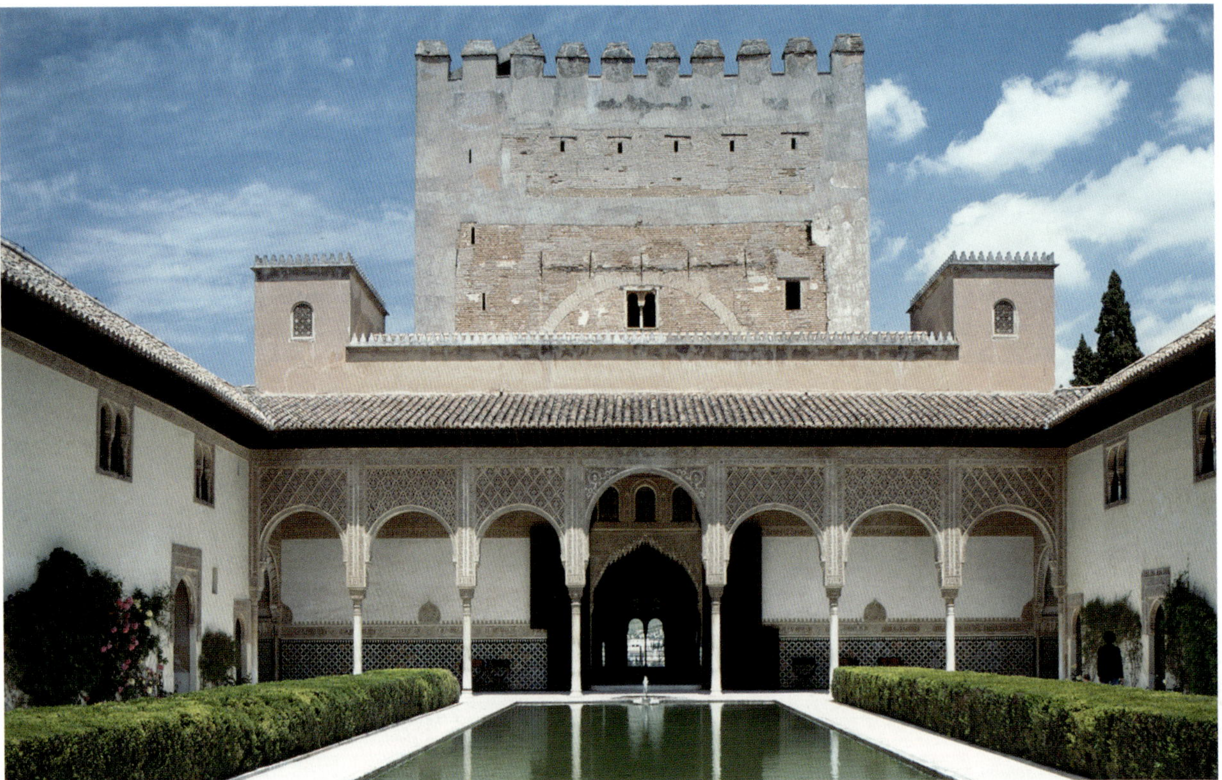

Plate 2.6 Court of the Myrtles, 1362–91. Comares Palace, Alhambra, Granada. Photo: © akg-images/De Agostini Picture Lib./G. Sioen.

embellishing many of the parts of the palace are the main sources of intelligence concerning when it was built and how it was used.

The Comares Palace was evidently begun by Yusuf, and inscriptions in the square Hall of the Ambassadors at the north end of the Court of the Myrtles imply he used this as his throne room; references to the Seven Heavens suggest the cupola was conceived as a heavenly reflection of the Nasrid court.[23] The Court of the Myrtles and the Palace of the Lions were completed or built by Muhammad V after his return to power in 1362. Inscriptions suggest that the Hall of the Two Sisters at the north end of the Court of the Lions may also have been intended to evoke the Seven Heavens.

On a neighbouring hill, but connected to the Alhambra, there is an earlier palace now known as the Generalife. Here there was a pleasure garden with watercourses and sunken quadrants planted with flowers or trees that could be viewed from the walkways and loggias above. This combination of walkways, water channels and division into four planted areas or quadrants that were often sunken

exemplified the Islamic system of formal gardens known as Chahar Bagh, also found in the Court of the Myrtles and the Court of the Lions.[24]

Both courtyards are built around hydraulic systems using water brought by aqueducts from the surrounding hills. The Court of the Lions (Plate 2.7) is focused on a central fountain supported by 12 stone lions that also spout water supplied by narrow watercourses from north, south, east and west. Originally the four areas between these watercourses were sunken gardens with orange trees.[25] The Court of the Myrtles (Plate 2.6) is arranged around a broad central watercourse which, in the sixteenth century and probably also in Nasrid times, had myrtle bushes and orange trees on either side.[26] At the Alhambra, gardens and vistas onto landscapes played a particularly important role. In one such viewpoint, the Mirador by the Hall of the Two Sisters, the inscription reads 'In this garden I am an eye filled with delight and the pupil of this eye is truly our Lord'.[27] Written in the first person as if it is the building itself that is speaking, actively engaging the visitor, this inscription reveals the high level of conceptual subtlety and sophistication of the Alhambra.[28] The gardens were clearly primarily

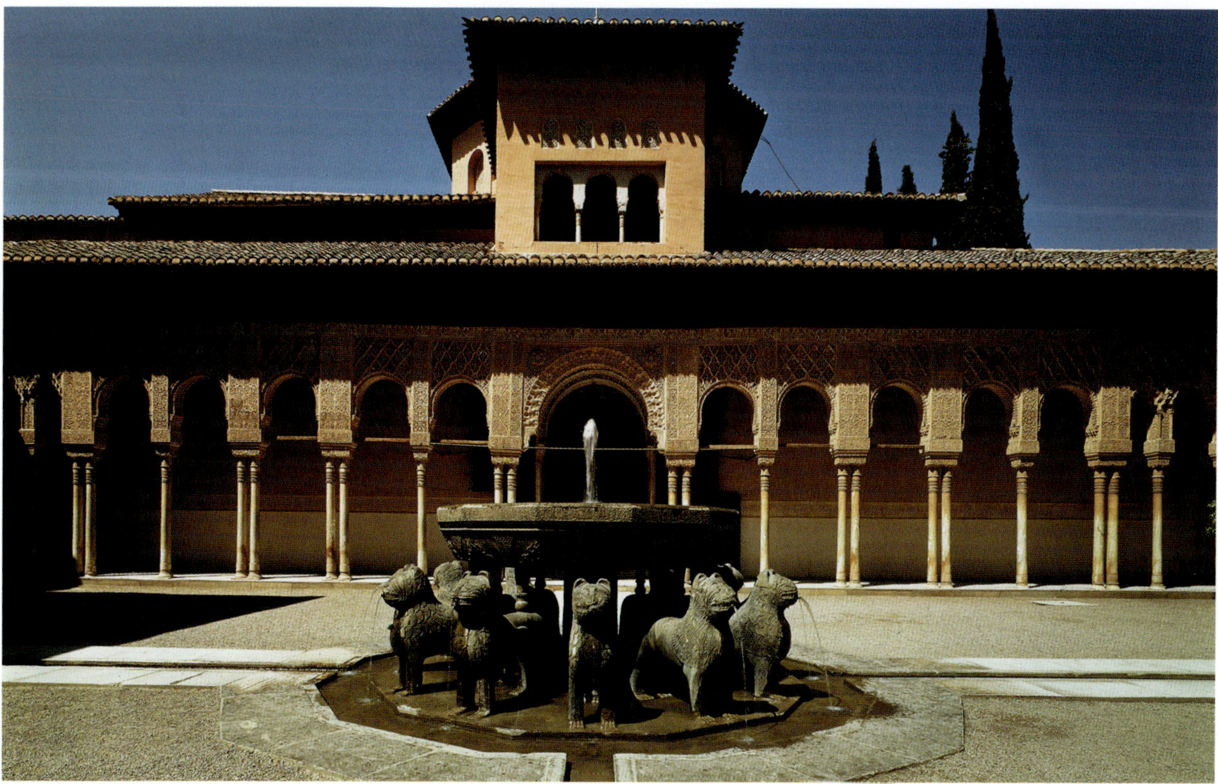

Plate 2.7 Court of the Lions, *c*.1362–91. Palace of the Lions, Alhambra, Granada. Photo: © Raffaello Bencini/Bridgeman Images.

intended for the pleasure of the sultan, but they may also have had connotations of Paradise: in Arabic, the word for Paradise and garden is the same.[29]

The interior surfaces of the building are particularly densely embellished, in keeping with long-standing Arabic traditions, but here perhaps also to conceal poor building materials.[30] Arabic inscriptions pervade the plasterwork, some praising the patron or reciting the Nasrid motto 'there is no conqueror but God'. A line of slightly horseshoe-shaped arches are placed at each end of the Court of the Myrtles with intricate geometric plaster decoration in the wall above, known as *sebka*. The lower part of the wall is decorated with geometric ceramic tiling patterns known as *alicatado*. The central arch behind the arcade, which opens into the apartments at the end, is a *muqarnas* arch, an arch decorated with stalactite-like plaster work. The square Hall of the Two Sisters at one end of the Court of the Lions has a *muqarnas* dome over an octagonal base, while at the other end of the courtyard the Hall of the Abencerrajes has a *muqarnas* dome in the shape of an eight-sided star (Plate 2.8). Poetic inscriptions alluding to power and victory by Ibn Zamrak, the

private secretary of Muhammad V, are inscribed in plaster around the Court of the Lions and around the bowl of the fountain itself. The capitals are inscribed with words of praise for the architect and for the patron Muhammad V, adding a level of depth and significance to the complex.

Intriguingly, even in this most impressive of Islamic buildings there is an element of cultural hybridity. On the eastern short side of the Court of the Lions, the Hall of Justice has three vaults decorated with narrative scenes stuck to the ceiling.[31] The painting style is reminiscent of European fourteenth-century wall paintings such as those at the papal palace at Avignon, but the technique of tempera on leather is an Islamic one. These scenes were probably painted by Muslim craftsmen, perhaps deriving designs from portable Christian objects decorated with narrative romances, such as caskets or tapestries.[32] There has been much debate about exactly which legends the narratives describe, but the game of chess on the south ceiling identifies the well-known Christian romance of Tristan and Isolde. Other scenes may be from Arthurian legends or perhaps the tale of the Christian

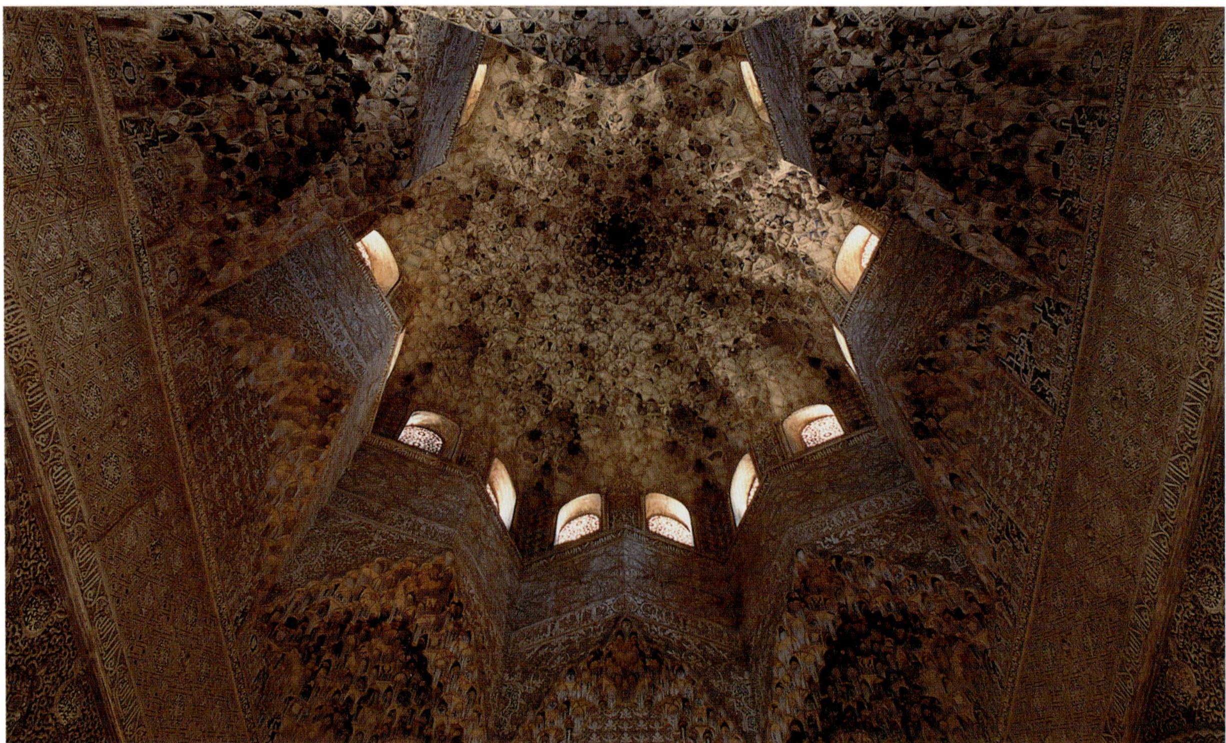

Plate 2.8 *Muqarnas* dome. Hall of the Abencerrajes, Alhambra, Granada. Photo: © Hervé Champollion/akg-images.

countess Blancaflor (who was Tristan's mother according to some versions) and her love affair with the Muslim prince Flor; in the centre are ten turbaned figures, perhaps part of the Flor legend, perhaps representations of Nasrid rulers or viziers (Plate 2.9).[33]

Whatever their precise meaning, the legends have been plausibly interpreted as 'frontier' narratives, representing the interface between Christian and Muslim, even if the narrative is weighted to make it clear that it is the Muslim who triumphs.[34] The most likely motive was that the foreignness of the paintings imparted a highly desirable air of luxury and cosmopolitanism, just as a Málaga or Manises lustreware bowl might in a Christian palace.[35] It has also been noted that a degree of hybridity was a feature of the courts of both Muhammad V and his Castilian counterpart and ally, Pedro I (r.1350–69), across the porous frontier separating Granada from Castile.[36] The inclusion of this European narrative is a minor detail in a building that otherwise depends upon Arabic traditions, so hybridity at the court of Muhammad V should not be overemphasised. It is much more obvious at the court of Pedro I.

Between its conquest in 1248 and the death of Pedro I in 1369, Seville was the capital of Castile, and the Grenadine border was hence in close proximity. Pedro grew up in Andalucia and may have considered Islamic visual culture to be no more 'foreign' than the Gothic traditions of northern Europe.[37] Muhammad V had visited the court of Pedro I in Seville in 1359 during his three-year exile. Pedro was instrumental in returning him to the throne, and Muhammad V in turn supported Pedro against his usurping half-brother Henry of Trastámara. Difficulties in identifying the origins and religious identities of the craftsmen who worked for these two rulers testify to the fluidity with which people, objects and ideas moved across frontiers.

Pedro I was accused by his enemies of maurofilia – a slander that implied a taste for and fascination with Islamic culture that was excessive and inappropriate for a Christian ruler.[38] In the 1360s, around the same time that Muhammad V may have begun additions to the Alhambra, Pedro the Cruel (another label applied by his enemies) built a new palace in the Alcazar, the historic Islamic palace complex in Seville which dated back to the tenth century.

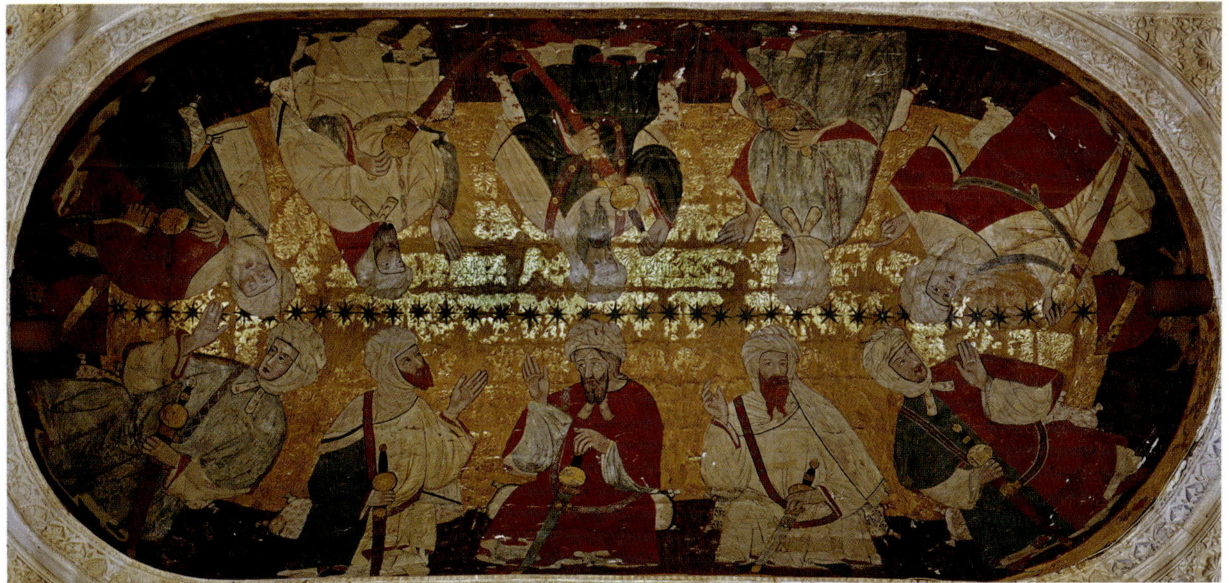

Plate 2.9 Ten turbaned figures, fourteenth century, tempera on leather. Hall of Justice, Alhambra, Granada.
Photo: © akg-images/Album/Oronoz.

6 Mudejar art and the Alcazar of Seville

Pedro's new palace has been seen as the epitome of mudejar art. The term 'mudejar' describes Muslims living in Christian territories, and was first used in the nineteenth century to describe art and architecture built by mudejar craftsmen for Christian patrons. In modern scholarship it is used broadly to describe objects and buildings outside Islamic territories that draw on Islamic artistic traditions. According to the inscriptions on the façade and the doors leading to the so-called Hall of the Ambassadors, it was built in 1364–66, though it has been significantly modified and restored since. The layout was that typical of an Islamic palace, with inward-facing bedrooms at either end of the hall or courtyard. The main courtyard, the Court of the Maidens (Plate 2.10), also used to have an Islamic-style sunken garden with citrus trees, water channels and a central walkway.[39] The arcades around it are decorated with intricate geometric plasterwork and the walls behind with tiles, both traditional in Islamic architecture. The typical Islamic horseshoe arches are found in the most important room attached to this courtyard, the Hall of the Ambassadors. In adjacent rooms, birds and chivalric themes were incorporated into the otherwise Islamic-style decoration.

The palace is literally as well as culturally bilingual, for it includes Arabic as well as Spanish inscriptions. The main palace façade includes in Arabic the Nasrid motto 'there is no conqueror but God'.[40] The Arabic inscriptions on the marquetry doors to the Hall of the Ambassadors that record the completion date of the palace use the Islamic rather than the Christian calendar. Inscriptions name those responsible for the doors as craftsmen from Toledo, still a centre for mudejar skills in the fourteenth century. By contrast, on the inside of the doors are biblical texts in Spanish.

Pedro here adopted and adapted Islamic architecture as his own. Although the very appropriation of the Alcazar palace demonstrated Castilian political domination, the reasons for Pedro's choice of the mudejar style and the message that conveyed, more than a century after the conquest of Seville, are uncertain.[41] An Islamic-style palace offered greater luxury and comfort than a European-style castle might, especially in Seville's hot climate. As the overlord of Muhammad V, Pedro could appropriate from a position of strength.[42] This mudejar building suggests that Islamic architectural style was in some measure transferable and not indelibly 'tainted' by its association with Muslim 'enemies'. Instead it suggests that by this time it may have been the Nasrid court that established elite tastes in the Iberian peninsula, though it should be remembered that some of the

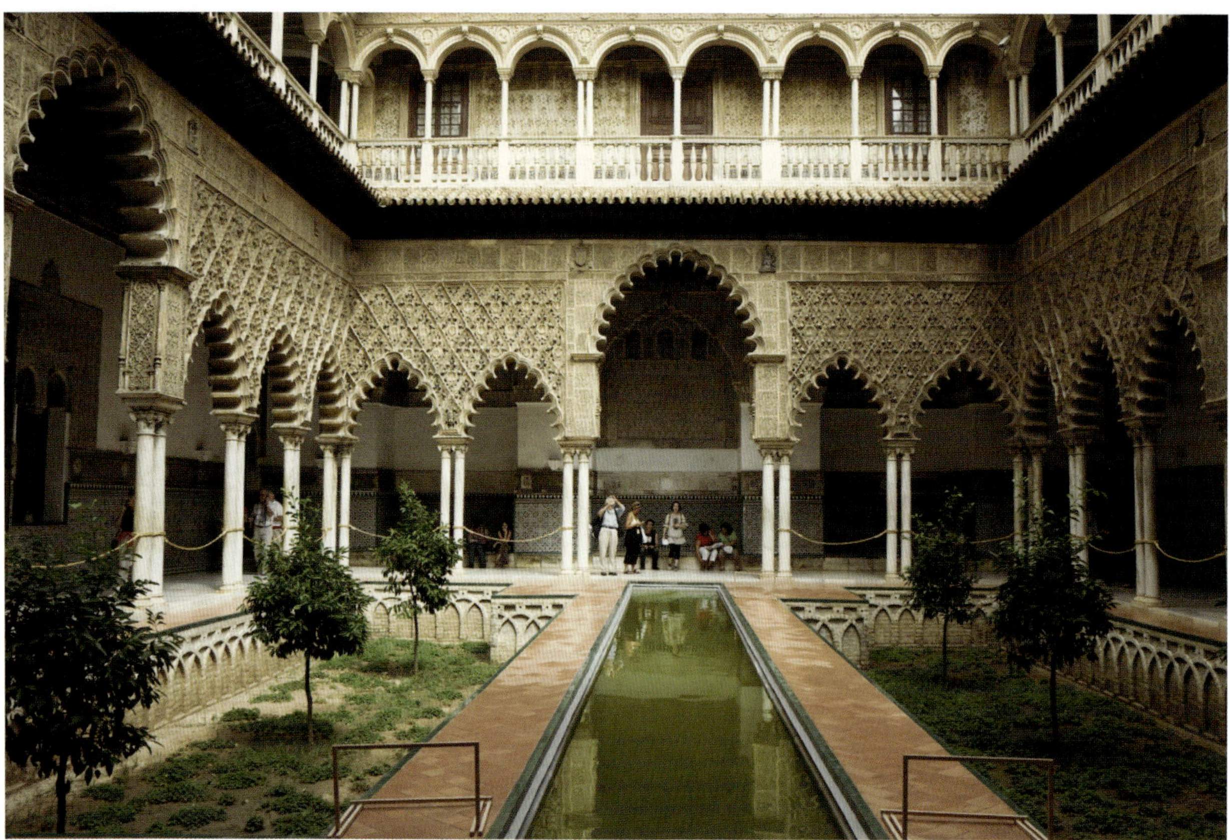

Plate 2.10 Court of the Maidens, 1359–69. Alcazar, Seville. Photo: © Ken Welsh/Bridgeman Images.

most famous parts of the Alhambra, including the Court of the Lions, were constructed after Pedro built his palace.[43] It has also been pointed out that the kingdom of Castile was bigger by far than the reduced territory of Nasrid Granada. There were many more building projects going on in Castile, and it is possible that some mudejar innovations originated on the Castilian side of the border.[44] During Pedro's brief reign, it has been argued, a mudejar architectural approach became a kind of Castilian court style.[45] This does not negate the idea that art might reflect and construct a cultural identity, but it does show the complexity of the process.

Mudejar specialisms such as *muqarnas* or *sebka* plasterwork, ceramic tiles and inlaid wooden ceilings and doors remained much in demand in Christian territories of Spain in the fifteenth and even the sixteenth centuries. The chapel of Lope Fernandez de Luna, Bishop of Zaragoza, was built in 1374–81 and adjoins Zaragoza Cathedral (La Seo). The remaining original exterior wall is encrusted with Islamic-style coloured ceramic tiles and raised brickwork in dense geometric patterns

(Plate 2.11), while the staircase leading to the chapel crypt has stepped, ziggurat-style arches overhead. The Aragonese capital of Zaragoza, like Seville, had an illustrious Islamic past and this chapel shows that its traditions remained alive far removed from the mudejar building projects of Pedro I. It also shows that Islamic decorative features were incorporated into Christian churches as well as secular buildings.

In neighbouring Castile, the Salón de la Galera in the royal palace of Segovia built in 1412 for Catherine of Lancaster, wife of Enrique III of Castile (r.1390–1406), has mudejar-style decorations. Between 1480 and 1492, and hence on the very eve of the reconquest of Granada, the second marquis of Santillana (d.1500), head of the aristocratic Mendoza family, built a new palace in Guadalajara in a hybrid style.[46] Northern European Gothic architect Juan Guas was lured from royal service to direct the project, while the distinctive, diamond-cut brickwork of the façade is an example of Italian-Renaissance-style rustication. Mudejar craftsmen decorated the ceilings in the Salón de Salvajes (room of the wild men) and Sala de Consejas

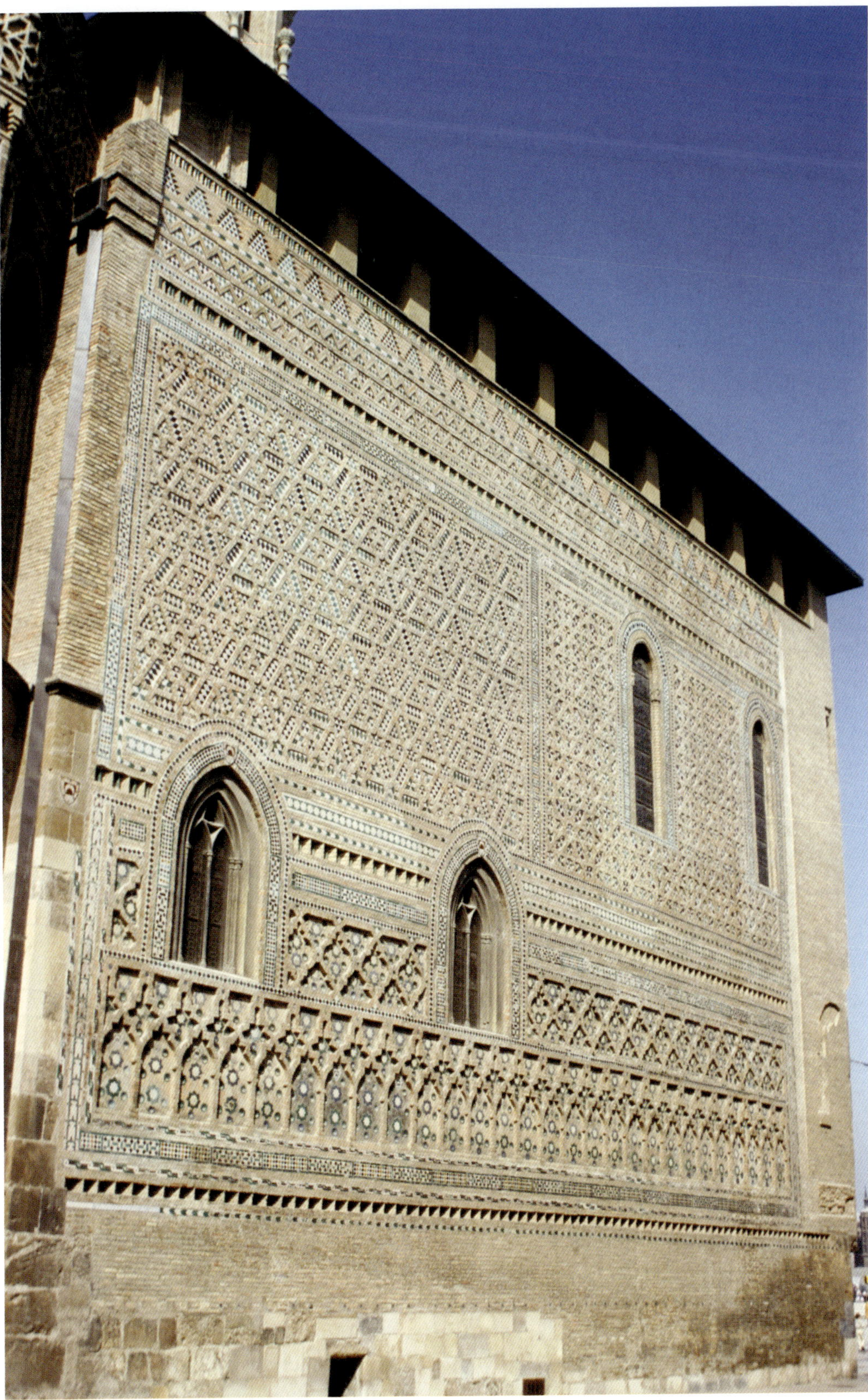

Plate 2.11 Mudejar wall, chapel of Lope Fernandez de Luna, 1374–81. Adjoining Zaragoza Cathedral (La Seo).
Photo: © Omniphoto/UIG/Bridgeman Images.

(council room) with distinctively Islamic plasterwork, both alas destroyed in the Spanish Civil War. This palace epitomises the hybrid approach to architecture, picking and choosing luxury features from different traditions for the purposes of prestige. The Casa de Pilatos in Seville was remodelled in 1520–39 in Italian Renaissance style but with mudejar tiles, plasterwork and inlaid wood. Mudejar art even had a limited afterlife in the New World. Some Mexican churches, such as that of Asunción de Nuestra Señora in Tlaxcala, have mudejar-style timber decoration incorporating eight-pointed stars, suggesting some craftsmen trained in traditional Islamic crafts also found work in the New World.[47]

7 Judaism

In 1215 the Fourth Lateran church council decreed that European Jews were required to wear some kind of identifying clothing. Christian prejudice against them in Europe was acute. Up until 1391, the Jewish communities in Castile and Aragon fared rather better. They were allowed a degree of self-government and were often prosperous professionals, craftsmen and tradesmen. Individual Jews took on financial roles and sometimes important offices at court. One of these was Samuel Halevi Abulafia (c.1320–60), treasurer, tax collector and adviser to Pedro I. He founded a synagogue in Toledo in 1357, which was later transformed into the Christian church dedicated to the Death of the Virgin and known as El Transito (Plate 2.12). The original synagogue demonstrates the same spirit of hybridity as Pedro I's Alcazar. The building has Islamic-style polylobed arches in the *mihrab* and in the upper zone, intricate plasterwork, an inlaid wood ceiling, tiled floor and Hebrew and Arabic texts running around the interior.[48] Here the Jewish Samuel may have adopted mudejar architectural forms to participate in the preferred culture of his master Pedro I, or perhaps the Islamic heritage of Toledo retained its cultural power long after its conquest. Nevertheless, the dedicatory inscription proudly lists the material objects provided for Jewish worship: the wooden tower for reading the law, the Torah scrolls, the lamps and a courtyard for rabbinical discussion.[49]

Halevi's synagogue was a Jewish commission for the use of Jews, albeit later adapted for Christian use. The Alba Bible produced in 1422–30 is an example of a Christian commission entrusted to a Jew: a translation of the Hebrew Bible (the Old Testament) made by Rabbi Moses Arragel of Maqueda near Toledo for Don Luis de Guzmán, Master of the military order of Calatrava. The purpose appears to have been to acquire an up-to-date text and concordance of Jewish and Christian interpretations of points of difficulty. This is interesting in its own right, particularly as the commission coincided with an edict passed by Pope Martin V (r.1417–31) requiring humanity and kindness towards European Jews.[50] For the Christian aspects, the rabbi was assisted by a relative of the patron and the Franciscan Brother Arias. Of the 513 folios, 334 are illustrated and follow a hybrid combination of Christian and Jewish conventions.

The Bible begins with a 25-folio (50 double-sided pages) prologue setting out the story of the commission and its scrutiny for error at the University of Salamanca and in the Franciscan monastery of Toledo on its completion. Also transcribed was an exchange of letters in which the rabbi refused to supervise the illustration of the manuscript on the grounds that it would be sinning against Jewish law and he knew nothing about illustration. Brother Arias promised to get the illustration done in Toledo if the rabbi just left blanks at the appropriate places. The rabbi's refusal may have been transcribed to protect him from criticism from his fellow Jews. Indeed images of God are included several times, for example in the Expulsion of Adam and Eve from the Garden of Eden (fol. 28 verso), and this is strictly forbidden in Judaism. Willingly or not, the rabbi cooperated with the pictorial programme in practice. His commentary sometimes refers to the illustrations, and some miniatures follow specific rabbinical texts such as Cain's murder of Abel by biting him in the neck (fol. 29 verso) or Jewish festivities such as Yom Kippur.[51] Rabbi Moses is depicted presenting the book to Don Luis in the dedicatory miniature and wearing a red badge, a reminder that he was a Jew (Plate 2.13).[52]

Half a century later, in the so-called Kennicott Bible, Jewish qualms about illustration appear to have been set aside, reflecting a much more permissive Jewish attitude towards the visual arts. This spectacular Hebrew Bible is a rare survival of Spanish Judaism, or of the Sephardic Jews as they are commonly known. It also incorporates the grammatical treatise

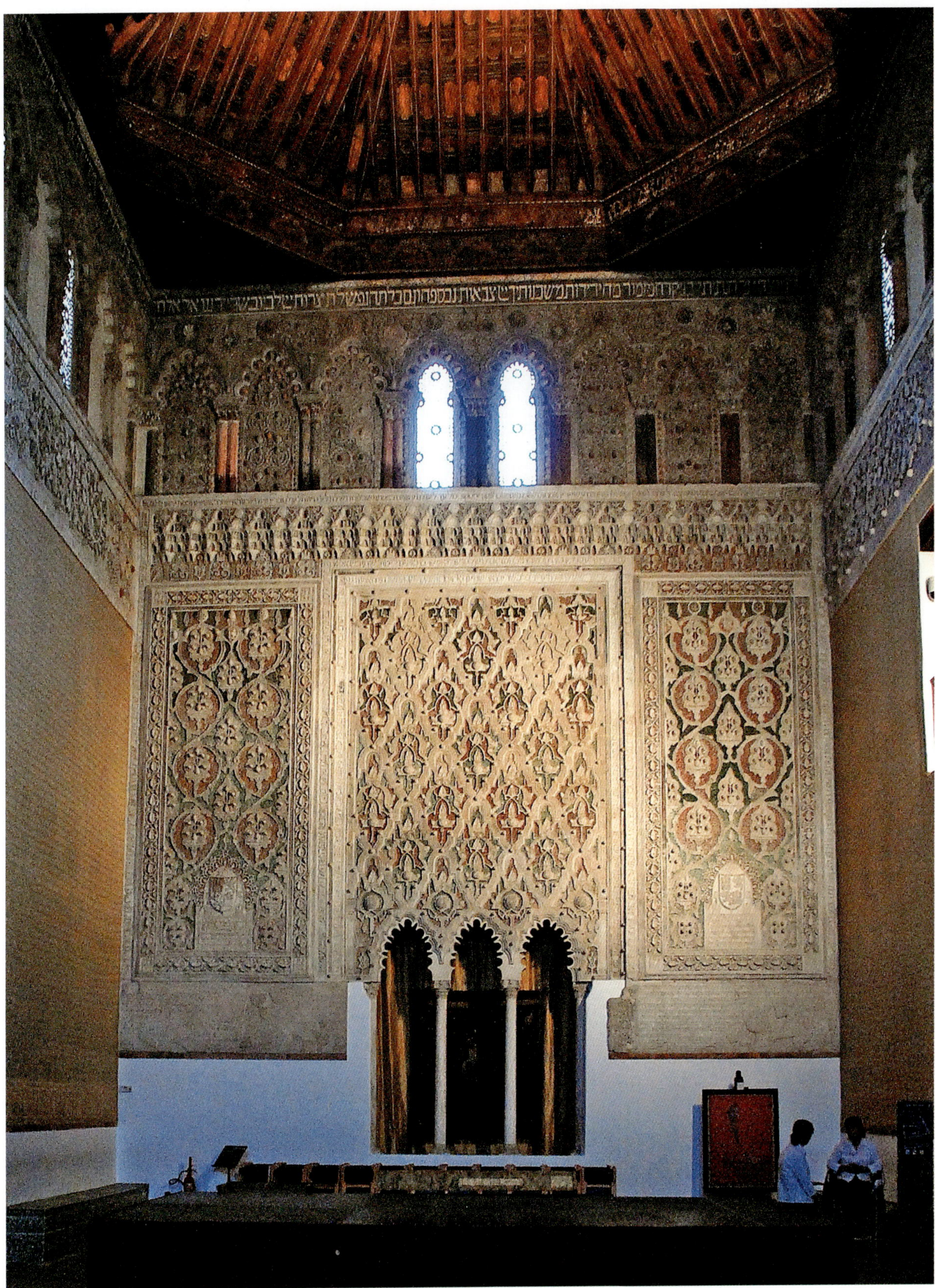

Plate 2.12 El Transito, 1357–60, Toledo. Photo: © akg-images/Bible Land Pictures/Z.Radovan/BibleLandPictures.com.

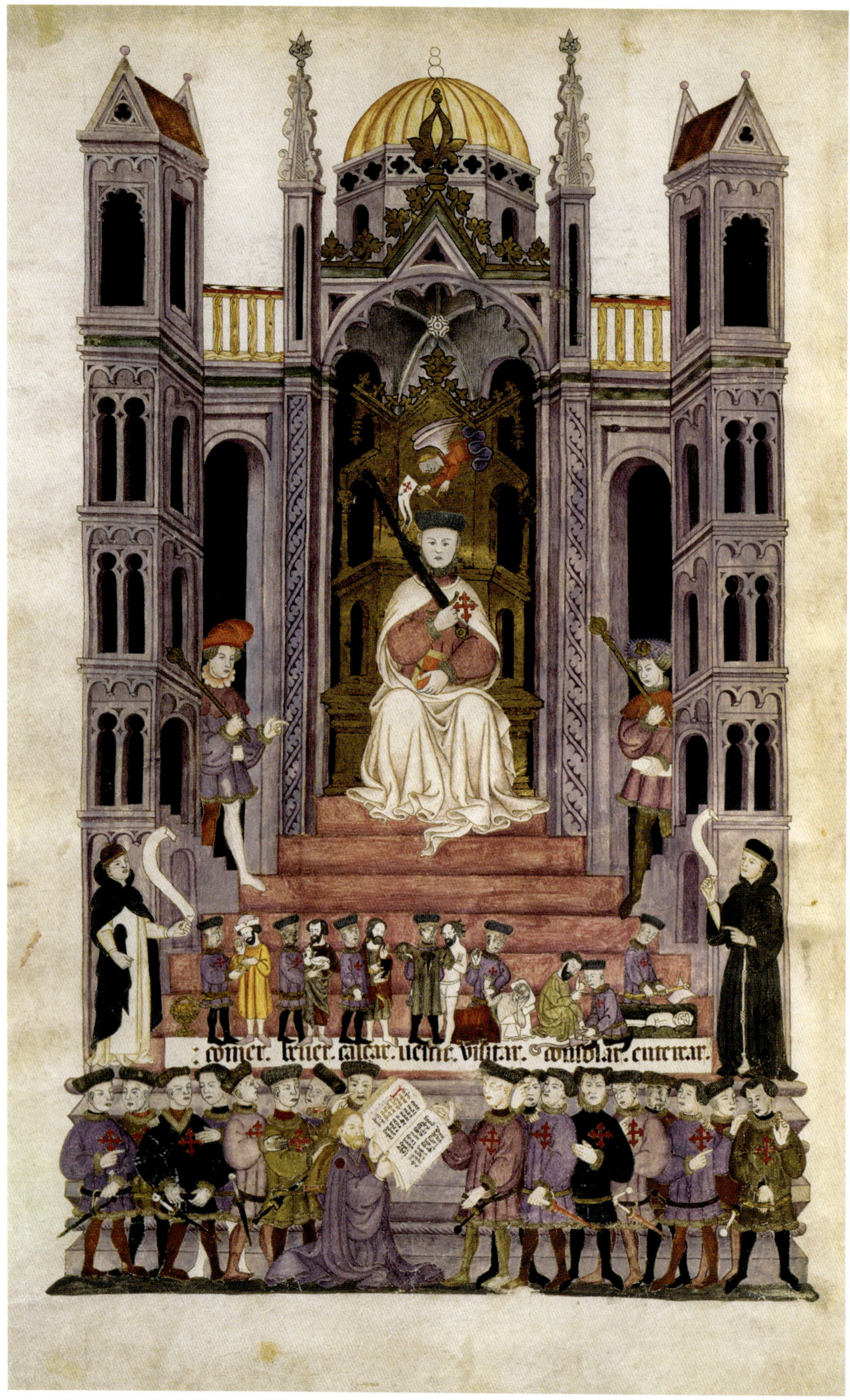

Plate 2.13 Rabbi Moses, dedicatory miniature in the Alba Bible, 1422–30. Collection of the Duke of Alba, Madrid. Photo: © akg-images/Album/ Oronoz.

of Rabbi Qimhi. This time it was a Jewish commission, and an inscription at the beginning of the book reveals that it was made in 1476 in the north coast Galician port of La Coruña. It was written in Hebrew by scribe Moses Ibn Zabara for Isaac, son of Don Solomon de Braga who, judging by his name, originally came from Portugal. At the end, a second inscription reveals the artist to have been Joseph Ibn Hayyim, about whom little is known.[53] This is a truly hybrid book combining Jewish, Islamic and Christian forms. Inside the front cover is a star inscribed within a circle, motifs found in Islamic visual art (see Plate 2.18). The grammatical text at the beginning is written in two columns set out on the page within the two 'windows' of an architectural frame. Some of these use the horseshoe arch and interlocking geometric ornament reminiscent of Islamic traditions. Folio 6 recto, however, contains motifs associated with Christian European manuscripts: rabbits, leaves and a monkey. The full page illustration on folio 120 verso shows the menorah, the seven-branched candlestick of Judaism. Folio 305 recto (Plate 2.14) depicts Jonah being swallowed by a whale, a common theme in Christian illumination but exceptional in the iconophobic traditions of Judaism. Marginal animals and figures also abound, sometimes mythical: there is a centaur on folio 86 verso, for example. While propagating a Jewish text with its traditions of commentary and vocalisation marks for reading aloud, this illuminator incorporated the rich heritage of Islamic decoration and Christian narrative art and marginal illumination.

Religious figurehead Saint Vincent Ferrer (c.1350–1419) placed huge emphasis on converting the Jewish population, while large-scale forced conversions accompanied the infamous massacre of Jews in 1391. In order to assimilate these uncatechised conversos – Jews converted to Christianity – into Christian society, the segregation of unconverted Jews was, if anything, intensified.[54] Doubt was subsequently cast on the authenticity of the faith of conversos.[55] It was this anxiety that gave rise to the notorious Spanish Inquisition in 1478 and it also had an impact on the visual arts.

During the fifteenth century some very celebrated conversos held high office in Castile. Alonso de Cartagena, Bishop of Burgos (1435–56), was a second generation converso of great distinction. His father, Pablo de Santa Maria (d.1435), had been an eminent

Jewish rabbi and scholar, who had converted around the time of the 1391 pogroms and who had preceded Alonso as Bishop of Burgos.

In 1442, Alonso established the chapel of the Visitation in Burgos Cathedral as a burial chapel. His tomb (Plate 2.15) was made during his lifetime and this is important because it must have reflected his own wishes.[56] His Gothic, lavishly detailed alabaster effigy was made at a time when even the eminent were usually commemorated only by stone effigies, if indeed they had an effigy at all. It places him on a par with some of the most distinguished men in the land, like the Archbishops of Toledo and the deposed King of Castile, Pedro I.

Reliefs of saints on tombs were not unknown in Iberian tomb conventions, but Bishop Alonso's tomb chest is surrounded by prominent, three-dimensional statues of saints, and this was unusual in alabaster tombs in Spain and elsewhere in Europe. At the head end of the tomb is the Visitation to which the chapel is dedicated. Below the effigy's right side are fundamental figures of the Catholic Church: the four church fathers Ambrose, Jerome, Gregory and Augustine, with Saints Peter and Paul between them. On the other side are saints chosen for their association with the city of Burgos or for the Bishop's own devotions. Religious images were anathema to practising Jews, as seen earlier. By unnecessarily including these statues, Alonso demonstrated his complete orthodoxy and the extent to which he, like his father, had thrown in his lot with Christianity. It put him above suspicion at a time when hostility towards Jewish conversos was increasing.

From the forced conversions of 1391 onwards, there was great anxiety about whether Spanish Jews professing Christianity were genuine in their new faith. This anxiety drove artistic and religious agendas alike. In 1478 the confessor to Queen Isabella, Hernando de Talavera, had decreed that every Christian should have images of the cross, of the Virgin and the saints, ostensibly with the purpose of 'arousing them to devotion', a function of religious art that had been current since the time of Pope Gregory the Great (r.590–604).[57] This decree originated in specific circumstances, however: the campaign to convert Jews in Seville. It is clear that the use of religious images was a test of orthodoxy for those

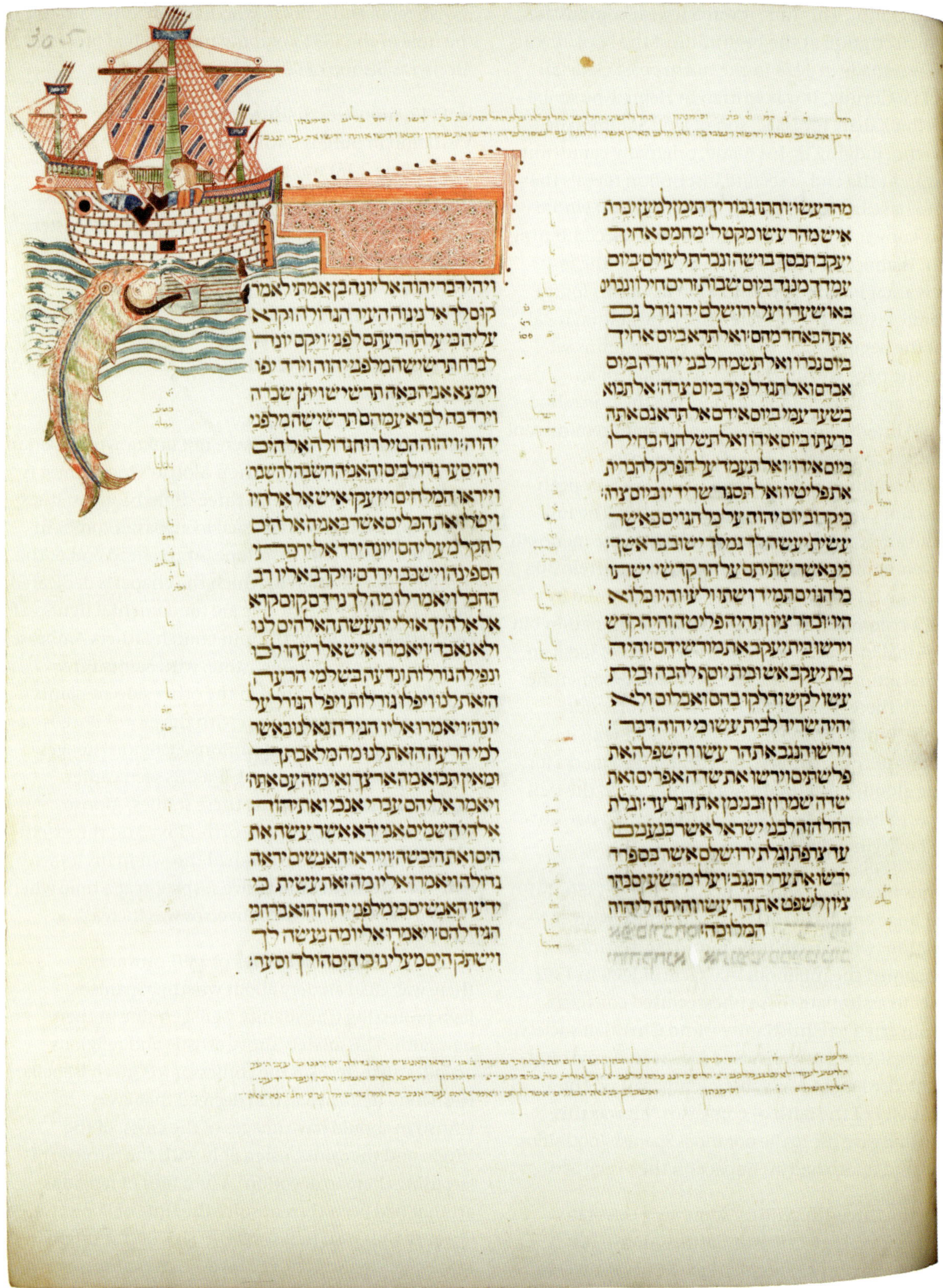

Plate 2.14 Joseph Ibn Hayyim, *Jonah Being Swallowed by the Whale*, in the Kennicott Bible, 1476. The Bodleian Library, University of Oxford, MS. Kennicott 1, fol. 305r.

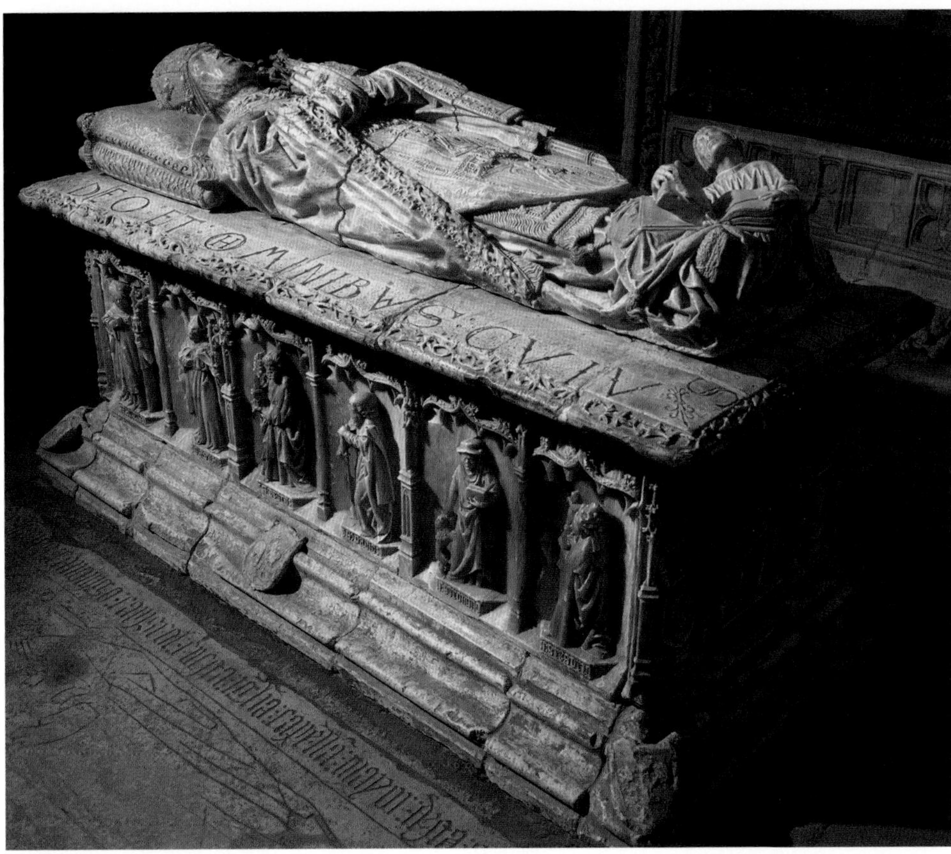

Plate 2.15 Unknown northern European sculptor, tomb of Alonso da Cartagena, Bishop of Burgos, alabaster, by 1447. Burgos Cathedral. Photo: © akg-images/Album/Oronoz.

claiming to have converted to the Christian faith; it demanded conformity not just in public but also in the home.

8 Christianity

European culture was dominated historically by a succession of 'tastemakers', a useful term coined by the social theorist Pierre Bourdieu to signify role models that others wished to emulate.[58] We have already seen that in fourteenth-century Spain one of these tastemakers was the Nasrid court of Granada. By the fifteenth century the focus had shifted to the Low Countries, the culturally rich territories of the powerful and wealthy Dukes of Burgundy and the Netherlands.[59] In 1496, the daughter of Ferdinand and Isabella, Joanna the Mad, married the Netherlandish ruler Philip the Handsome (r.1494–1506), which eventually led to the uniting of the two realms under their son Charles V. Philip's sister, Margaret of Austria, married the heir of Ferdinand and Isabella the following year. This was the culmination of

a long trading partnership with the Burgundian Netherlands. From the second third of the fifteenth century, imported Netherlandish art and immigrant Netherlandish craftsmen had begun to transform Christian Iberian culture. This is nowhere clearer than in the burial chapel of Isabella's father, Juan II, at the Cistercian monastery of Miraflores near Burgos (Plate 2.16).

At Miraflores there is no obvious trace of the Islamic architectural or decorative features that had so appealed to Isabella's forebears. Instead, both furnishings and architecture are derived from the Burgundian Netherlands. Nevertheless, Islamic art may underlie some of its designs. The alabaster tomb of Juan II of Castile was designed in 1486 and made in 1489–93 by sculptor Gil de Siloe, thought to be an expatriate from the Low Countries. The tomb chest on which the effigies lie is in the shape of an eight-pointed star. This distinctive star made up of two superimposed squares is common in Islamic art as we have seen (Plates 2.4 and 2.8).

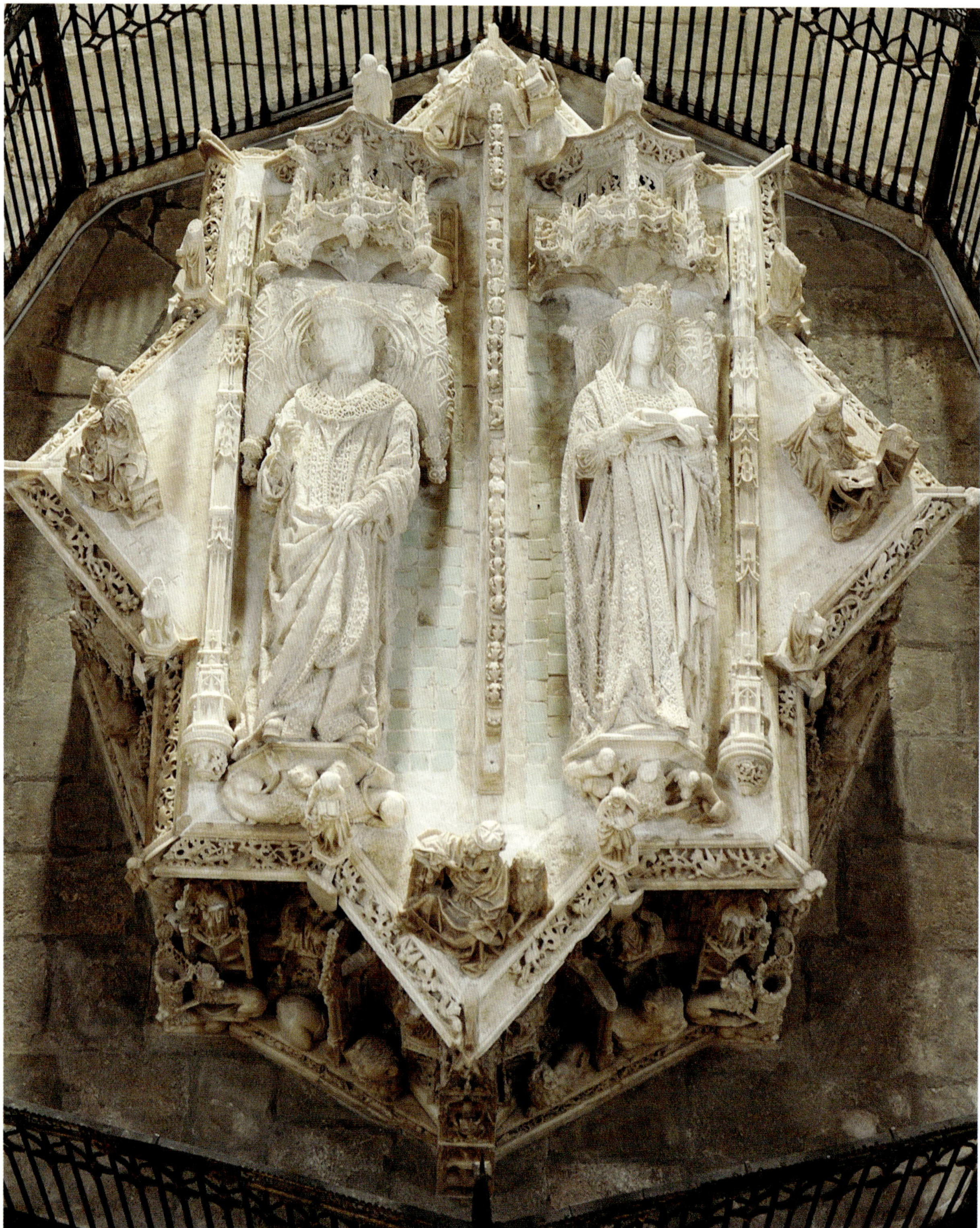

Plate 2.16 Gil de Siloe, tomb of Juan II and Isabella of Portugal, designed 1486, made 1489–93, alabaster. Cistercian monastery of Miraflores, Burgos. Photo: © Juanma Aparicio/age fotostock.

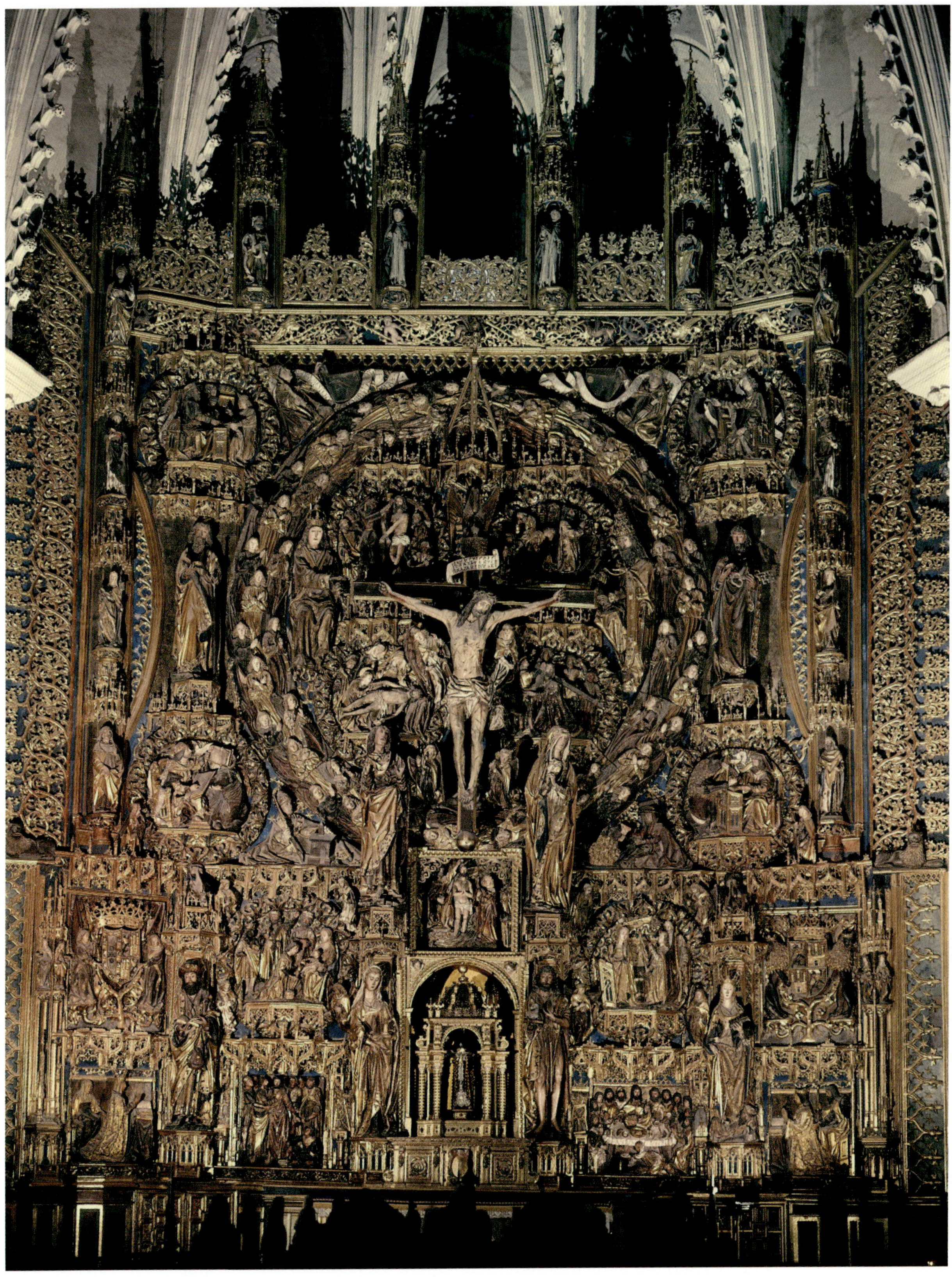

Plate 2.17 Gil de Siloe and Diego de la Cruz, Miraflores altarpiece, 1496–99. Cistercian monastery of Miraflores, Burgos.
Photo: © 2016 Album/Scala, Florence.

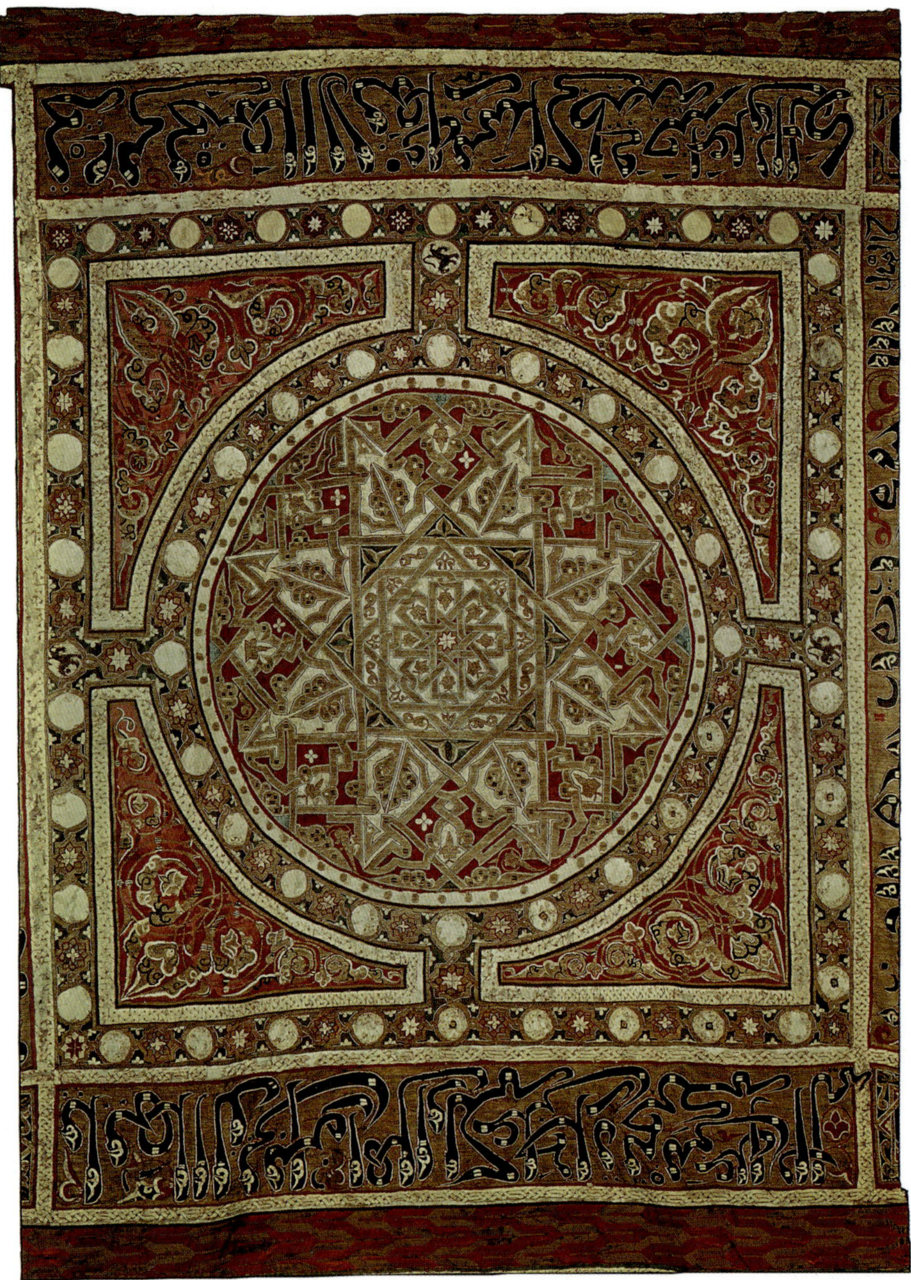

Plate 2.18 Islamic standard reputedly captured at the Battle of Las Navas de Tolosa, 1212, 330 × 221 cm. Las Huelgas, Burgos. Photo: © akg-images/ Album/Oronoz.

Juan's tomb was designed during the final campaign to reconquer Granada. Juan II had also won a key victory over Nasrid forces at the Battle of Higueruela in 1431, and to commemorate it he commissioned a huge painting of the battle on canvas 'in imitation of the ancient Caesars' to hang in the Alcazar in Segovia.[60] It seems plausible that an eight-pointed star with Islamic associations was adopted and 'Christianised' as much later propaganda of conquest in Juan's tomb.

The star tomb chest is populated by statues of the three Christian theological virtues of Faith, Hope and Charity; the four cardinal virtues thought necessary for virtuous secular rule, Justice, Prudence, Fortitude and Temperance; and Old Testament exemplars such as Abraham and Samson. On top are the writers of the four Gospels, Matthew, Mark, Luke and John, and there were previously additional figures of saints at each of the points of the star, now lost or replaced.

The carved wooden altarpiece on the altar of Miraflores was also designed and made by Gil de Siloe in 1496–99 in conjunction with his habitual collaborator, the painter and polychromer Diego de la Cruz, who was almost certainly also from the Low Countries (Plate 2.17).[61] This enormous and unusual altarpiece cost a great deal to make – over a million maravedis in Castilian currency. It centres on a Crucifixion within a large medallion.

A small medallion or 'oculus' is sometimes found in Spanish carved altarpieces, such as the one in Zaragoza Cathedral, but medallions are also often used in Islamic textile design.[62] For example, an Islamic battle standard kept at the royal monastery of Las Huelgas – long associated with the Battle of Las Navas de Tolosa in 1212, though probably made later – has an eight-pointed star within an enclosing medallion (Plate 2.18).[63] The front cover of the Kennicott Bible has a similar motif, as seen already. The making of tomb and altarpiece coincided with the final campaign to conquer Granada, so it seems possible that the star and medallion designs might have been appropriated at Miraflores for triumphalist Christian motives. Nevertheless, both forms are also found in European art: tapestries from northern Europe sometimes had narratives set within medallions, for example.[64]

The organising principles of this densely packed altarpiece could not be more different from the coherent spatial illusionism and simple narrative sequence of carved wooden altarpieces made in the Low Countries. Whereas Netherlandish carved altarpieces read strictly from left to right, here the eye meanders, revolving around the subsidiary scenes adapted to their medallions like designs on a lustreware dish. It may not be entirely fanciful to detect the impact of Islamic design in this unique work of art.

9 The rhetoric of opposition

The rhetoric of opposition and the struggle for power between Muslim and Christian inhabitants of the Iberian peninsula and the aspiration by Christian territories to (re)conquer al-Andalus are key themes in Spanish culture, particularly surrounding the final Christian conquest of Granada in 1492. The monastery of San Juan de Los Reyes in Toledo was built in 1477–92 by Ferdinand and Isabella in thanks for their victory at the Battle of Toro, which marked the end of the civil war over Isabella's claim to the throne. Initially they intended it to serve as their burial place. The exterior is to this day adorned with chains hung there in 1485–86 on the instructions of Isabella herself as a potent visual symbol of the Christian prisoners freed during the preliminary battles of the conquest of Granada.[65]

Portugal was also engaged in the offensive against the Muslims. Four tapestries, now in the Collegiate Church of Our Lady of the Assumption in Pastrana, Spain, commemorate a campaign into North Africa led by Afonso V of Portugal (r.1438–81) in 1471. Three depict the conquest of the Moroccan town of Asilah and the last the fall of Tangier. The first in the series, the *Landing at Asilah*, has a woven inscription claiming that the expedition served the ideological purpose 'to combat the Moors for the faith of Christ' and promote 'the exaltation of the Catholic faith', but in reality the motives also included securing trade through the Strait of Gibraltar and taking revenge for an ignominious defeat back in 1437 where Afonso's uncle was taken hostage.[66]

Commissioned most likely in the 1470s in the Low Countries and perhaps on behalf of Afonso himself, the tapestries are sometimes associated with the foremost tapestry merchant of the Low Countries, Pasquier Grenier of Tournai. The tapestries give a sense of place and differentiate one set of protagonists from the other using generic cultural signifiers. In the *Fall of Tangier* (Plate 2.19), the Muslim exiles leaving the city on the right-hand side of the tapestry wear turbans or carry baskets on their heads, and there is an Arabic-style inscription around the hem of the robe of one man, for example (Plate 2.20). Whoever designed and wove these tapestries is unlikely to have been familiar with North African cities or warriors, though they could have been supplied with detailed drawings or instructions. These tapestries presumably bore similar propaganda purposes to Juan II's canvas painting of the Battle of Higueruela – to bear witness to the triumph of Portugal and the advance of Christianity into the very heartlands of Islam.

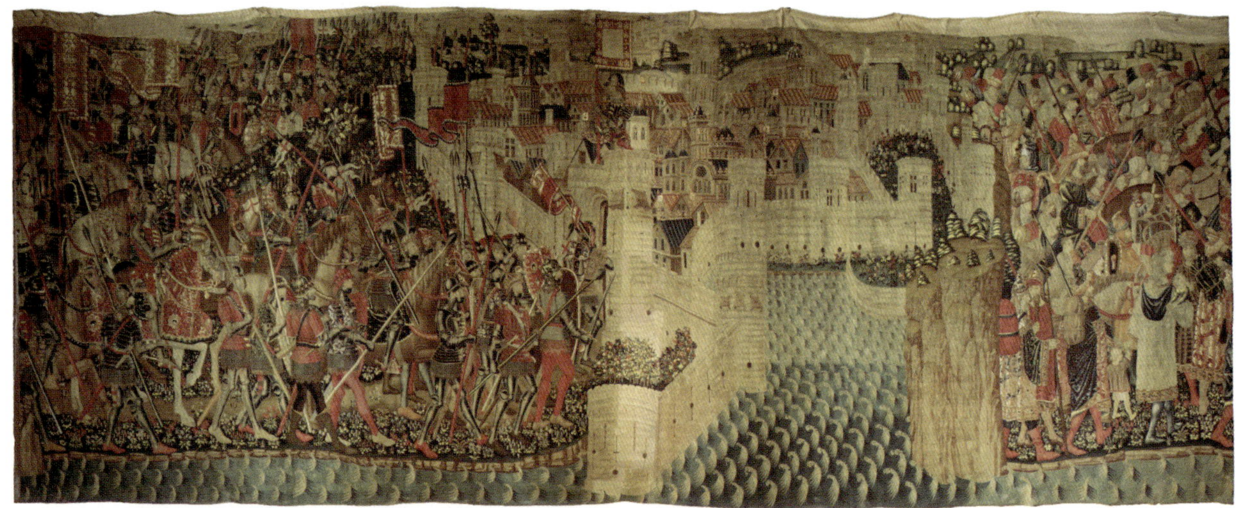

Plate 2.19 Tournai workshops, *The Fall of Tangier, c.*1471–75, silk and wool, 404 (left) / 387 (right) × 1082 cm. Collegiate Church of Our Lady of the Assumption, Pastrana. Photo: © Paul Maeyaert/Bridgeman Images.

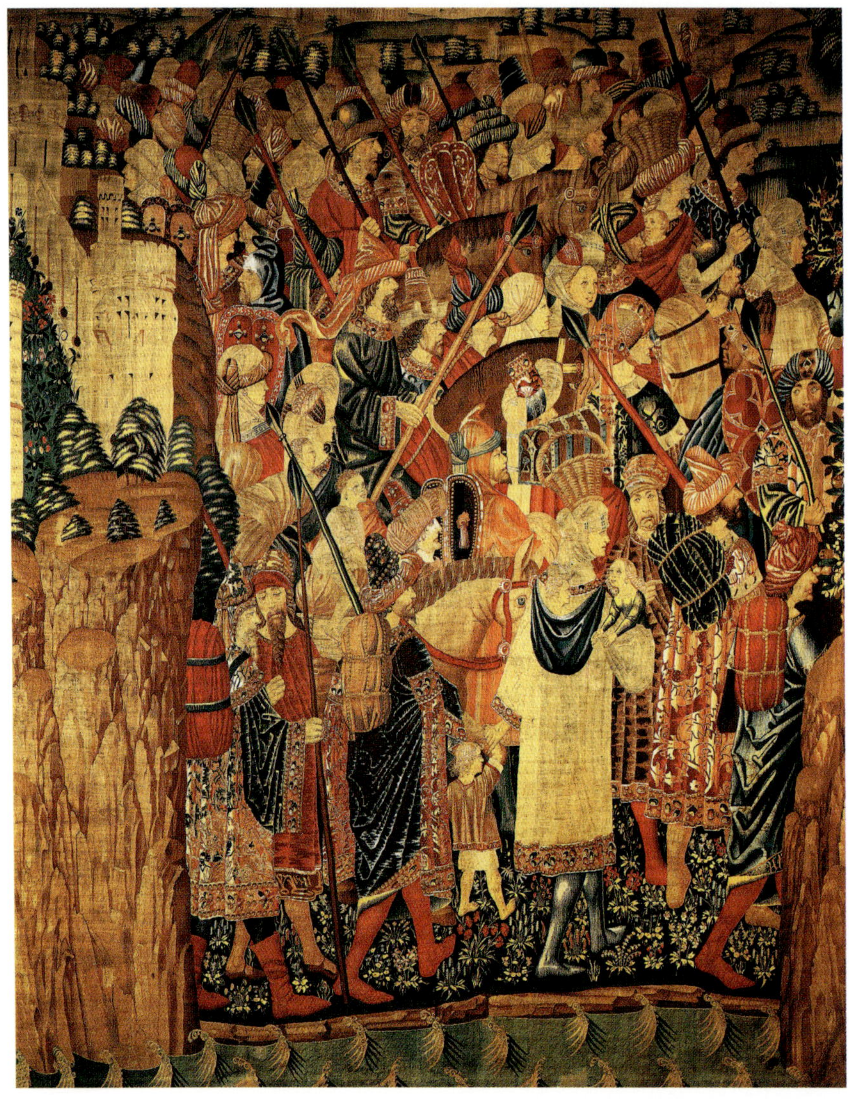

Plate 2.20 Tournai workshops, *The Fall of Tangier* (detail from Plate 2.19). Photo: © De Agostini/Getty Images.

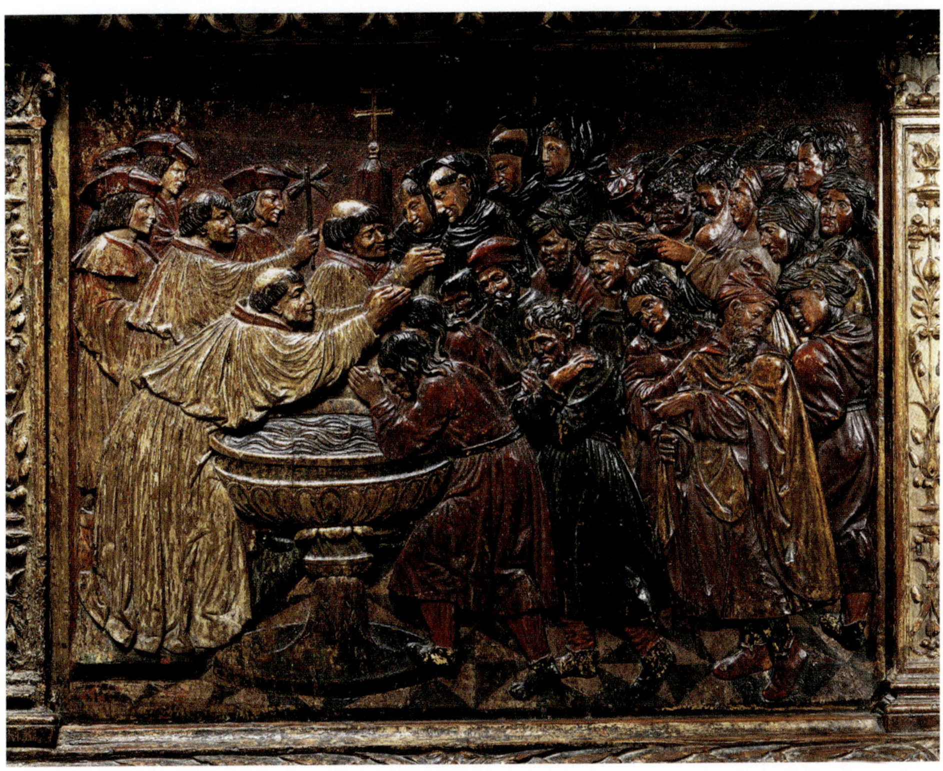

Plate 2.21 Felipe Vigarny (or Bigarny), *The Baptism of the Muslim Men*, part of the main altarpiece of the Royal Chapel, 1519, polychromed wood. Granada Cathedral. Photo © Prisma/UIG via Getty Images.

10 The New World

Ferdinand and Isabella were buried in the new Royal Chapel or Capilla Royal in defeated Granada, for which the Burgundian sculptor Felipe Vigarny (or Bigarny) carved a new polychromed wooden high altarpiece in 1519. The principal reliefs show conventional representations of saints and scenes from the death of Christ. In the lowest zone or *banco* are reliefs depicting the end of the Nasrid kingdom of Granada, including two scenes representing the baptism of converted Muslims. In *The Baptism of the Muslim Men* (Plate 2.21), the baptismal font forms a symbolic divide between the court officials and white-clad Christian baptisers and the submissive Muslims waiting to be baptised, hemmed in by black-clad friars. One Muslim is having his turban unwound in preparation for baptism, a symbolic shedding of Islamic dress. In *The Baptism of the Muslim Women*, the women are mostly heavily shrouded, but one or two begin to reveal their faces, perhaps again as a sign of baptism. The conquest of Granada was justified, and sanctioned by the Church, in terms of 'winning back' Islamic territories into Christian control and converting the 'infidel'; these scenes serve to document this belief.

In 1519 the adventurer Hernán Cortés and a band of soldiers first landed in what is now Mexico. By June 1521, the legendary Aztec ruler Moctezuma II (r.1502–20) was dead, his capital city Tenochtitlán was in ruins and thousands of Aztecs had been massacred by the conquistadores. Although in theory Mexico was incorporated into the vast empire of Charles V, Holy Roman Emperor and ruler of Spain, it was only in 1535 that the first viceroy arrived from Spain to establish a proper government. The conquest of the Inca Empire was no less violent. Following an exploratory expedition to Peru, in 1529 Francisco Pizarro was granted authority by the Spanish crown to conquer it. In November 1532, the Spaniards first encountered and imprisoned the Inca ruler Atahuallpa and staged a massacre. Atahuallpa famously tried to ransom himself with gigantic quantities of gold, which the Spanish duly collected before executing him nevertheless. In 1535 Pizarro established his coastal capital of Lima. There followed a civil war between the conquistadores. Pizarro himself was assassinated in 1541 and effective government from Spain was established only in 1548.

It is sometimes claimed that the Christian Spanish in the New World were able to apply a model for ruling conquered peoples from their experience at home.[67] Whether this is true or not, this new encounter involved considerable cultural shock on both sides, for the indigenous Amerindians and the Spanish invaders. The sophistication of Aztec and Inca societies was recognised by the conquistadores, who expressed admiration for indigenous skills and systems of government. On the other hand, centuries of living alongside Jews and Muslims was no preparation for the sudden exposure to Aztec and Inca religious beliefs, which lacked the familiar authority symbol of a sacred book and involved the practice of human sacrifice. This was as horrifying to Christian Europeans as European brutality and duplicity were to the indigenous peoples.

The conquistadores romanticised their conquests of Mexico and Peru by drawing parallels with the defeat of Muslim Spain.[68] In practice, greed for gold led to a lamentable exploitation of resources and peoples. It was true, however, that the spread of Christianity constituted one official justification for the conquest. In 1522, the pope charged the Franciscan friars with the task of converting the indigenous 'Indians', and as a result the Franciscan Fray Pedro of Ghent (*fl.*1523–72) and two companions were the first missionaries to arrive in Mexico in 1523. They carried a mandate from Charles V himself, whom Pedro had served before becoming a Franciscan and whom he met on board the ship from Santander on his way to the New World.[69] The following year, 12 Franciscans arrived to spearhead the missionary movement, followed in 1526 by the Dominicans and in later years the Augustinians. The role of these often utopian friars in working among and championing the indigenous population constitutes a less well-known narrative of the conquest, and one that had implications for art, a powerful reason for exploring these connections here.

Art played a critical role in the missionary movement to convert and instruct the peoples of the New World in Catholic Christianity and to furnish new Catholic churches. Art also had a role to play in the debate over the rights of indigenous peoples in the New World. Indigenous artistic ability was one criterion by which the capacities, and rights, of these newly encountered societies were assessed, valued and ruled: as free and civilised adults, as the equivalent of children or, worse, as slaves to be owned and exploited. For Bartholomé de Las Casas, the Dominican missionary in many ways sympathetic to Aztec Mexico, 'the very ancient, vaulted and pyramid-like buildings' of the Indians, as they were dubbed, revealed their 'prudence and good polity'.[70] For the unsympathetic Dominican Juan Ginés de Sepúlveda (d.1573), who argued the case for uncompromising Spanish rule from the safety of Spain, manual skill meant little – even ants could build impressive structures, he pointed out.[71]

11 Art and conversion in Mexico

Since the time of Pope Gregory the Great, Christian images had been used to teach and inspire devotion. When the missionary Saint Augustine of Canterbury (d.604) was sent by Pope Gregory to evangelise England in 597, he is supposed to have brought with him a painted image of Christ.[72] Likewise, Hernán Cortés appears to have set sail equipped with a series of statues of the Virgin and Child, which he installed en route for Tenochtitlán in an attempt to introduce indigenous peoples to the Christian faith.

The friars also used art. An annotated print published in 1579 shows a preacher (A) pointing to a series of pictures (B) narrating the death of Christ in order to instruct his audience of Mexicans (C), while underneath the pulpit is a subdued monster symbolising the defeat of paganism (Plate 2.22).[73] This is an engraving made in the European tradition – the Mexicans are clad in togas! The print accompanies a Latin text intended to convince a European audience of the civilising power of Christian preaching among the Amerindians.[74] The author was Diego Valadés, a Franciscan friar and artist who was born in Mexico, probably of mixed blood. He had first-hand experience of the school run by Fray Pedro of Ghent from 1548 and also of the college of Santa Cruz, founded by the first Bishop of Mexico, the Franciscan Juan de Zumárraga, to train elite Amerindians for the priesthood. His book was published in Italy, where he was briefly procurator general of the Franciscan order, and provides an insight into the role of art in the earlier work of the friars in the New World.

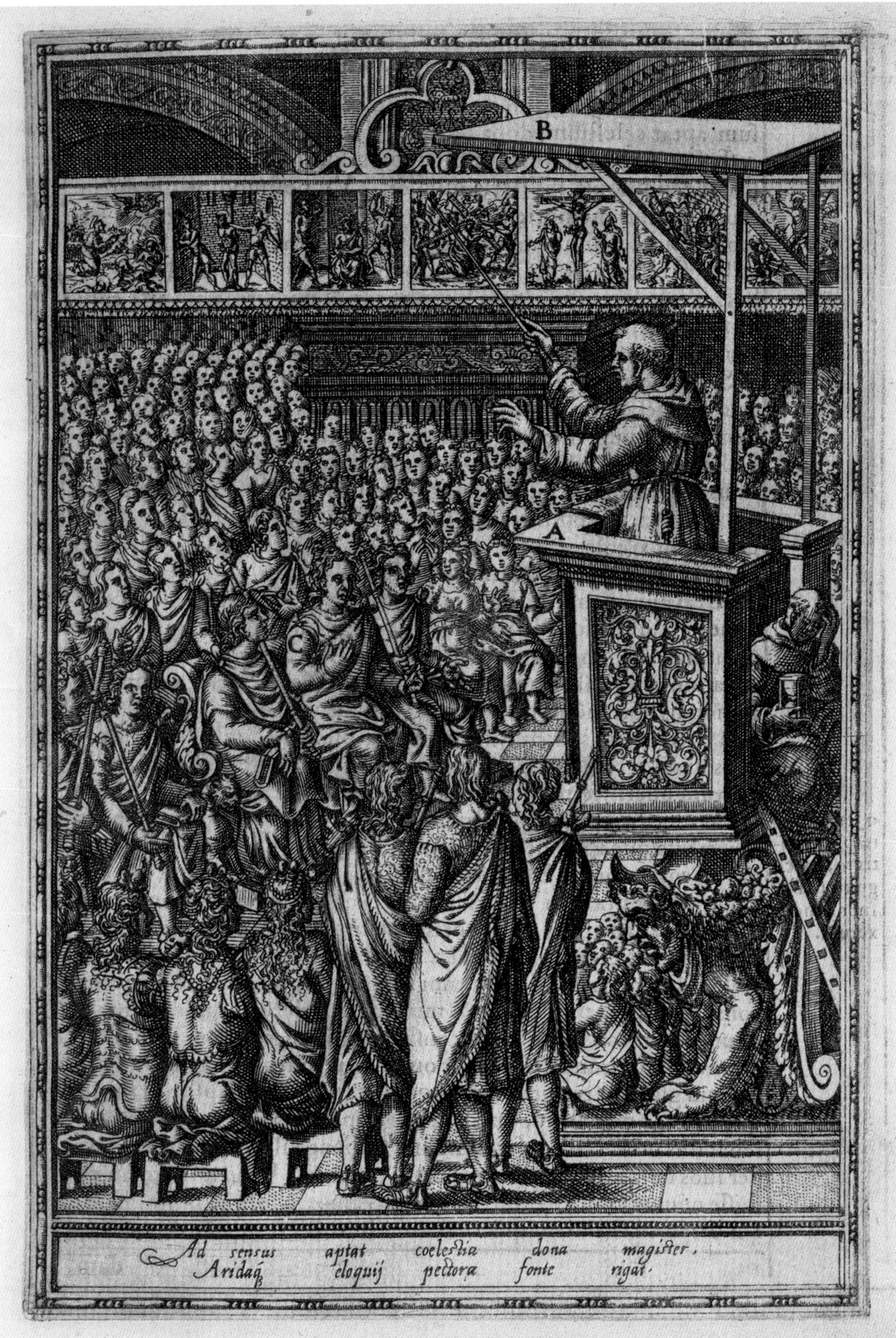

Plate 2.22 Diego Valadés, 'A friar preaching', copper engraving in *Rhetorica christiana*, Perugia, P. P. Petrutio, 1579. Bibliteca Nacional Collection, Madrid. Photo: © akg-images/Album/Oronoz.

According to Valadés, indigenous traditions disposed Aztecs to visual persuasion. He described how they used to make their confession not verbally but by putting little stones on pictures of the sins they had committed.[75] Pictograms constituted a traditional mode of communication in Aztec society and continued to be used for recording the payment of tributes, for chronicling history and even for catechisms. Valadés also claimed that tapestries were used to teach Christian doctrine, including representations of the Apostles' Creed, the Ten Commandments, the seven deadly sins, the seven works of mercy and the seven sacraments.[76] Whether indigenous peoples formed by a very different culture would have received any of this in the way that those who taught it intended is a moot point, but specifically Christian art was also produced by indigenous Amerindians, however they understood it.

As vast numbers of monasteries, churches and chapels were established in Mexico, the friars were also faced with the problem of how to furnish them with the kind of religious art customary in Catholic Europe. As European artists had not yet begun to arrive in the New World in any significant number, one solution was to train indigenous artists. Fray Pedro of Ghent set up the school of San José de Belén de los Naturales (Saint Joseph of Bethlehem of the Indians) at the convent of Saint Francis in Tenochtitlán. It taught liturgical singing and the alphabet in the Aztec language Nahuatl and also provided training that adapted a range of indigenous Aztec crafts such as manuscript painting, murals and feather pictures for the production of Catholic art. According to some sources, Pedro himself may have taught art.[77] Designs were often taken from European prints, which were portable enough to be imported from Europe from an early date.

Featherwork was an indigenous Aztec technique that carried considerable cultural prestige and hence was considered particularly appropriate to be harnessed to the service of God. The amantecas, or workers in feather, were high-status individuals based in Tenochtitlán who made items such as ceremonial cloaks and shields for the ruler. Feathers constituted part of the tribute paid by Aztec villages to their ruler and were valued for their vivid colours. Missionary

Las Casas described the range of featherwork produced by Aztec converts, from pictures to bishops' mitres:

> To sum up, out of feathers they have made and still make, every day, statues, altar-pieces, and many other things of ours; they also interpose bits of gold at suitable places, making the work more beautiful and charming so that the whole world may wonder at it. They made trimming for chasubles and mantles, covers or silk cases for crosses, for processions and for divine service, and mitres for bishops.[78]

The *Mass of Saint Gregory* is one of the most famous surviving feather pictures (Plate 2.23). The inscription round the edge reveals that the governor Don Diego, under the supervision of Fray Pedro of Ghent, had it made in 1539 for Pope Paul III (r.1534–49).[79] Don Diego was a high-ranking Aztec convert and relative of Moctezuma II, appointed to his office by the first viceroy of Mexico, Antonio de Mendoza. The inscription authenticates this work as a product of Fray Pedro's School of Saint Joseph. The subject is Pope Gregory the Great experiencing a vision of Christ while he was saying mass. In European and particularly in Netherlandish artistic representations of this theme, Christ was often accompanied by Instruments of the Passion, that is the implements used to injure Christ before and at his Crucifixion.

Exercise

Examine the feather picture of the mass of Saint Gregory carefully (Plate 2.23). What do you think is particularly European about it apart from its subject matter? Can you spot anything that is or could be Amerindian?

Now, compare the feather picture of the mass of Saint Gregory with the engraving by Israhel van Meckenem (Plate 2.24). Do you think the design for the feather picture was taken from this engraving?

Discussion

The balance and symmetry of the design in the featherwork look quite European, and so does the illusionistic lettering around the edge. Another European element is perspective: Christ's tomb and the altar appear to recede into space. The spatial recession is not consistent though – the background is very dominant and there is no real floor, suggesting that there was a limit to the impact of European perspective. The blue background is very bright; is it intended to suggest the open air? In Europe, mass was celebrated in a church, whereas in Mexico the mass was celebrated in outdoor structures, so this could be an indigenous detail. There are two pineapples on the edge of the tomb, which is a more obvious local detail.

None of the figures matches up closely enough for this engraving to have served as a design to be copied, though it might have helped to inspire the composition of the feather picture.

The gift of this picture to Pope Paul III had a strong rationale. In 1537, Pope Paul III had sided with the missionaries against the Spanish government and declared that the peoples of the New World were fully rational beings, had souls and were capable of receiving the sacraments. Crucially, this meant that they could not be exploited as 'natural slaves' and had rights. The subject of the picture would have been understood by an ecclesiastical audience to refer to the pope and to the mass which Paul III had now decreed Indians were entitled to receive.[80] Prowess in art was also seen as one of the attributes of free humanity. As Julián Garces, Bishop of Tlaxcala, wrote to Pope Paul in 1537, 'who would be so presumptuous and brazen to affirm that they [the Amerindians] are incapable of faith if we see how capable they are in the mechanical arts'.[81] The feather picture demonstrated to its intended European audience that Fray Pedro's craftsmen at the School of Saint Joseph were every bit as capable as a standard western European artist and confirms Pope Paul's conclusion that they were also just as capable of freedom and salvation.

The most famous religious image of conquered Mexico, and indeed in the whole of Latin America, is also the work of an indigenous painter: the painting of *Our Lady of Guadalupe*, named after the miraculous image kept in the Spanish Monastery of Guadalupe in Extremadura in western Spain (Plate 2.25). According to a legend first recorded in 1648, a converted Aztec called Juan Diego received a vision of the Virgin of Guadalupe in 1531 on the site of an Aztec shrine and claimed that she requested that a shrine be built to her there. The miraculous image of the Virgin was, according to the legend, imprinted on the cloth in which Juan Diego brought flowers to the Bishop of Mexico to testify to his vision.[82]

Although the miraculous painting was supposed to date from 1531, the first evidence for it came in the 1550s. In 1556, the leader of the Franciscan order in Mexico, Francisco de Bustamente, delivered a sermon in the chapel of Saint Joseph of Bethlehem criticising Alonso de Montúfar, Dominican Archbishop of Mexico between 1554 and 1572, for encouraging the new cult. His argument was that the cult kindled idolatry and undid the good work of the friars, for the painting was known to have been painted by an indigenous artist. This was subsequently corroborated by witnesses, where the painter is named Marcos.[83] This is of interest because Marcos de Aquino was one of three celebrated Mexican painters with whom the conquistador Bernal Díaz compared celebrated painters of the past and of his own day.[84] The surviving picture is supposed to bear the date 1556 and the initials M. A. in an underlayer of paint.[85]

The image follows closely the painted conventions of a western European apocalyptic Virgin as revealed in Revelation 12: 1: 'clothed with the sun and with the Moon under her feet and upon her head a crown of 12 stars'. It constitutes an indigenous version of lower-cost religious paintings on linen, common in Spain and the Low Countries. Here the image is painted on cloth made from fibres from the maguey plant. While often represented with fair hair in the European tradition, here, famously, the Virgin's hair and skin are darker, which it is claimed identifies her with indigenous physical types.[86] The painter Marcos gives credence to Franciscan friar Toribio Motolinía's claim regarding indigenous Mexicans that 'by merely observing and seeing how things are made many of them became experts in crafts that in Spain it takes many years to learn'.[87]

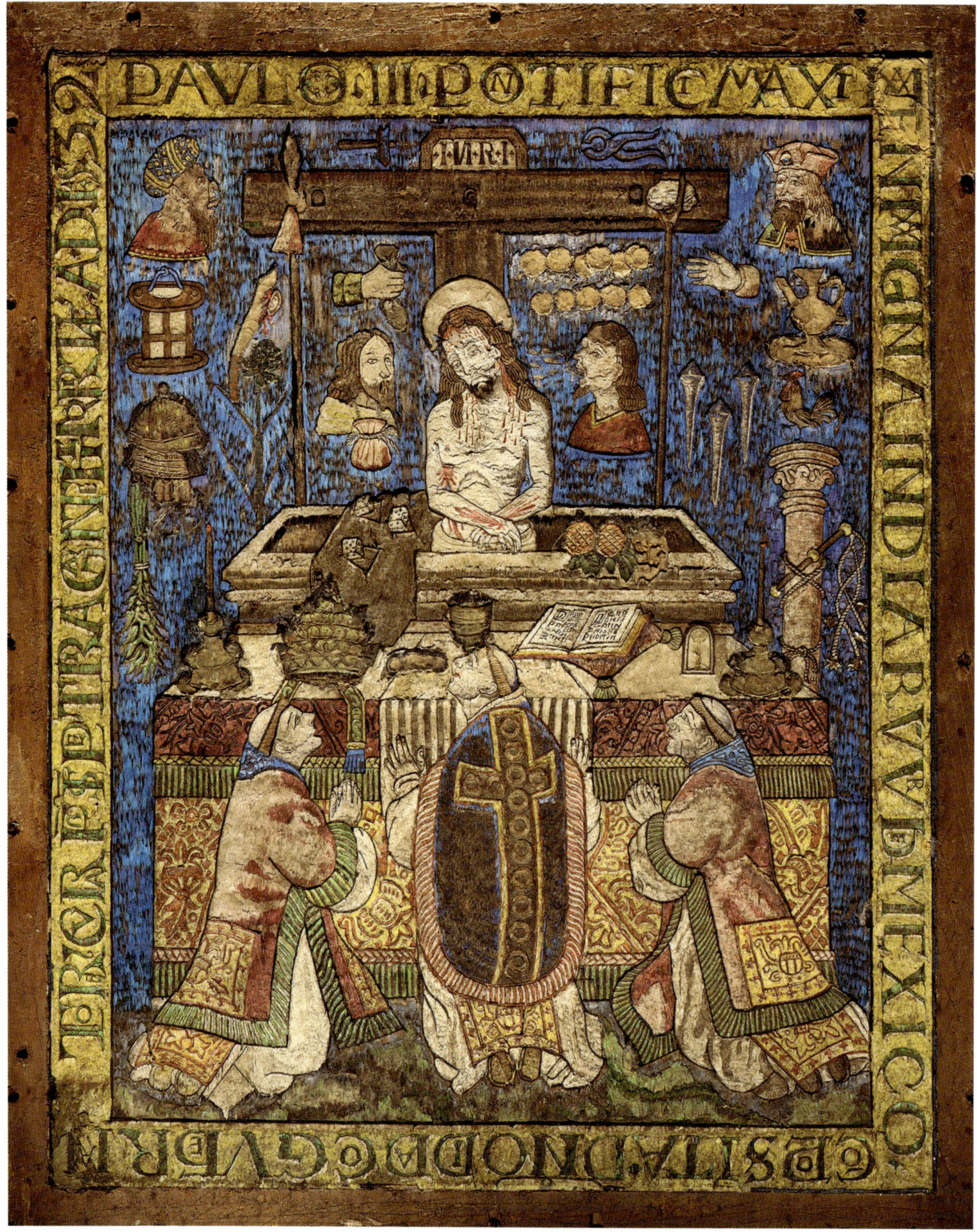

Plate 2.23 *Mass of Saint Gregory*, 1539, feather on wood, 68 × 56 cm. Musée des Jacobins, Auch. Photo: © akg-images/Bernard Bonnefon.

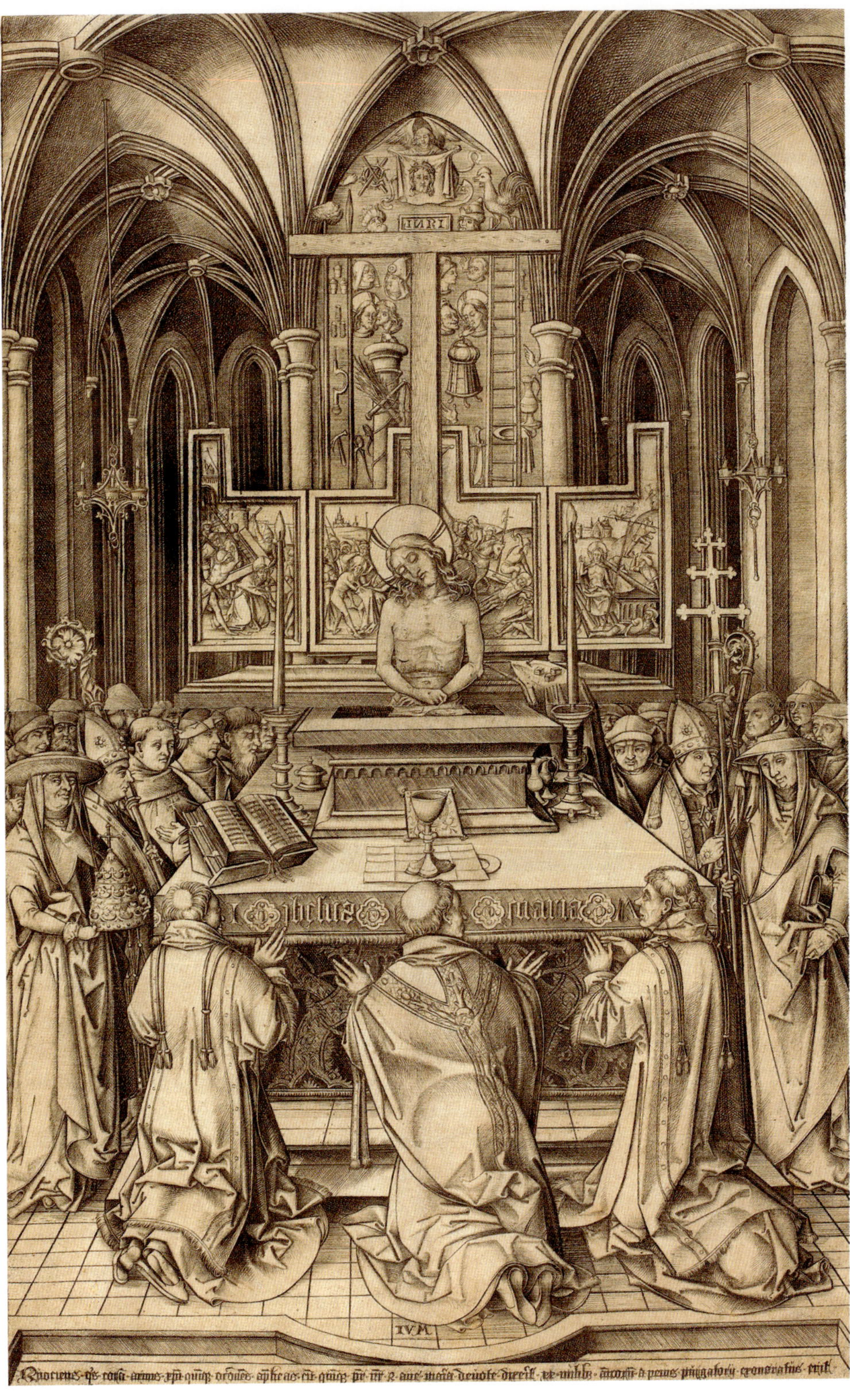

Plate 2.24 Israhel van Meckenem, *Mass of Saint Gregory*, c.1490–1500, engraving. Photo: © akg-images/Liszt Collection.

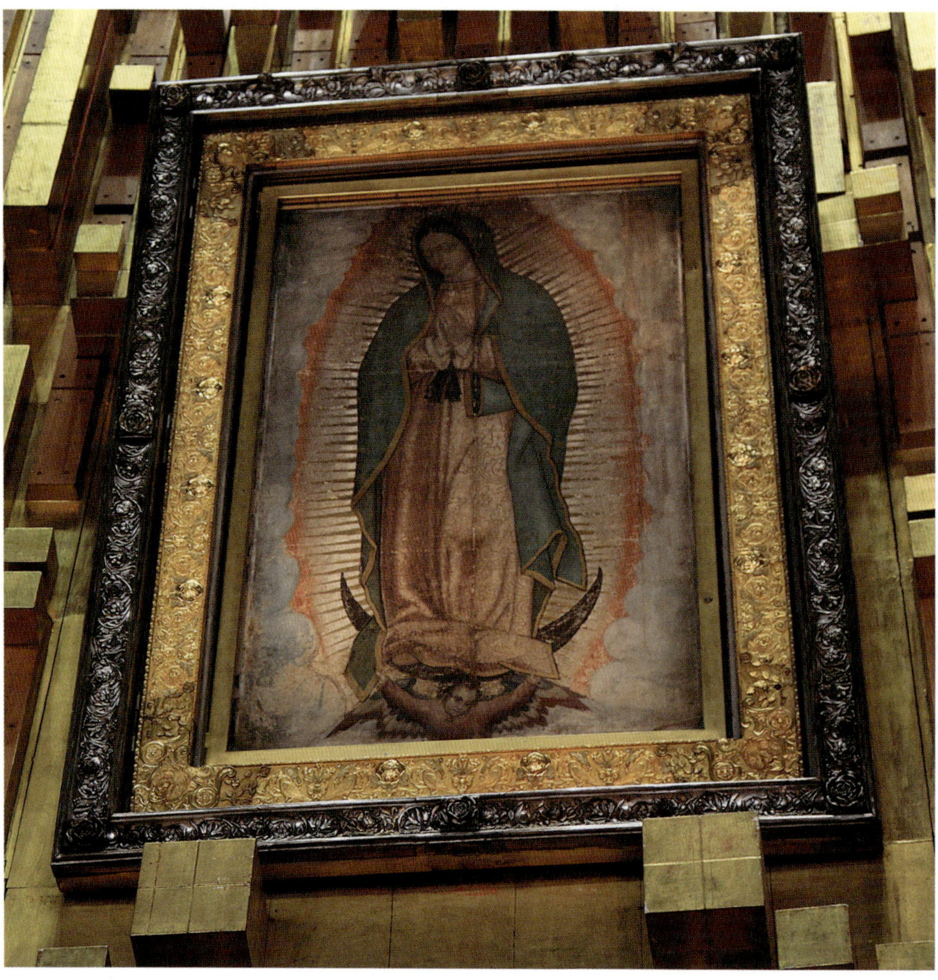

Plate 2.25 *Our Lady of Guadalupe,* mid-sixteenth century, oil and tempera on maguey fibre cloth, 170 × 105 cm. Shrine of the Virgin of Guadalupe, Mexico City. Photo: Wendy Connett/Alamy.

12 Peru

Lima, the conquistadores' capital in Peru, was a new city founded by Francisco Pizarro, which consequently had no local artistic traditions and little even by way of indigenous population. Situated on the coast, it was the main trading port for the viceroyalty of Peru in particular with Seville, which held the monopoly of trade with the New World from 1543; the archdiocese of Lima was also a suffragan (or subsidiary) to the archdiocese of Seville.[88] It is not surprising, then, that initially the Spanish settlers, clerics and friars imported religious art from Seville to evangelise the population and stock the new churches, among them the burial chapel of the conqueror of Peru, Francisco Pizarro himself.

In 1551, Francisco Pizarro's daughter, Francisca, received permission to erect an altarpiece in the choir chapel of Lima Cathedral where her father was buried.[89] Francisca was resident in Spain and had the

altarpiece made there and exported from Seville. The life-size statue of the Virgin and Child (Plate 2.26) still in the choir chapel belongs to this commission. It has been attributed to Roque de Balduque, a Netherlandish expatriate probably from 's-Hertogenbosch (in French, Bois-le-Duc), who settled in Seville in the 1530s. Both Virgin and Christ gaze benignly outwards, the Virgin highly idealised, the Child in an attitude of blessing. These are dynamic images actively engaging with and conveying spiritual benefits upon the viewers, who at this date and in this prestigious location are likely to have been mostly expatriate Spaniards rather than indigenous converts. Through this statue, Catholic Spanish imagery is transplanted uncompromisingly into the new territory.

A second statue of the Virgin and Child by Roque in the Dominican church in Lima was made for Fray Domingo de Santo Tomás, the Bishop-elect of

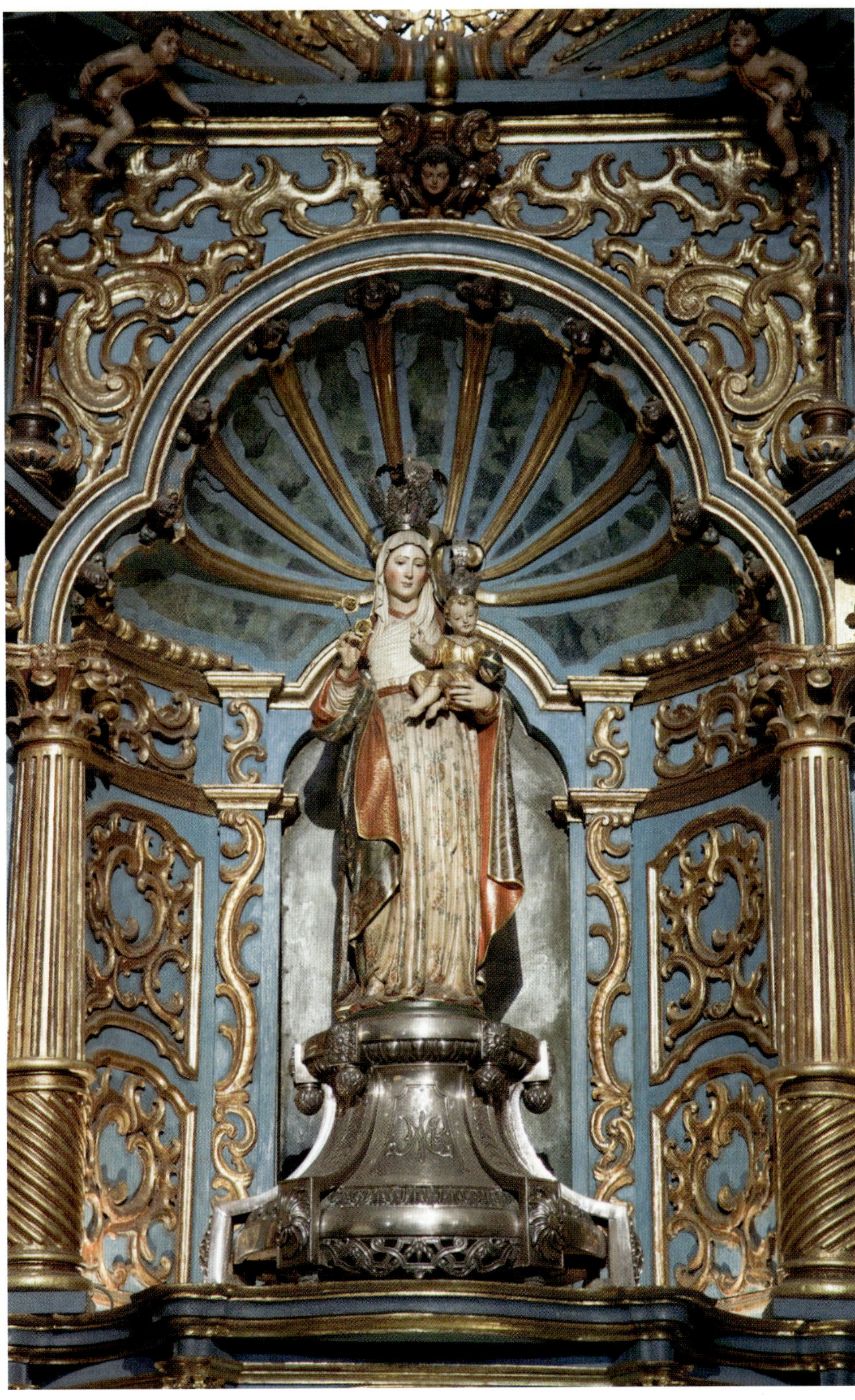

Plate 2.26 Roque de Balduque, *Statue of the Virgin and Child*. Basilica Cathedral, Lima. Photo: © Getty Images/Danita Delimont.

Chuquisaca, who was originally from Seville. It was part of a consignment of works of art and books that travelled to Lima in 1559 with a group of emigrating friars. Here, the original rich polychromy is partially intact and adds to the lifelike effect.

The will of Roque de Balduque shows that at the time of his death he was still owed money for some large pictures (presumably painted reliefs) that he had sent to be sold in the 'Indias', understood to mean the New World.

As the work of a Netherlandish migrant living in Seville, exported to conquered Peru and serving an audience of Spaniards and converts, these Lima statues epitomise the cross-cultural, character of Spanish art in the period up to 1550.

Conclusion

The cultural heritage of Spain is inextricably bound up with its complicated past and the encounter between Islamic, Jewish, Christian and New World cultures. Stereotypically, the impact of Islam has been understood in terms of the Iberian Christian convention of ceramic tiling and an Islamic-inspired density of decoration often referred to as *horror vacui* (a repudiation of empty spaces). This chapter has revealed a much more complicated pattern of appropriation, translation and hybridity with regard to the visual arts of al-Andalus. The demand for luxury goods and skills crossed cultural and religious boundaries in a way that suggests consumers of other faiths were either adept in detaching desired objects from dubious cultural origins or ignorant or careless of them.

The legacy of Iberian Jews extended far beyond surviving Hebrew Bibles and converted synagogues, for it is clear that Christian art was fundamentally shaped by the problems created by the forced conversion of Jews to Christianity. The wealth generated by conquests in the New World served to pay for Catholic works of art both in the New World and in Spain. Far more important was the ongoing debate among Spanish settlers, missionaries, rulers and intellectuals surrounding the degree to which the indigenous cultures of the New World, visual or otherwise, might legitimately be tolerated and adapted and the degree of hybridity acceptable within Christian traditions. This was a long-running debate that neither began nor

ended in the New World and to a degree was arguably rather futile, for experience in Spain should have shown that cultural heritage possessed both enduring power and adaptability.

Notes

[1] For converting mosques to churches see Harris, 1997 and Remensnyder, 2000.

[2] Hattstein and Delius, 2004, p. 222.

[3] Ecker, 2003, pp. 115, 135, note 8.

[4] Melville and Ubaydli, 1992, p. 189.

[5] Harris, 1997.

[6] Ecker, 2003, p. 122; Marks, 2015, p. 262.

[7] Fairchild Ruggles, 2008, pp. 91–3.

[8] Stern, 1976, p. 1.

[9] Dodds, Menocal and Krasner Balbale, 2008, pp. 84–5; Barton, 2009, p. 39.

[10] Dodds, Menocal and Krasner Balbale, 2008, pp. 85, 88–9.

[11] Davies, 2007.

[12] Glick, 1969.

[13] Barton, 2009, pp. 110–11.

[14] Ray, 2000, p. 41.

[15] Mann, Glick and Dodds, 1992, p. 229, catalogue no. 78.

[16] Marks, 2015.

[17] Rosser Owen, 2010, pp. 92–3; Ray, 2000, p. 78, catalogue no. 163, Victoria and Albert Museum, acquisition number 243-1853.

[18] Trusted, 2007, pp. 120–1.

[19] Grabar, 1978, pp. 141, 128–9.

[20] Grabar, 1978, p. 136; Fairchild Ruggles, 2000, pp. 191–3.

[21] Grabar, 1978, pp. 110, 136.

[22] For the variety of views see Robinson, 2008, p. 197; Echevarra, 2008, p. 204.

[23] Grabar, 1978, p. 143.

[24] Fairchild Ruggles, 2008, p. ix.

[25] Fairchild Ruggles, 2008, pp. 154–5.

[26] Fairchild Ruggles, 2008, p. 154.

[27] Fairchild Ruggles, 2000, pp. 203, 214.

[28] Bush, 2015, pp. 15–16.

[29] Fairchild Ruggles, 2008, p. 96; Fairchild Ruggles, 2000, p. 214.

[30] Grabar, 1978, p. 169.

[31] Dodds, 1979.

[32] Dodds, 1979; Luyster, 2008.

[33] Robinson, 2008.

[34] Robinson, 2008.

[35] Luyster, 2008, pp. 360, 366.

[36] Rodriguez Porto, 2008, pp. 256–7.

[37] Ruiz Souza, 2006.

[38] Rodriguez Porto, 2008, p. 234.

[39] Fairchild Ruggles, 2008, pp. 47, 157–8; Rosser Owen, 2010, p. 84.

[40] Marín Fidalgo, 1995, p. 26; Fairchild Ruggles, 2004, p. 91.

[41] Mann, Glick and Dodds, 1992, pp. 253–61.

[42] Fairchild Ruggles, 2004, p. 97.

[43] Ruiz Souza, 2006.

[44] López Guzmán, 2009, p. 102.

[45] Dodds, Menocal and Krasner Balbale, 2008, pp. 241–5.

[46] The most complete account is Layna Serrano, 1997.

[47] Egerton and Pérez de Lara, 2001, p. 43, figure 2.7.

[48] Dodds, 1992.

[49] Mann, 2000, pp. 76–8.

[50] Fellous, 2000, p. 209.

[51] Nordström, 1967, pp. 58–9; for festivals see Fellous, 2000, p. 220; Mann, 2000, pp. 25–8.

[52] Fellous, 2000, p. 227.

[53] Roth, 1957.

[54] Nirenberg, 2002.

[55] Gampel, 1992.

[56] Gómez Bárcena, 1998, pp. 50–3.

[57] Pereda, 2001.

[58] Bourdieu, 1984, pp. 247–56 (especially p. 255).

[59] Belozerskaya, 2002.

[60] de Colmenares, 1969–70, pp. 578–9. Also cited in Smith, 1989, p. 125.

[61] His one signed painting is clearly Netherlandish in style. See Dotseth, Anderson and Roglan, 2008, pp. 46–7.

[62] The Zaragoza altarpieces was begun by Pere Joan in 1434 and completed by Hans of Swabia in 1477. See Lacarra Ducay, 2000.

[63] Hattstein and Delius, 2004, p. 268.

[64] Yarza Luaces, 2007, pp. 11–13.

[65] Gilman Proske, 1951, p. 138.

[66] de Bunes Ibarra, 2011.

[67] Fletcher, 1992, p. 7.

[68] Pagden, 1993, pp. 93–4.

[69] Verlinden, 1986, p. 116.

[70] Elliott, 1970, p. 45.

[71] Elliott, 1970, p. 45.

[72] Bede, 1969, pp. 73–7.

[73] Valadés, 1579; Egerton and Pérez de Lara, 2001, pp. 116–19.

[74] Moffitt Watts, 1991.

[75] Moffitt Watts, 1995, p. 148.

[76] Moffitt Watts, 1991, p. 423.

[77] Lovera de Navarro, 1992, pp. 70–2.

[78] Newall, 2017, p. 56.

[79] Pierce, Ruiz Gomar and Bargellini, 2004, pp. 94–102.

[80] Gallori, 2013, p. 65.

[81] Russo, 2014–15, p. 357.

[82] Brading, 2001, especially pp. 54–7.

[83] Brading, 2001, pp. 268–71; Poole, 1996, pp. 58–64.

[84] Díaz, 1963, p. 230; Newall, 2017, pp. 53–5.

[85] Pierce, Ruiz Gomar and Bargellini, 2004, p. 84.

[86] Bailey, 2005, pp. 5–6.

[87] Steck, 1951, p. 295.

[88] Bernales Ballesteros, 1999.

[89] Bernales Ballesteros, 1977, p. 362; Bernales Ballesteros, 1999, pp. 25–9.

Bibliography

Bailey, G. A. (2005) *Art of Colonial Latin America*, London, Phaidon.

Barton, S. (2009) *A History of Spain*, Basingstoke, Palgrave Macmillan.

Bede, the Venerable (1969 [731]) *The Ecclesiastical History of the English People*, Colgrave, B. and Mynors, R. A. B. (eds), Oxford, Oxford University Press.

Belozerskaya, M. (2002) *Rethinking the Renaissance: Burgundian Arts across Europe*, Cambridge, Cambridge University Press.

Bernales Ballesteros, J. (1977) 'Esculturas de Roque de Balduque y su círculo en Andalucía y América', *Anuario de estudios Americanos*, vol. XXXIV, pp. 349–71.

Bernales Ballesteros, J. (1999) 'La escultura en Lima siglos XVI–XVIII', in de Lavalle, J. A. (ed.) *Escultura en el Perú*, Lima, Banco de Credito del Perú, pp. 1–134.

Bourdieu, P. (1984) *Distinction: A Social Critique of the Judgement of Taste* (trans. R. Nice), Routledge & Kegan Paul.

Brading, D. A. (2001) *Mexican Phoenix: Our Lady of Guadalupe, Image and Tradition across Five Centuries*, Cambridge, Cambridge University Press.

Bunes Ibarra, M. Á. de (2011) 'The Pastrana tapestries and Portuguese expansion in North Africa', in de Bunes Ibarra, M. Á., La Rocca, D. J., Rodrigues, D. and Maes De Wit, Y., *The Invention of Glory: Alfonso V and the Pastrana Tapestries* (trans. P. Sutton), Madrid, Fundación Carlos de Amberes: El Viso, pp. 15–27.

Bush, O. (2015) 'Entangled gazes: the polysemy of the New Great Mosque of Granada, *Muqarnas*, vol. 32, special issue, pp. 97–133.

Colmenares, D. de (1969–70 [1640]) *Historia de la insigne ciudad de Segovia y compendio de las historias de Castilla*, Segovia, Academia de Historia y Arte de San Quirce, vol. 1.

Davies, W. (2007) 'The early Middle Ages and Spanish identity', in Pryce, H. and Watts, J. L. (eds) *Power and Identity in the Middle Ages: Essays in Memory of Rees Davies*, Oxford, Oxford University Press, pp. 68–84.

Díaz, B. (1963) *The Conquest of New Spain* (trans. J. M. Cohen), London, Penguin.

Dodds, J. (1979) 'The paintings in the Sala de Justicia of the Alhambra: iconography and iconology', *The Art Bulletin*, vol. 61, no. 2, pp. 186–97.

Dodds, J. D. (1992) 'Mudejar tradition and the synagogues of medieval Spain: cultural identity and cultural hegemony', in Mann, V. B., Glick, T. F. and Dodds, J. D. (eds) *Convivencia: Jews, Muslims and Christians in Medieval Spain*, New York, G. Braziller, pp. 113–32.

Dodds, J., Menocal, M. R. and Krasner Balbale, A. (2008) *The Arts of Intimacy: Christians, Jews, and Muslims in the Making of Castilian Culture*, New Haven, CT and London, Yale University Press.

Dotseth, A., Anderson, B. and Roglan, M. (eds) (2008) *Fernando Gallego and His Workshop: The Altarpiece from Ciudad Roderigo*, Tucson, AZ, University of Arizona Museum of Art; Dallas, TX, Philip Wilson Publishers.

Echevarra, A. (2008) 'Painting politics in the Alhambra', *Medieval Encounters*, vol. 14, special issue on the Alhambra, pp. 197–218.

Ecker, H. (2003) 'The great mosque of Córdoba in the twelfth and thirteenth centuries', *Muqarnas*, vol. 20, pp. 113–41.

Egerton, S. Y. and Pérez de Lara, J. (2001) *Theatres of Conversion: Religious Architecture and Indian Artisans in Colonial Mexico*, Albuquerque, NM, University of New Mexico Press.

Elliott, J. H. (1970) *The Old World and the New 1492–1650*, Cambridge, Cambridge University Press.

Fairchild Ruggles, D. (2000) *Gardens, Landscape and Vision in the Palaces of Islamic Spain*, University Park, PA, Pennsylvania State University Press.

Fairchild Ruggles, D. (2004) 'The Alcazar of Seville and Mudejar architecture', *Gesta*, vol. 43, no. 2, pp. 87–98.

Fairchild Ruggles, D. (2008) *Islamic Gardens and Landscapes*, Philadelphia, PA, Pennsylvania State University Press.

Fellous, S. (2000) 'Cultural hybridity, cultural subversion: text and image in the Alba Bible 1422–33', *Exemplaria*, vol. 12, no. 1, pp. 205–30.

Fletcher, R. (1992) *Moorish Spain*, London, Phoenix.

Gallori, C. T. (2013) 'Collecting feathers: a journey from Mexico into Italian collections (sixteenth–seventeenth century)', in Bracken, S., Galdy, A. M. and Turpin, A. (eds) *Collecting East and West*, Newcastle upon Tyne, Cambridge Scholars Publishing, pp. 60–81.

Gampel, B. R. (1992) 'Jews, Christians and Muslims in medieval Iberia: convivencia through the eyes of Sephardic Jews', in Mann, V. B., Glick, T. F. and Dodds, J. D. (eds) *Convivencia: Jews, Muslims and Christians in Medieval Spain*, New York, G. Braziller, pp. 11–37.

Gilman Proske, B. (1951) *Castilian Sculpture: Gothic to Renaissance*, New York, Hispanic Society of America.

Glick, T. F. (1969) 'Acculturation as an explanatory concept in Spanish history', *Comparative Studies in Society and History*, vol. 11, no. 2, pp. 136–54.

Gómez Bárcena, M. J. (1998) *Escultura Gótica funeraria en Burgos*, Burgos, Excma. Diputacíon Provincial de Burgos.

Grabar, O. (1978) *The Alhambra*, London, Allen Lane.

Harris, J. A. (1997) 'Mosque to church conversions in the Spanish re-conquest', *Medieval Encounters*, vol. 3, no. 2, pp. 158–72.

Hattstein, M. and Delius, P. (eds) (2004) *Islam, Art and Architecture*, Cologne, Könemann.

Lacarra Ducay, M. C. (2000) *El retablo mayor de San Salvador de Zaragoza*, Zaragoza, Librería General, Gobierno de Aragón, Departamento de Cultura y Turismo.

Layna Serrano, F. (1997) *El Palacio del Infantado en Guadalajara*, Obras Completas 4, Guadalajara, Aache.

López Guzmán, R. (2009) 'Relaciones artísticas entre el Sultanato Nazarí y el Reino de Castilla', in Cosmen Alonso, M. C., Herráez Ortega, V. and Gómez-Calcerrada, M. P. (eds) *El intercambio artístico entre los reinos hispanos y las cortes europeas en la Baja Edad Media*, Léon, Universidad de Léon, pp. 83–102.

Lovera de Navarro, N. (1992) 'Contributions of the Franciscan brother Peter of Ghent to the painting and architecture of New Spain during the sixteenth century', in Vandenbroek, P. (ed.) *America, Bride of the Sun: 500 years of Latin America and the Low Countries*, Antwerp, Royal Museum of Fine Arts, pp. 69–75.

Luyster, A. (2008) 'Cross cultural style in the Alhambra: textiles, identity and origins', *Medieval Encounters*, vol. 14, special issue on the Alhambra, pp. 341–67.

Mann, V. B. (ed.) (2000) *Jewish Texts on the Visual Arts*, Cambridge, Cambridge University Press.

Mann, V. B., Glick, T. F. and Dodds, J. D. (eds) (1992) *Convivencia: Jews, Muslims and Christians in Medieval Spain*, New York, G. Braziller.

Marín Fidalgo, A. (1995) *Visitors Guide: Real Alcazar of Seville*, Madrid, Aldeasa.

Marks, L. U. (2015) 'The taming of the haptic space, from Málaga to Valencia to Florence', *Muqarnas*, vol. 32, special issue, pp. 253–78.

Melville, C. and Ubaydli, A. (1992) *Christians and Moors in Spain, Volume 3: Arabic Sources (711–1501)*, Warminster, Aris & Phillips.

Moffitt Watts, P. (1991) 'Hieroglyphs of conversion: alien discourses in Diego Valadés's *Rhetorica christiana*', *Memorie Domenicane*, vol. 22, pp. 405–33.

Moffitt Watts, P. (1995) 'Language of gesture in sixteenth-century Mexico: some antecedents and transmutations', in Farago, C. (ed.) *Reframing the Renaissance: Visual Cultures in Europe and Latin America 1450–1650*, New Haven, CT, Yale University Press, pp. 140–51.

Newall, D. (ed.) (2017) *Art and its Global Histories: A Reader*, Manchester and Milton Keynes, Manchester University Press in association with The Open University.

Nirenberg, D. (2002) 'Conversion, sex and segregation: Jews and Christians in medieval Spain', *American Historical Review*, vol. 107, no. 4, pp. 1065–93.

Nordström, C. O. (1967) *The Duke of Alba's Castilian Bible*, Uppsala, Acta Universitatis Upsaliensis, new series 5.

Pagden, A. (1993) 'Lus et factum: text and experience in the writing of Bartholomé de las Casas', in Greenblatt, S. (ed.) *New World Encounters*, Berkeley, CA, University of California Press, pp. 85–100.

Pereda, F. (2001) 'Through a glass darkly: path to salvation in Spanish painting at the outset of the Inquisition', in Kessler, H. L. and Nirenberg, D. (eds) *Judaism and Christian Art: Aesthetic Anxieties from the Catacombs to Colonialism*, Philadelphia, PA and Oxford, Pennsylvania State University Press, pp. 263–90.

Pierce, D., Ruiz Gomar, R. and Bargellini, C. (eds) (2004) *Painting a New World: Mexican Art and Life 1521–1821*, Denver, CO, Denver Art Museum.

Poole, S. (1996) *Our Lady of Guadalupe: The Origins and Sources of a Mexican National Symbol 1531–1797*, Tucson, AZ, University of Arizona Press.

Ray, A. (2000) *Spanish Pottery 1248–1898 with a Catalogue of the Collection in the Victoria and Albert Museum*, London, Victoria and Albert Museum.

Remensnyder, A. G. (2000) 'The colonization of sacred architecture: the Virgin Mary, mosques and temples in medieval Spain and early sixteenth century Mexico', in Farmer, S. and Rosenwein, B. H. (eds) *Monks and Nuns, Saints and Outcasts: Religion in Medieval Society, Essays in Honour of Lester K Little*, Ithaca, NY and London, Cornell University Press, pp. 189–219.

Robinson, C. (2008) 'Arthur in the Alhambra? Narrative and Nasrid courtly self-fashioning in the Hall of Justice ceiling paintings', *Medieval Encounters*, vol. 14, special issue on the Alhambra, pp. 164–98.

Rodriguez Porto, R. M. (2008) 'Courtliness and its Trujamanes: manufacturing chivalric imagery across the Castilian–Grenadine frontier', *Medieval Encounters*, vol. 14, special issue on the Alhambra, pp. 219–66.

Rosser Owen, M. (2010) *Islamic Arts from Spain*, London, Victoria and Albert Museum.

Roth, C. (1957) *The Kennicott Bible*, Oxford, Bodleian Library.

Ruiz Souza, J. C. (2006) 'Architectural languages, functions, and spaces: the Crown of Castile and Al-Andalus', *Medieval Encounters*, vol. 12, no. 3, pp. 360–87.

Russo, A. (2014–15) 'An artistic humanity: new positions on art and freedom in the context of Iberian expansion 1500–1600', *Res: Anthropology and Aesthetics*, vols. 65/66, pp. 353–63.

Smith, C. (1989) *Christians and Moors in Spain, Volume 2: 1195–1614,* Warminster, Aris & Phillips.

Steck, F. B. (ed.) (1951) *Motolinía's History of the Indians of New Spain*, Washington, DC, Academy of American Franciscan History.

Stern, H. (1976) *Les mosaïques de la grande mosquée de Cordoue*, Berlin, de Gruyter.

Trusted, M. (2007) *The Arts of Spain: Iberia and Latin America 1450–1700*, London, Victoria and Albert Museum.

Valadés, D. (1579) *Rhetorica christiana*, Perugia.

Verlinden, C. (1986) 'Fray Pedro de Gante y su época', *Revista de Historia de América*, vol. 101, pp. 105–31.

Yarza Luaces, J. (2007) *La Cartuja de Miraflores II: el retablo*, Cuadernos de Restauración de Iberdrola, vol. XIII, no. 2.

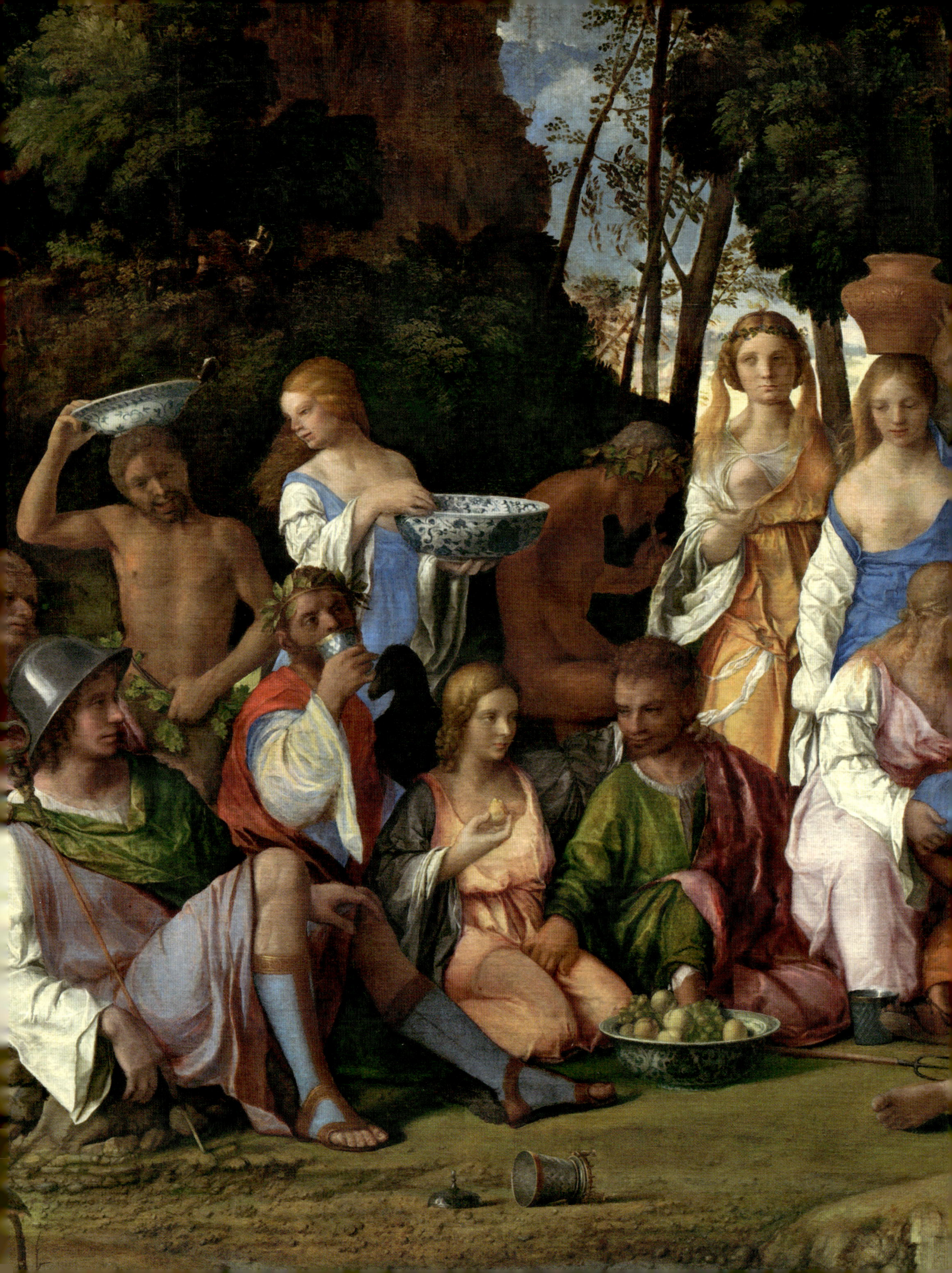

Chapter 3

Collecting the world: art, nature and representation

Leah R. Clark

Introduction

Domenico Ghirlandaio's fresco of Saint Jerome in the church of Ognissanti in Florence depicts the saint as a Christian scholar in a contemporary Italian space (a study) framed by classical architecture, in which humanistic enterprises such as reading and writing lead to the pursuit of knowledge and an understanding of God (Plate 3.2). This painting, in many ways, presents a quintessential illustration of the 'Renaissance' study with its emphasis on learning and its reference to classical antiquity. But when looking more closely at the image, another story is told: the oriental carpet that adorns Jerome's desk and the maiolica *albarelli* (drug jars) and crystal vases gracing the shelves point to an international luxury trade that stretched from China through Persia and across the Mediterranean. The fresco was painted in 1480 and, in the decade that followed, Christopher Columbus would set sail for the New World, and Vasco da Gama would discover a sea route to Asia, both of which would open up even more routes and provide Europeans with more foreign objects to acquire and place in their studies and the domestic settings of their homes. These discoveries would also shift the balance of powers within Europe and the world at large.

Even before Columbus encountered the New World, Europeans had long been in contact with other cultures through trade and diplomacy. In most cases a 'non-European' object was not entirely non-European, as centuries of cross-cultural interaction had resulted in cross-fertilisation of motifs, ideas, shapes and forms.[1] Similarly, most European objects are not solely European, but represent this chequered history of interaction with other cultures. In this chapter attention will be paid to the complex processes of interaction where influence went three ways – from Europe, into Europe and within Europe. Some questions that will be addressed throughout this chapter are: what effects did the collection of objects from other cultures have on the perception of the objects themselves and the image of the cultural area in question? What in turn do these objects tell us about the culture that collected them? What is meant by 'European' collections of 'art' and 'foreign' objects for this period?

Renaissance art collections are usually studied with a focus on paintings or classical antiquities, where the complex mythological or biblical subject matter is seen as a reflection of the humanist pursuits of patrons and a renewed interest in antiquity.[2] This chapter, instead, approaches collecting from a global perspective, investigating the role that foreign objects and cultures played in collecting practices and the formation of

Plate 3.1 (Facing page) Giovanni Bellini, *Feast of the Gods* (detail from Plate 3.10).

knowledge about the world outside Europe. The acquisition of foreign goods and their display became the means by which Europeans bolstered their claims to power. But this study also underlines that European collections were not that lavish or even noteworthy, when compared with contemporary princely collections from around the globe. The chapter also goes beyond the confines of interior spaces to pursue how collecting was expanded out of doors as creatures from around the world were put on display.

This chapter will explore the diverse contexts in which works of art were produced, consumed and interpreted within a framework of cross-cultural encounters. These encounters were sometimes first-hand, but more often in this time period, they were second- or third-hand. Indeed, the mobility of objects meant that the objects themselves were often the sites of encounter, as individuals confronted the visual and material cultures of distant lands through holding an object in their hands or observing its representation depicted in a painting.

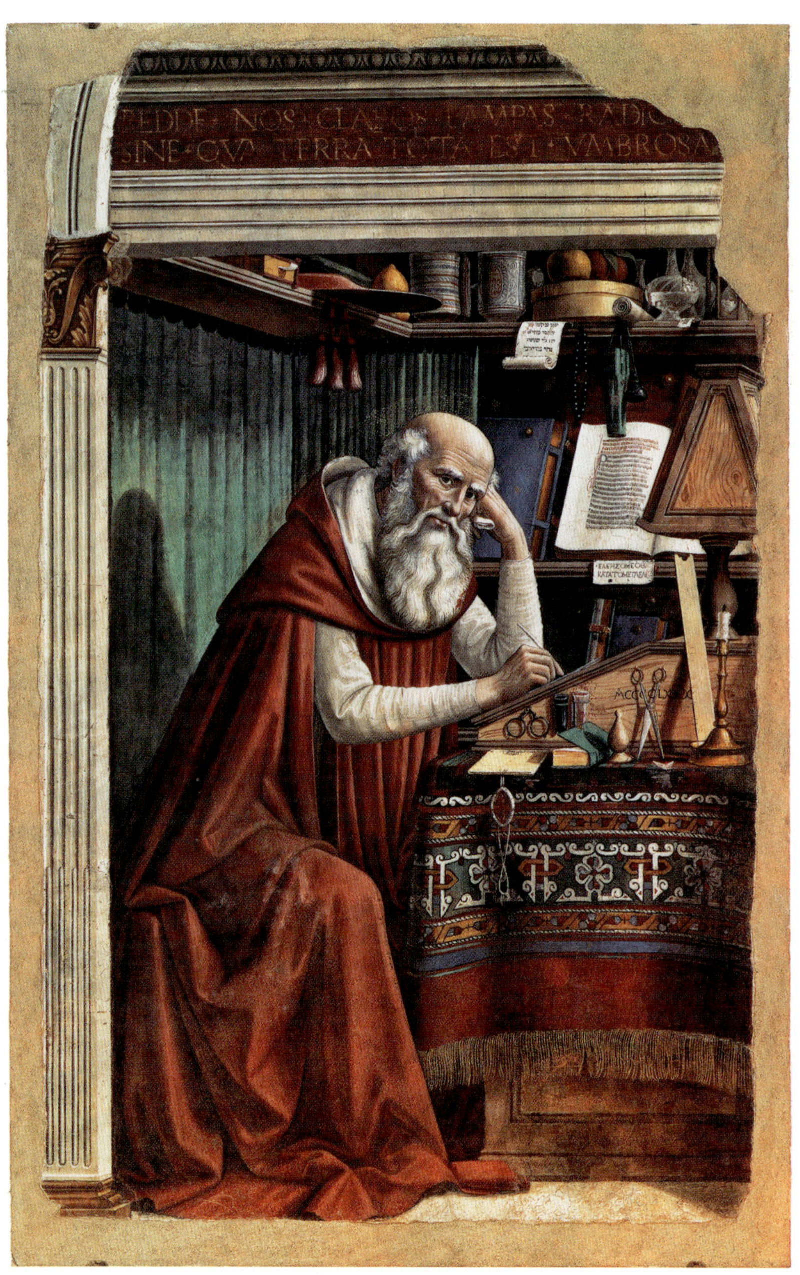

Plate 3.2 Domenico Ghirlandaio, *Saint Jerome in His Study*, 1480, fresco, 184 × 119 cm. Church of Ognissanti, Florence. Photo: Getty.

1 European collecting practices and the wider world

Ghirlandaio's fresco (Plate 3.2) marks an increasing interest, which emerged across Europe in the fifteenth century, in acquiring foreign goods, from Islamic carpets and metalwork to glass, ceramics and even Chinese porcelain. Ghirlandaio's fresco is located within a church and thus a sacred setting, but Saint Jerome is depicted in a secular space – that of the study – underlining a significant shift in the history of collecting. This shift has often been emphasised as reflective of the move towards more secular ways of understanding the world in the Renaissance. Marvellous objects that represented the miraculous works of God, from relics of saints and precious stones to elephant tusks, ostrich eggs and unicorn horns, were commonly housed in church treasuries in the medieval period. In the Renaissance, due to increased trade, these items also made their way into patrician and aristocratic homes, becoming part of a secular collecting culture.[3] This relocation of precious and rare things from the church to the home was not simply a change of setting, but a reflection of shifting attitudes to the world of goods and the world at large.

The increased interest in collecting luxury goods within a secular context might have been novel for Europeans, but it was not for Eastern rulers. Indeed, foreign courts – from the Mamluks and Ottomans in the Mediterranean, to the Aqqoyunlu and the Timurids of central Asia and Persia, to the rich empires in India and China – often outdid European courts in a type of collecting which was globally competitive. Eastern courts' access to raw goods such as diamonds and gems and to the manufacture of luxury objects such as ceramics and metalwork meant that they served as models worthy of emulation.[4] The emergence of these practices in Europe thus was part of a longer history of collecting and the circulation of goods. In the period studied in this chapter (*c.*1450–1550), European access to networks and trade routes increased but at a different pace, resulting in new power dynamics. For example, by the early sixteenth century, Portugal's monopoly over trade routes to India meant that luxury items that were still deemed rare in Italy had become commonplace on the streets of Lisbon, reflecting Portuguese power.[5]

The study

In Europe, collectors built dedicated spaces in their homes to display a variety of objects. In Italy, this room or study was usually referred to as a *studiolo* and emerged in the fifteenth century, while in German-speaking countries such a room became popular in the sixteenth century and was called a *Kunstkammer* (chamber of art) or *Wunderkammer* (chamber of wonders).[6] In the sixteenth and seventeenth centuries, these spaces were also referred to as cabinets of curiosities, to reflect both the inquisitive impetus that led to their formation and the curious things that could be found within.[7]

European collecting spaces and associated practices took many forms. Aristocratic families who ruled courts acquired goods to reflect their magnificence and power, as well as to demonstrate taste and knowledge, dedicating whole rooms to collecting where the walls were decorated with complex painting programmes and cabinets filled with precious objects. Increasingly, collecting became a pastime that merchants, humanists and others undertook, where goods were collected and displayed to show sophistication, worldly knowledge and a successful business.[8] In homes of the middling sorts, a closet or a small room could serve as a study and a collecting space, similar to a monastic cell (as in Plate 3.2). But many middle-class homes simply housed their collectables in one part of the bedchamber (bedrooms were more public rooms than they are today) or throughout their home, placed on shelves, above doorframes and in cabinets.

Vittore Carpaccio's depiction of Saint Augustine (Plate 3.3) situates him in an idealised interior space, but alludes to contemporary practices.[9] The painting reveals how objects associated with collecting could spill out between the rooms of a house. Saint Augustine sits at a desk scattered with books and writing utensils, with an astrolabe hanging above (to the right). On the left wall, books line the upper shelf and below collectables are displayed, including Etruscan vases, sculptures and a metalwork candlestick, while the right shelf showcases different types of vases. At the far end, an altar marks religious activities, and to the left, a door opens onto a smaller study where a book wheel is placed atop a table.

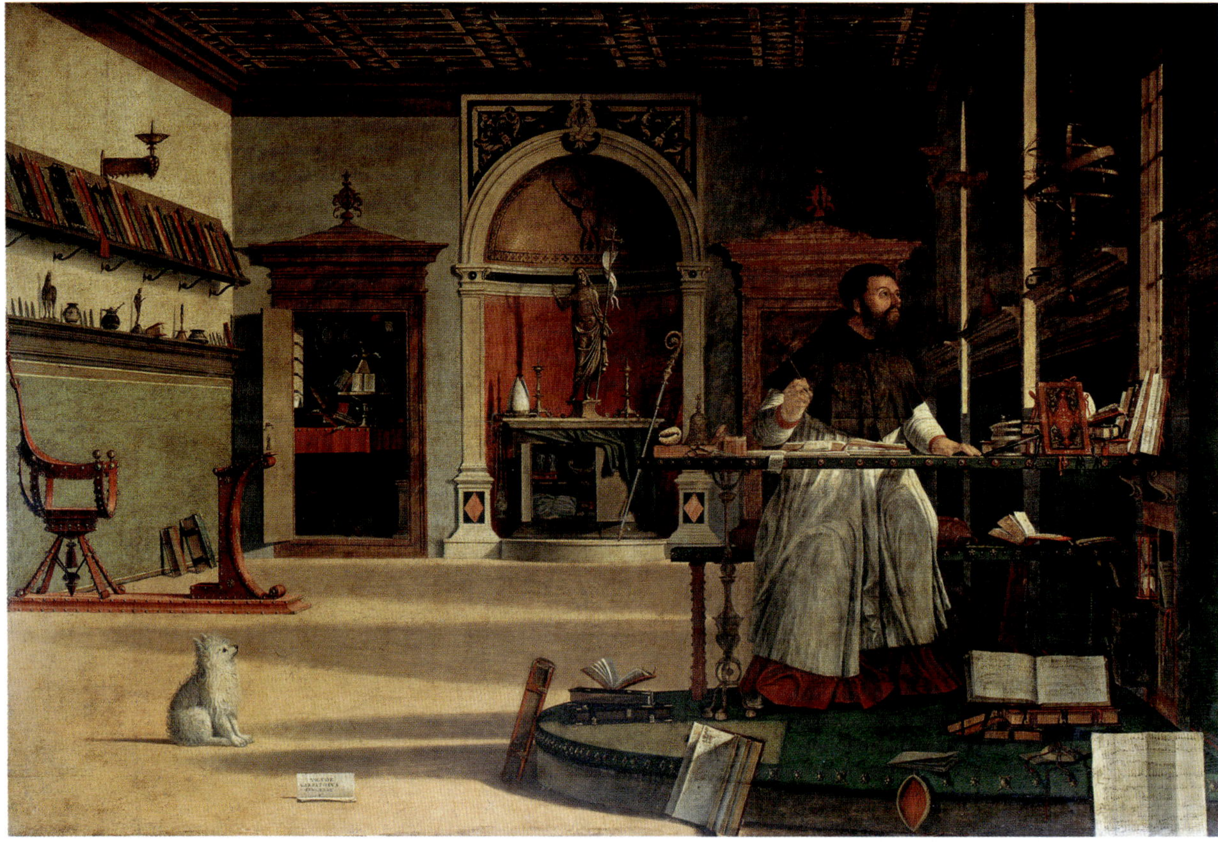

Plate 3.3 Vittore Carpaccio, *Vision of Saint Augustine*, 1502, tempera on canvas, 141 × 210 cm. Scuola di San Giorgio degli Schiavoni, Venice. Photo: Getty.

The door into the smaller study has a lock and key, reflecting contemporary practices. In Leon Battista Alberti's treatise on the family (*Della famiglia*), written between 1433 and 1441, one of the speakers notes that he ensured that his 'books and records and those of [his] ancestors' were 'locked up and arranged in order in [his] study, almost like sacred and religious objects'.[10] The study thus served numerous functions, from a space for cerebral and spiritual activities such as contemplation and business, to a treasury where the most precious objects and documents of the family were stored.

Marvellous objects

When foreign objects entered European collections, they also encountered a new system of value and were culturally redefined. As such, their function also shifted. Art is a category that requires some rethinking for this period. In the first half of the

sixteenth century, Giorgio Vasari was writing his treatise on the *Lives of the Most Eminent Painters, Sculptors, and Architects* where he privileged Florentine artists who looked to antiquity and employed classical principles in their works.[11] His text also reflected a growing interest in the liberal, intellectual capacity of artists over the manual labour of craftsmen. The emergence of collecting spaces which exhibited paintings certainly contributed to, and was influenced by, this new conception of art. However, this is only half the story. At the same time, collectors were eager to amass not only man-made artworks but odd and natural specimens as well. One way of understanding the selection criteria of objects and the motivation behind collecting is to consider the concept of the 'marvellous'. Objects that were considered marvels were things that were unique and rare and were often understood to have resulted from exceptional conditions or circumstances, such as through some divine force. With increased humanist interests in understanding the world, coupled with expanding trade routes, the religious component did not necessarily disappear, but was complemented with new secular concerns about the world and, increasingly in the sixteenth century, with secular power.

Raffaello Borghini's description of Bernardo Vecchietti's villa in Florence in the late sixteenth century underlines how the vast array of objects housed in the study could provide astonishment:

> A great marvel to see is a study with five shelves where small statues of marble, bronze, clay and wax are arranged in a beautiful order. Fine stones of many sorts are arranged there, vases of porcelain and of rock crystal, seashells of many kinds, pyramids of precious stone, jewels, medals, masks, fruit and animals frozen in very fine stone [fossils], and so many new and rare things coming from India and from Turkey as astonishes whoever sees them. Beyond some further rooms, in another part of the villa, is a similar study completely stocked with silver and gold vases and prints and drawings by the most excellent masters that sculpture and painting have had. Precious distilled waters and very efficacious oils are there ... very beautiful knives from the Orient, Turkish scimitars, worked in various ways, and a large number of cups and different porcelain vases.[12]

Exercise

What does Borghini single out as noteworthy? Are these objects easy to classify? What would you put into the 'art' or 'nature' category? Does he mention origins and places of manufacture?

Discussion

Borghini mentions wonders of nature such as fossils, but he also mentions works that might be classified as 'art' today: statues, prints and drawings. He also references vases of porcelain, oils and knives but he does not seem to categorise these items in one camp or the other. His reference to the most excellent masters of sculpture and painting, however, points to a particular emphasis on artistic skill, although he mentions silver and gold vases in the same sentence, which also indicates material value. The line between nature and art is sometimes blurred: Borghini lists fossils, rock crystal and seashells together with porcelain. Works that were natural but reworked by human hands were seen as novelties, such as fine gems carved with figures. The emphasis on novelty meant that the criteria for collecting did not follow a division of 'high' and 'low' art, but origins could play an important role in determining value. He specifies some items coming from India and Turkey, but he is less precise with his reference to 'the Orient' reflecting an unspecific geographical place, associated with luxury and mystery.

Objects worthy of collection could therefore have different registers of value, according to novelty or rarity, material make-up or artistic intervention. This is reflected in contemporary inventories of the time, such as that of the Florentine merchant-banker Lorenzo de' Medici taken in 1492, where a 'unicorn horn' (likely a narwhal tusk) was valued at an extraordinary price, while works by great masters such as a sculpture by Donatello or a painting by Fra Angelico were valued considerably lower.[13] Most collections housed a mix of *naturalia* (oddities of nature) and *artificilia* (works fashioned by human hand), manifesting the idea that the collection was a microcosm reflecting the larger world (macrocosm). For rulers, amassing a great collection of rare objects from foreign lands could demonstrate their knowledge and even possession of those lands as well as wealth, status and power. Equally, rulers' collections of paintings by great masters demonstrated their ability to recruit the best artists and extolled their court as a centre for learning and the arts. It was therefore not unusual to see paintings by famous painters such as Jan van Eyck or Titian in the same collection that housed Bengali textiles, rhinoceros horns, coconuts, Turkish shoes, carved African ivories, Syrian metalwork, oriental carpets and Mexican shields.

Gifts and trade

Representations of prized possessions, such as those found in depictions of gift ceremonies, underline the novelty of objects associated with the East. Cross-

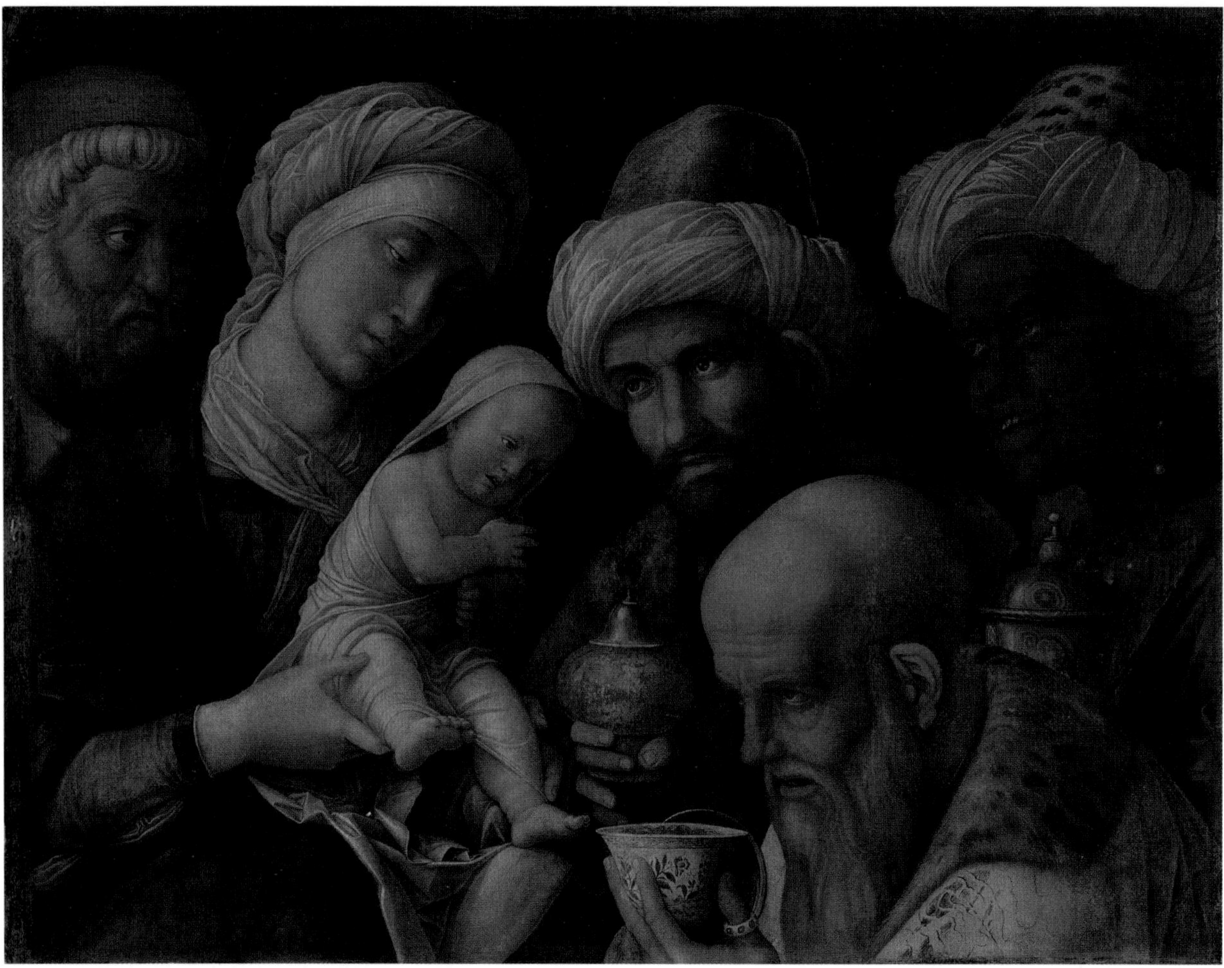

Plate 3.4 Andrea Mantegna, *Adoration of the Magi*, c.1495–1505, distemper on linen, 49 × 66 cm. Getty Museum, Los Angeles. Photo: Digital image courtesy of the Getty's Open Content Program.

cultural associations with gifts, the evocation of distant lands and the emphasis on diplomacy are most evident in paintings of the magi – the ultimate example of gift-givers. The *Adoration of the Magi* (Plate 3.4) by Andrea Mantegna allows the viewer to feel as if they are a privileged member of this intimate ceremony, providing an opportunity for a close-up depiction of these rare gifts. These particular gifts resemble the types of highly prized foreign objects that would have been exchanged between rulers and found in the *studioli* of the elite. Melchior holds a Turkish censer for perfuming the air, while the agate receptacle held by Balthasar (the black magus adorned with jewels) may have been modelled on objects of Persian manufacture. The blue and white bowl full of coins is probably one of the earliest representations of Chinese porcelain in the West.[14] The gifts represented

in Mantegna's *Adoration* thus had a close tie to real gifts that were mediators between international courts in the fifteenth century and represent the types of commodities that were readily available in foreign lands, but still valued as precious collectables in Europe.

Merchants were in a particularly good position to acquire foreign goods, such as Carlo Helman, who was originally from Antwerp but resided in Venice. His house spoke to his professional and personal interests and networks, serving as both his home and his office, with dedicated spaces to conduct business and house his merchandise, while the living quarters were decorated with his art collection, including paintings by famous Venetian masters such as Titian, Giovanni Bellini and Paolo Veronese. His study reflected his trading with Turkey as it was full of Turkish artefacts,

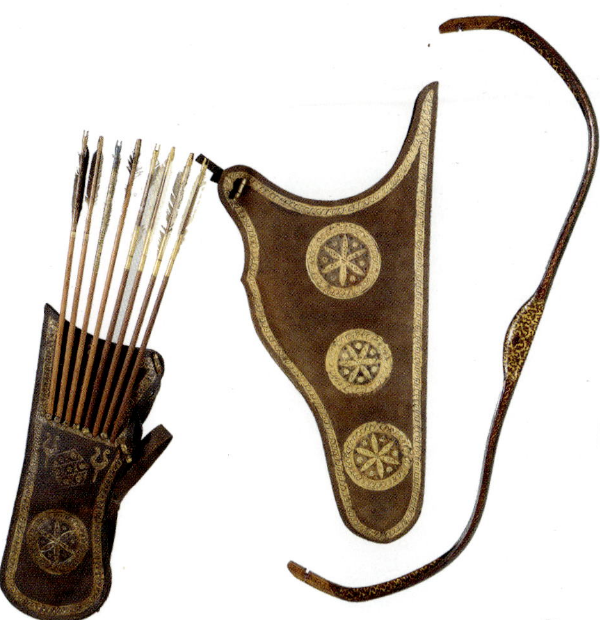

Plate 3.5 Quiver with arrows and a bow with bowcase, Turkish, 1569, leather, wood, gilding, paint. Germanisches Nationalmuseum, Nuremberg. Photo: Monika Runge/GMN.

from weapons (a quiver and two Turkish bows) and clothing (including a courtly woman's dress) to travelling equipment and even 'a book in the Turkish manner with portraits of Turks in it' (probably a costume book).[15] One cabinet in his study contained additional 'Turkish and Indian things' as well as a rhinoceros horn, demonstrating an interest in both material artefacts and natural specimens from the world around him. He probably acquired these objects in Venice via trade routes, although many Venetians did travel and even lived in the Levant as part of their training and work. His study, then, had multiple functions: as a place for contemplation and reading, as well as a showcase of his successes in trade and his experiences of travel, shown off to visitors and privileged clients.

While the specific Turkish artefacts from Helman's study are no longer traceable, a collection of Turkish objects brought back from Constantinople as part of an embassy of the Holy Roman Empire in 1569 by Stephan III Praun give an idea of what these artefacts would have looked like (Plate 3.5). They are now housed in Nuremberg and include a quiver with arrows, a purse, red leather slippers and a bow with bowcase.[16] The patterns on these artefacts were associated with

the East and were often copied by artists on a range of material goods, from ceramics to book illustrations to paintings, becoming incorporated into European material cultures, demonstrating how cultural transfer could take place through material artefacts.

2 Exchange and diplomacy

Artefacts from distant lands made their way into European collections usually through three major routes: through trade networks, through voyages of discovery and through international diplomacy. The acquisition of foreign artefacts was therefore closely related to political and diplomatic negotiations, as well as to expansion. In the Mediterranean, two major Islamic empires, the Mamluks (present-day Egypt and Syria) and the Ottomans (present-day Turkey), were continuously in diplomatic negotiations with European powers, which resulted in the exchange of numerous gifts, from silverware to textiles to ceramics to animals. While the political climate was often fraught and religious divides could produce tensions, the shared interest in lavish and rare objects meant that numerous objects passed between European rulers and these Islamic polities. As such, these gifts were certainly not always a sign of peace, but often were used to broker relations and ease tensions.[17]

For instance, in the fifteenth century the Mamluks were in territorial struggles with the neighbouring Ottomans, as well as in competition to gain trade deals with European powers. The Mamluks' dominance over the 'spice' trade in this century meant that they had luxury objects in abundance, traded along the silk roads, which they then gifted as diplomatic gifts as a means of brokering territorial and commercial deals. In 1473, during political and trade negotiations, the Mamluk Sultan Qaytbay of Cairo (r.1468–96) sent Doge Niccolò Tron of Venice (r.1471–73) 20 pieces of porcelain, medicinal herbs, fine sugar and a civet horn. Similarly, in 1487, Qaytbay's ambassadors in Florence presented Lorenzo de' Medici with porcelain, Valencian vases, textiles, spices, a horse, a fat-tailed sheep and a prized giraffe (Plate 3.6).[18] This was a particularly important moment for both parties. The Medici, a famous merchant-banking family, were de facto rulers of Florence who were seeking greater control of the city, while the Republic of Florence was involved in complex negotiations with other

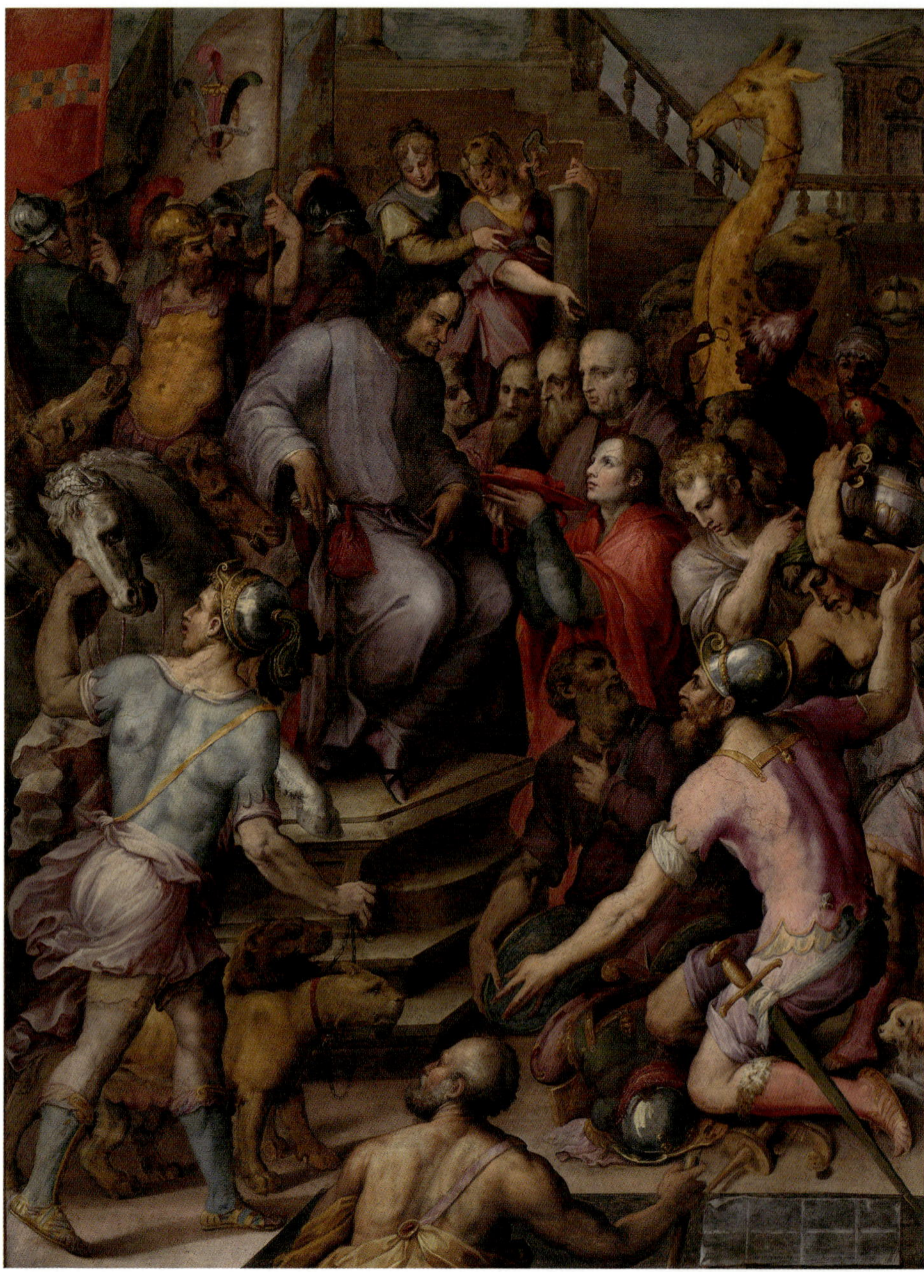

Plate 3.6 Giorgio Vasari, *Lorenzo de' Medici Receiving Gifts from His Ambassadors*, c.1556, ceiling fresco. Palazzo Vecchio, Florence. Photo: Getty.

Italian states, following a particularly tumultuous period of alliances, counter-alliances and wars. The Mamluks too were eager to settle a trade deal with the Florentines before the Ottomans could interfere. Italian states like Florence and Venice and the empires of the Ottomans and Mamluks were well aware of how access to trade routes and the exchange of goods were central to their economy and the health of their state. At the same time, the pope was also calling for a crusade to reclaim the Holy Land. Gifts, then, were bound up in complicated relations that included trading networks, acquisition of luxury goods, religious wars and territorial struggles. The processions of foreign embassies and the lavish ceremonial exchange of gifts in European cities worked to display the power of both giver and receiver. The gift of luxury objects and exotic animals publicly demonstrated a ruler's power and his or her access to important trade routes, as well as advertising potential commodities to be traded in future.

Diplomatic gifts exchanged between East and West in the fifteenth and sixteenth centuries were not new, but a continuation of practices of diplomacy that dated back to antiquity. What was new for Europeans was the increased access to these luxury goods, however commonplace they were for foreign courts. Lists of lavish gifts, from textiles to ceramics and slaves to camels, were frequently compiled to track the numerous objects the Mamluks gave and received from courts all over the world. For example, the Mamluks received Chinese porcelain from Yemen in the hundreds (400 or 500 in some lists) but when regifted to European courts, the Mamluks never exceeded 30 pieces at a time. Placed in perspective, European access to these goods was rather meagre.

Those who did have access to these commodities, such as merchants, found that their status rose considerably because of this. Merchant families such as the Fuggers of Augsburg or the Medici of Florence became extraordinarily wealthy and powerful through their importation of foreign goods that filled their own *Wunderkammern* and *studioli* as well as supplying those of the princely elite. Collecting was a multifaceted process, whereby collections were assembled gradually over time through a complex system of exchange, involving gift-giving, commerce, patronage and inheritance – networks were thus important. The Fuggers had offices in all the major trading ports and hubs from Lisbon, Madrid, Vienna, Frankfurt, Antwerp, Amsterdam, Paris, Venice and Rome to the Levant, the Yucatán and Brazil. They also financed commercial ventures out of Lisbon to as far afield as India, Ceylon and Africa. The family's own collections reflected this vast network – a microcosm of their global reach. The Fuggers' relationships with the princely elites of Europe, particularly Charles V and Albrecht V, Duke of Bavaria (r.1550–79), as well as their close ties to well-known humanists and scholars, meant that they not only provided commercial goods, but were instrumental in the conceptual formation of a culture around collecting.[19]

3 Materials and motifs

A particularly sought-after item by European princes, as well as by the Ottoman and Mamluk sultans in the fifteenth and sixteenth centuries, was Chinese porcelain. Blue-and-white Chinese porcelain did not come directly to Italy from China, but through Persia, and was then gifted to Europeans by the Mamluks and Ottomans.[20] Sending porcelain to Italian elites, like the Mamluks did throughout the fifteenth century, was a form of advertisement, promoting a costly new product that had begun arriving in their territory in sufficient amounts to export. It was valued not only because it was rare in Europe, but also because its material properties were assumed to be magical, and was considered to be a precious stone, a marvellous liquid that solidified underground, or a mixture of water and crushed shells. Porcelain was transported along the silk roads accompanied by other precious items sought by European rulers, such as diamonds, precious gems, silk and spices. Part of the value of the porcelain thus lay in the fact that it had come from afar, and its journey told tales of diplomatic entanglements, mercantile routes and travel.

The Medici family is often singled out as having the largest collections of Chinese porcelain in Europe in the fifteenth century. By the death of Lorenzo de' Medici in 1492, 52 items were recorded in his inventory.[21] While this is noteworthy for Italy and Europe, it pales in comparison with the collections of other princes from around the world, such as those of the Mamluks, demonstrating the often-skewed perspective when discussing European collections. Lorenzo's collection was displayed on shelves in his bedchamber and would have been highly admired and shown to numerous diplomatic and political figures who had the privilege to visit the Medici palace in Florence. This collection would have bolstered the family's fame and status, particularly at a moment where they were trying to gain more power within Italy. Lorenzo was well known for his collection of hardstone vases and antique gems, but he also collected paintings and tapestries. Some of Lorenzo's porcelain was gifted, as mentioned, by the Mamluk sultan, but he also had inherited some pieces which his forebears probably received through their vast trading networks. In the sixteenth century, the Medici family's power increased dramatically and they became Grand Dukes of Tuscany. The family's fascination with porcelain would eventually lead Francesco de' Medici (r.1574–87) to experiment with materials, producing the first European version of porcelain in 1575.[22]

Some of the Chinese porcelain pieces in the Medici collection were placed in metallic mounts, a common practice across Europe, not only for ceramics but applied

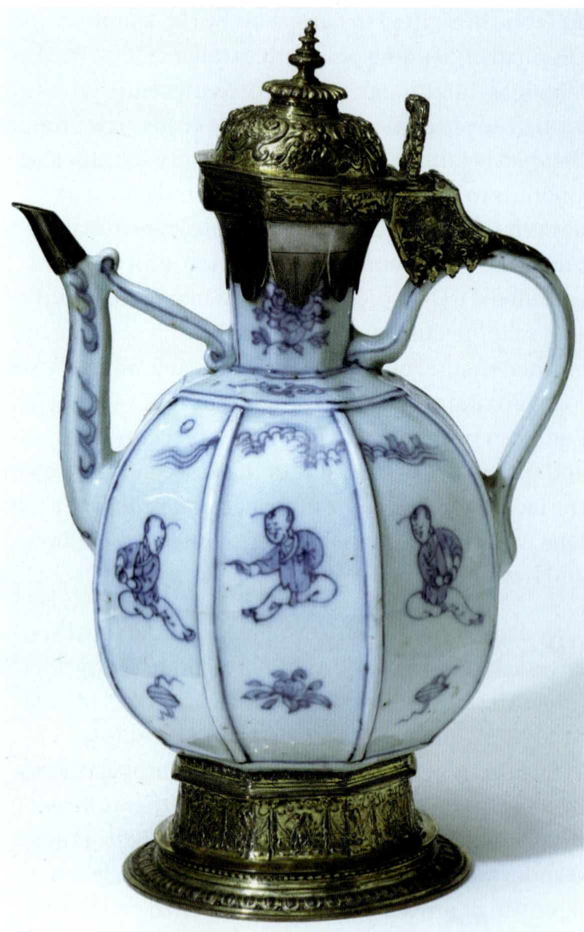

Plate 3.7 Ewer, *c.*1560–86, porcelain, China (Jingdezhen), with gilt-metal English mounts. Victoria and Albert Museum, London, 7915-1862. Photo: © Victoria and Albert Museum, London.

to ostrich eggs, coconuts and other extraordinary works of nature, allowing for easier handling of the vessels. The addition of mounts was certainly not exclusively a European practice, as metallic mounts were prevalent in Iran, Ottoman Turkey and the Mughal Empire, where porcelain was collected in large numbers and was often exchanged as part of intercultural diplomacy. The addition of mounts could transform an object's shape, form and function and could also serve to repair a broken piece. In many cases, the addition of a spout or a handle would allow for better functionality, but may have served an aesthetic function, as in the Ottoman context, where precious and semi-precious stones were inlaid on to the sides of the ceramic. In an English example, metal mounts facilitated the pouring of a porcelain ewer (Plate 3.7). Such mounts encourage new ways to consider the reception of Chinese porcelain.

How should such an object be categorised? Is it Chinese or English? The object has undergone not only a visual transformation but also a material one, as well as a shift in cultural identity. The object is thus a hybrid – not only a Chinese dish, but also an English one – and therefore becomes part of the local material culture of that region.[23]

Imitation porcelain

By the end of the fifteenth century, from Iznik to Damascus and finally to Spain and Italy, potters sought to replicate both the material and design motifs of porcelain, which provide useful case studies to explore the notions of cultural transfer and hybridity. A drug jar (*albarello*) now in Paris (Plate 3.8) was made in Syria, most likely Damascus.

Exercise

Look closely at Plate 3.8 and take note of some of the key visual components of the drug jar. What sorts of motifs are visible (floral, geometric, vegetal, animal)? Do any of these decorations hint at where the jar was made or where it was intended to be used or sold? Are the decorations sharply defined or blurred? What colours are used?

Discussion

At the centre of the jar there is an emblem, which looks like the fleur-de-lis, sitting slightly crooked. This emblem was used in Florence, where it was known as the florin, and the jar was probably created for export to Florence. Beside the florin, on either side (only half visible in the photograph) are birds with their wings spread. The jar is made up mostly of floral designs which loop together to create a continuous flow around the jar. There are bands around the jar, one delineating the neck, with a scroll pattern, which is repeated again, roughly three-quarters of the way towards the bottom of the jar. The floral scrolls and flying birds are typical of Syrian wares inspired by Persian pottery and Chinese porcelain.[24] The blue-and-white motifs are fairly clearly articulated, but in some places the blue is slightly blurred, demonstrating some problems in the firing process and suggesting some experimentation.

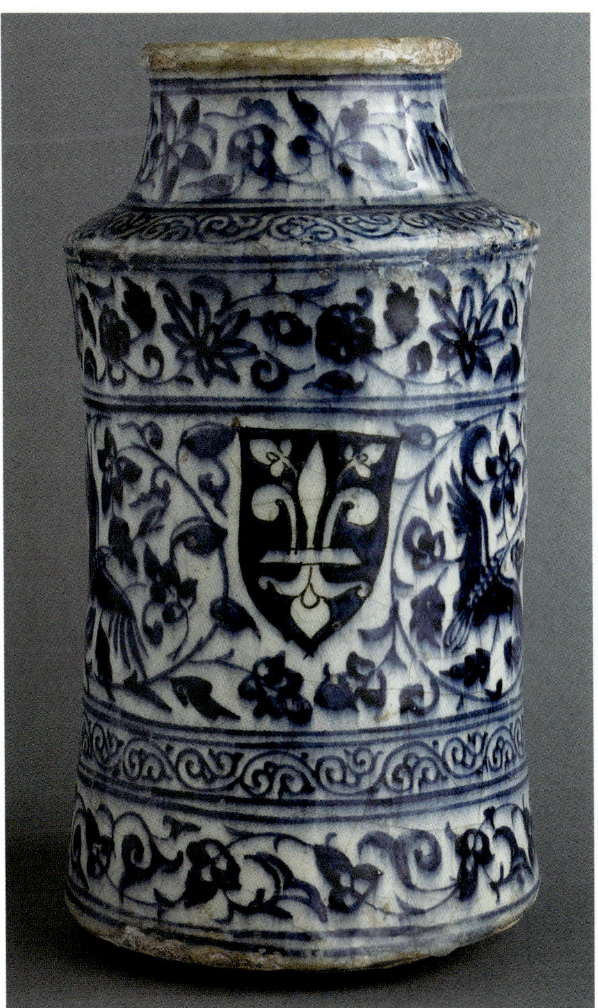

Plate 3.8 *Albarello* (drug jar), *c.*1400–50, fritware, Syria (Damascus). Musée des Art Décoratifs, Paris. Photo: © RMN-Grand Palais (Musée du Louvre)/Jean-Gilles Berizzi.

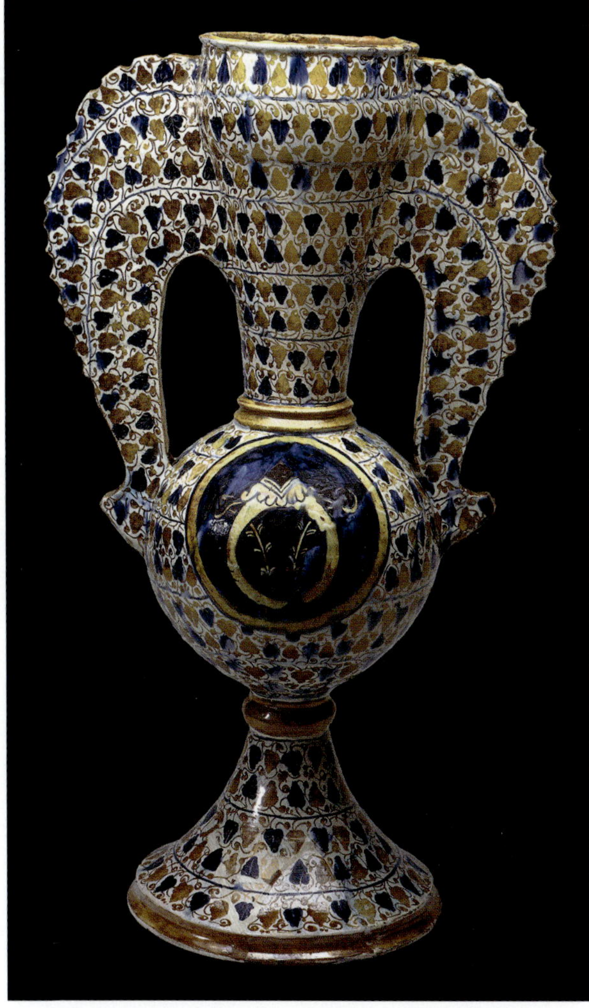

Plate 3.9 Jar, *c.*1465–80, tin-glazed earthenware, height 57 cm, Spain (Valencia). British Museum, London, G.619. Photo: © The Trustees of the British Museum.

This example can be seen to be a 'hybrid' object – a reflection of two distinct cultural motifs coming together – but also a more complex, entangled one, reflecting interconnecting histories of numerous cultures (Italian, Syrian, Persian, Chinese). *Albarelli* were found in homes as well as in apothecaries and were associated with the East because they held costly spices. They often appear in paintings of the period of the domestic interior, such as in Ghirlandaio's fresco (Plate 3.2). This sort of ware was sometimes referred to in Italy as *porcellana domaschina* (damascene porcelain), implying blue-and-white ware made in Damascus and not authentic Chinese porcelain, but the term 'damascene' was also used to describe metal objects in a style associated with Syrian production (see Plates 3.15 and 3.16).

In Spain, as mentioned in Chapter 2, Muslim and Christian potters working in Valencia also produced lustre pottery which was admired for its metallic sheen and motifs inspired by Islamic wares (Plate 3.9; see also Plates 2.4 and 2.5). These were often personalised by adding arms, intended for the export market, as in the case of Plate 3.9, where Medici insignia appear on both sides of the vase. Such Spanish lustreware became so popular in Italy that it provided the impetus for Italian potters to make their own, known as maiolica. By the end of the fifteenth century, this new kind of tin-glazed pottery became extremely fashionable, varying in decorations from those that mimicked Spanish, Syrian and Chinese wares to those depicting classical motifs and stories. The novelty of these new wares was continuously stressed by contemporaries who often noted that they preferred them to silver or gold, underlining how their rarity and technology were key to their value.[25]

Alfonso d'Este's *camerini*

The technological feat of producing these ceramics was indeed something that appealed to collectors. Approaching collecting in terms of technology and cross-cultural relations can provide new insight into familiar works of art usually associated with the *studiolo*. In 1511, Alfonso d'Este, Duke of Ferrara (r.1505–34), began designing a series of paintings for his *studiolo*, located in a suite of rooms known as the *camerini* (Plates 3.10 and 3.12). The humanist Mario Equicola set the intellectual programme for the paintings and it is the classical subject matter that is usually the focus of discussion when studying this cycle.[26] Giovanni Bellini's *Feast of the Gods,* executed in 1514 for this space (but reworked later by Titian and Dosso Dossi), depicts an episode recounted in the first book of Ovid's *Fasti* where ancient gods and goddesses feast (Plate 3.10). While the overall subject matter is certainly important, prominently displayed

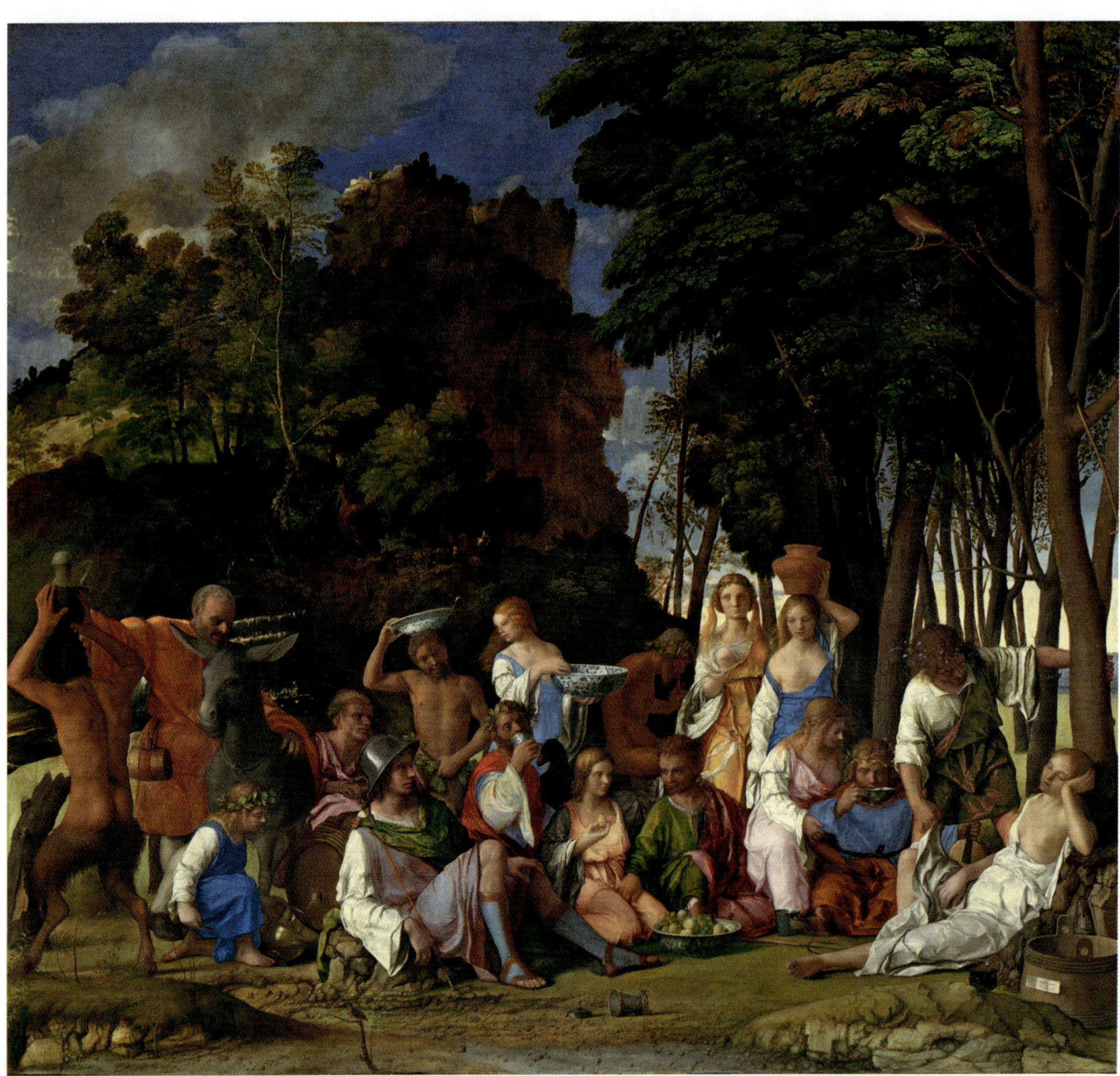

Plate 3.10 Giovanni Bellini, *Feast of the Gods*, c.1514–29, oil on canvas, 170 × 188 cm. National Gallery, Washington, DC. Photo: Bridgeman Images.

in this painting are three pieces of Chinese porcelain, significant from a cross-cultural perspective and providing insight into Alfonso's collecting interests.

The sixteenth-century biographer Paolo Giovio noted that not only did Alfonso admire ceramics, he was keen on making them himself.[27] Alfonso sought to have porcelain made in Ferrara, inviting a Venetian ceramicist to move there to experiment, while he also eagerly collected glassware and imitation porcelain. Titian, the painter who took over after Bellini for the cycle of paintings, was also involved in ceramic making. In 1520 he made designs for maiolica and was also asked to procure glass vases in Murano and jars for the duke's spice cabinet. Venetian glass was a highly collected item in Italy, visible in Jerome's study on the upper shelf (see Plate 3.2) and in Bellini's painting (see Plate 3.10). The glass factories were located on the Venetian island of Murano and the Venetian Senate was eager to safeguard its technical secrets. Today glass is still known as a Venetian speciality, even though its technology was borrowed from the East and thus it is a reflection of cross-cultural interaction.[28]

Throughout Alfonso's *camerino* paintings close attention is paid to particular types of vases and cups: in Bellini's *Feast of the Gods*, a glass jug is being filled towards the bottom left, while the central figure holds a large porcelain bowl, similar to one housed in the Victoria and Albert Museum today dating from the Ming dynasty (a reference to the dynasty's

reign in China, 1368–1644) (Plate 3.11). It is thought that Bellini may have painted a specific bowl he saw in Venice or one that he had himself received from the Turkish Sultan Mehmed II (r.1444–46 and 1451–81) when he travelled to Constantinople.[29] Recent archival documents, however, have revealed that Alfonso's mother, Eleonora d'Aragona, Duchess of Ferrara (r.1473–93) also had a large art collection, including a significant amount of Chinese porcelain, which he might have inherited and could very well be represented in the painting.[30] Hardstone vases and glass vessels were also on display in some of the nearby rooms.[31] The *camerino* paintings thus represented and indeed celebrated Alfonso's tastes and interests, which included collecting and making ceramics as well as the cultivation of exotic animals (as depicted in another painting for the space (Plate 3.12)).

This desire to acquire luxury products from around the world reflected an increasing interest in, and imperative for, rulers to seek out new trade routes, sending explorers on missions to see what they could find. These missions would ultimately shift the balance of power, whereby countries who led in explorations soon had a vast array of products at their fingertips. These groundbreaking discoveries of sea routes would open up new commercial opportunities, as in the case of custom-made porcelain pieces, and resulted in cultural transfers of motifs and iconography. When Vasco da Gama set sail from Portugal in 1497 to explore sea routes to Asia, he was

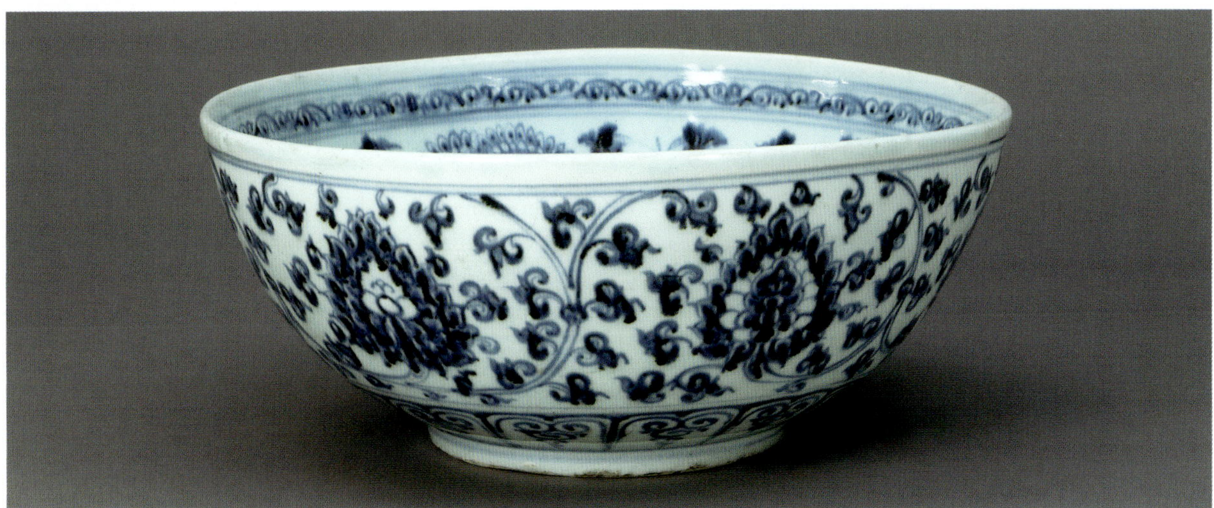

Plate 3.11 Bowl, *c.*1368–98, porcelain painted in underglaze blue, China (Jingdezhen). Victoria and Albert Museum, London, C.18-1957. Photo: © Victoria and Albert Museum, London.

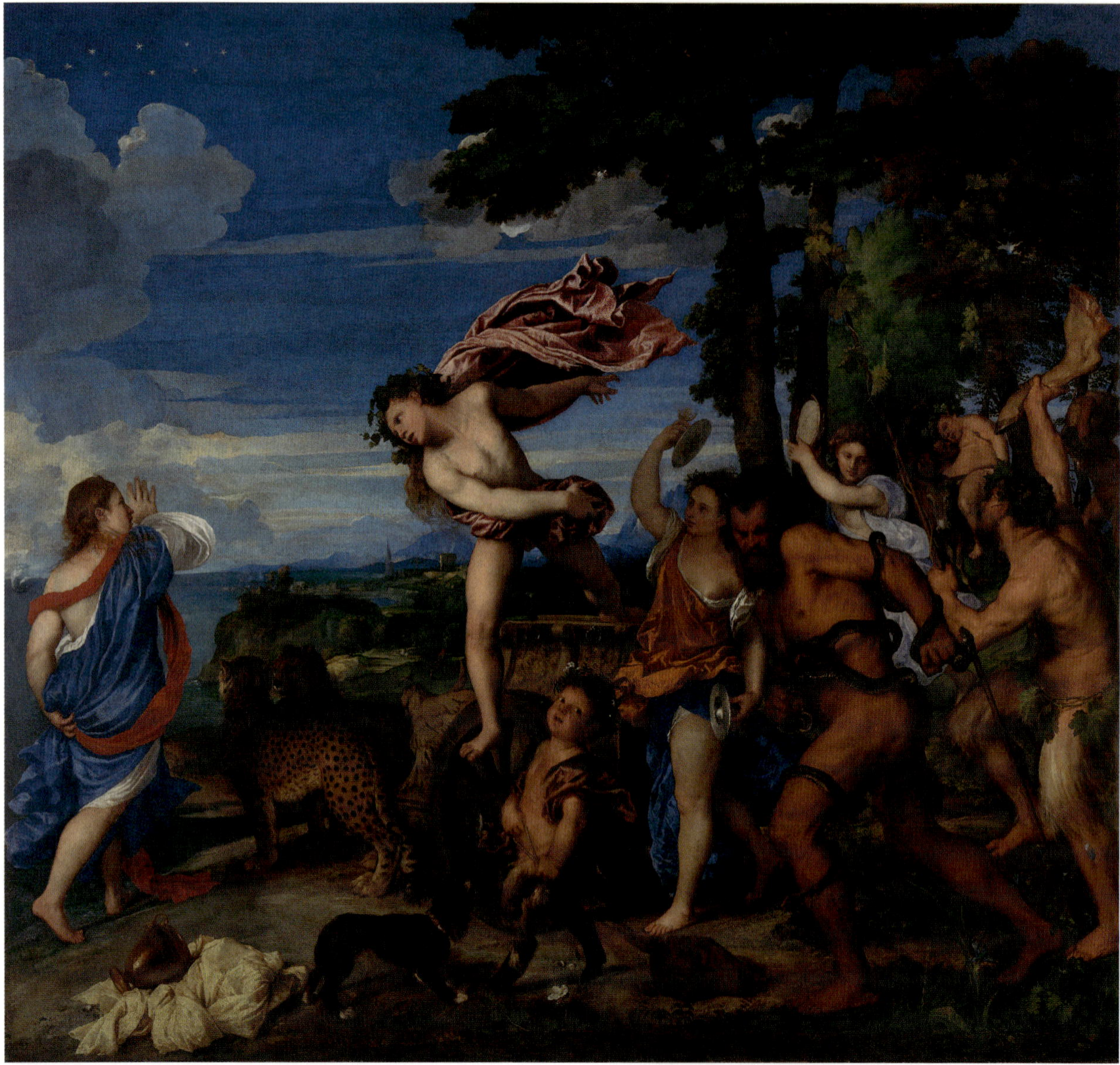

Plate 3.12 Titian, *Meeting of Bacchus and Ariadne*, c.1520–23, oil on canvas, 177 × 191 cm. National Gallery, London. Photo: National Gallery.

requested to bring back two things Europeans most desired, spices and porcelain. A pilgrim flask (Plates 3.13 and 3.14) demonstrates how complex and far-flung these cross-cultural ties had become by the time of Philip II – King of Spain (r.1556–98) and Portugal (r.1580–98). The pilgrim flask is made out of Chinese porcelain, composed of a unique clay coming from Chinese soil and fired in kilns in Jingdezhen in south-eastern China, where most porcelain had been made since the fourteenth century. The blue that makes up the recognisable blue-and-white variety of porcelain is,

however, made from cobalt pigment from ore mined in Persia. Finally, the iconography is significant. On one side is a seated scholar attended by a servant in a rocky landscape, a combination of Persian and Chinese motifs, but a subject appealing to Europeans. On the other side appear the arms of Spain, probably copied from a Spanish coin.[32]

The pilgrim flask thus exemplifies the extent of Philip's power, but also its status as a complex cultural object, reflecting the ways in which the world had become connected through the commercial and political

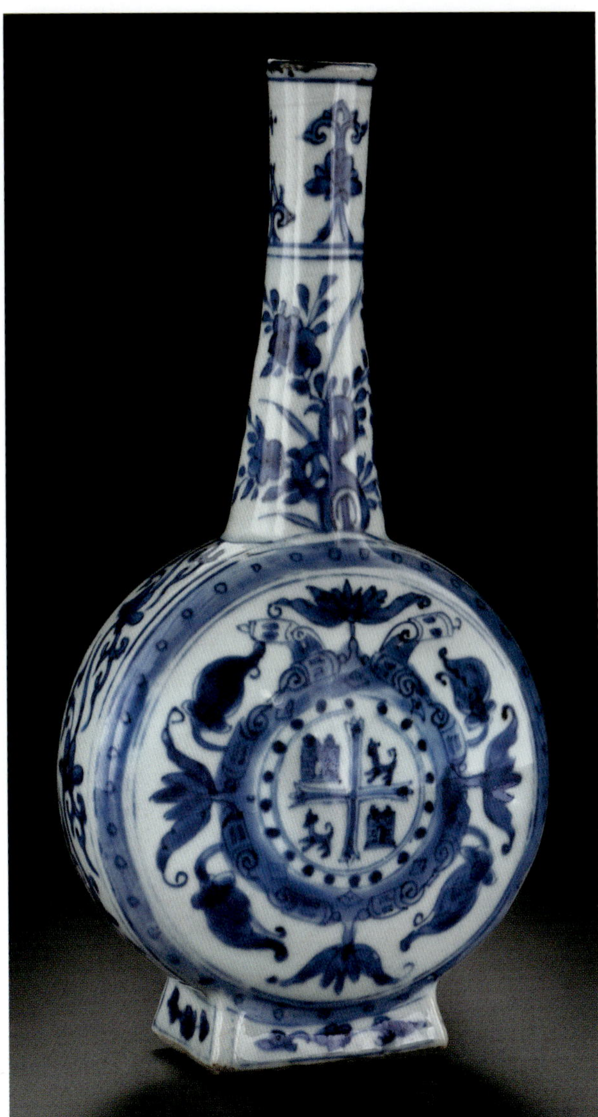

Plate 3.13 Pilgrim flask with the arms of King Philip II of Spain, *c.*1573–1620, porcelain, height 30 cm, China (Jingdezhen). The Peabody Essex Museum, Massachusetts, purchased 1988, inv. no.: E82416. Photo: © 2010 Peabody Essex Museum, Salem, MA. Photographed by Dennis Helmar.

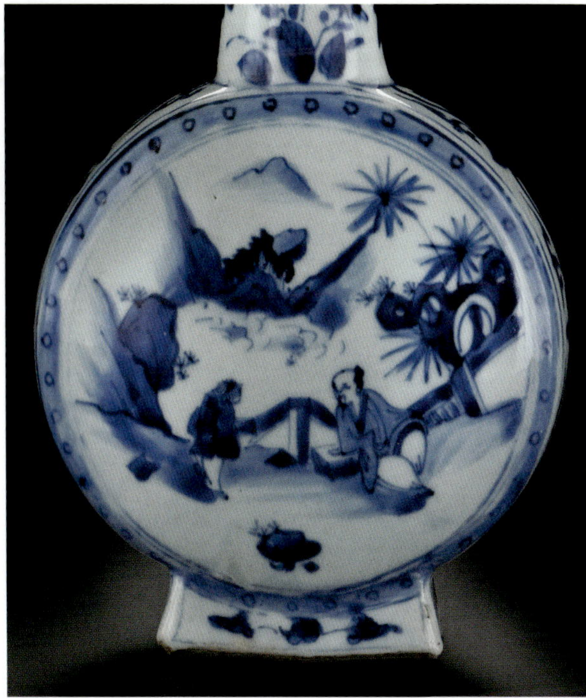

Plate 3.14 Reverse of pilgrim flask showing recumbent sage and an attendant on a terrace, *c.*1573–1620, porcelain, height 30 cm, China (Jingdezhen). The Peabody Essex Museum, Massachusetts, purchased 1988, inv. no.: E82416. Photo: © 2010 Peabody Essex Museum, Salem, MA. Photographed by Dennis Helmar.

interests of Spain's ruling family. Spain's expansion into the New World meant that a sovereign such as Philip had Peruvian and Mexican silver mines to plunder, as well as control over a significant maritime trade, which brought pepper and spices from India, silk and silver from China and Japan, and slaves from Africa. Philip II's collections reflected this power, containing over 1500 paintings, along with manuscripts, tapestries, jewellery, prints, books,

natural specimens and an incredible amount of porcelain, amounting to over 3000 pieces.

Veneto-Saracenic metalwork

One final example of transcultural production, that of metalwork, provides evidence of how Italian and Mamluk artisans worked closely together and were influenced mutually by each other. The provenance of numerous metalwork pieces in European collections has caused problems for scholars for centuries. Metalwork was traditionally a Mamluk craft, decorated with figural motifs and shaped into perfume burners, bowls and candlesticks. Many of these objects were made into shapes that would appeal to a European market, in some cases sporting European coats of arms. One instructive example is a candlestick with a coat of arms, probably belonging to the Boldu family, Venetian merchants active in trade with the Levant (Plate 3.15). A similar candlestick can be found depicted on the

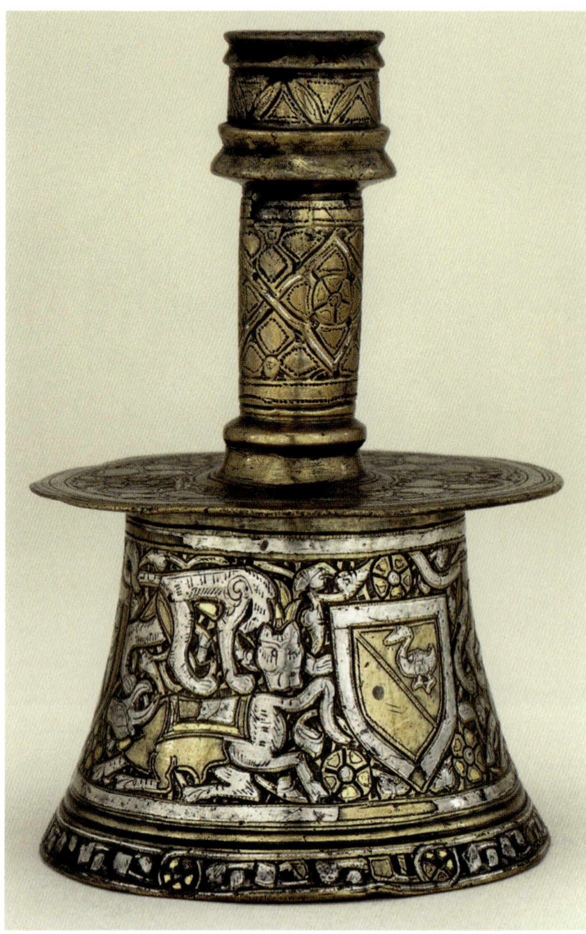

Plate 3.15 Candlestick, c.1423, cast brass engraved and inlaid with gold and silver, height 13 cm, Syria (Damascus). British Museum, London, 1878,1230.721. Photo: © The Trustees of the British Museum.

lower left shelf in Carpaccio's painting (see Plate 3.3). It is still widely debated by scholars how such works were produced. It has been suggested that they were produced by Mamluk/Muslim craftsmen in Venice or made abroad in Syria for European consumption; as such they are often referred to as 'Veneto-Saracenic'.[33] These hybrid objects demonstrate the interconnected modes of production between Italian and Mamluk craftsmen and suggest a coexistence and sharing of ideas across cultures. A very popular form was the perfume burner (Plate 3.16). The function of these types of objects could change depending on context: they were used for burning incense in the Islamic world, while in Italy they could perfume the air by being hung up, but they were also used as hand warmers and collectors' items.

This section has examined how objects coming from afar influenced local production and tastes. It was through the collection of foreign artefacts that individuals became interested in their materials, provenance and artistic qualities. They were prized alongside paintings by famous painters such as Titian and Bellini and must be studied together with these works to understand their larger significance. These objects were associated with the 'East' and were largely the result of centuries of cross-cultural relationships, but in the next section the 'discovery' of the New World will be examined to demonstrate how it affected collecting and contributed to knowledge of an expanding world.

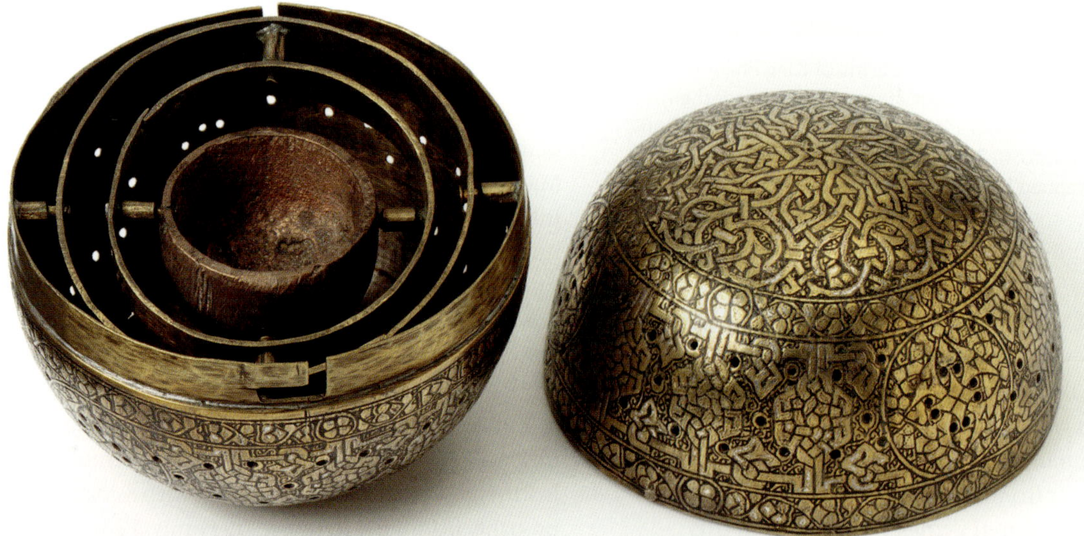

Plate 3.16 Perfume burner, c.1450–1500, brass, pierced, engraved and silver damascened with black lacquer infill, Italy (Venice) or Syria. Victoria and Albert Museum, London M.58-1952. Photo: © Victoria and Albert Museum, London.

4 Encountering the New World

With the discovery of the Americas by Columbus in 1492, new objects made their way into European collections, reflecting interests in this new continent, but also raising issues around how it was to be conceived, interpreted and understood. From the beginning, material objects became fundamental to exchanges between the New and Old Worlds. Following diplomatic customs of the Old World, Columbus presented gifts – 'some red caps and some glass beads … and many other things of little value' to the New World inhabitants, who in return presented 'parrots and cotton thread in balls, and spears and many other things'.[34] The numerous voyages that followed meant that thousands of American artefacts made their way into Europe before the eighteenth century, although fewer than 300 survive today.

What did Europeans make of these artefacts and how did they contribute to knowledge and conceptions of the New World? It is important to underline that for most Europeans the numerous tribes and peoples of the Americas were not distinguished from one another, resulting in a vague understanding of the indigenous peoples and an even more ambiguous conception of New World geography (particularly when the New World was still thought to be part of Asia). In Europe, a formalised concept of 'art' was only beginning to emerge at this time, as a result of new collecting practices and the emergence of art collections and academies of art. Thus the concepts of 'Amerindians' and 'Amerindian art' are European constructs – they will be used here to refer to the New World inhabitants and their material culture in a generalised sense, but they do not reflect the plurality of the peoples of what is now known as North and South America and their vast and diverse material cultures. These terms, however, do signal the European approach to collecting the products of this New World and point to the complexities of trying to apply European vocabulary such as 'art' retrospectively to works that in their original context would have had diverse functions. Artefacts such as featherworks and shields have been classified either as ethnographic specimens or works of art, when neither of those categories are entirely suitable. Examining Amerindian art thus provides a useful example, as Christian Feest has put it, to understand how 'changes in the perception of "Indians" and the conceptual

development of "art"' occurred.[35] Vocabulary that references the place of manufacture can be extremely misleading in Renaissance documents, as is demonstrated by the use of the terms 'Indiana', 'alla Indiana' and 'dell'Indie' for a wide range of objects that sometimes came from India, but often referred to items from Africa, China, Japan, the Levant and even Europe.[36] This semantic confusion reflects a geographic confusion, an issue that will be underlined throughout this section.

The response to Amerindian artefacts and the reasons for collecting them varied across Europe. The economic and political power of Spain's ruling family, the Habsburgs, and their close associations with the explorers of the New World meant that they were some of the most active collectors of American objects. Their collections demonstrate how interest and curiosity in the world intersected with expansion and a need to reflect the empire's dominions. One particularly instructive example is the collector Margaret of Austria, Duchess of Savoy (r.1507–15, 1518–30), Emperor Charles V's regent and governor general of the Netherlands, who held significant political power in Europe in the sixteenth century.[37] She had a large art collection, ranging from devotional paintings to dynastic portraits to New World artefacts, as well as a range of *naturalia*, including corals, precious stones and a bird of paradise. The changes to her collections over time reflect shifts in perceptions of the New World and Europe's role in shaping its destiny. Margaret's marriage to Juan, the heir of Ferdinand II of Aragon (r.1479–1516) and Isabella I of Castile (r.1474–1504), required her to live at the royal court in Spain from March 1497 to September 1499, a particularly important time for exploration in the New World. It was at this time that the Spanish monarchy was marvelling at and reflecting on Columbus's first two voyages to the 'Indies' (1492 and 1496), from which he returned with New World treasures. Margaret would have also been at court when Columbus prepared for and departed on his third voyage in April 1498.

In 1507 Margaret was made Regent of the Netherlands, ruling on behalf of her brother's son Charles (later Emperor Charles V). By this time she was living in the Palace of Savoy in Mechelen: her first husband Juan had died, as had her second, Philibert II, Duke of Savoy (r.1497–1504). Two inventories were taken of her collections in the palace in Mechelen – one in 1516 and one between 1523 and 1524 – and the differences between the two suggest that her collection of New World artefacts grew significantly during this period. This is due to the fact that many of her New World objects were received as gifts from her nephew, Emperor Charles V, in 1523. These artefacts were part of the treasures the explorer Hernán Cortés had presented to Charles, originally received from the Aztec ruler Moctezuma II (r.1502–20) in 1519. Margaret's collection of New World artefacts included ceremonial costumes and shields decorated with plumes, gold and gems, as well as necklaces, bracelets, feather fans, a staff and a sword, among other things amounting to 170 Amerindian artefacts in total in her possession.[38]

Margaret's artefacts were part of a targeted display of the treasures of the New World and provide a useful example in understanding how the larger public came to know about this new continent and its material and visual culture. First exhibited in Seville, the gifts from Cortés were exhibited across Spain before they were displayed in Brussels in 1520. How did Europeans describe these artefacts? Those who had a chance to see these fantastic objects, ranging from jewels, silver, gold, shields, clothes, necklaces and feather objects, were astounded and, in many cases, at a loss for words. After seeing the gifts in Spain, Peter Martyr, a historian at the Spanish court, wrote: 'I do not know how to describe the panaches, the plumes, the feather fans. If ever artists of this sort were ever ingenious, then these savages certainly are … in my opinion, I have never seen anything whose beauty can more delight the human eye.'[39]

Featherwork

Peter Martyr, like many Europeans, was struck by the featherwork (sometimes referred to as feather mosaics), a particular art form that came to be associated with the New World. Featherwork became the material means – something tangible – through which Europeans could begin to envisage this new continent.[40] Featherworking was a refined art made by *amantecas* (feather artists) in Meso-America (the mix of cultures including the Maya, Mexica and Mixtecs located in what is now Mexico and Central America). A featherwork shield (Plate 3.17) dating from around

1520, once believed to have been one of the items gifted by Cortés, was one of many shields travelling in early Spanish shipments from Meso-America.[41] The shield's designs are made out of a variety of American feathers, which gives it its bright colours, glued on to agave paper (a plant indigenous to North America, from which tequila is made). The animal and the glyph exiting its mouth were symbolic of war in Aztec Mexico. European observers, however, would not have picked up on this symbolism, but probably prized it for its colours, skill and New World origins.

Comparing the shield (Plate 3.17) with a featherwork that incorporates Christian motifs (Plate 3.18) demonstrates how quickly artists in the New World began creating combined European/Meso-American objects. While both featherworks are certainly different, there are some similarities: both combine text/glyph and image and both convey a symbolic meaning. The commissioning of works of art in the New World employed an Old World practice, which customised New World objects to suit European needs. These novel objects, however, were the beginning of a new conception of, and mandate for, the Americas. In 1523 for example, the Franciscan Fray Pedro of Ghent travelled to the Americas with the idea that through the use of images and the training of local artists to produce these kinds of hybrid Christian-Aztec objects, he would convert and Christianise this New World.

In the case of Plate 3.18, the material of featherwork is certainly Meso-American, as is the technical skill involved, but the subject matter is European and in particular Christian. For Cortés, these artefacts represented the coming together of these two cultures and his successful campaigns in the New World – no longer simply voyages of discovery but potentially of possession, control and a means of displaying European power. One scholar, Alessandra Russo, has suggested Christianised featherwork is categorised not as European or Meso-American, but as 'Cortesian' to reflect how such objects were made in response to the artistic world introduced by the Spaniards and to underline the political processes of interaction in the creation of New Spain.[42] Interpreting this object as a hybrid can operate on two levels: one might choose to see it as a visual encounter between two artistic traditions, but one might also choose to read it

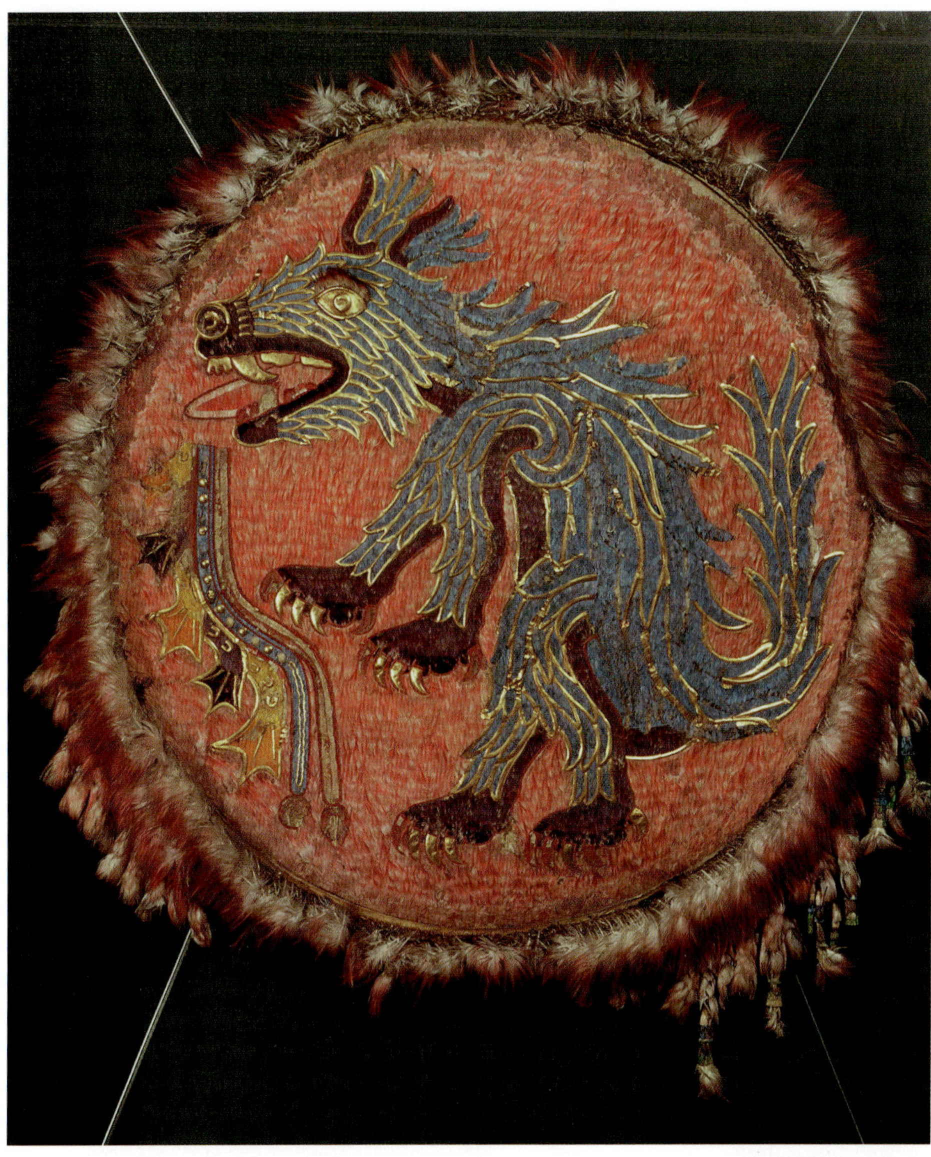

Plate 3.17 Featherwork shield, *c.*1520, feathers, sheet-gold, agave paper, leather and reed, Mexico. Weltmuseum, Vienna. Photo: Bridgeman Images.

according to certain political and religious agendas and emphasise the unequal power relationships at play.[43]

By the second decade of the sixteenth century, featherwork was an extremely highly sought item among collectors and princes and resulted in many being shipped from the New World. For example, a tribute list from the 1520s listed 117 featherworks, including 68 shields, capes, garments, headdresses, fans and figures, which were then given to churches, convents and individuals in Spain.[44] But the collection of featherwork was not restricted to Spain: Cosimo I de' Medici (r.1537–74) owned a number of featherworks and New World objects in Florence,

while they were also largely collected in Germany and Austria.[45] The collection of featherwork in Europe also raises questions around how to approach interpretation: did this reflect an early modern interest to syncretise the New and Old Worlds, or were these works exoticised and seen as marvels of nature?[46]

As these New World works were increasingly collected and celebrated across Europe, the question around their makers and their 'humanity' became central to Spanish power in the New World. In 1537, Pope Paul III (r.1534–49) issued a papal bull that decreed that Amerindians should not be enslaved and had rights to their own property, declaring that 'Indians

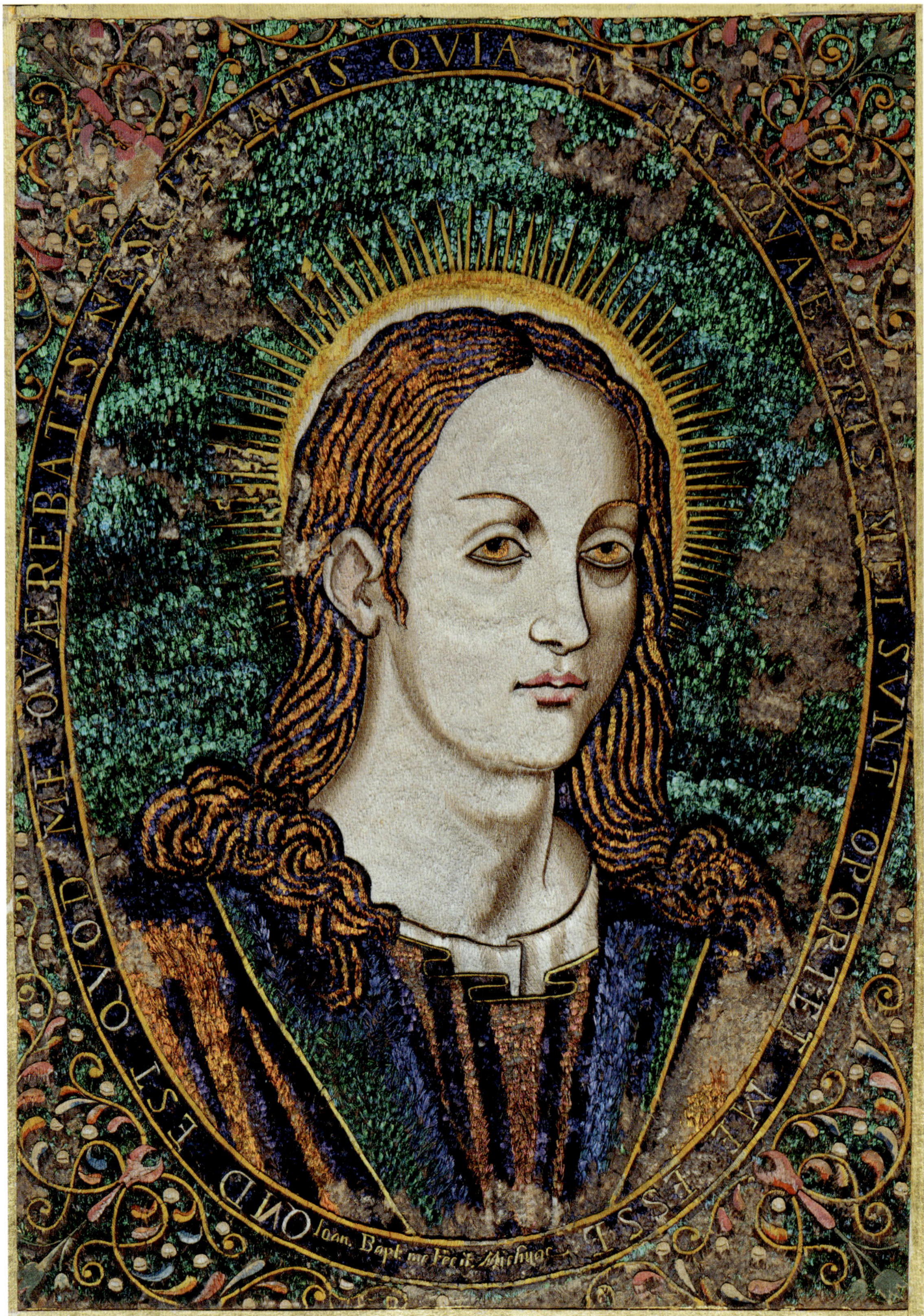

Plate 3.18 Juan Bautista Cuiris, *Portrait of Christ*, c.1550–80, feathers on copper support, 25 × 18 cm, Mexico (Michoacán). Kunsthistorisches Museum, Vienna. Photo: KHM-Museumsverband.

and all other people who may later be discovered by Christians' were endowed with 'nature and faculties'.[47] This decree was nullified two years later and led to numerous heated discussions resulting in economic and practical repercussions in the New World itself, while at home in Europe it had a role to play in conflicting and contradictory perceptions and representations of New World peoples.

5 Representing nature

This chapter so far has looked at how material objects from both the 'East' and 'West' were collected and how the interests in the New World resulted in a less clear line between subjects and objects. This last section will now turn to examine how nature figured in collecting habits, the pursuit of knowledge and expansion. A whole new approach to nature emerged largely due to the fundamental changes that took place in the fifteenth century, from the discovery of new continents and new peoples to the establishment of new trading routes.[48] This interest in the natural world was not only in the purview of princes and discoverers. In the sixteenth century, there emerged growing networks of humanists, courtiers, diplomats, merchants and artists, who were keen on obtaining and sharing news on the latest discoveries of people and the flora and fauna of the New World, in addition to procuring interesting natural specimens from within Europe and as far afield as India.[49] Acquaintance and engagement with nature thus varied, from the prized elephants and giraffes that were gifted among princes to the smaller specimens circulating among middle-class collectors, to the representations of nature and peoples found in the sketchbooks of artists such as Albrecht Dürer and Leonardo da Vinci.

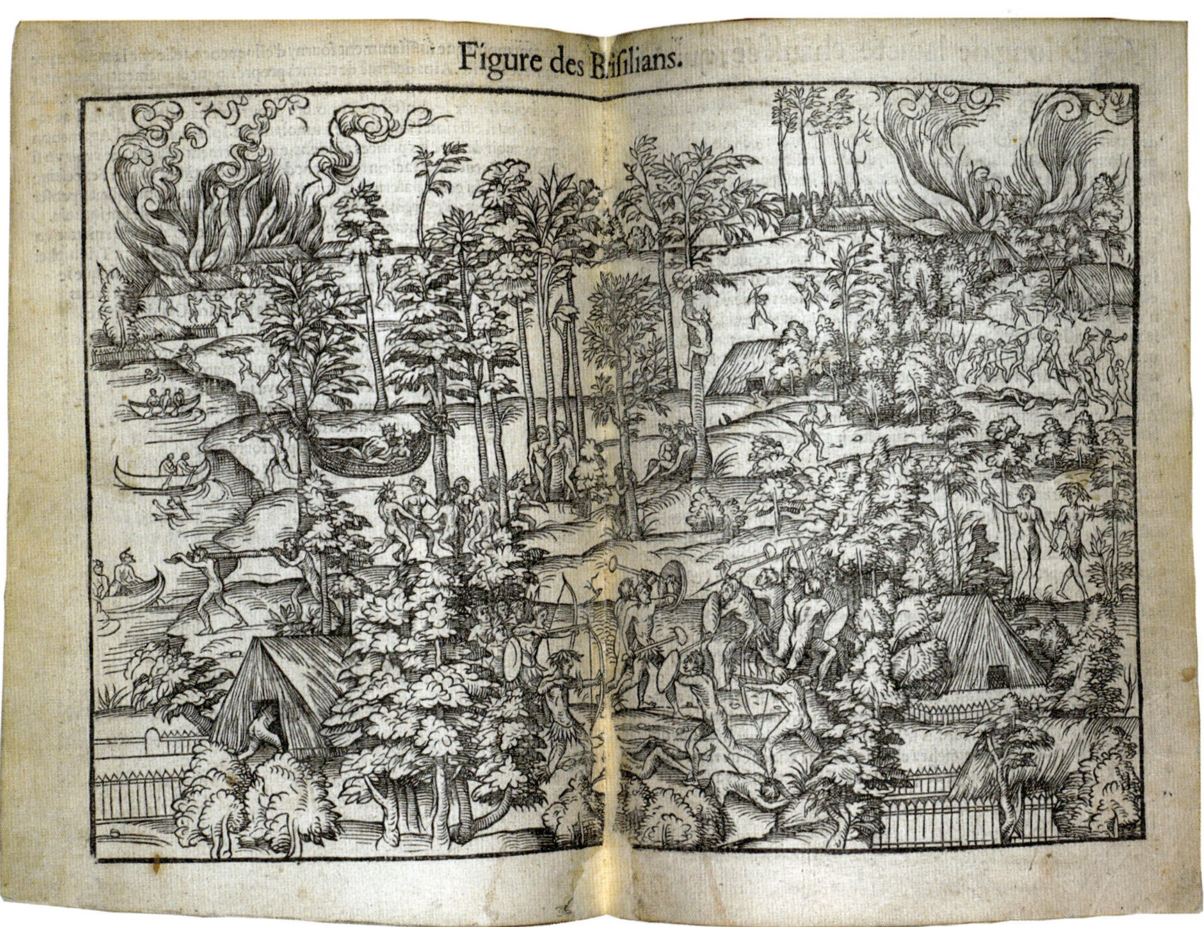

Plate 3.19 'Figure des Brasilians', woodcut in *C'est la deduction du sumptueux ordre, plainsantz spectacles…*, Rouen, 1551. The British Library, London, 811.d.26. Photo: The British Library Board.

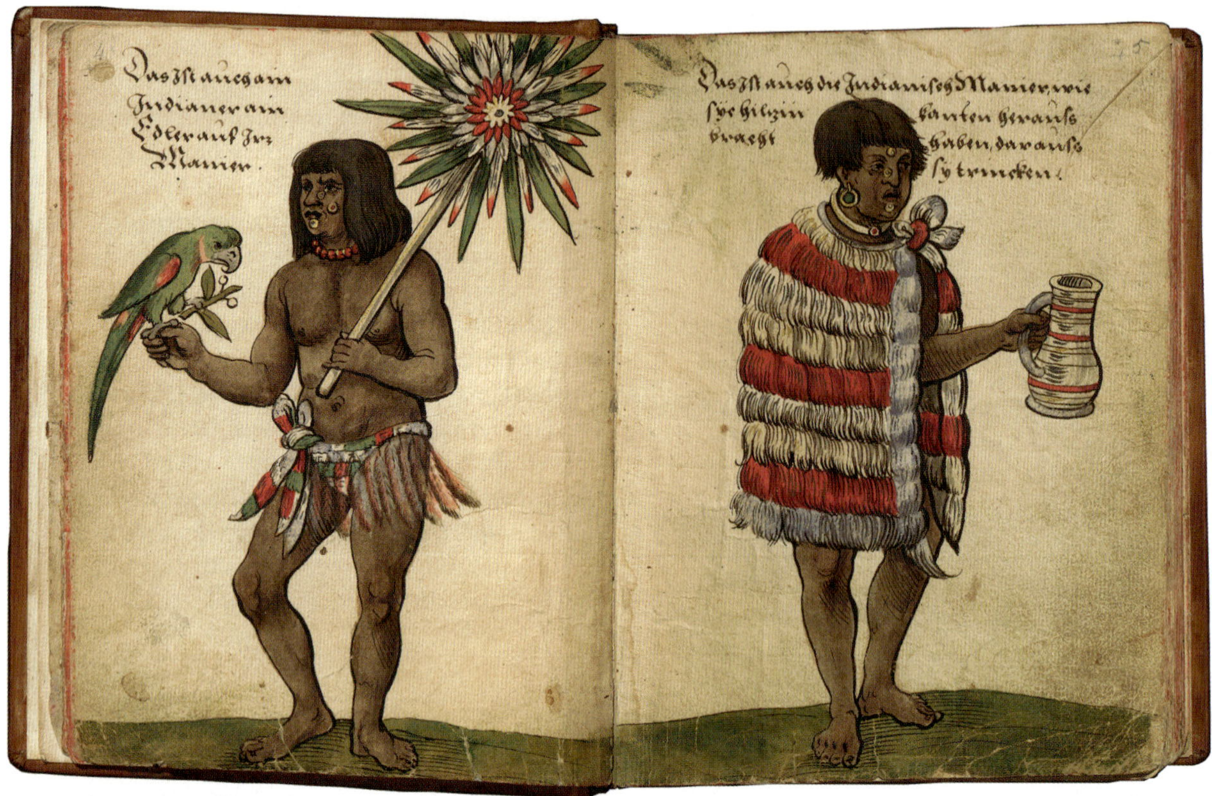

Plate 3.20 Christoph Weiditz, illustration of Amerindians, 1529, watercolour on cotton and linen paper, double page spread, 15 × 40 cm. Germanisches Nationalmuseum, Nuremberg. Photo: GMN.

With the discovery of the Americas, Europeans now found themselves having to engage with a new-found cultural diversity, as well as new flora and fauna which were difficult to describe within the confines of European categories and concepts.[50] As more and more European countries attempted to claim a part of the New World for themselves, a greater interest grew in having indigenous peoples of the Americas sent back to Europe to sovereigns where they could be put on show as signs of possession, along with the material artefacts acquired. Representations of New World inhabitants provide less an ethnographic documentation of Amerindians and more of an insight into Europeans' shifting conceptions of themselves in relation to the wider world. Before 1492, mythic constructions of monstrous inhabitants at the edge of the world resulted in a gamut of representations, from wild men to Edenic images of Adam and Eve (see Plate 0.8).[51] In a time when the geographic specificity of the New World was still undergoing definition, New World inhabitants became represented through generalised types, drawing on existing concepts, with little attention to factual accounts and first-hand experiences. This was not aided by early written descriptions of the New World that confused older associations of the East with the Americas.

In 1550, a Brazilian village was reconstructed for the triumphal entry of King Henri II (r.1547–59) into Rouen, France. Here 300 naked men and women (50 of whom were real Amerindians) 'performed' New World life by hunting and gathering food, complete with a mock battle scene. An engraving of the 'village' draws on pre-existing concepts of Paradise fused with recycled images of the New World.[52] Here 'Brazilians' canoe, make fire, camp, fight and engage in amorous activities; dotted throughout the image are identifiable 'Adam and Eve' types (Plate 3.19). Charles V also used indigenous peoples (probably Aztecs) as performers at his court, who were drawn by the German artist Christoph Weiditz in 1529 (Plate 3.20). In these depictions, feathers are used to indicate the performers' New World identity. In these examples, the collection of nature and courtly entertainment became fused; history and natural history became one and the same thing, allowing rulers to write history by drawing on biblical imagery of Paradise with their New World conquests, creating a new articulation of the world and their role within it.

Weiditz's figures also underline how clothing, ornaments and weapons – that is artefacts that were making their way into collections – soon became the key signifiers of the New World, rather than physiognomic characteristics such as facial features.[53] These objects came to be incorporated into representations of 'Calicut' by German artists, thus suggesting to viewers that India could be reached by going either east or west. Calicut was the old designation for the present state of Kerala in India, where Vasco da Gama had landed in 1498, but the term was often used to refer to unspecified locations in both the Americas and India. Amerigo Vespucci had argued that the lands discovered in the west were indeed a New World and not part of Asia, but this was still widely debated. Confusion thus was widespread about where 'Indians' were actually from, which was confounded by visual generalisations and textual tales, so for the early sixteenth century, the distinction between the Americas and Asia is anachronistic.[54]

Drawings by Hans Burgkmair the Elder demonstrate the cross-fertilisation of New World objects and clothing with representations of the peoples of Africa and Asia. In one drawing (Plate 3.21), dating from around 1520, New World feather coverings are accompanied by a Brazilian club and an Aztec turquoise shield (similar to one housed in the Weltmuseum, Vienna today), yet the man is depicted with African physiognomy. This palimpsest of objects from all over the Americas demonstrates a general trend: New World objects that were exhibited, collected and represented confused rather than clarified existing understandings of peoples from around the world. The anthropologist William Sturtevant has employed the term 'Tupinambization' to refer to the erroneous use of feathers in a wide range of imagery to signal the New World (Tupinambá was a term to reference the people of Brazil).[55] The use of feathers as a hallmark was often an indication of larger cultural misunderstandings.

This strange mix and miscomprehension also appears in Dürer's descriptions of the things he saw and acquired in the Low Countries. In 1520, Dürer, among other artists, was witness to the display of New World artefacts sent back to Europe by Cortés and he recorded in his notebook a sense of wonder and admiration for the artistry of the peoples of the Americas. Besides seeing the Mexican treasures from Cortés, Dürer also acquired exotic animals, Chinese porcelain, a Turkish whip, a 'Calecutish wooden shield', 'several feathers, Calecutish things', '2 Calecutish ivory salt cellars', 'Calecutish clothes, one of them silk', and a 'small Calecutish target, made of fishskin and two gloves for their fighting'.[56] Out of all the items, the shields and cloth were probably the only things that were Asian; the salt cellars were likely Afro-Portuguese, while the feathers were most probably New World artefacts.

Salt cellars are particularly intriguing objects as they were among many ivory carvings that were produced in Africa for European consumption, as a result of Portuguese trade and travel in Africa (beginning in the 1470s).[57] Once in Europe, they were collected as prestige items, used at feasts or proudly displayed in the collections of rulers from Florence to Dresden. The three main areas of production of ivories occurred in the regions of the Congo, Benin and Sierra Leone, all of which had different and varying degrees of interaction with the Portuguese.[58] Many of these ivory sculptures included portraits of the Portuguese depicted from an African perspective, and thus provide insight into how Europeans were represented and imagined. The Benin salt cellars in particular depict specific Portuguese dress that suggests close contact with Europeans, while also conveying symbolic motifs (Plate 3.22). For example, the Portuguese were often depicted with gaunt, aged faces, in contrast to the idealised youthful faces of Benin royalty, suggesting that the Portuguese were sickly or close to death. In African belief, bodies of water were passages to the afterlife. As navigators who had arrived by sea, the Portuguese were thus interpreted as ancestral spirits, but these religious connotations from the carvers would not have been recognised by the European collector. Some African ivories also incorporated European motifs and thus can be seen as hybrid objects, reflecting the interaction between the Portuguese and Africa, which has resulted in the label 'Afro-Portuguese ivories'. These ivories were among many items of commerce that the Portuguese brought back to Europe, naming them

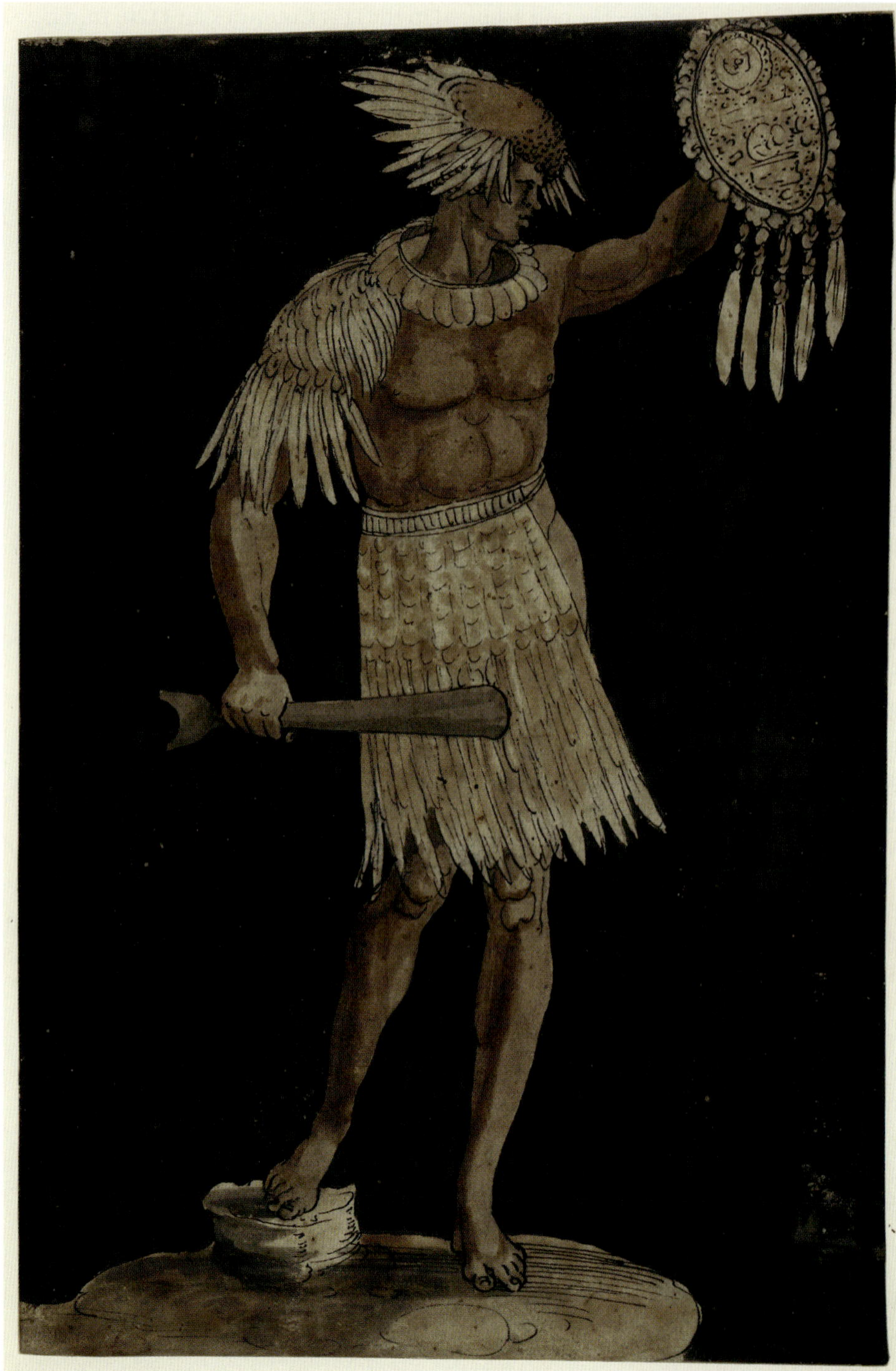

Plate 3.21 Hans Burgkmair the Elder, *Youth Dressed in a Feather Skirt*, c.1520, pen and black ink, with brown, black and grey wash on paper, 24 × 16 cm. British Museum, London, SL,5218.128. Photo: © The Trustees of the British Museum.

peca (item of trade). The same term was used for slaves, however, which points to the blurring of subjects and objects and the acceptance at that time that Africans as slaves could be traded and sold just as any other commodity, something that would set into motion the slave trade for centuries to follow. In this case, the relationship undergirding hybridity resulted in sinister consequences.

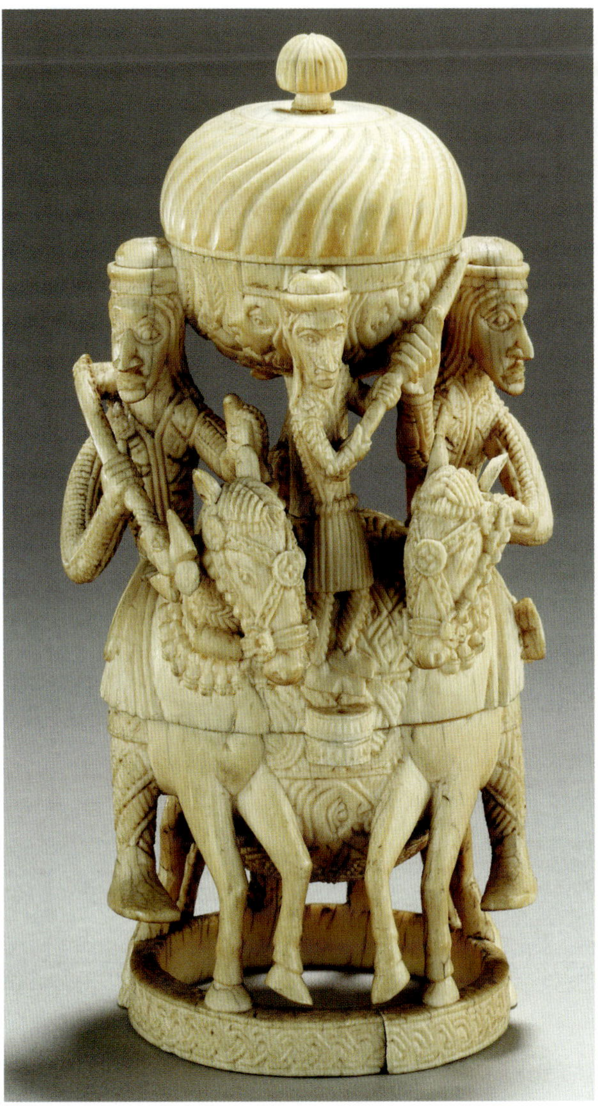

Plate 3.22 Benin salt cellar, c.1525–1600, ivory, height 22 cm, Africa (present-day Nigeria). British Museum, London, Af1856,0623.162a-c. Photo: © The Trustees of the British Museum.

Exotic animals

Aside from feathers and peoples being traded, interest in understanding the wider world resulted in the exchange of animals between rulers, from giraffes and elephants to parrots and monkeys.[59] Collections of exotic animals, known as menageries, extended the microcosm/macrocosm analogy of the *studiolo* by bringing collecting habits outdoors and reflected a ruler's power and his or her diplomatic ties. The most famous of these exotic gifts was arguably the rhinoceros that was gifted to King Manuel I of Portugal

(r.1495–1521) from the Sultan Muzaffar II of Gujarat (r.1511–26) in 1515. Manuel in turn sent the large animal as a diplomatic gift to the Medici Pope Leo X (r.1513–21). Unfortunately it never made it to Rome alive as the ship that was carrying it sank, but it was reported to be washed ashore and stuffed and sent on to Rome in February 1516. In its short stay on European shores, the animal created a sensation, particularly because it was the first rhinoceros to reach Europe since Roman times. The animal was also made famous by its portrait executed by Dürer in the form of a woodcut (Plate 3.23).

Dürer never set eyes on the creature, but instead probably copied the image and the description from a now lost report. When describing his drawing of it, however, he employed the term 'abkunterfet' in German that implied 'copied from life' as a way to imply he had actually seen it and to create a sense of a first-hand encounter.[60] The animal's shape is fairly typical of a rhinoceros, but Dürer has portrayed him wearing strange armour and sporting fish scales and an odd tail, reflecting the artist's unfamiliarity with the animal. Nevertheless, the woodcut soon circulated across Europe and was followed by two later editions in 1540 and 1550, serving as the main source for depictions of the species of animal for centuries to come. While Dürer did not portray the rhinoceros from life, he did sketch a number of animals that he had seen at the royal zoo in Brussels, including several drawings of lions, a baboon and a lynx (Plate 3.24). In these drawings, Dürer has paid attention to the different types of fur of each animal, as well as their shapes. In the case of the baboon, he added watercolour and noted down the weight and size too. Like the depictions of New World inhabitants, some representations of nature accurately reflected real specimens, while others were often a combination of what was known and what was observed. Dürer himself received gifts of nature: coral, coconuts and feathers, snail shells, a tortoise shell, a large fish scale and precious stones.[61]

The rhinoceros also underlines how keen rulers were to collect rare animals. Once the sea route to Asia was opened by Vasco da Gama, many exotic specimens came through the Portuguese. At least 13 Asian elephants were imported into Portugal, some of which Manuel I sent on to other European rulers as gifts as examples of his power and overseas dominions. The

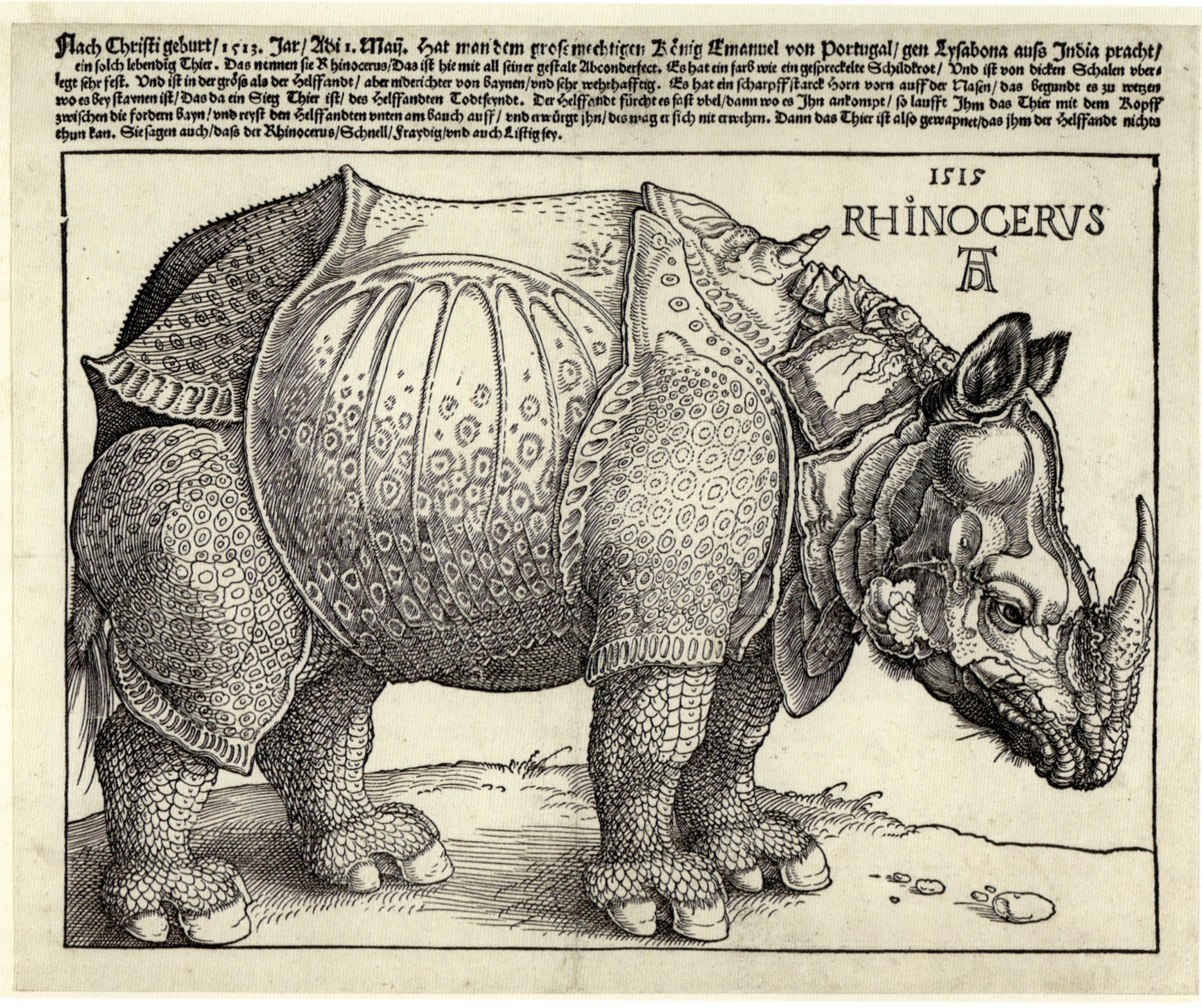

Plate 3.23 Albrecht Dürer, *Rhinocerus* (Rhinoceros), 1515, broadside print of woodcut and letterpress, 21 × 30 cm. British Museum, London, 1895,0122.714. Photo: © The Trustees of the British Museum.

most famous of these was Hanno the elephant who, accompanied by his Hindu mahout, was sent to Pope Leo X. Catherine of Austria (r.1525–57), Queen of Portugal and wife of Manuel's son, King John III (r.1521–57), became renowned for her ability to procure rarities, including exotic animals, through her vast network of merchants, agents, viceroys and household officials scattered throughout Portuguese trading networks as far as Goa, Cochin and Malacca. She herself kept a large menagerie, which symbolically reflected her and her husband's rule over the flora and fauna of the world, as well as their ability to domesticate nature. [62]

Effigies of these exotic animals were also highly sought, as a way to make their presence more permanent. For those who did not own or did not have access to the live animals, it offered a chance to see them. In the early sixteenth century, Duke Alfonso d'Este of Ferrara was particularly keen on procuring a portrait of Hanno the elephant, writing numerous times to acquire it. In further hopes of obtaining the effigy, Alfonso provided a portrait of a tiger from his menagerie, as a pre-emptive counter-gift. [63] Like his interests in Chinese porcelain, Alfonso's predilection for collecting foreign animals is evident in another painting commissioned for his *camerino* where cheetahs from his menagerie are depicted (see Plate 3.12). Alfonso's father, Ercole I d'Este (r.1471–1505), also kept a menagerie including an elephant, which he had received from Cypriot merchants, while his mother, Duchess Eleonora d'Aragona, had a giraffe

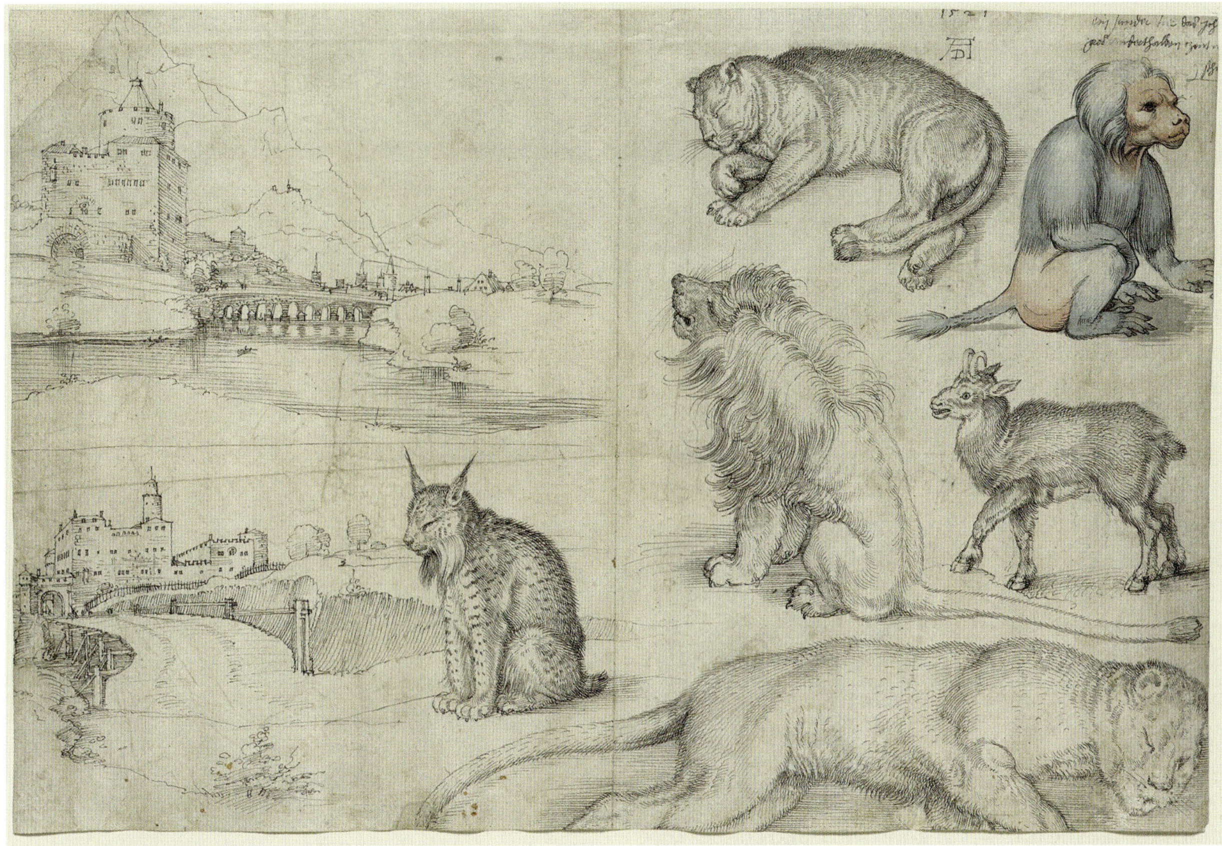

Plate 3.24 Albrecht Dürer, sketches of animals and landscapes, 1521, pen and black ink with blue, grey and rose wash on paper, 27 × 40 cm. Sterling and Francine Clark Art Institute, Williamstown, Massachusetts. Photo: Bridgeman Images.

depicted on the walls of her balcony in Ferrara. Well known was Lorenzo de' Medici's giraffe, gifted by Sultan Qaytbay, who gained a reputation in Florence, depicted in numerous paintings of the time, including a fresco by Giorgio Vasari in the Palazzo Vecchio (see Plate 3.6).[64] Such a painting, executed after Lorenzo's death, worked to bolster Medici power and underline the family's ability to court favour with foreign rulers, as well as tame nature.

Artists played an important role in the study of nature and their representations of nature could be based on first-hand encounters or based on alternative sources, such as stuffed specimens, oral or written accounts and depictions by other artists, or, in some cases, a mixture of reality and fiction. Art rendered knowledge visible and images could generate a new understanding of the natural world, but not always a completely accurate one.

Conclusion

This chapter has looked at how the practices of collecting and the objects collected were not simply reflective of larger global relationships, but were also instrumental in those exchanges. In some cases, it was the spaces of collection and the knowledge produced there that sought to define the terms of those relationships. The chapter has also underlined the complexities of interaction, from the proffering of diplomatic gifts between European princes and their Islamic neighbours to the display of New World artefacts and peoples, something that would in turn influence new conceptions of what it meant to collect. The emphasis on the universality of the collection became more important in the sixteenth century, when overseas expansion began to be dominated by specific countries and ruling families. As control of trade routes and lands became more and more restricted to the powerful few, collections opened up the opportunity for individuals to partake in some form of possession of foreign lands, even if it meant simply admiring a print of a New World inhabitant. These encounters through objects also gave rise to greater possibilities of cultural transfers and in turn multiple hybridities.

By focusing on the objects of exchange this study has pointed to the ways those objects could represent divisions as well as points of contact. Interaction with foreign objects and representations could clarify and articulate difference, but just as easily also promote confusion and misunderstandings. The term hybridity has been used throughout to highlight the complicated nature of transcultural relationships and the material evidence of cultural encounter. Cultural transfers and translations are processual – they occur over time and space. It is important to remember to pay particular attention to the specifics of time and place and not to apply retrospective or anachronistic readings onto things of the past. The examples studied here have shown that curiosity could lead to technical innovations, the transfer of knowledge and coexistence of different faiths and cultures, but that there was also a darker side to curiosity, which led to the objectification and in some cases the annihilation of entire cultures.

Notes

[1] Farago, 2010; Molà and Ajmar-Wollheim, 2011 (extract reproduced in Newall, 2017, pp. 92–102).

[2] Campbell, 2006; Clark, 2013; Thornton, 1997; Findlen, 1989; Christian, 2010.

[3] North, 2010; Shelton, 1994.

[4] Frankopan, 2016; Contadini, 2010; Contadini, 2013; Golombek, Mason and Bailey, 1996.

[5] Jordan Gschwend and Lowe, 2015.

[6] Kauffman, 1994.

[7] Impey and MacGregor, 1997.

[8] Mack, 2002; Thornton, 1997; Ruvoldt, 2006.

[9] Fortini Brown, 1999; Campbell, 2006, pp. 32–5; Nagel and Wood, 2005.

[10] Alberti, 1969, p. 209.

[11] Vasari, 1868.

[12] Borghini, 2007, p. 50.

[13] Stapleford, 2013, p. 96.

[14] Carr, 1997; Lightbown, 1986, pp. 445–6.

[15] Thornton, 1997, pp. 78–82.

[16] Thornton, 1997, p. 80.

[17] Um and Clark, 2016.

[18] Behrens-Abouseif, 2014, pp. 113–14; Mack, 2002, p. 23; Newall, 2017, pp. 62–4.

[19] Meadow, 2002.

[20] Kerr, 2004; Carswell, 2000; Finlay, 1998; Finlay, 2010; Mack, 2002.

[21] Fusco and Corti, 2006.

[22] Hess, 2004b.

[23] Pierson, 2012; Pierson, 2013.

[24] Mack, 2002, pp. 98–104.

[25] Syson and Thornton, 2001, pp. 201–4, 215.

[26] Colantuono, 2010; Fehl, 1973; Hope, 2012; Hope, 1971a; Hope, 1971b.

[27] Giovio, 1553, pp. 18–19.

[28] Hess, 2004a.

[29] Carswell, 1993.

[30] This is part of a current project I will be publishing shortly. Eleonora's inventory can be found in the Archivio di Stato di Modena.

[31] Marchesi, 2012.

[32] Finlay, 2010.

[33] Behrens-Abouseif, 2005; Contadini, 2006; Contadini, 2010; Spallanzani, 1978, pp. 47–8.

[34] Feest, 1993, p. 2; Mullaney, 2000.

[35] Feest, 1993, p. 2.

[36] Markey and Keating, 2010.

[37] MacDonald, 2002.

[38] MacDonald, 2002.

[39] MacDonald, 2002, p. 660.

[40] Russo, Fane and Wolf, 2015.

[41] Feest, 1990; Russo, 2011.

[42] Russo, 2011.

[43] Dean and Leibsohn, 2003.

[44] Shelton, 1994.

[45] Markey, 2016.

[46] Russo, Fane and Wolf, 2015, p. 13.

[47] Farago, 2010, p. 25.

[48] Eichberger, 1998.

[49] Findlen, 1994.

[50] Feest, 2014.

[51] Milbrath, 1991.

[52] Yaya, 2008.

[53] Mason, 1994.

[54] Feest, 2014; Leitch, 2009.

[55] Leitch, 2009; Sturtevant, 1988.

[56] Feest, 2014, p. 294; Dürer, Troutman and Alexander, 1971; Newall, 2017, pp. 57–9.

[57] Lowe, 2015.

[58] Blier, 1993.

[59] Lach, 1970, pp. 123–78.

[60] Silver, 2009; Smith and Findlen, 2002, p. 2.

[61] Eichberger, 1998.
[62] Jordan Gschwend, 1995; Pérez de Tudela and Gschwend, 2007.
[63] Shearman, 1987.
[64] Joost-Gaugier, 1987.

Bibliography

Alberti, L. B. (1969) *The Family in Renaissance Florence/I libri della famiglia*, Columbia, SC, University of South Carolina Press.

Behrens-Abouseif, D. (2005) 'Veneto-Saracenic metalware', *Mamluk Studies Review*, vol. 9, no. 2, pp. 147–72.

Behrens-Abouseif, D. (2014) *Practising Diplomacy in the Mamluk Sultanate: Gifts and Material Culture in the Medieval Islamic World*, London, I.B. Tauris.

Blier, S. P. (1993) 'Imaging otherness in ivory: African portrayals of the Portuguese *c.*1492', *The Art Bulletin*, vol. 75, no. 3, pp. 375–96.

Borghini, R. (2007) *Il riposo*, Toronto, University of Toronto Press.

Campbell, S. (2006) *The Cabinet of Eros: Renaissance Mythological Painting and the Studiolo of Isabella d'Este*, New Haven, CT and London, Yale University Press.

Carr, D. W. (1997) *Andrea Mantegna, the Adoration of the Magi*, Los Angeles, CA, J. Paul Getty Museum.

Carswell, J. (1993) '"The feast of the gods": the porcelain trade between China, Istanbul and Venice', *Asian Affairs*, vol. 24, no. 2, pp. 180–5.

Carswell, J. (2000) *Blue and White: Chinese Porcelain Around the World*, London, British Museum Press.

Christian, K. W. (2010) *Empire without End: Antiquities Collections in Renaissance Rome, c.1350–1527*, London and New Haven, CT, Yale University Press.

Clark, L. R. (2013) 'Collecting, exchange, and sociability in the Renaissance studiolo', *Journal of the History of Collections*, vol. 25, no. 2, pp. 171–84.

Colantuono, A. (2010) *Titian, Colonna and the Renaissance Science of Procreation: Equicola's Seasons of Desire*, Farnham and Burlington, VT, Ashgate Publishing.

Contadini, A. (2006) 'Middle-Eastern objects', in Ajmar-Wollheim, M. and Dennis, F. (eds) *At Home in Renaissance Italy*, London, Victoria and Albert Museum, pp. 308–21.

Contadini, A. (2010) 'Translocation and transformation: some Middle Eastern objects in Europe', in Saurma-Jeltsch, L. E. and Eisenbess, A. (eds) *The Power of Things and the Flow of Cultural Transformations: Art and Culture between Europe and Asia*, Berlin, Deutscher Kunstverlag, pp. 42–64.

Contadini, A. (2013) 'Sharing a taste?: material acquisitions and intellectual curiosity around the Mediterranean, from the eleventh to the sixteenth century', in Norton, C. and Contadini, A. (eds) *The Renaissance and the Ottoman World*, Farnham and Burlington, VT, Ashgate Publishing, pp. 23–61.

Dean, C. and Leibsohn, D. (2003) 'Hybridity and its discontents: considering visual culture in colonial Spanish America', *Colonial Latin American Review*, vol. 12, no. 1, pp. 5–35.

Dürer, A. (1971) *Diary of His Journey to the Netherlands, 1520–21* (trans. P. Troutman and S. Alexander), London, Lund Humphries.

Eichberger, D. (1998) '*Naturalia* and *artefacta*: Dürer's nature drawings and early collecting', in Eichberger, D. and Zika, C. (eds) *Dürer and His Culture*, Cambridge, Cambridge University Press, pp. 13–37.

Farago, C. J. (2010) 'On the peripatetic life of objects in the era of globalisation', in Sheriff, M. D. (ed.) *Cultural Contact and the Making of European Art since the Age of Exploration*, Chapel Hill, NC, University of North Carolina Press, pp. 17–41.

Feest, C. F. (1990) 'Vienna's Mexican treasures: Aztec, Mixtec, and Tarascan works from sixteenth century Austrian collections', *Archiv für Völkerkunde*, vol. 44, pp. 1–63.

Feest, C. F. (1993) 'European collecting of American Indian artefacts and art', *Journal of the History of Collections*, vol. 5, no. 1, pp. 1–11.

Feest, C. F. (2014) 'The people of Calicut: objects, texts, and images in the age of proto-ethnography', *Boletim do Museu Paraense Emilio Goeldi*, vol. 9, no. 2, pp. 287–303.

Fehl, P. (1973) 'The worship of Bacchus and Venus in Bellini's and Titian's bacchanals for Alfonso d'Este', *Studies in the History of Art*, vol. 6, pp. 37–95.

Findlen, P. (1989) 'The museum: its classical etymology and Renaissance genealogy', *Journal of the History of Collections*, vol. 1, no. 1, pp. 59–78.

Findlen, P. (1994) *Possessing Nature: Museums, Collecting and Scientific Culture in Early Modern Italy*, Berkeley, CA, Los Angeles, CA and London, University of California Press.

Finlay, R. (1998) 'The pilgrim art: the culture of porcelain in world history', *Journal of World History*, vol. 9, no. 2, pp. 141–87.

Finlay, R. (2010) *The Pilgrim Art: Cultures of Porcelain in World History*, Berkeley, CA, Los Angeles, CA and London, University of California Press.

Fortini Brown, P. (1999) 'Carpaccio's St Augustine in his study: a portrait within a portrait', in Schnaubelt, J. C. and Fleteren, F. V. (eds) *Augustine in Iconography: History and Legend*, New York, Peter Lang, pp. 507–47.

Frankopan, P. (2016) *The Silk Roads: A New History of the World*, London, Bloomsbury Paperbacks.

Fusco, L. and Corti, G. (2006) *Lorenzo de' Medici: Collector and Antiquarian*, Cambridge, Cambridge University Press.

Giovio, P. (1553) *La vita di Alfonso da Este, Duca di Ferrara*, Florence.

Golombek, L., Mason, R. B. and Bailey, G. A. (1996) *Tamerlane's Tableware: A New Approach to Chinoiserie Ceramics of Fifteenth and Sixteenth-Century Iran*, Costa Mesa, CA, Mazda Publishers; Toronto, Royal Ontario Museum.

Hess, C. (2004a) 'Brilliant achievements: the journey of Islamic glass and ceramics to Renaissance Italy', in Hess, C. (ed.) *The Arts of Fire: Islamic Influences on Glass and Ceramics of the Italian Renaissance*, Los Angeles, CA, J. Paul Getty Museum, pp. 1–34.

Hess, C. (ed.) (2004b) *The Arts of Fire: Islamic Influences on Glass and Ceramics of the Italian Renaissance*, Los Angeles, CA, J. Paul Getty Museum.

Hope, C. (ed.) (2012) *Il regno e l'arte: i camerini di Alfonso I d'Este, terzo duca di Ferrara*, Florence, L.S. Olschki.

Hope, C. (1971a) 'The "Camerini d'Alabastro" of Alfonso d'Este-I', *The Burlington Magazine*, vol. 113, no. 824, pp. 641–50.

Hope, C. (1971b) 'The "Camerini d'Alabastro" of Alfonso d'Este-II', *The Burlington Magazine*, vol. 113, no. 825, pp. 712–21.

Impey, O. and MacGregor, A. (1997) *The Origins of Museums: The Cabinet of Curiosities in Sixteenth and Seventeenth-Century Europe*, New York, Ursus Press.

Joost-Gaugier, C. L. (1987) 'Lorenzo the Magnificent and the giraffe as a symbol of power', *Artibus et Historiae*, vol. 8, no. 16, pp. 91–9.

Jordan Gschwend, A. (1995) 'In the tradition of princely collections: curiosities and exotica in the *Kunstkammer* of Catherine of Austria', *Bulletin of the Society for Renaissance Studies*, vol. 13, no. 1, pp. 1–9.

Jordan Gschwend, A. and Lowe, K. (2015) *The Global City: On the Streets of Renaissance Lisbon*, London, Paul Holberton Publishing.

Kauffman, T. D. (1994) 'From treasury to museum: the collections of the Austrian Habsburgs', in Elsner, J. and Cardinal, R. (eds) *The Cultures of Collecting*, London, Reaktion Books, pp. 137–54.

Kerr, R. (2004) 'Chinese porcelain in early European collections', in Jackson, A. and Jaffer, A. (eds) *Encounters: The Meeting of Asia and Europe, 1500–1800*, London, Victoria and Albert Museum, pp. 45–51.

Lach, D. F. (1970) *Asia in the Making of Europe*, Chicago, IL and London, University of Chicago Press.

Leitch, S. (2009) 'Burgkmair's peoples of Africa and India (1508) and the origins of ethnography in print', *The Art Bulletin*, vol. 91, no. 2, pp. 134–59.

Lightbown, R. (1986) *Mantegna: With a Complete Catalogue of the Paintings, Drawings, and Prints*, Oxford, Phaidon Christie's.

Lowe, K. (2015) 'Made in Africa: West African luxury goods for Lisbon's markets', in Jordan Gschwend, A. and Lowe, K. (eds) *The Global City: On the Streets of Renaissance Lisbon*, London, Paul Holberton Publishing, pp. 163–73.

MacDonald, D. (2002) 'Collecting a new world: the ethnographic collections of Margaret of Austria', *The Sixteenth Century Journal*, vol. 33, no. 3, pp. 649–63.

Mack, R. E. (2002) *Bazaar to Piazza: Islamic Trade and Italian Art, 1300–1600*, Berkeley, CA, Los Angeles, CA and London, University of California Press.

Marchesi, A. (2012) 'Robe che si trovano nello studio overo camerino di marmo, et nel adorato di Sua Excellentia: Presenze e assenze di oggetti d'arte nell'inventario Antonelli del 1559', in Hope, C. (ed.) *Il regno e l'arte: i camerini di Alfonso I d'Este, terzo duca di Ferrara*, Florence, L. S. Olschki, pp. 203–34.

Markey, L. (2016) *Imagining the Americas in Medici Florence*, Philadelphia, PA, Pennsylvania State University Press.

Markey, L. and Keating, J. (2010) '"Indian" objects in Medici and Austrian-Habsburg inventories: a case-study of the sixteenth-century term', *Journal of the History of Collections*, vol. 23, no. 2, pp. 283–300.

Mason, P. (1994) 'From presentation to representation: Americana in Europe', *Journal of the History of Collections*, vol. 6, no. 1, pp. 1–20.

Meadow, M. A. (2002) 'Merchants and marvels: Hans Jacob Fugger and the origins of the Wunderkammer', in Smith, P. H. and Findlen, P. (eds) *Merchants and Marvels: Commerce, Science, and Art in Early Modern Europe*, New York and London, Routledge, pp. 182–99.

Milbrath, S. (1991) 'Representations of Caribbean and Latin American Indians in sixteenth-century European art', *Archiv für Völkerkunde*, vol. 45, pp. 1–38.

Molà, L. and Ajmar-Wollheim, M. (2011) 'The global Renaissance: cross-cultural objects in the early modern period', in Adamson, G., Riello, G. and Teasley, S. (eds) *Global Design History*, New York and London, Routledge, pp. 11–20.

Mullaney, S. (2000) 'Imaginary conquest: European material technologies and the colonial mirror stage', in Erickson, P. and Hulse, C. (eds) *Early Modern Visual Culture: Representation, Race and Empire in Renaissance England*, Philadelphia, PA, Pennsylvania State University Press, pp. 15–43.

Nagel, A. and Wood, C. S. (2005) 'Interventions: toward a new model of Renaissance anachronism', *The Art Bulletin*, vol. 87, no. 3, pp. 403–15.

Newall, D (ed.) (2017) *Art and its Global Histories: A Reader*, Manchester and Milton Keynes, Manchester University Press in association with The Open University.

North, M. (2010) 'Introduction – artistic and cultural exchanges between Europe and Asia, 1400–1900: rethinking markets, workshops and collections', in North, M. (ed.) *Artistic and Cultural Exchanges between Europe and Asia, 1400–1900*, Farnham and Burlington, VT, Ashgate Publishing, pp. 1–8.

Pérez de Tudela, A. and Jordan Gschwend, A. (2007) 'Renaissance menageries: exotic animals and pets at the Habsburg courts in Iberia and central Europe', in Enenkel, K. A. E. and Smith, P. J. (eds) *Early Modern Zoology: The Construction of Animals in Science, Literature and the Visual Arts*, Leiden, Brill, pp. 418–47.

Pierson, S. (2012) 'The movement of Chinese ceramics: appropriation in global history', *Journal of World History*, vol. 23, no. 1, pp. 9–39.

Pierson, S. (2013) *From Object to Concept: Global Consumption and the Transformation of Ming Porcelain*, Hong Kong, Hong Kong University Press.

Russo, A. (2011) 'Cortés's objects and the idea of new Spain', *Journal of the History of Collections*, vol. 23, no. 2, pp. 229–52.

Russo, A., Fane, D. and Wolf, G. (eds) (2015) *Images Take Flight: Feather Art in Mexico and Europe (1400–1700)*, Munich, Hirmer.

Ruvoldt, M. (2006) 'Sacred to secular, east to west: the Renaissance study and strategies of display', *Renaissance Studies*, vol. 20, no. 5, pp. 640–57.

Shearman, J. (1987) 'Alfonso d'Este's Camerino', in Chastel, A. (ed.) *'Il se rendit en Italie': études offertes à André Chastel*, Rome, Edizioni dell'elefante; Paris, Flammarion, pp. 209–29.

Shelton, A. A. (1994) 'Cabinets of transgression: Renaissance collections and the incorporation of the New World', in Elsner, J. and Cardinal, R. (eds) *The Cultures of Collecting*, London, Reaktion Books, pp. 177–203.

Silver, L. (2009) 'Cultures and curiosity', in Anderson, J. (ed.) *Crossing Cultures: Conflict, Migration and Convergence*, Melbourne, Miegunyah Press, pp. 242–6.

Smith, P. H. and Findlen, P. (eds) (2002) *Merchants and Marvels: Commerce, Science, and Art in Early Modern Europe*, New York and London, Routledge.

Spallanzani, M. (1978) *Ceramiche orientali a Firenze nel Rinascimento*, Florence, Cassa di Risparmio di Firenze.

Stapleford, R. (2013) *Lorenzo de' Medici at Home: The Inventory of the Palazzo Medici in 1492*, Philadelphia, PA, Pennsylvania State University Press.

Sturtevant, W. (1988) 'La Tupinambisation des Indiens d'Amerique du Nord', in Thérien, G. (ed.) *Les figures de l'indien*, Montreal, UQAM, pp. 295–306.

Syson, L. and Thornton, D. (2001) *Objects of Virtue: Art in Renaissance Italy*, Los Angeles, CA, J. Paul Getty Museum Publications.

Thornton, D. (1997) *The Scholar in his Study: Ownership and Experience in Renaissance Italy*, New Haven, CT and London, Yale University Press.

Um, N. and Clark, L. R. (2016) 'Special issue: the art of embassy – situating objects and images in the early modern diplomatic encounter', *Journal of Early Modern History*, vol. 20, no. 1, pp. 3–18.

Vasari, G. (1868) *The Lives of the Most Eminent Painters, Sculptors, and Architects*, London, Bell and Daldy.

Yaya, I. (2008) 'Wonders of America: the curiosity cabinet as a site of representation and knowledge', *Journal of the History of Collections*, vol. 20, no. 2, pp. 173–88.

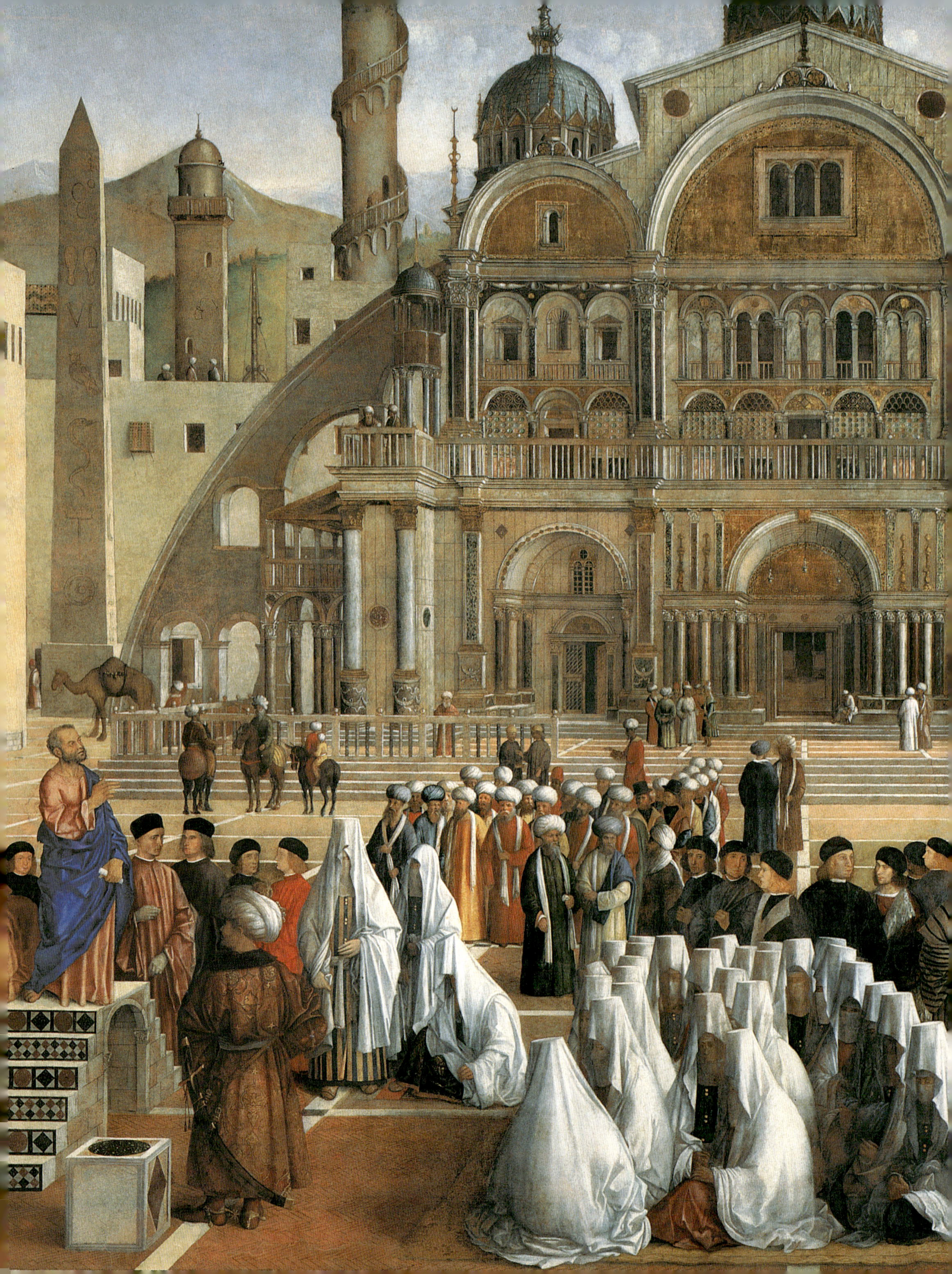

Chapter 4

Aspects of art in Venice: encounters with the East

Paul Wood with Kathleen Christian and Leah R. Clark

Introduction

The Venice Biennale is the longest-running of the major international exhibitions that have come to play such an important part in the contemporary practice of art. Inaugurated as long ago as 1895, the fiftieth exhibition in 2003 included work by the African American artist Fred Wilson. Wilson's display set out to address the multicultural, multi-ethnic make-up of Venice itself, from the Renaissance to the twentieth century. His installations included an opulent chandelier in Murano glass – black glass. There were also numerous figures of the 'blackamoor' types used to advertise Venetian consumer products from the seventeenth century to the present day and images of Renaissance paintings depicting non-European figures. In the Biennale catalogue, Wilson's rereading of Venetian history was expressly linked to the contemporary situation: 'As the world of today struggles again with issues of immigration, ethnicity and race, the topic of diversity in historical Venice is particularly resonant.'[1]

Much of the interest in continuing to study Renaissance art in the early twenty-first century lies in a comparable sense of 'looking again'. At a point when the nature of the Western canon is coming under greater scrutiny than at any time in its history, it follows that the vaunted 'rebirth' of

that tradition is itself going to be a suggestive site for encountering and challenging received meanings and interpretations. In historical representation, consciously or otherwise, the horizon of the present is always drawn around the continent of the past. Not only is our map of the societies and cultures that produced Renaissance art being substantially redrawn, but our sense of what counts as 'art' itself is subject to redescription. In a way that echoes the decentring of painting and sculpture from the contemporary practice of the arts (exemplified by, among others, Wilson's Venice installation), our sense of Renaissance cultural practice is now moving to re-embed painting and sculpture in a matrix of ritual and building, mechanical reproduction, material culture, design and consumption, from which the modern system of the arts detached it.[2] The hierarchical distinctions of the canon have come to seem out of tune with our own cultural hybridity in an epoch of globalisation. That said, no one could sensibly argue with claims for the relevance of an understanding of Renaissance art to the subsequent Western tradition. What stands at issue are the terms of that understanding. As new historical enquiry begins to shed light on the complexity and diversity of Renaissance experience, the consequences for a sense of Western cultural identity, as historically grounded in the Renaissance, are considerable.[3]

Plate 4.1 Gentile Bellini, *Saint Mark Preaching in Alexandria* (detail from Plate 4.23).

Recurring figures in recent studies of Venetian culture are the collage, the montage or, in another variant, the palimpsest. The sense conveyed is of Venetian culture as layered and as a site of marked juxtapositions.[4] This is apparent in the very make-up of the Renaissance city itself, reflected in its inhabitants as well as its visual culture, a fact noted by contemporaries. At the end of the fifteenth century, Philippe de Commynes, the French ambassador to Venice, remarked that 'most of the people are foreigners'. And this perception of a society in which northerners (Flemish and Germans), Dalmatians, Greeks, Muslims, Jews and mainland Italians mingled with indigenous Venetians was further highlighted in the sixteenth century by the Venetian writer Francesco Sansovino: 'Peoples from the most distant parts of the world gather here to trade and conduct business, [people who] differ among themselves in appearance, in customs and in languages.'[5]

Renaissance Venice was a corporate society, long thought to be structurally hierarchical. At the top were the patricians, the *nobile*, with a legally enshrined monopoly on political power. From them a doge was elected, who was head of state for life but was prevented from accumulating wealth and power on the model of, say, the Medici in Florence. Below the patricians was a larger, but still numerically small, layer of citizens, the *cittadini*. And below them was the vast majority, almost 90 per cent, of the *popolani* (the people).[6] Within the overall framework of prosperity, the secret of continuing stability can however be found in critical points of flexibility within the hierarchy. Of particular significance for the arts is the fact that, despite political power as such being reserved for the hereditary patrician class, the citizens played an extremely powerful role as a kind of permanent civil service. Among the institutions for which they were responsible were the *scuole*: lay – albeit deeply religious – confraternities, in the larger cases extremely wealthy, which were responsible for a wide range of activities approximating to what we would think of as social services. As well as providing many commissions for artists, the *scuole* played an important role in maintaining the social cohesion which, allied to naval supremacy, underwrote Venetian power and prosperity.

In an age of great social upheaval and almost continuous wars, the city-state, according to its own officially sanctioned 'Myth of Venice', remained stable and survived for over 1000 years, from the end of the Roman Empire to Napoleon.[7] Underlying this stability was economic power. Controlling a trading empire based in the eastern Mediterranean, but stretching into northern Europe and Asia, Venice enjoyed great wealth. This wealth encouraged innovation as well as cultural diversity, and information was no less important to the accumulation of wealth than the trade in spices and exotic goods. In the late fifteenth century, Venice became a centre for the new technology of printing. Venetian printers were also engaged in map-making, not least nautical maps of the main sea routes and ports around which Venetian trade was organised. It has been established that 'in the course of the fifteenth century more books were printed in Venice than in any other city in Europe'.[8] And the diversity which marked contemporary Venetian life was mirrored in the printing industry. Considerable numbers of ancient Greek texts were produced, alongside books of Jewish history and translations of Arabic works, as well as costume books which offered visual representations of the appearance of different peoples. Peter Burke notes that Venice was 'a centre of printed information about the "East" linked to travels of merchants and others', concluding that 'the information structure was related to, if not a simple expression of, the economic, social and political system'.[9]

1 Between East and West

When one thinks of the term 'Renaissance', its governing sense is of a rebirth of the art, architecture, literature, science and philosophy of antiquity. Alone among major Italian cities however, Venice had no antiquity. There are no significant classical ruins or inscriptions in the Venetian lagoon, the city having been the creation of refugees during the period of the barbarian invasions in the fifth century, after the collapse of the Roman Empire. The Venetian Renaissance of the fifteenth and sixteenth centuries had to construct its sense of antiquity.[10]

The Renaissance in Venice is also distinctive because of the city's closely interconnected relationship not only with northern Europe, but also with the Mamluk Sultanate and Ottoman Empire (in present-day Egypt, Syria and Turkey). This was a time before Columbus's voyages to America, before the Portuguese opened a sea route to Asia, when the ports of North Africa and the eastern Mediterranean were among the most active centres of world economic and cultural development. For several hundred years, particularly from the eleventh to the late fifteenth centuries, Venice was a maritime power. Its naval dockyard, the Arsenal, became the largest industrial complex in late medieval Europe. Venice's geographical location and close relationship with the Byzantine Empire, centred on Constantinople, gave it distinct advantages in the fierce competition that developed in the eleventh century between the Italian seafaring powers of Genoa, Amalfi and Pisa for access to the wealth of 'the East'. Eventually, Venice established trading 'colonies' or *fondachi* (a *fondaco* is a semi-permanent, enclosed settlement where merchants lived) in overseas trading hubs, for example Alexandria, Beirut and Damascus. Sea routes to these outposts gave Venice access to a network that joined together sub-Saharan Africa, the Levant, western and central Asia, the Persian Gulf, India and China.[11] Venice's long-standing and far-reaching network made it the single most important trading centre between western Europe, Africa and Asia, a status it held until it began to be eclipsed in the sixteenth century.

It is important to pause here for a moment however, to reflect on this concept of 'the East'. In Renaissance studies it has conventionally been used to refer to a range of societies stretching from Turkey to China, with a particular emphasis on Islam.[12] Sometimes the lands of the Eastern Orthodox Church, that is the Byzantine Empire, were also included.[13] Increasingly however, scholars are recognising the problems inherent in simplistic 'East–West' or 'Christian–Muslim' dichotomies, and are beginning to acknowledge the complexities and contradictions informing economic, political and cultural relationships between Europe and its neighbours in the early modern period. Years of coexistence, mutual trade and shared interests in new materials and markets often overrode religious and territorial conflict. The 'East' is a term that is often employed but one that has to be used carefully if crucial distinctions are not to be collapsed. In the present chapter the focus is successively on the impact of three quite distinct societies upon Venetian material and visual culture: Orthodox Christian Byzantium, the Ottoman Empire centred on present-day Turkey and the Mamluk Sultanate which stretched from Egypt to Syria. With all of these, Venice was involved not only culturally but also politically, diplomatically and economically.[14]

Due to its geographical situation, early modern Venice even looked different.[15] With its power based on the *Stato da Mar* (the 'empire of the sea'), the city was literally built on the water. The palaces of the wealthy merchants that stood beside the Grand Canal and other waterways were highly distinctive. For most of the fifteenth century, the dominant elements were a characteristic admixture of the Gothic and the Islamic. Architecture remains largely beyond the scope of the present chapter, but it is nonetheless worth pausing to note the appearance of these buildings. Early palace façades incorporated a diverse collection of Gothic arches and tracery, topped by Islamic-inspired cresting along rooflines. The pointed ogee arch, seen for example on the façade of the Ca' d'Oro begun in 1421 (Plate 4.2), is itself a hybrid. Found in English Gothic, though less usual in continental Europe, it also occurs in Asian architecture. The architectural historian Deborah Howard has argued that 'the intention behind the introduction of the ogee arch and its adoption as a trademark by the Venetian merchant class was to allude to a mental image of the Orient'[16] – a 'mental image' composed out of myriad individual memories of trade in the East, characteristic Islamic forms in mosques and markets, ornaments and furniture, descriptions in travellers' tales, even the double curves found in the hulls of the galleys themselves. But by the later fifteenth century, the palace of the diplomat Giovanni Dario adopted features of a more typical Renaissance façade, drawing on developments elsewhere in mainland Italy (Plate 4.3). However, even here the classical columns and the rounded arches are mixed in with expensive imported coloured marbles and set in circular mounts which may have been observed by Dario on diplomatic missions to the Mamluk court in Cairo. The palace itself was even host to envoys from the Ottoman sultan in 1515 and 1516.[17]

This layered architectural heritage is to be seen most vividly on the two great buildings which stand adjacent to each other on the Piazza San Marco, the central ceremonial space of Venice (Plate 4.4) The basilica of San Marco and the Palazzo Ducale marry Gothic tracery and arches with, respectively, Byzantine domes and mosaics, and coloured tiles in an Islamic lozenge pattern. Traces of centuries of interaction with the eastern Mediterranean abound throughout the city, forming a marked contrast to the

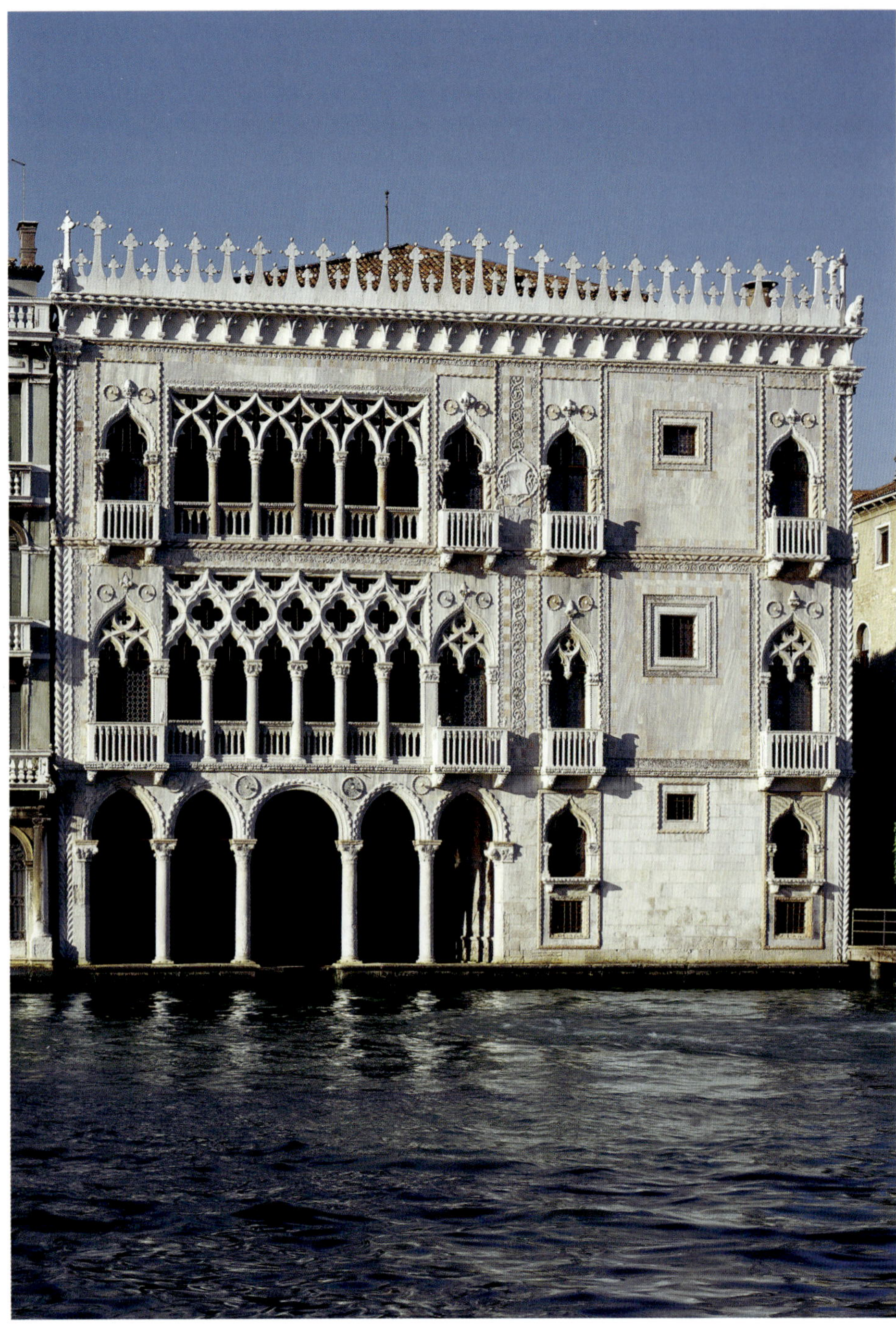

Plate 4.2 Ca' d'Oro, Venice, façade, begun 1421. © 2017. Photo: Scala, Florence.

rational composition of the façades of the classically influenced *renovatio* movement which emerged in the early sixteenth century.[18] The specific character of Venice as a physical space is thus inscribed by the sedimented experience of cultural otherness, manifest in both form and colour: ogee arches, Gothic pinnacles, asymmetrical façades, overhanging balconies, narrow canals and streets, coloured marble and painted plaster.[19]

One of the most important cultural influences on Venice thus came not from Islam and not even from the Western Christian tradition of Rome, itself the conduit for so much of what we consider to be the Renaissance. From its earliest days until the twelfth century, Venice had stood at the western limit of the Eastern Christian Empire, centred on Byzantium.[20] The first permanent Venetian trading post was established in Byzantium in 1082, though commercial links had

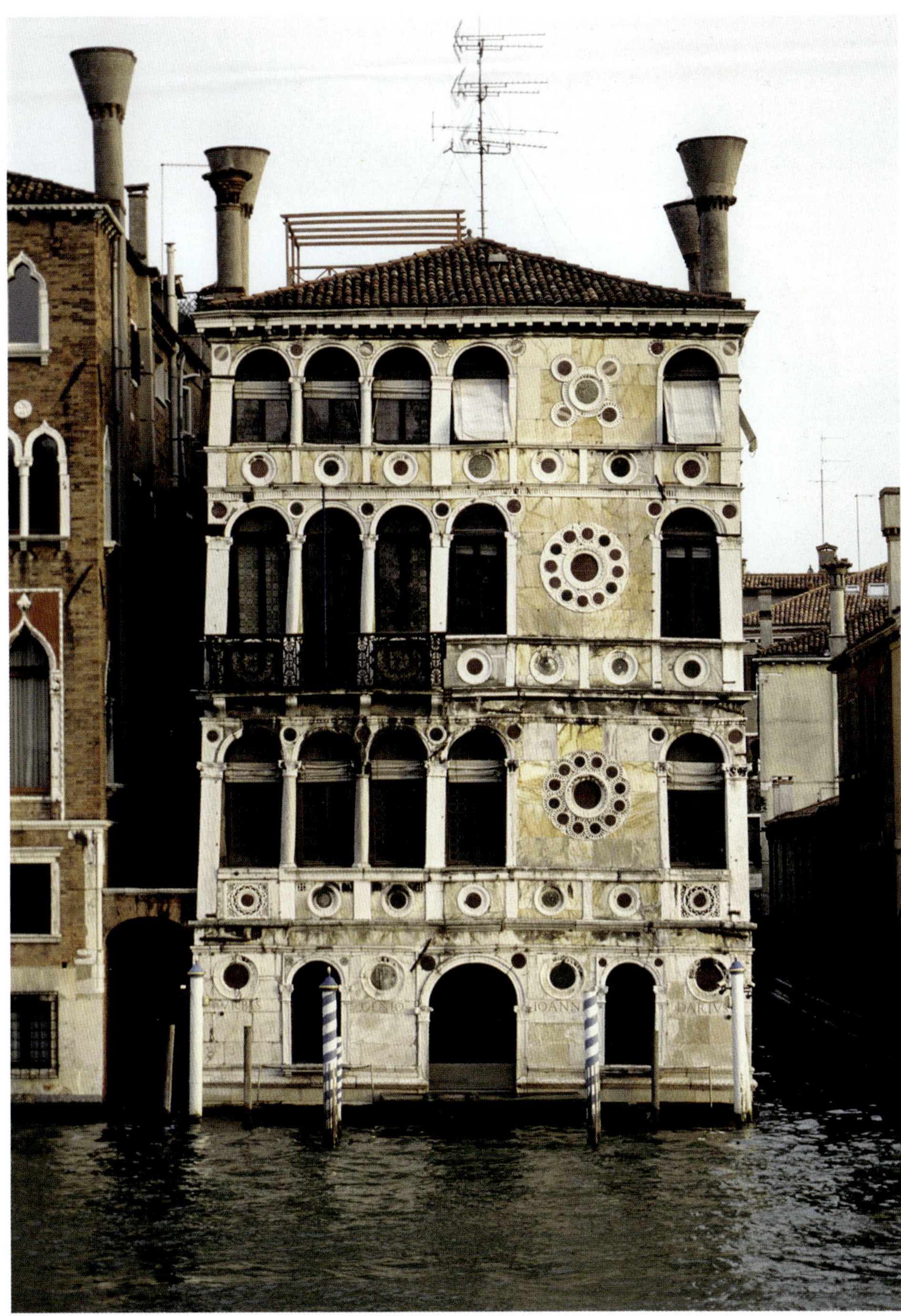

Plate 4.3 Ca' Dario, Venice, façade, 1480s. Photo: © Sarah Quill/ Bridgeman Images.

existed long before that. However, as the Byzantine Empire declined and that of Venice expanded, the balance of power and influence gradually changed, until crisis point was reached in 1204. In that year, the Venetian doge succeeded in diverting the Fourth Crusade from its destination in the Holy Land to Constantinople. After a siege, the Venetians ruthlessly sacked the city. As a consequence, huge amounts of booty made their way to Venice, ranging from

jewels, metalwork and precious objects of Islamic craftsmanship, to bronze and marble sculptures as well as porphyry columns and sheets of marble for use in the decoration of buildings.

The basilica of San Marco is the single most important transmitter of Byzantine influence into Venetian culture. It was first established in the ninth century to house the relics of Venice's patron saint, Saint Mark,

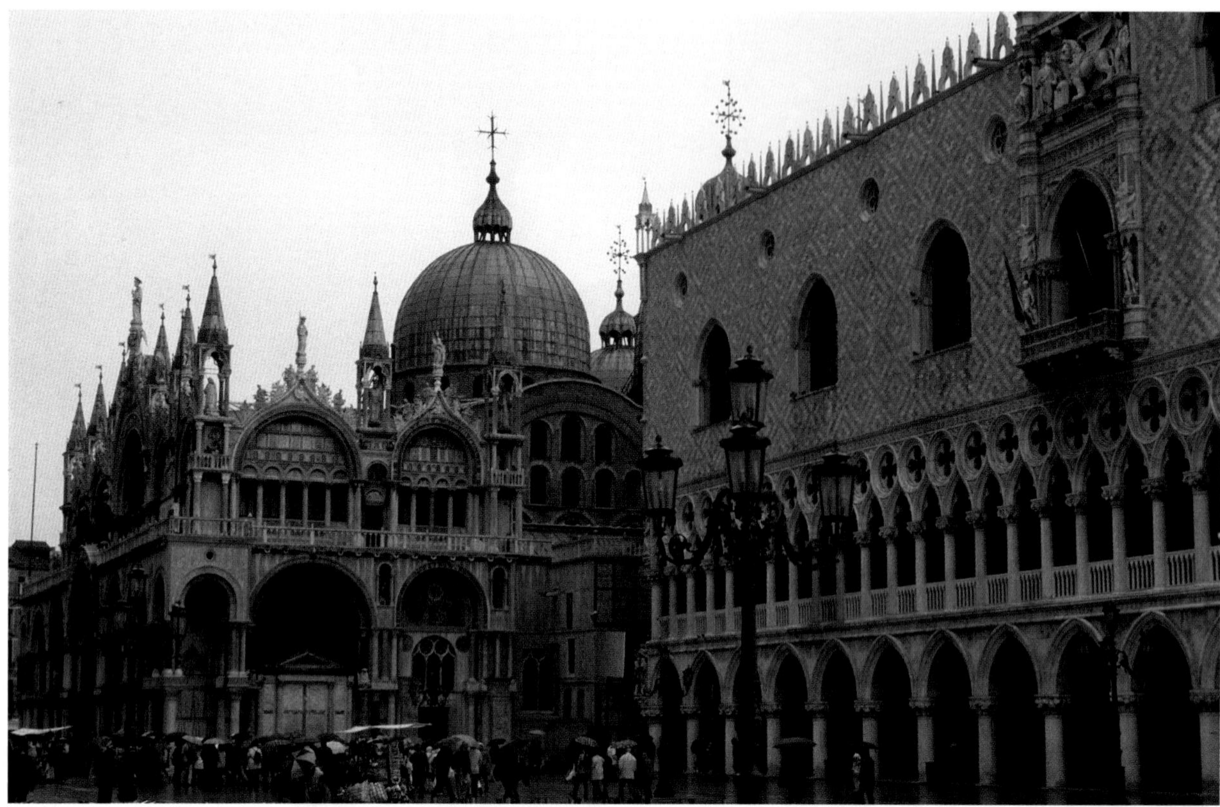

Plate 4.4 Exterior view of the basilica of San Marco and the Palazzo Ducale from the Piazzetta. Photo: Paul Wood.

which were transferred to the city from Alexandria in 829. Both in its external architectural form and in its interior, San Marco is distinct from the conventions of Italian and northern churches alike, with their characteristic decorative schemes of fresco, stone sculpture and stained glass. San Marco began to assume its present form in the late eleventh century, based directly on the plan of the Church of the Holy Apostles in Constantinople, that is, a Greek cross with five domes marking each arm and the central crossing point. Thereafter, it was in a continuous process of expansion and embellishment until the fifteenth century and beyond. Mosaic decoration had started in the late eleventh or early twelfth centuries, but a surge of work followed in the wake of the capture of Constantinople. In addition to the four life-size bronze horses of classical antiquity, shipped over and set above the main entrance, the domes, arches and vaults of the interior were decorated with mosaics by artists brought from Constantinople, often working with glass tesserae themselves appropriated for the purpose. Outside, mosaics above the portals told the story of the transportation of the saint's relics from Alexandria to

Venice. In addition to the pictorial mosaics, Byzantine effects were present throughout San Marco in the many columns of marble and porphyry, as well as sheets of coloured, patterned marble, stripped from Constantinople and used to decorate the walls and the elaborately patterned floor.

Constantinople was retaken by the Greeks from Venetian domination after less than 60 years, and a new dynasty was secured: the Palaeologus. But two centuries later, not just Italy but the whole of Christendom was convulsed by news of the final collapse of the Byzantine Empire. Constantinople fell to the Ottoman Turks in 1453, under the leadership of Mehmed II (r.1444–46 and 1451–81). Despite calls for a new crusade to repel the infidel, there was in fact no collective response. One of the immediate effects for Venice, however, was an increase in the numbers of the Greek community there, as Christian refugees fled from Muslim expansion. The result of the influx of scholars, coupled with a rapid expansion of the printing industry, was that in the second half of the fifteenth century Venice became a major centre of Greek learning in western Europe.

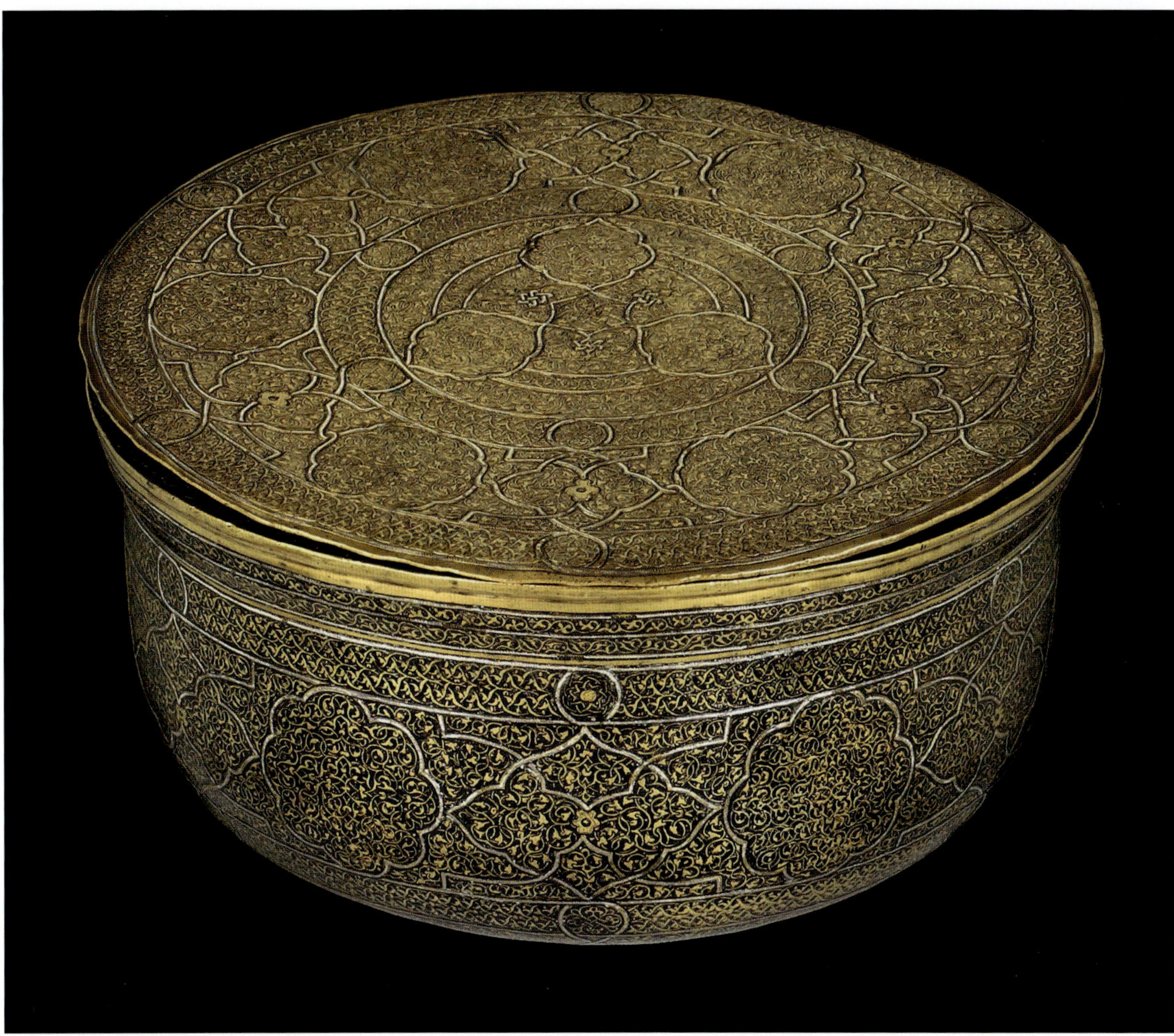

Plate 4.5 Mahmud al-Kurdi, bowl-shaped box with cover of engraved brass inlaid with silver, fifteenth century, height 8 cm, diameter 16 cm. Courtauld Institute of Art, O.1966.GP.204. © The Samuel Courtauld Trust, The Courtauld Gallery, London.

Venice was also a gateway through which, in a two-way traffic, the manufactured goods of Europe spread out to the East and a vast range of imported goods and designs – cotton and alum, spices and carpets, metalwork and perfumes, colours, shapes and ideas – entered the European consciousness.[21] The exchange of material culture gave rise to shared consumer tastes, so much so that it is sometimes not known today whether particular objects were produced in Europe or outside of it. Such is the case with examples of so-called 'Veneto-Saracenic' metalwork (Plate 4.5). These are typically brass objects – candlesticks, bowls, basins and perfume burners – which have been decorated with inlaid silver

that is stylistically Islamic, including for example arabesque motifs and interlocking knotwork patterns (also see Chapter 3, Plates 3.15–3.16). There is little documentary evidence surrounding the production of these objects and art historians have looked to the works themselves for evidence of their place of origin.[22] In the nineteenth century, it was suggested that these were decorated by Muslim craftsmen in Venice. This was largely discounted until recently, when archival evidence confirmed the presence of an Armenian from Damascus in Venice in 1563 who was working in metal inlay, and may have passed on the trade to Venetian craftsmen, although this theory is still debated.[23]

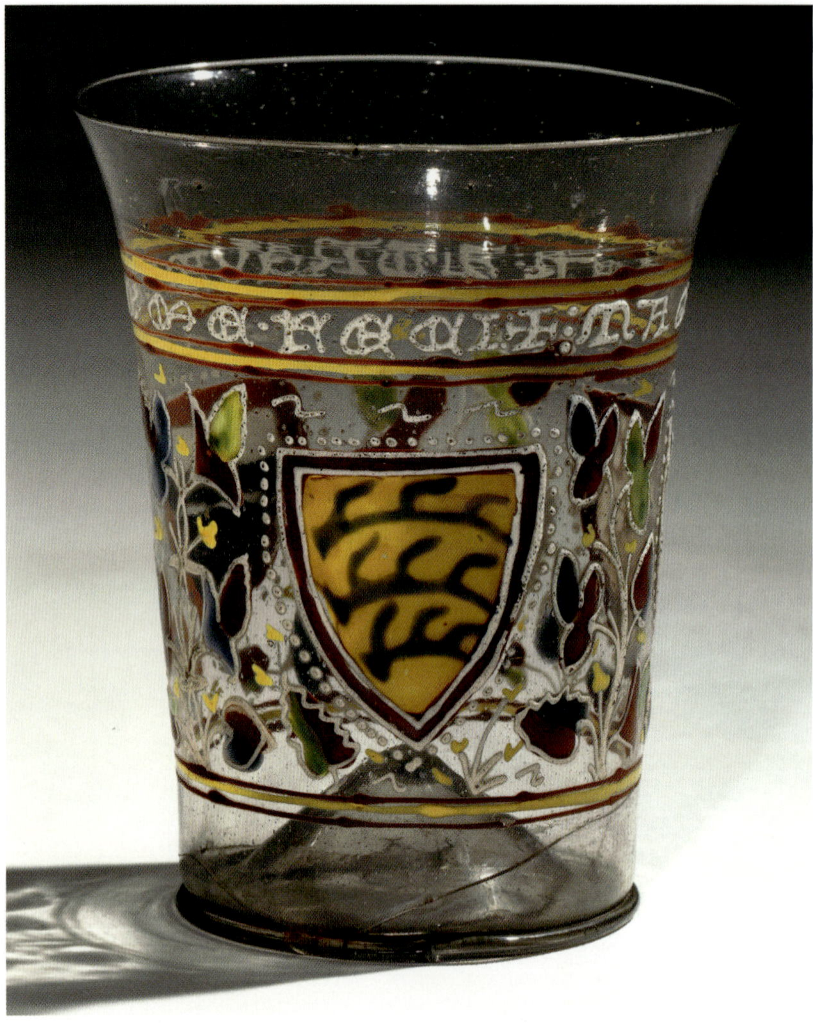

Plate 4.6 Aldrevandin beaker, Venice, c.1330, glass and enamel, height 13 cm. British Museum, London, 1876,1104.3. Photo: © The Trustees of the British Museum.

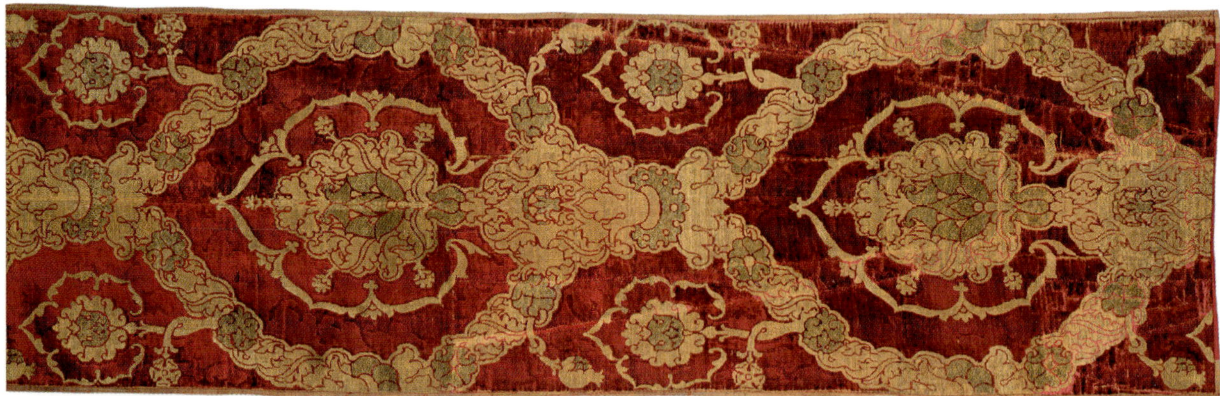

Plate 4.7 Detail of length of velvet, sixteenth century, silk with metal thread, 58 × 376 cm. The Metropolitan Museum of Art, New York, Rogers Fund, 1912, acc. no.: 12.49.8. © 2017. Image copyright: The Metropolitan Museum of Art/Art Resource/Scala, Florence.

The application of the silver inlay differs among surviving examples, which also indicates several different places of manufacture, leading more recent scholars to categorise these objects into types: metalwork made in Mamluk territories; inlay applied in Syria to pre-existing European vessels; European imitations; signed vessels. The second type would have involved a rather complex cross-cultural process, whereby undecorated vessels in European shapes made in northern Europe were shipped to Syria to be decorated (damascened) and then sold to European consumers, some even containing arms of European families, many Venetian (Chapter 3, Plate 3.15). By the sixteenth century, craftsmen in Venice were producing imitations, but combining the arabesque with *all'antica* motifs, and using a different technique of inlay. The final type is particularly intriguing, composed of a series of vessels that include inscriptions, identifying the maker Mahmud al-Kurdi (Mahmud the Kurd) written in Arabic, coupled with a transliteration in Roman characters.[24] A bowl in the Courtauld Gallery (Plate 4.5) is an example of this latter kind (although intriguingly missing the final part of the artist's name, 'the Kurd'). It is not certain where al-Kurdi was based, but the presence of Roman characters suggests an intended European audience. Arguably however, the more significant point is that these uncertainties around the provenance of such objects ought to be regarded less as a problem than as an indicator of how closely artistic contact and exchange flourished across the eastern Mediterranean.

In Venice, imported goods inspired local craft industries that eventually became key elements of Venice's economy, as well as the city's aesthetic identity. Gilded and enamelled glass produced in Egypt and Syria under the Mamluks at the end of the medieval period had a great impact on Venetian taste, so that by the fourteenth century enamelled glass was produced locally, an example of which is the 'Aldrevandin' beaker, whose maker's name appears on the rim (Plate 4.6).[25] Glass is still bought today by tourists in Murano as a quintessentially Venetian product, yet historically it was a technique developed by Islamic glassblowers and imported to Venice, possibly via Byzantium. It is a technology that encapsulates cross-cultural transfer and exemplifies how Venetians learned to mimic luxury products from abroad and make them their own.[26] Indeed, by

the sixteenth century Venetians were even producing glass mosque lamps and exporting them to the Islamic world.[27]

Silk was another specialist product of Venice developed first through the imitation of imports from abroad, then manufactured for export in the form of original, exquisitely crafted designs. Silk textiles had been produced competitively in Italy since the twelfth or thirteenth centuries, after the technique, first invented in ancient China, was imported via Byzantium and the Islamic world. Thereafter, the silk industry in Venice developed hand in hand with the growth of trans-Mediterranean trade.[28] The importance of luxury textiles in diplomatic gift-giving, their portability and use as a near-universal form of currency, as well as the ability of vivid designs and colours to set trends across cultures, made them particularly prone to cross-fertilisation.[29] Venetian weavers developed their own specialisms on the global market, becoming leading producers of velvets, including gold-brocades and patterns that used piles of different heights. Venetian silk became popular in the Islamic world and the Mamluk and Ottoman export markets were especially significant. While it is now difficult to trace the provenance of textiles from this era, one exquisite example of a high-end textile thought to have been woven in Venice in the sixteenth century is a length of red velvet enhanced with metal-thread brocade and multi-height pile (Plate 4.7). The pattern combines an artichoke motif with a double frame of pointed ogees, the same Asian-inspired, arched shapes favoured in Venetian palace architecture (Plate 4.2). In this case the inner ogees are pinched at the bottom, another borrowing from Asian designs.[30]

2 Mehmed II and Venice

Venice's relationship with its major rival in the Mediterranean, the Ottoman Turks, extended well beyond commercial trade. One of the most intriguing instances of exchange concerned not goods, but an artist: the Venetian painter Gentile Bellini. He became the focal point of a diplomatic mission to the court of Sultan Mehmed II, conqueror of Constantinople, whose portrait Bellini painted from life in 1480 (Plate 4.8). Gentile was a member of a family of artists and together with his younger brother, Giovanni, was part of a workshop headed by his father, Jacopo.[31]

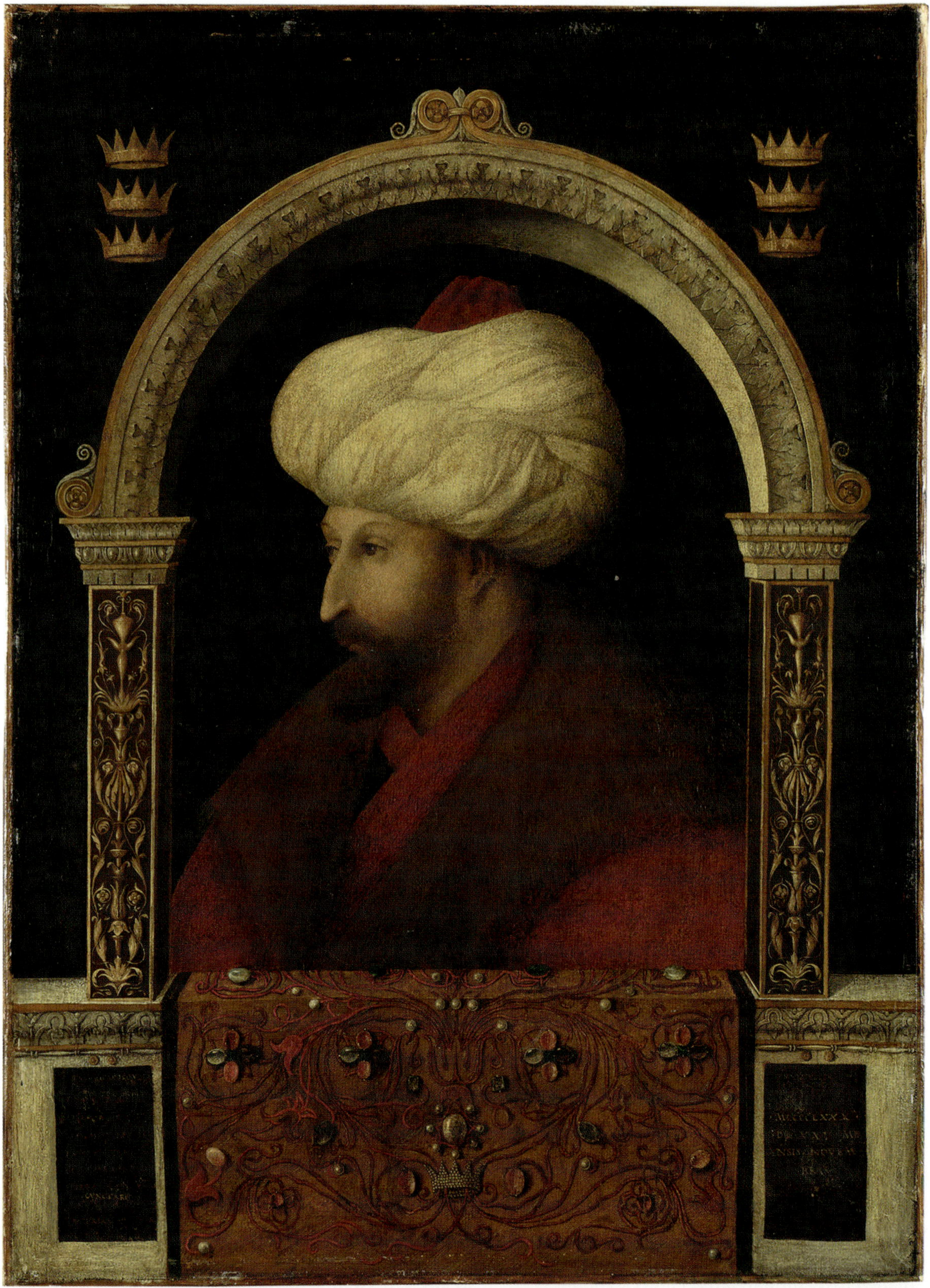

Plate 4.8 Gentile Bellini, *Portrait of Mehmed II*, 1480, oil on canvas, 70 × 52 cm. National Gallery, London, Layard bequest, 1916, acc. no.: 6352. © 2017. Copyright The National Gallery/Scala, Florence.

Gentile had taken over the family workshop after the death of Jacopo in *c.*1470 and subsequently gained the most important commissions for the decoration of the Grand Council Chamber in the Palazzo Ducale in 1474, as well as others for the *scuole grandi*. He has been described as the 'impresario' of Venetian art in the late fifteenth century, and received a knighthood from the Holy Roman Emperor. So it was not just any painter who travelled to Constantinople in 1479. But then, this was not just any court. In the second half of the fifteenth century, the Ottomans emerged not only as a serious rival to the Venetian empire as well as to the Mamluk sultanate in the Mediterranean, but for the next 100 years represented a real challenge to the hegemony of Western Christendom as such. These are curious conjunctions. What was an Italian painter doing in an Ottoman court? Why did an Islamic monarch want to have his portrait painted by a European, Christian artist? It could be said that, in a sense, this modest picture figures not just a man, but the relationship between two cultures.[32]

Mehmed II had ascended to the Ottoman throne for the second time in 1451, aged 19.[33] His original tenure as an adolescent had been unsuccessful and his father had needed to come out of retirement and reassume power. After his father's death, Mehmed did not fail for a second time. He immediately began building his military power, and a policy of expansion rapidly led him to the siege of Constantinople. The city was by then almost all that remained of the former Byzantine Empire. The large Ottoman army and navy, estimated at 80–100,000 men, faced a defending force of only about 7,000. Despite the imbalance of forces, the siege lasted 55 days, but on 29 May 1453, a date perceived as one of European history's turning points, Constantinople fell to the Turks.

News of the fall of Constantinople set off a panic in Christian Europe. Nonetheless, the immediate reaction, to unite in a crusade to retake Constantinople from Islam, foundered on the reefs of internecine squabbling and self-interest on the part of individual states. Before the end of the year, Venice had concluded a treaty which established a permanent embassy in Turkish Constantinople, and secured the continuing domination of Venetian trade in the eastern Mediterranean (something for which collective excommunication by the papacy for betraying Christendom was deemed a fair price to pay).[34] The peace lasted a decade, but was then followed by a draining 15-year war between Venice and

the Ottomans which broke out in 1463. This history has a bearing on Bellini's portrait. By 1478, Venetian wealth and trade had become so adversely affected as a result of the war that peace negotiations were opened. The experienced diplomat Giovanni Dario (owner of the palace in Plate 4.3) travelled to Constantinople charged with acceding to as many demands as were necessary to preserve Venetian trade in the region. The terms of the treaty concluded on 25 January 1479 were harsh for Venice, including financial reparations for the costs of the war and the payment of an annual rent for trading within the Ottoman Empire.

On the positive side for the Venetians, the permanent ambassador, or *bailo*, in Constantinople was re-secured. Mehmed, meanwhile, had built up the city from the impoverished and depopulated shell it had been after the conquest a quarter of a century earlier into a new capital of 60–70,000 inhabitants. For well over 100 years, from the fall of Constantinople until the last quarter of the sixteenth century, fear of 'the Turk' was mixed with admiration for their social system, which seemed to grant them in equal measure irresistible military power and enviable cultural riches.[35] The same Mehmed who was responsible for thousands of executions and was in one report described as 'feared and dreaded, ruthless and cruel … a second Nero and far worse'[36] also spoke several foreign languages (Arabic, Persian, as well as some Greek and Serbian), wrote poetry in Ottoman Turkish and possessed considerable knowledge of the literature and philosophy of antiquity. An eyewitness, subsequently quoted in a contemporary Venetian chronicle, reported that before the siege of Constantinople, Mehmed enjoyed daily readings from 'ancient historians such as Laertius, Herodotus, Livy and Quintus Curtius and from chronicles of the popes and Lombard kings'.[37] Kritovoulos of Imbros, a Greek scholar, recounted how he 'used to read philosophical works translated into Arabic from Persian and Greek and discuss the subjects which they treated with the scholars of his court'.[38] Mehmed's knowledge of history stimulated his imagination, leading him to fashion himself as a new Alexander the Great, reversing the direction of Alexander's celebrated conquests by imposing Eastern domination on the West.[39]

One of Mehmed's most important projects was the construction of a new palace complex in Constantinople – the Topkapı Palace – from which the Ottoman Empire was administered. Although many

Christian churches were taken over and converted into mosques, the Orthodox Church had been re-established, and a degree of multiculturalism with Christians and Jews existed within the overall Islamic culture of the city. At the same time, in his artistic and cultural choices, Mehmed drew together European and non-European visual traditions into a combination defined by the architectural historian Gülru Necipoğlu as Roman–Byzantine, Italian Renaissance and Timurid–Turkmen, in reference to the Timurid and Turkmen dynasties in central Asia. Under Mehmed, Constantinople re-emerged as a cosmopolitan capital of trade and diplomacy, and he in his turn sought to project the image of a sovereign who fused together the best elements of several traditions.[40]

For many centuries, societies in central Asia had been among the richest in the world and in the aftermath of cultural cross-fertilisation in Eurasia brought about by the Pax Mongolica, Islamic rulers had been open to artistic and intellectual currents from as far afield as Europe and China. However, even if Mehmed's interest in Europe had been shared to some extent by a minority among his Islamic predecessors and contemporaries, the extent of his focus on Europe, and on Italy in particular, was distinctive. His attention to ancient models and his sponsorship of Italian artists and European visual types and conventions were developed with a view to the eventual incorporation of Rome, and the rest of Italy, into a universal empire.[41] According to the then widespread view of world history as rooted in the Old Testament book of the prophet Daniel, the four pagan empires of Babylon, Persia, Greece and Rome were to be followed by a fifth empire uniting the world. It was not unusual for Renaissance scholars in the late fifteenth and early sixteenth centuries to worry that with Christendom prey to internecine warfare, this empire would be Islamic. In the event, Mehmed's only successful incursion into Italy was the capture of Otranto in the kingdom of Naples in 1480, which, although a major victory, could not be followed up due to his death in 1481. Nonetheless, Ottoman power continued to be a significant threat to Europe well into the sixteenth century. In 1521 a report by the Venetian ambassador stated that the sultan 'holds in his hands the keys to all of Christendom', and as late as 1576, it was still being lamented that 'the fall of such an empire by the hands of men is therefore the vainest thing to think of'.[42]

In discussions with the Venetian delegation during the peace negotiations of 1478–79, Mehmed's interest in European culture became clear, including his interest in the tradition whereby rulers reinforced their power through the circulation of portraits of themselves on coins and medals. Soon after the end of the war, Mehmed sent requests to Venice for a 'good painter who knows how to paint portraits', as well as for a sculptor and a bronze founder. This was only the first of several requests for artists – painters, bronze casters, woodworkers and builders – that Mehmed would send to Florence and Venice.[43] After 1453, Venice had lost a string of important colonies in the eastern Mediterranean, with consequent damage to its overseas trade. For both military and commercial reasons, Venice needed to secure its accommodation with the Turks. Complying with Mehmed's artistic desires, in terms of both palace decoration and the dissemination of his own image, was a useful means to this greater end. In short, the Venetian government would have done all it could to satisfy Mehmed's desire to propagate his image, including loaning out artists as a form of diplomatic gift-giving. A painter and sculptor were soon on their way. The bronze caster was a relatively little-known Paduan sculptor, Bartolomeo Bellano. But the painter was Gentile Bellini, the leading artist in Venice. Bellini's *Portrait of Doge Giovanni Mocenigo* (Plate 4.9), completed just before the summons to Constantinople, shows the doge facing left, in profile, his elevated status conveyed by the flat gold ground, the gold collar and the characteristic horned hat, the *corno ducale*, embossed with geometric designs. Following an established formula, only the doge's face is lightly modelled, conveying just sufficient information for the painting to qualify as a portrait rather than a stereotype. There seems little doubt that Gentile Bellini's ability to fulfil contemporary requirements for an individuated likeness, combined with a classically legitimated sense of the gravity of office, led to his being chosen for the mission to Constantinople.

Gentile's output at the Ottoman court included several portraits, a view of Venice, a Madonna and Child, as well as other works described only as 'luxurious things'.[44] In some ways, however, what is surprising about his year and a half long sojourn in the Ottoman capital is what he did not do. Gentile produced no images of Ottoman society, no paintings of contemporary Ottoman architecture or social life to equate with those on which

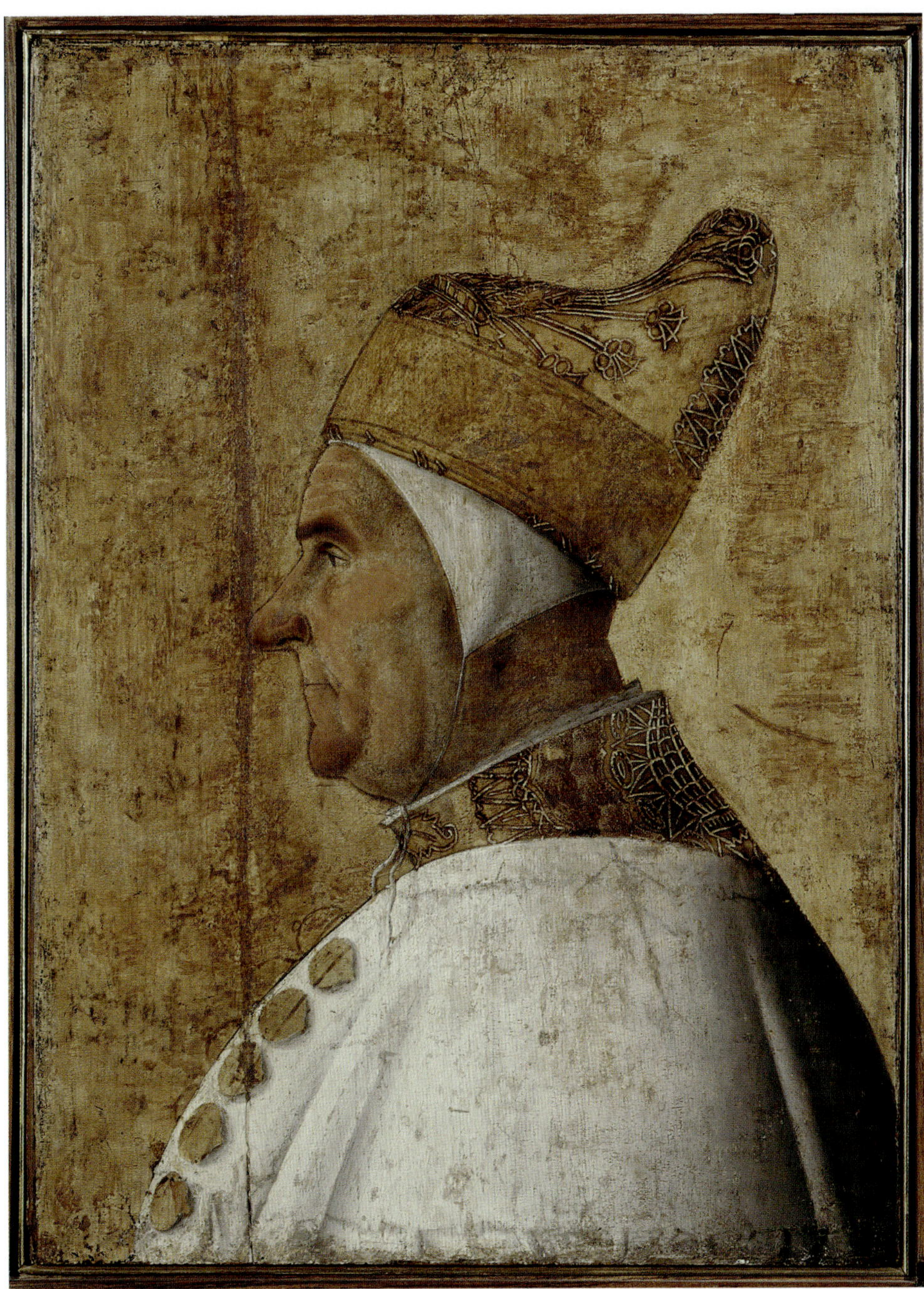

Plate 4.9 Gentile Bellini, *Portrait of Doge Giovanni Mocenigo*, *c.*1478, panel, 63 × 46 cm. Museo Correr, Venice. © 2017. Photo: Scala, Florence.

his reputation in Venice rested. He did, however, make several studies of individual Turkish people in daily costume, which formed the basis for many subsequent depictions of Turks and other Eastern figures in European art (Plate 4.10).

Although Gentile was the best known, he was not the first European artist involved with the Ottoman court. Slightly earlier another painter, Matteo de' Pasti, had together with an 'engineer' been arrested as a spy by the Venetians in Crete, en route to Constantinople, for allegedly having in his possession a map of Italy.[45] More successful was the Venice-born Costanzo da Ferrara (Costanzo de Moysis), who was there during the late 1470s, sent by the king of Naples.[46] The principal work of Costanzo's to have survived is his portrait medal of Mehmed cast in two versions, one of *c.*1478 and another of 1481 (Plates 4.11 and 4.12 show the obverse and reverse of the 1481 version, respectively). This image of a powerful man provides

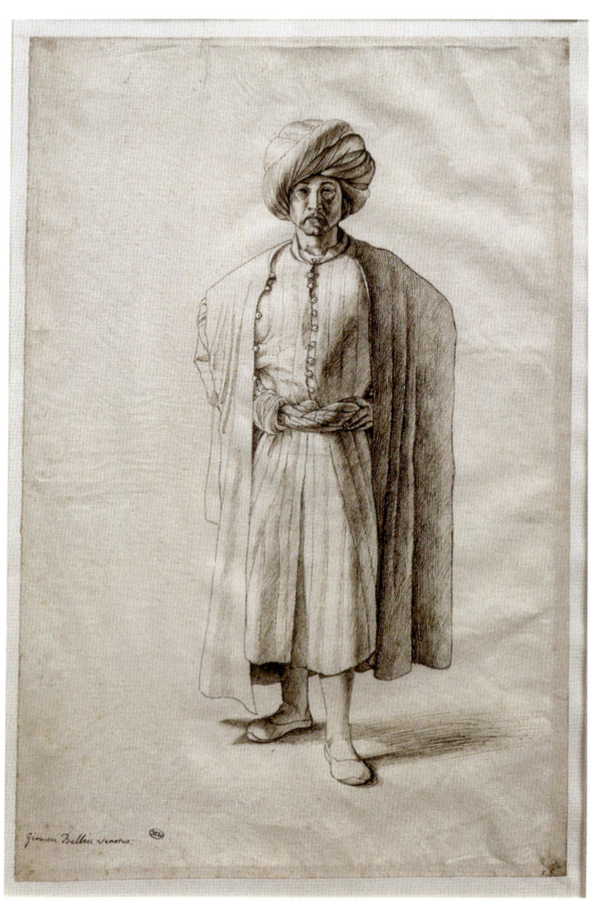

Plate 4.10 Workshop of Gentile Bellini, *Standing Ottoman*, late fifteenth century, ink on paper, 30 × 20 cm. DAG, Louvre, Paris. Photo: © RMN-Grand Palais (Musée du Louvre)/Michèle Bellot.

an interesting instance of the way images of the sultans entered art, often built up from a single actual observation. Costanzo's model was Pisanello's earlier portrait medallion of the Byzantine Emperor, John VIII Palaeologus, made at the time of the Council of Orthodox and Catholic Churches held in Ferrara and Florence in 1438–39 (Plate 4.13). The portrait of Mehmed is comparable to Pisanello's image of the Byzantine Emperor, not least through its use of exotic headgear to signify otherness. The reverse of the medal shows an equestrian image of the sultan (Plate 4.12). This has its roots in a sheet of drawings by Pisanello, apparently life studies of the Byzantine Emperor's entourage. They show an image of the emperor standing, clad in a full-length cloak, some details of the cloak's embroidered hem, and another of the emperor mounted on horseback and wearing the characteristic Timurid hat.[47] This last observed image, adapted for the circular proportions of Pisanello's medal, was in turn used as the compositional basis for the equestrian

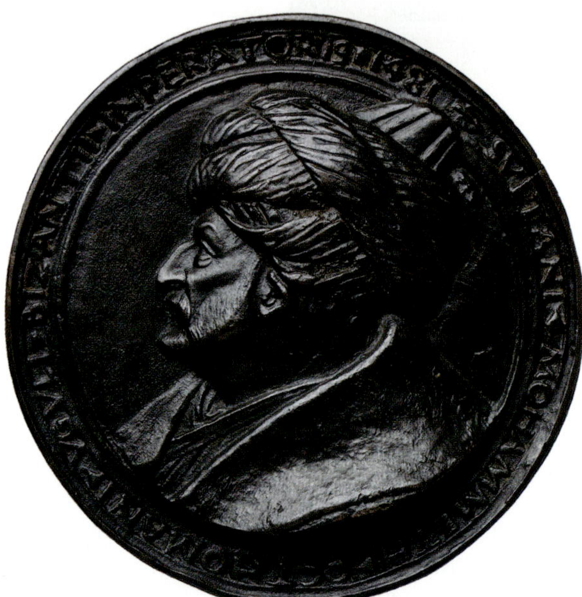

Plate 4.11 Costanzo da Ferrara, medal of Mehmed II, 1481, obverse (portrait), bronze, diameter 12 cm. Ashmolean Museum, Oxford, HCR8016. © Ashmolean Museum, University of Oxford.

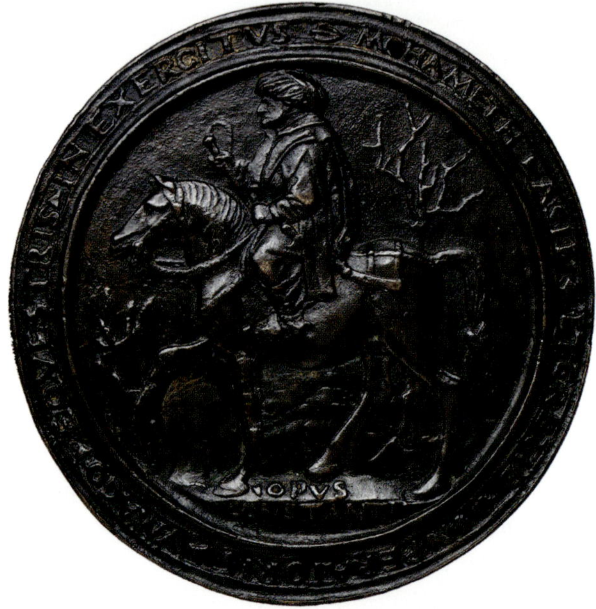

Plate 4.12 Costanzo da Ferrara, medal of Mehmed II, 1481, reverse (equestrian figure), bronze, diameter 12 cm. Ashmolean Museum, Oxford, HCR8016. © Ashmolean Museum, University of Oxford.

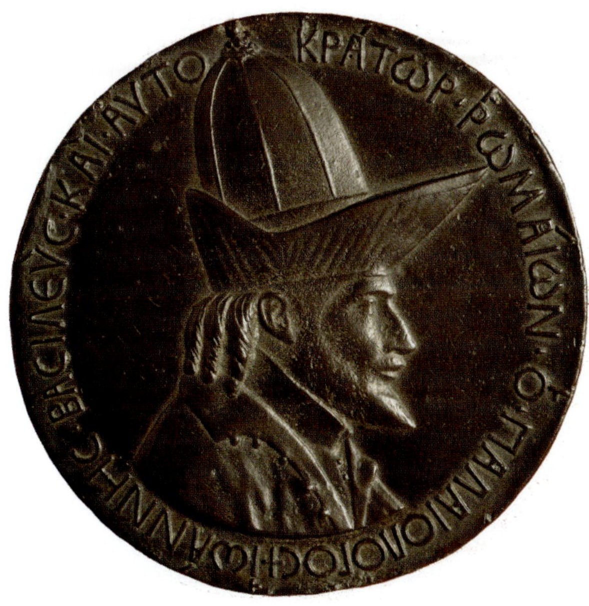

Plate 4.13 Pisanello, medal of Emperor John VIII Palaeologus, obverse, 1438–39, bronze, diameter 10 cm. Bargello, Florence. © 2017. Photo: Scala, Florence – courtesy of the Ministero dei Beni e delle Attività Culturali.

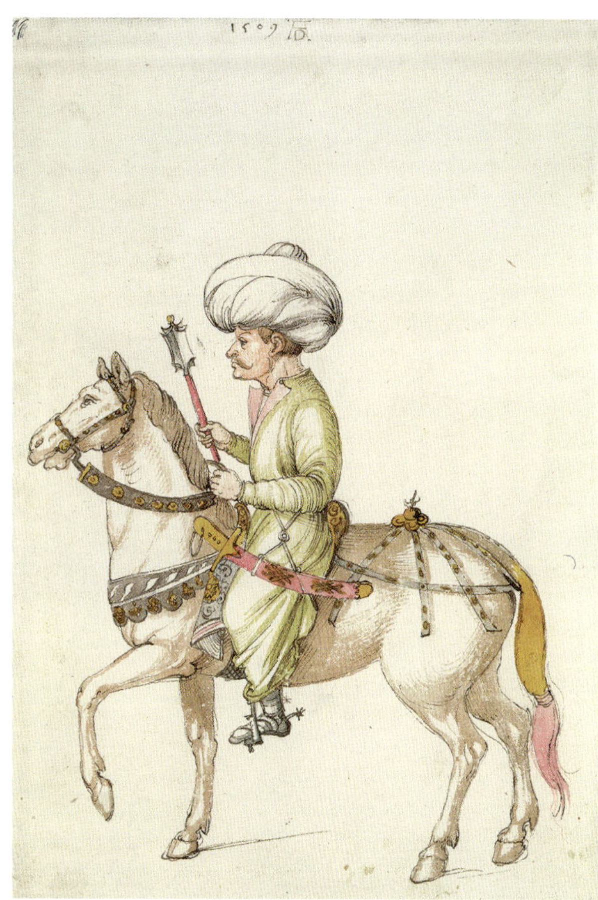

Plate 4.14 Albrecht Dürer, *Ottoman Rider*, c.1495, ink and watercolour on paper, 30 × 21 cm. Albertina, Vienna, Graphisches Sammlung, no. 3196, D 171. Photo: © Albertina/ Bridgeman Images.

portrait on the reverse of Costanzo's medal of Mehmed 40 years later. Subsequently, this image became transformed into a generic representation of an 'Ottoman rider' by no less a figure than Dürer during his first visit to Venice in 1495 (Plate 4.14). Rosamond Mack has remarked of this kind of borrowing that 'artists tended to adapt a small repertory of authentic images to a variety of representational uses', concluding that what they reveal, despite the level of commercial contacts in the Mediterranean and beyond, is 'a limited vision of the Orient'.[48]

Dürer seems also to have had access to Gentile Bellini's studio in 1495 and to have seen work in progress on his monumental painting of a *Procession in the Piazza San Marco* (see below, Section 3, Plate 4.19). Dürer was interested in collecting exotic types for subsequent incorporation into his own pictures, and to this end made a copy of one of Bellini's preparatory studies of Ottoman figures in the background of the San Marco painting, presumably sketched from life during Gentile's earlier sojourn in Constantinople (Plate 4.15). Dürer went on to incorporate many of the oriental types he collected in Venice into subsequent compositions. Sometimes these were positive, as in the *Map of the Northern Sky* he made in 1515. The

four corners of Dürer's print show eminent scientist-philosophers of the ancient world, including, along with Ptolemy of Egypt, 'Azophi Arabus' – testimony to the status of Arabic learning. More often, however, such figures function as negative signifiers of the Other in his paintings (see Chapter 1, Plate 1.21) and his woodcuts and engravings of a variety of biblical scenes. *The Martyrdom of Saint John the Evangelist* from the *Apocalypse* series of 1496–98 is notable for its inclusion of a black African and a Jew as well as three turbaned Orientals variously observing and presiding over the Christian saint's agonies (Plate 4.16).[49] Dürer's time in Venice gave him the opportunity to encounter a mixture of cultures as well as to acquire foreign goods. In a final letter before leaving the city, he recounts spending 100 ducats on colours he was able to buy there, and also of managing to purchase two expensive oriental carpets for his friend and patron, the Nuremberg humanist, Willibald Pirckheimer.

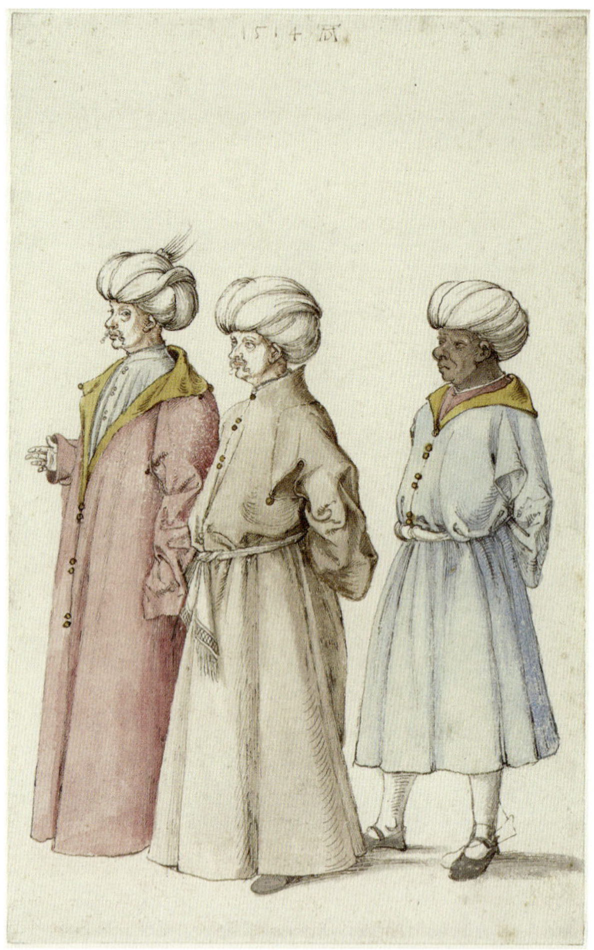

Plate 4.15 Albrecht Dürer, *Three Orientals*, c.1495 (signed and dated 1514 by another hand), pen and black and brown ink with watercolour on paper, 31 × 20 cm. British Museum, London, PD 1895-9-15-974. © The Trustees of the British Museum.

Gentile Bellini also produced a portrait medal of Mehmed, probably in collaboration with Bellano during their time in Constantinople.[50] It was slightly smaller than Costanzo's, albeit very similar in format, and gave a markedly less robust image of the sultan. The outstanding work to survive from Gentile's mission to Constantinople, however, is his oil portrait of Mehmed (Plate 4.8), dated in its inscription at the bottom right to 25 November 1480. By this time, Mehmed the Conqueror – the title he had assumed on capturing Constantinople a quarter of a century before – was almost 50 years old and in ill health. He had retired within the confines of the palace and was principally preoccupied with its decoration and with the cultivation of a garden. The sultan is represented in the painting in the bust-length profile familiar from the medals, and also from contemporary portraits of eminent Venetians. The image, however, has a pensive, scholarly air, more marked even than Gentile's medal and quite dissimilar to Costanzo's thicker-set, somewhat belligerent-looking figure. In all three, the sultan is depicted wearing the distinctive Ottoman tāj, the turban consisting of a length of white material wound around a stiff, ribbed cap in red felt. He also wears a similar garment, a kind of shirt with a cross-over collar, under a deep-red kaftan with a broad fur collar. In the painting, the archway in which he is framed is represented in a European perspectival style, with decoration suggestive of classical candelabra and tracery. But draped over the lintel is an opulent velvet cloth of gold decorated with jewels, in imitation of a practice sometimes followed in honorific textiles, even if this particular cloth has no known parallels in surviving examples.[51] Apart from the date, the now largely illegible inscription, written in the Latin language of western Europe, rather than Ottoman Turkish, has been interpreted to read 'Victor ac dom[in]-ator orbis' – conqueror and ruler of the world. The significance of the crowns, for all the prominence of their placement, is unclear. On the reverse of Bellini's portrait medal there are three of them, and they are usually taken to refer to the three components of the Ottoman Empire (Greece, Trebizond and Asia) brought together at the conclusion of the Veneto-Ottoman wars in 1479.[52] However, it has also been suggested that the six crowns in Bellini's oil portrait represent the six previous Ottoman sultans, with Mehmed himself symbolised by the seventh crown, made of pearls, at the bottom centre of the jewelled textile right at the front of the painting.[53]

Bellini left Constantinople in January 1481 and Mehmed was dead within a year. His successor, Bayezid II, seems to have sold off the Venetian art Mehmed had commissioned for the Topkapı Palace. Bayezid may have been unsympathetic towards European figural art, yet continued to receive portraits as gifts and thought highly enough of European engineering to invite both Leonardo and Michelangelo to submit designs for a bridge across the Golden Horn.[54] Legend has it that Sultan Mehmed's portrait was bought in the marketplace on behalf of a Venetian merchant who subsequently transported it home. Interestingly, however, Bellini's painting did leave a trace in Ottoman art.[55] There survives a portrait attributed to Sinan Beg

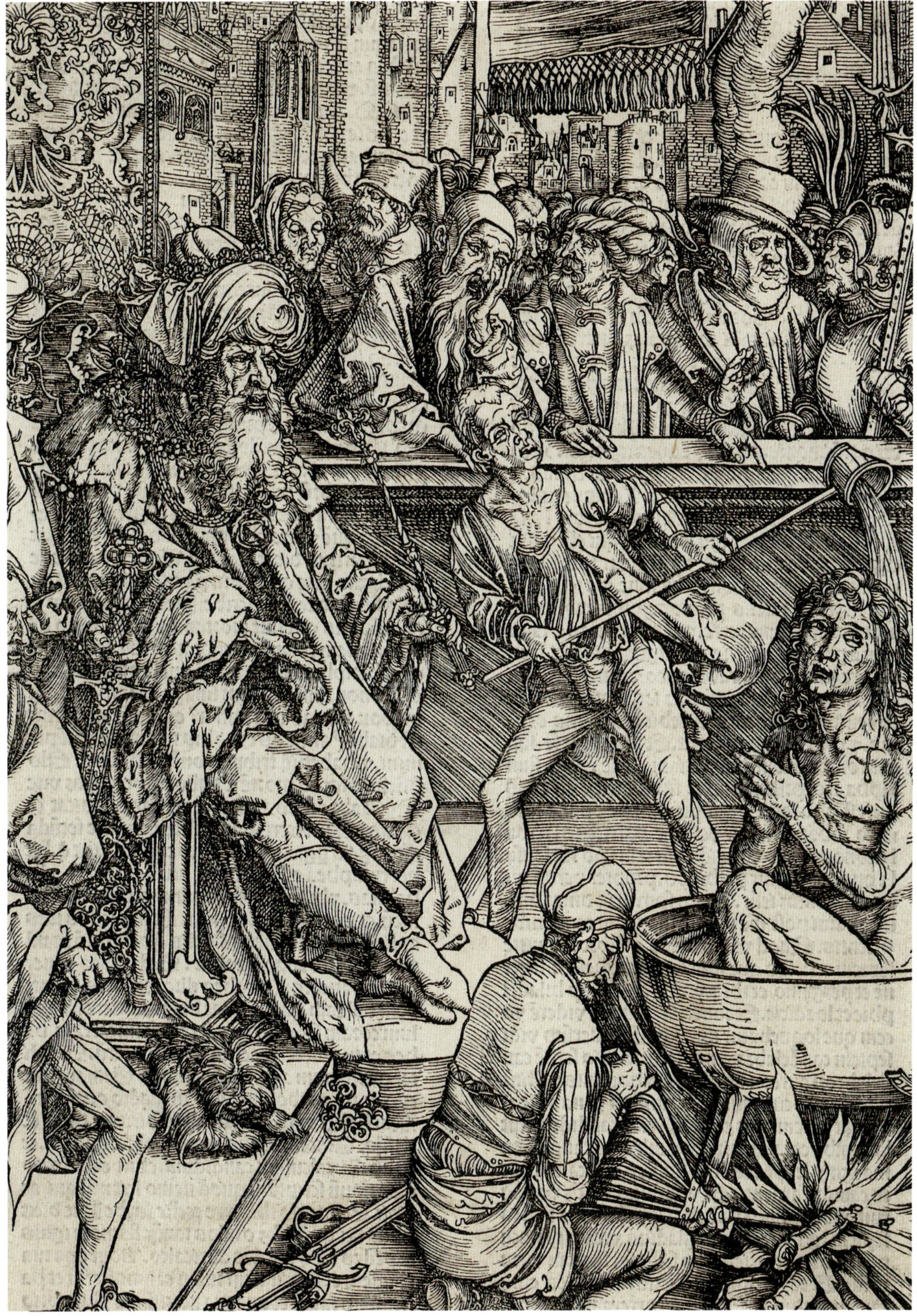

Plate 4.16 Albrecht Dürer, *The Martyrdom of Saint John the Evangelist*, from the series *The Revelation of Saint John (Apocalypse)*, 1498, woodcut, 40 × 29 cm. British Museum, London, PD 1895-1-22-559. © The Trustees of the British Museum.

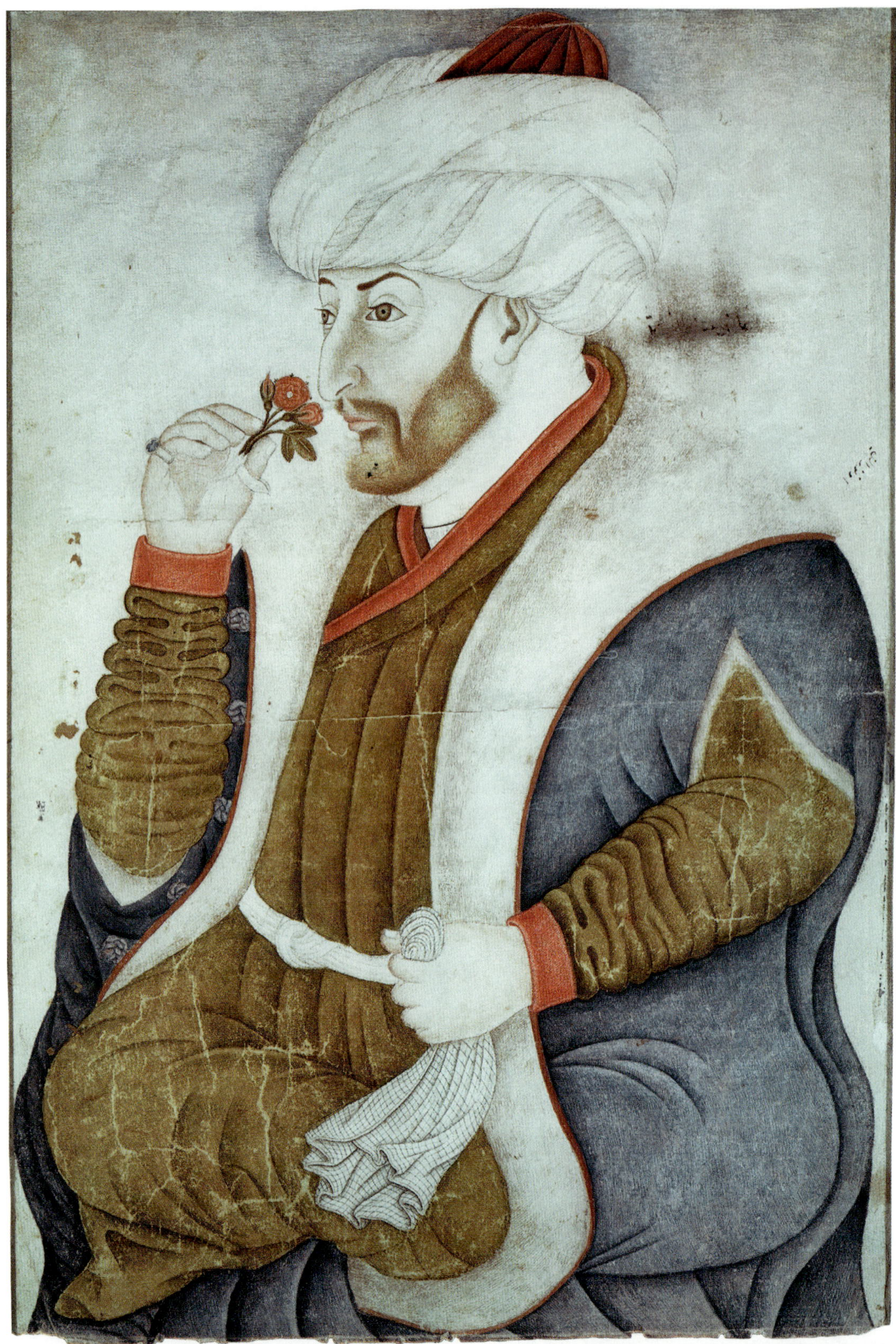

Plate 4.17 Attributed to Sinan Beg or Şiblizade Ahmed, *Portrait of Mehmed II*, 1475, gouache on paper, 39 × 27 cm.
Topkapı Serail Library, Istanbul, nr. H. 2154-10a. Photo: © akg images/Maurice Babey.

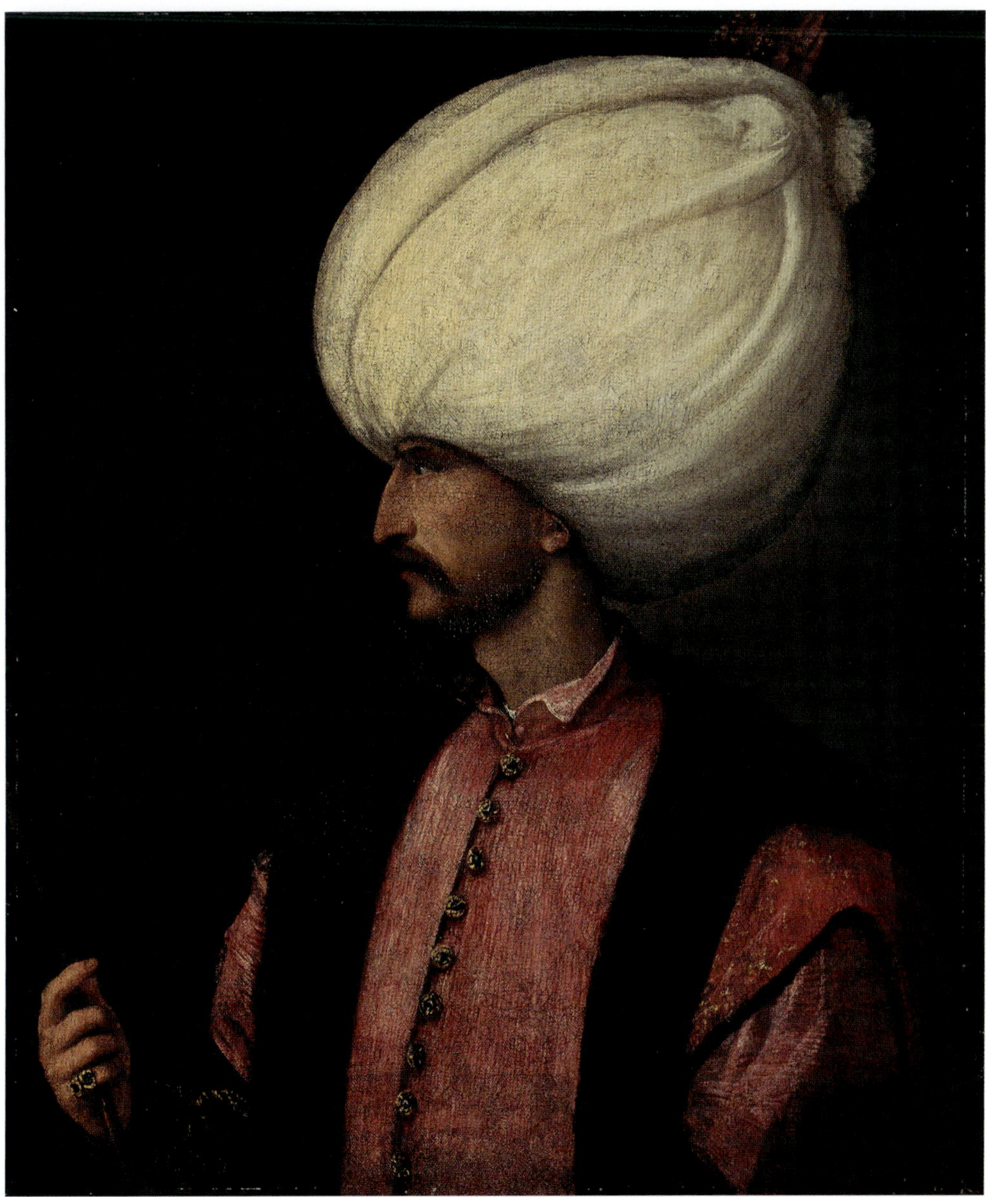

Plate 4.18 Studio of Titian, *Süleyman the Magnificent*, *c.*1530–40, oil on canvas, 99 × 85 cm. Gemäldgalerie, Kunsthistorisches Museum, Vienna. Photo: © akg-images.

(or his pupil, Şiblizade Ahmed) from the same time which draws upon the visual conventions of Timurid royal portraiture in its kneeling pose, as well as the refined accessories of the scented rose and handkerchief. At the same time, the portrait relies on a sense of realism borrowed from Italian conventions. It looks back to the composition used by Bellini and employs European-style shading to suggest volume in areas such as the handkerchief, turban and face, in contrast to the Ottoman convention for flat, unmodelled planes (Plate 4.17).[56]

This story of the portrait image of the Ottoman sultan is inseparable from the larger story of diverse societies and their complex interaction. A generation later, when the pressure of the Turks on Christendom reached its highest point, the studio of Titian produced another profile image of a Turkish sultan: Mehmed's descendant, Süleyman the Magnificent (Plate 4.18). By the sixteenth century, headgear had become a major visual signifier of the 'Oriental', as is evident in costume books and prints from the time. In the portrait of Süleyman, it reaches a climax: the fact of its authorship by the most eminent workshop of the day, its unstable mix of authority and otherness, of majesty and caricature, say much about the ambiguous power of 'El Gran Turco', as he was widely known, in the European imagination of the time.[57]

3 Mamluk motifs and an 'Oriental mode'

Venetian trade, together with the colonies of merchants established throughout the eastern Mediterranean, meant a constant interplay and importation of ideas and stories, as well as objects, textiles and raw materials into Venice itself. The result of the merging of thousands of individual responses was a distinctively inflected society bearing witness to 'the profound cultural impact of centuries of trade with the Islamic world'.[58] In the early fifteenth century, Jacopo Bellini had already drawn turbaned figures and exotic animals in his sketchbooks, which were essential in establishing a visual repertoire for the representation of these complex interactions. Later in the fifteenth century, and in the early years of the sixteenth, a deepening response to Islamic motifs, dress and peoples continued to impact on Venetian material culture and led to a distinct 'Oriental mode' for Venetian pictorial art. This section will go on to explore examples of this art, but will begin with two images of the heart of the city, or rather its hearts (plural): the political and religious focus on Piazza San Marco, with the Palazzo Ducale and the basilica (Plate 4.4), and the economic and commercial centre of the Venetian empire at Rialto.

Gentile Bellini's *Procession in the Piazza San Marco* of 1496 (Plate 4.19) points to the unique societal organisation of Venice. The ethos of the ordered totality, as enshrined in the 'Myth of Venice', encompassing a multiplicity of distinctions, but encompassing and subsuming them nonetheless, underwrites the picture's composition. Bellini's piazza is dominated by the façade of San Marco, in front of which a procession makes its way from right to left. Bellini in effect orchestrates the multiplicity of cultural influences on the fabric of Venice, from the golden Byzantine mosaics and domes, and the Gothic arches of the basilica, to the Islamic pink and white lozenge-shapes and decorative tile work of the Doge's Palace.

Bellini's picture was originally painted for the meeting room of the Scuola Grande di San Giovanni Evangelista, whose members process across the front of the square. The organised quality of the painted representation stands unequivocally for the ordered nature of Venetian society – its diversity rendered equal in the sight of the Church.[59] Along with ladies, gentlemen and citizens in recognisable costumes, there is a group of German merchants in the middle distance to the right of the canopy; four Greek merchants in their distinctive black-brimmed hats standing in the middle of the square to the left; in the distance, in front of the basilica to the right, are three turbaned Turks. In the row of first-floor windows along the far left of the square, well-dressed women, two of them apparently veiled in Islamic style, look out from balconies, over which are draped more than 30 rich oriental carpets, stressing Venice's trading empire.

The real subject of the picture, however, is none of this urban spectacle. Its main point, and the point also of the other eight paintings in the *scuola*'s great albergo, or meeting room, is to commemorate the Miracles of the True Cross. The Scuola Grande di San Giovanni Evangelista's prize possession was a fragment of the True Cross, donated in the previous century by the Grand Chancellor of Cyprus, who had in turn received it from the Patriarch of Constantinople. The reliquary was taken out and borne in procession on key feast days – such as the one depicted here: 25 April, the feast day of Saint Mark, patron saint of Venice. The key figure in the painting is a merchant from Brescia, in Venice for the vigil, and doubtless also on business. While there, the merchant received notice of a near fatal accident to his son, and he is just visible, through a gap in the procession to the right of centre, kneeling and praying to God for his son's survival as the relic of the True Cross passes by. On his return to Brescia, the merchant found his boy healed: a miracle. God's presence in the world is confirmed. This is what Bellini represents: the divine at work in the cosmopolitan life of Venice.

Something of the same holds for another picture originally part of the same cycle in the Scuola's meeting room, painted by Vittore Carpaccio two years earlier (Plate 4.20). Here, Carpaccio depicts another miracle, this time in the economic and commercial heart of Venice, the Rialto, adjacent to the busy Grand Canal. Once again the key to the picture is displaced to the margins, the sacred being embedded in the flow of secular life. At the far left, in the first-floor loggia, an exorcism is taking place. A possessed man is being healed by the miracle-working fragment of the True Cross, as commercial and social life rolls on with barely a blink. Another varied cast of characters is discernible. Along the bank of the canal, immediately

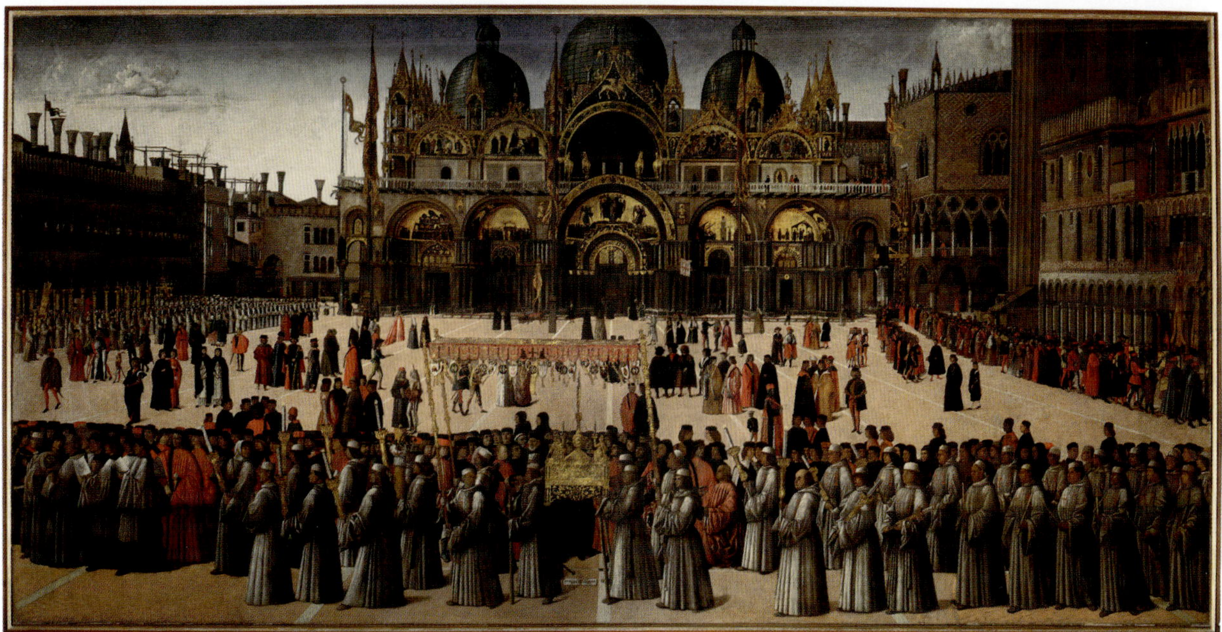

Plate 4.19 Gentile Bellini, *Procession in the Piazza San Marco*, 1496, oil on canvas, 367 × 745 cm. Accademia, Venice. © 2017. Photo: Scala, Florence – courtesy of the Ministero dei Beni e delle Attività Culturali.

before the bridge, can just be seen the columns of an open loggia where the merchants met. Outside it, two white-turbaned figures in long robes, one white, one orange, can just be made out. In the foreground, at the far left, in black-brimmed hats and sumptuous brocade robes, stand figures thought to be Armenian or Greek merchants. And unmissable, right in the centre foreground and acting as a kind of counter-focus to the decentred miracle, is a working man, albeit no ordinary workman: a distinctively attired African gondolier.

This gondolier was either a slave or more likely a freedman, an ex-slave. Recent research has argued that the slave trade was crucial to Venice's early economic growth, as early as the eighth century.[60] Most were from central and eastern Europe, often described as 'Tartars' or 'Circassians' from the area around the Black Sea, but slaves were also brought to Europe from coastal areas of Africa, and there is evidence that their specialist skills as oarsmen were recognised as a qualification for this distinctly Venetian profession.[61] After the fall of Constantinople, there was a decline in the Black Sea slave trade (not that the traffic died out – they were simply used by the Ottomans) and an increase in the use of slaves from Africa. The numbers increased as European attitudes turned against the

enslavement of fellow Christians, and increasing Ottoman power militated against the use of Muslim slaves. By 1600, however, Venetian slavery had died out – not least because of competing demand from Portuguese, Spanish, Dutch, British and French colonies, as well as the Muslim states. After that time, freed slaves continued to live in Venice, mostly, though not exclusively, working as domestic servants. Although Africans were never as numerous as other communities, such as Jews, Turks and Germans, the imagery of black people entered into Venetian popular culture and has never really left it (as the Fred Wilson installation mentioned at the start of this chapter testifies).

In the Scuola di San Giorgio degli Schiavoni, the *fondaco* of the merchants from Dalmatia, between 1502 and 1508, Carpaccio painted three scenes from the life of Saint George as part of an overall scheme of nine pictures. Whereas the two paintings from San Giovanni Evangelista by Bellini and Carpaccio represent the diversity of Venetian society itself, these pictures form part of an overtly 'Oriental mode' in Venetian art. The narrative mode as a whole functioned as a visual counterpart to the historical chronicles which recounted the city's foundation and prosperity.[62] In the late fifteenth century,

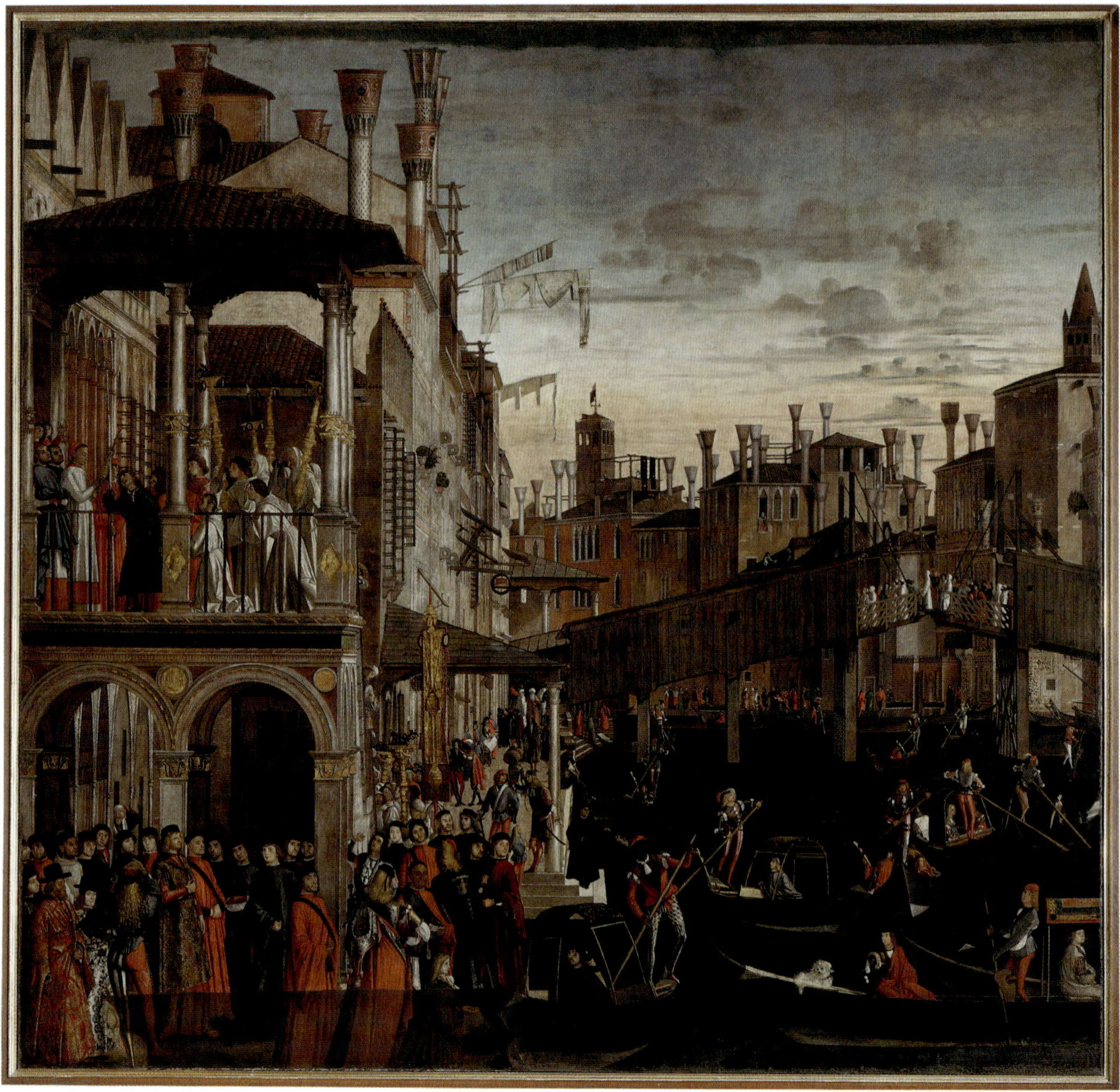

Plate 4.20 Vittore Carpaccio, *Miracle at Rialto (The Exorcism)*, 1494, oil on canvas, 365 × 389 cm. Accademia, Venice. © 2017. Photo: Scala, Florence – courtesy of the Ministero dei Beni e delle Attività Culturali.

contemporary political developments seem to have stimulated artists to address a newly pressing theme, namely the Other to Venice's imperium, in the shape of expansionist Islam. In these works, certain Venetian artists 'attempted to reproduce an Islamic setting, with figures dressed in Muslim garb, exotic animals – camels, monkeys and giraffes – and, on occasion, architecture of Islamic inspiration'.[63] In contrast to Bellini's portrait of Mehmed II or his individual costume studies, these pictures involve a conscious attempt to imagine Islamic culture and society.

The representation of the world of Islam takes, however, a specific form. One curious feature of this development is that Venetian artists seem to have shied away from representing contemporary Ottoman society as such. Whereas verbal reports on Ottoman society abounded, and although isolated Ottoman figures can be found in Venetian art, sometimes situated in the heart of Venice itself, there are no known images of the lived environment of the Ottoman world. More 'realistic' depictions of Ottomans and their daily lives came to be known only

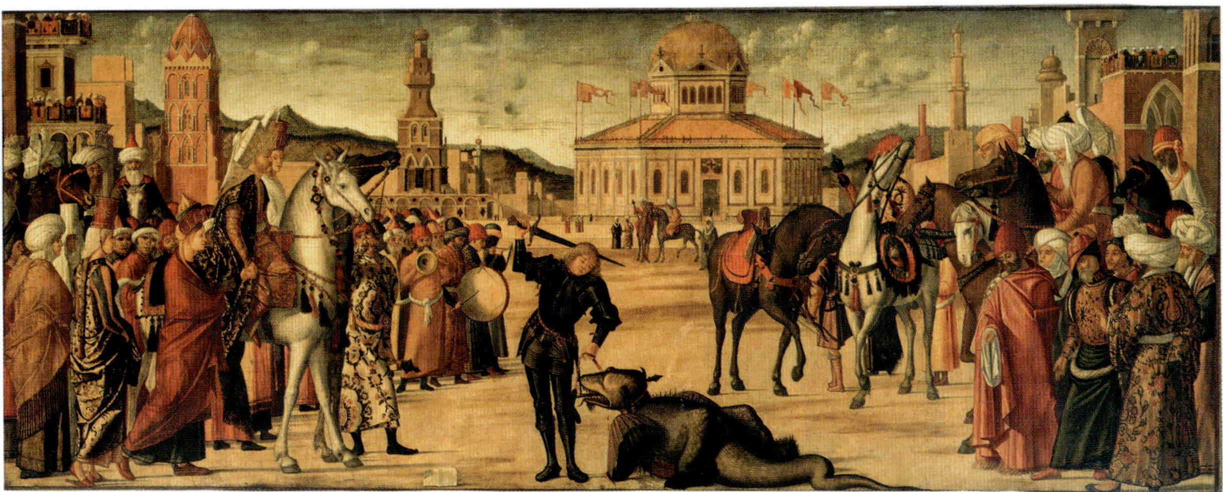

Plate 4.21 Vittore Carpaccio, *The Triumph of Saint George*, c.1507–08, oil and tempera on canvas, 141 × 360 cm. Scuola di San Giorgio degli Schiavoni, Venice. © 2017. Photo: Scala, Florence.

in the mid-sixteenth century, through printed images.[64] Appearing earlier, however, are plentiful images of the early Christian world of the Holy Land. And in the late fifteenth and early sixteenth centuries, the Holy Land lay not in Ottoman territory but in the empire of the Mamluks, the other eastern Mediterranean Islamic culture, based in present-day Syria and Egypt. So Venetian artists, representing the trials and victories of the early Christian Church, imagined them against a partly factual, partly made-up background of known architecture and non-Christians in Mamluk costume.

Thus, Carpaccio's *The Triumph of Saint George* (Plate 4.21) shows a crowd of Mamluk figures witnessing the triumph of the Christian knight against a background of buildings based on woodcut images of the Dome of the Rock and the Church of the Holy Sepulchre in Jerusalem. Traditionally, the Saint George story was set in the Eastern Christian Empire, including Palestine. The dragon motif was established in the thirteenth-century Golden Legend, wherein the killing of the dragon results in the conversion of the people to Christianity. It does not take an enormous leap of the imagination to read the dragon that is about to succumb to George's *coup de grâce* as a figure for the pagan unbelief that the Church is poised to overcome. This reading is reinforced in the final painting of the series, *Saint George Baptising the Pagans* (Plate 4.22). To the left, musicians wearing the Mamluk *zamt* (a tufted bonnet) stand on a plinth covered in an Islamic

carpet; to the right, conspicuously bare-headed figures are baptised into the Christian faith, their elaborate Mamluk headgear cast aside at the foot of the stairs they have mounted. The meeting house of the Dalmatian confraternity of Saint George was in a building owned by the Knights of Saint John of Jerusalem, themselves a crusader organisation. The Dalmatians had been in the frontline of the Venetian struggle against the Turks in the Adriatic, and their presence in Venice marked them as, essentially, refugees from Ottoman expansion. The occasion of the commission to decorate the meeting room was their receipt of an important relic of Saint George in honour of their exploits under the flag of Venice. This was a gift from the commander of the Venetian forts in Dalmatia before they fell to the Turks in 1499, who in turn had received it from no less a figure than the Patriarch of Jerusalem. It can readily be seen, therefore, how the Saint George legend of the defeat of pagan unbelief by the action of a virtuous Christian knight becomes a resonant motif at a point where Venetian Christian culture perceives itself threatened by the apparently unstoppable expansion of the Islamic Ottoman Empire.

A similar cluster of concerns underwrites the enormous painting by Gentile Bellini of *Saint Mark Preaching in Alexandria* (Plate 4.23). This picture turned out to be Gentile's last and, although the design and most of the actual work is his, some of the

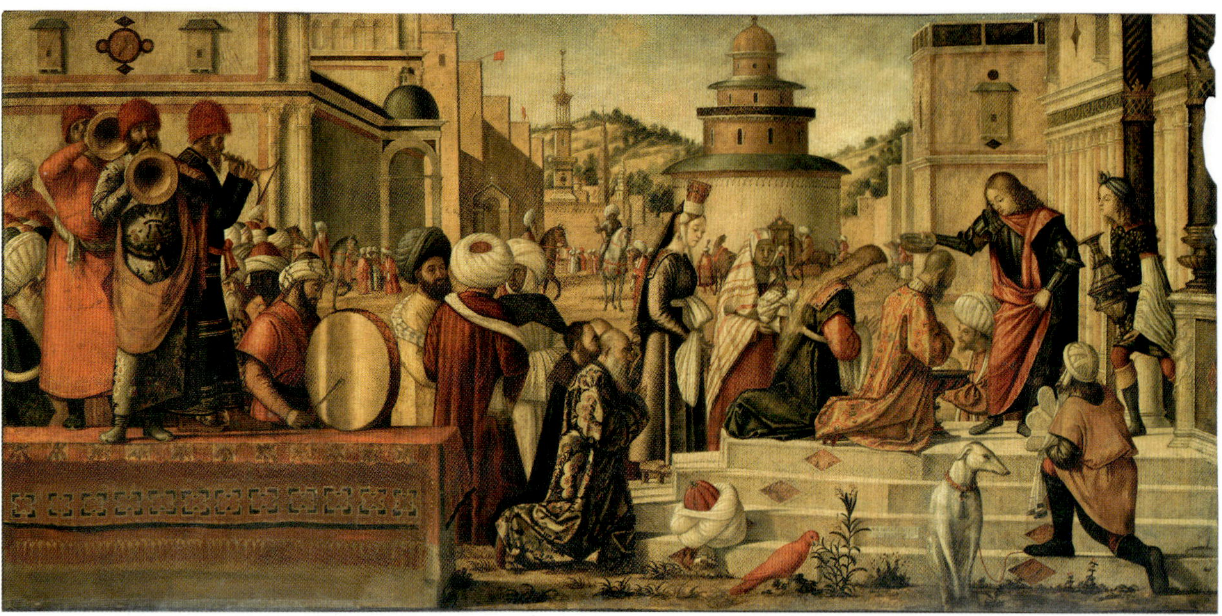

Plate 4.22 Vittore Carpaccio, *Saint George Baptising the Pagans (Selenites)*, *c.*1507–08, oil and tempera on canvas, 141 × 285 cm. Scuola di San Giorgio degli Schiavoni, Venice. © 2017. Photo: Scala, Florence.

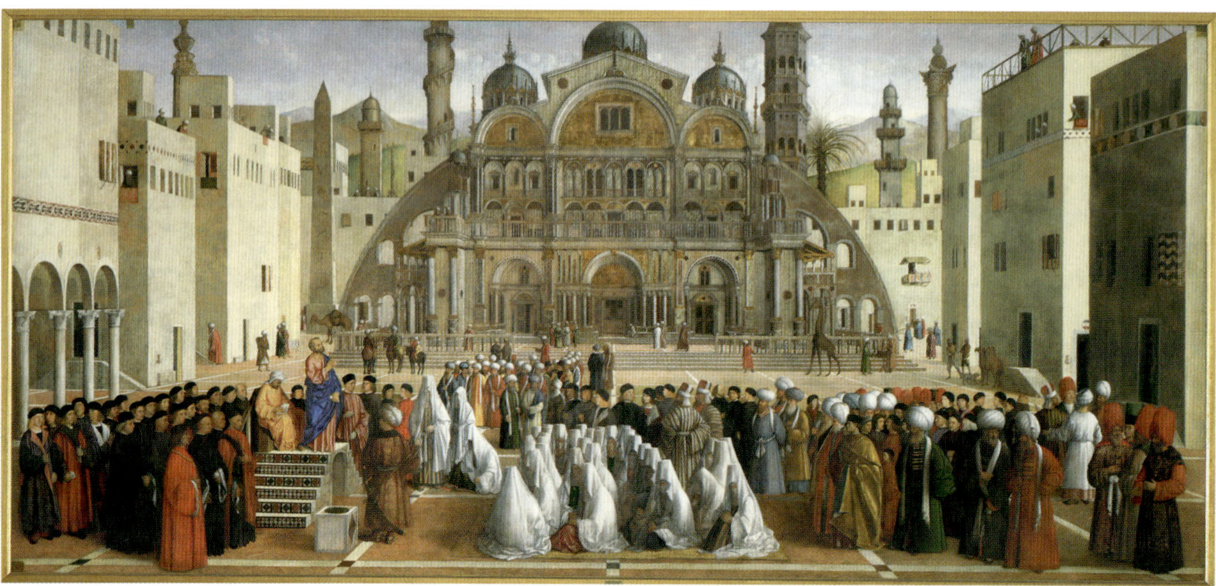

Plate 4.23 Gentile Bellini, *Saint Mark Preaching in Alexandria*, *c.*1504–07, oil on canvas, 347 × 770 cm. Pinacoteca di Brera, Milan. © 2017. Photo: Scala, Florence – courtesy of the Ministero dei Beni e delle Attività Culturali.

foreground figures and the buildings to right and left of the central square were completed after his death by his brother Giovanni. The Scuola Grande di San Marco had been rebuilding its premises after a fire in 1485, and Bellini put himself forward to decorate the albergo as early as 1492. The commission, however,

was not finalised until 1504, by which time Bellini had behind him the success of his *Procession in the Piazza San Marco*. The new painting was intended to evoke that earlier triumph, which was indeed 'specifically cited as the standard which he promised to surpass'.[65] The added ingredient in this commission, of course, is

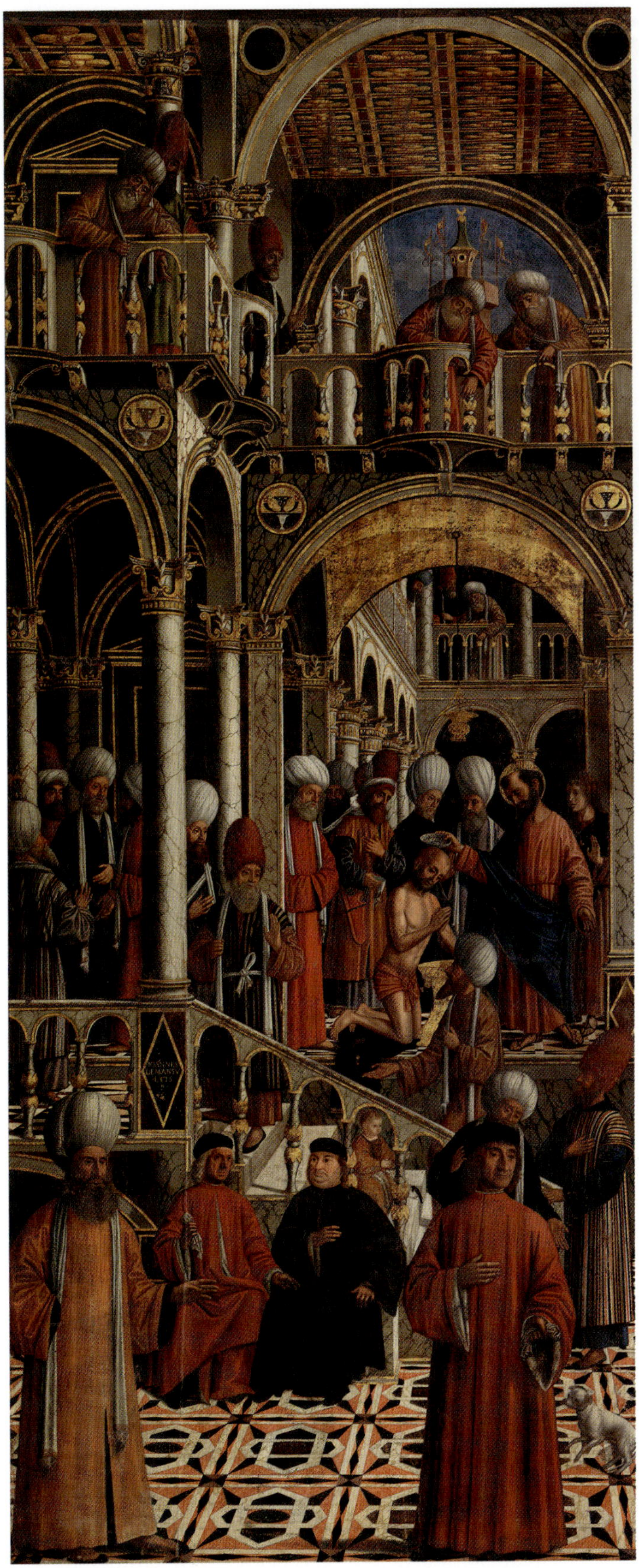

that Saint Mark is the patron saint of Venice itself. Preaching to the infidel – and indeed, dying for the cause – represents a powerful ideological message in early sixteenth-century Venice.

This was not the first work to dramatise Saint Mark's attempts to win over the infidels in a plausibly Egyptian setting: precedence goes to a project of the late 1490s by Cima da Conegliano and Giovanni Mansueti for the silk-weavers guild. Indeed, Mansueti went on to work on the Scuola Grande di San Marco commission after Gentile's death, with three further orientalising paintings on episodes from the life of Saint Mark (Plate 4.24). Mansueti's rather cluttered paintings draw on what was by then an established repertoire of motifs, including a variety of Islamic headgear and the Mamluk coat of arms, albeit set in unlikely classical architecture. By contrast, in the grandeur of its conception and coherence of design, Gentile's picture of *Saint Mark Preaching in Alexandria* represents a culmination of the 'Orientalist mode' in Venetian painting. Taken in conjunction with the *Procession in the Piazza San Marco*, this painting represents a kind of mapping of Venice onto its Other: the Piazza San Marco onto the Alexandrian square, the basilica onto the imaginary pagan temple. It is as if by assimilating the exotic – and threatening – into the familiar, the all too real threat of the Islamic Other could be negotiated and absorbed at the level of the imagination.

In his pioneering work on Venetian Orientalism, Julian Raby investigated a number of possible sources for this complex imagery of Islamic society that was fashioned by Venetian artists.[66] 'Fashioned' is an appropriate term because such images are not only the product of direct experience. As already noted, Bellini did not produce

Plate 4.24 Giovanni Mansueti, *Saint Mark Baptising Anianas*, commissioned 1518, completed on his death in 1526, oil on canvas, 335 × 125 cm. Pinacoteca di Brera, Milan. Photo: © akg-images/ Cameraphoto.

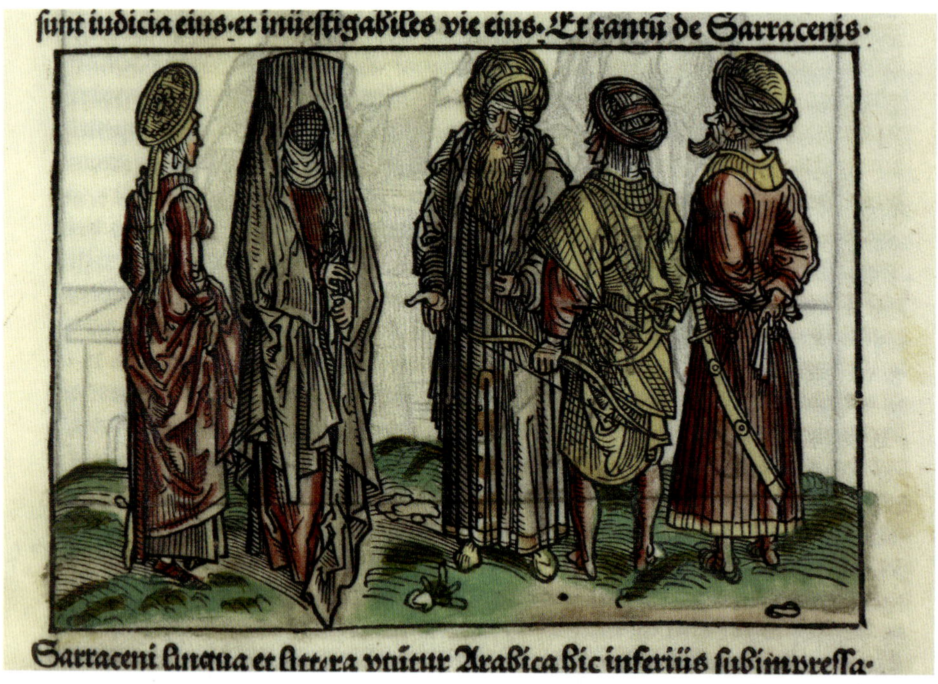

Plate 4.25 Erhard Reuwich, *Saracens*, woodcut in Bernhard von Breydenbach, *Peregrinatio in Terram Sanctam*, 1486. The British Library, London, shelfmark G.7202. Photo: © The British Library Board.

any large-scale image of Ottoman society from his visit to Constantinople, and none exists by any other hand. However, in addition to individual portraits and costume studies by Gentile Bellini and Costanzo da Ferrara, another important visual resource was provided by the German woodcuts of Erhard Reuwich. These accompanied Bernhard von Breydenbach's *Peregrinatio in Terram Sanctam*, an account of his pilgrimage to the Holy Land in 1483, published three years later in Mainz (Plate 4.25).

Exercise

Look carefully at *Saint Mark Preaching in Alexandria* (Plate 4.23). What particular elements in Gentile's painting situate the narrative in the 'exotic' setting of Alexandria?

Discussion

Exotic animals, such as camels and a giraffe, can be seen, as well as a palm tree. Close attention is also paid to costume. A clear contrast is intended between the dress of the Venetians behind Saint Mark and that of the crowd in front of him, particularly the heavy white veils of the women and the large turbans and sumptuous robes worn by the men. The white-veiled figures are

probably derived from Reuwich's woodcuts. The architecture of the buildings lining the square is also noteworthy, with their monochrome, largely undecorated façades and small windows to keep the buildings cool. Tall minarets in the background indicate an abundance of mosques, while to the left is an ancient Egyptian obelisk inscribed with hieroglyphs. As with the *Procession in the Piazza San Marco*, textiles or carpets are visible hanging from windows, but here the figures looking on from roofs and windows wear turbans and robes.

The picture is thus a composite put together to produce the effect of an Oriental scene.[67] Many of the architectural details are topographically accurate: the pillar in the right-hand background is the column of Diocletian in Alexandria, known as 'Pompey's pillar' and marking the site of a pagan temple destroyed by early Christians. The top of the famous Pharos lighthouse, one of the Seven Wonders of the World, demolished in 1480 by Sultan Qaytbay (r.1468–96), appears at the far left. The obelisk to the left of the central temple had been brought to Alexandria by the Roman Emperor Augustus from Heliopolis.[68] Yet the defining feature of the painting, rather than its circumstantial detailing, is of a somewhat different order: it is an imaginative recycling of Bellini's own previous masterpiece. The composition of the piazza flanked by the receding orthogonals of the side buildings (these apparently rendered plainer by Giovanni), the band of figures across the foreground, parallel to the picture plane, but above all, the fantastic temple dominating and defining the scene as Other, are all adapted from the *Procession in the Piazza San Marco*. The façade, with its arches and domes, unmistakeably evokes the basilica of San Marco, shorn of its Gothic tracery, but with the addition of enormous curving buttresses. Probably drawing on a visual memory of the basilica of Hagia Sophia, which Gentile would have seen in Constantinople a quarter of a century earlier, this formidable synthesis serves to situate the scene in a realm at once exotic and familiar. In sum, the giant picture with its hundreds of figures and colossal architecture aspires to nothing less than a displaced affirmation of Christian Venice's sway over the realm of the infidel: imagined, moreover, at precisely the moment when that actual hegemony was threatened as never before.

One final example of imagery in Venetian art that was inspired by contact with the Islamic world can be found in an arresting picture, now in the Louvre, of the official reception of an ambassador (Plate 4.26). The artist is unknown. For a long time, the location of the scene also remained unknown to Western art historians, themselves largely unfamiliar with Islamic societies. It has now been realised, however, that both the clothing and the architecture indicate a Mamluk location. The turbans are not Ottoman: they include the bearskin-type hats of the military, the large, often white, turbans lacking the Ottoman tāj in the middle, and the elaborate horned, so-called 'waterwheel' turban – used for example by Mansueti in his Saint Mark series of paintings. Also, the dome and minarets of the Umayyad Mosque in Damascus have now been identified. The city of Damascus was an important trading centre, situated at the end of Asian caravan routes, as well as a staging post for Western pilgrims en route to the Holy Land. Other features of the picture, such as the bathhouse in the centre, with glass tiles in its dome, the walled garden

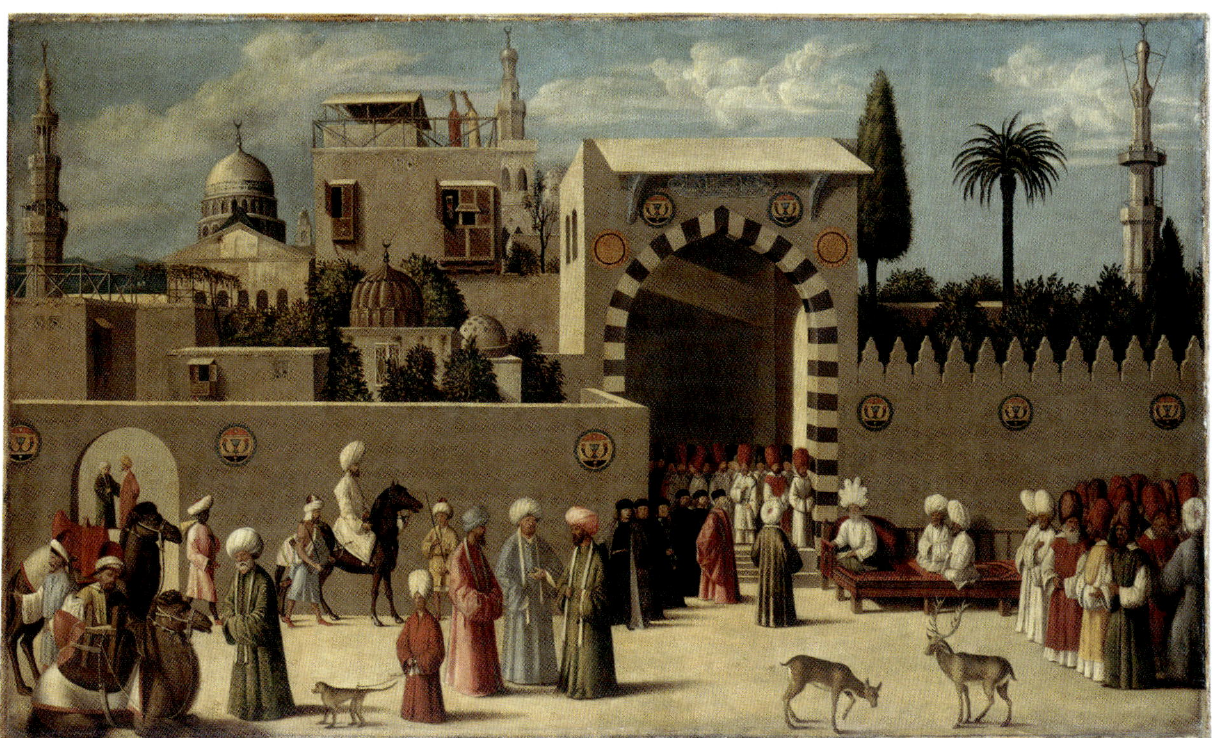

Plate 4.26 Unknown Venetian, *Reception of an Ambassador in Damascus*, between 1488 and 1516, oil on canvas, 175 × 201 cm. Musée du Louvre, Paris. Photo: © RMN-Grand Palais (Musée du Louvre)/Thierry Le Mage.

and rooftop terraces, all bespeak first-hand knowledge of such a scene. Indeed, it has been suggested that the mosque was viewed from the Venetian merchants' *fondaco* itself. Local colour is further provided by Mamluk insignia on the walls and gateway, and, not least, the camels and palm tree. The scene represents an official reception by the local governor or *na'ib*, shown seated on a low platform with two other dignitaries behind him, of a Venetian ambassador – standing in a red gown with other black-clad Venetians to the left of the gateway.

The Damascus reception was for long considered the single most important source for the Venetian 'Oriental mode' of Carpaccio, Cima, Mansueti, Gentile and others.[69] However, further research now indicates that it follows, rather than predates, such works. Recent conservation treatment of the painting has revealed the date '1511' in Roman numerals (MDXI), in the middle ground on the wall between the horse's legs.[70] This date has helped further situate the painting, not just spatially in Damascus, but temporally within a particular moment of intense diplomatic negotiations and intrigue between Venice and the Mamluks. In July 1510, a Cypriot messenger and two Venetian merchants based in Aleppo were intercepted on the north-west bank of the Euphrates, carrying compromising messages from Isma'il I, Shah of Persia (r.1501–24), to the Venetian consuls in Alexandria and Damascus, Tommaso Contarini and Pietro Zen. This caused a serious upheaval in diplomatic relations between the Mamluks and Venetians, known as the 'Zen Affair'. It resulted in the confiscation of goods and house arrest for the Venetian community living in Damascus, as well as the imprisonment of Zen and Contarini themselves. It is now thought that the picture may represent the reconciliation of this conflict, and the reception of Zen's successor as Venetian ambassador, Nicolò Malipiero.[71] If so, there would be an echo of the way in which Gentile Bellini's portrait of Sultan Mehmed II, with which this discussion of the 'Oriental mode' in Venetian art began, marked the ending of an earlier dispute between Venice and its trading partners in the Ottoman world.

A notable feature of the Venetian Orientalist paintings examined above is their keen attention to costume, as one of the principal topics of interest in these works. In the sixteenth century, Venetian fascination with the details of foreign fashions sparked a new and highly popular genre of imagery, the 'costume book', printed books illustrating costumes worn by diverse peoples of the world. Nine costume books were published in Venice between 1540 and 1610, about a third of all such books produced in Europe.[72] The significance of this is largely due to Venice's reputation as a 'theatre of the world', where people, as Giulio Ballino noted in 1569, 'use all languages and are dressed in different ways'.[73] One particularly instructive example of a costume print was published in 1602 and engraved by Ambrogio Brambilla, but likely followed earlier designs made by Martino Rota from earlier in the sixteenth century (Plate 4.27). In this print, viewers are asked specifically to compare the 28 female costumes as a way to define cultural identities.

Exercise

Can you identify the pictorial strategies that Brambilla is using to allow the viewer to contrast and compare the costumes? How are the images of women identified and organised, and how does the print differentiate between them?

Discussion

By using a grid, and employing the same profile silhouette, the viewer is asked to focus specifically on the contours of difference: from appendages such as hair and hats, to hemlines. The print begins with the dress worn in a number of Italian cities, which vary slightly from one another. But difference becomes exaggerated as you move down the page. Not only does the headgear become more elaborate, but the dresses become shorter and, in some cases, are more revealing. You may have noticed that there is less attention to difference in physiognomy, thus the emphasis is on dress.

As Bronwen Wilson has argued, this sort of comparison, effectively transmitted through print, makes socio-cultural difference legible and visible. Hence, the proliferation of costume books in Venice, illustrating different costumes from around the world, actually worked to emphasise geographical and national boundaries rather than annul them. It is significant that physiognomy and skin colour are secondary to

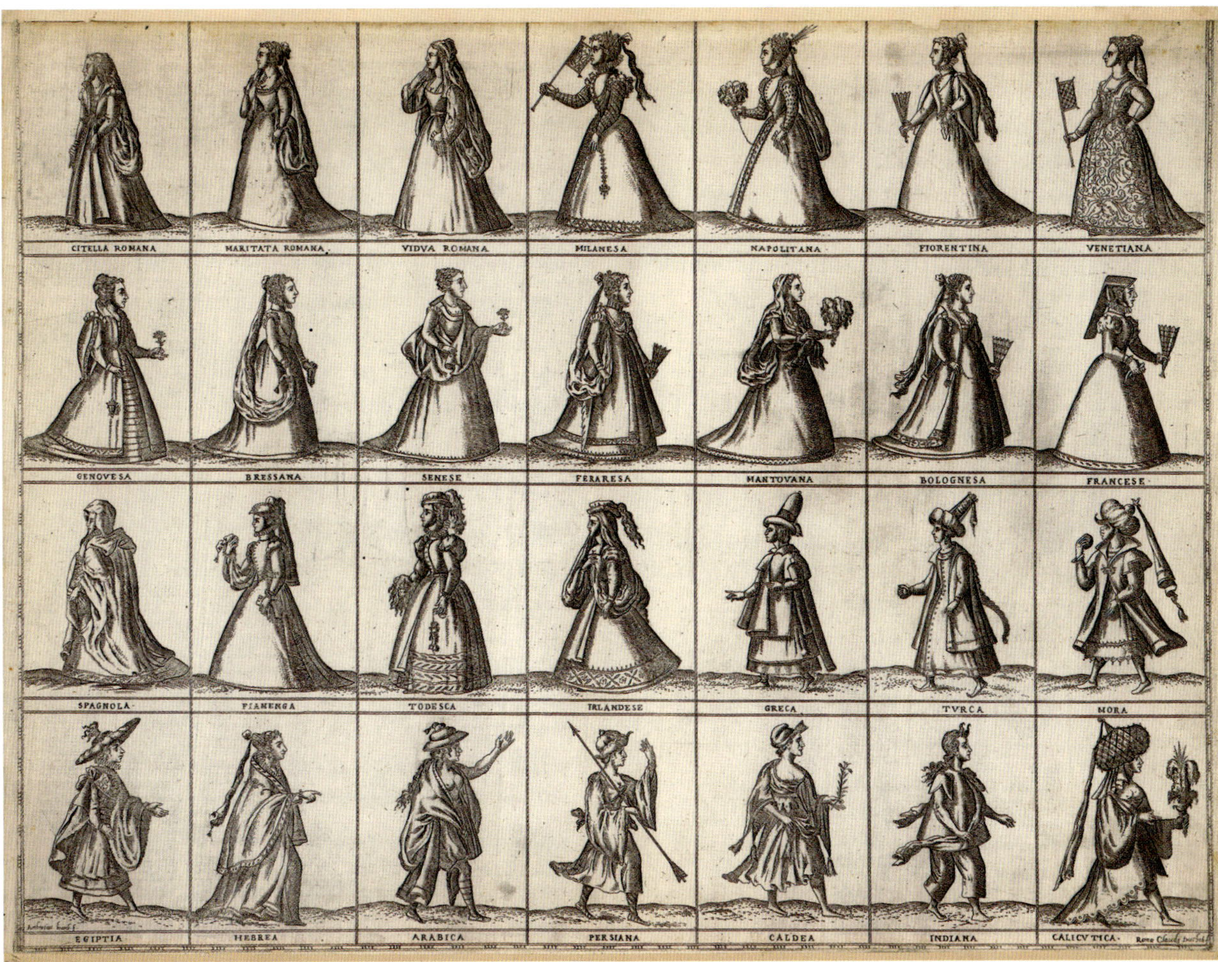

Plate 4.27 Ambrogio Brambilla, 'Female costumes', engraving, 54 × 51 cm, from the series *Speculum Romanae magnificentiae*, Rome, Claudio Duchetti, 1580–85. British Museum, London, PD 1947,0319.26.180. © The Trustees of the British Museum.

costume in communicating difference in such prints. It is important to underline that this is a time before the emergence of racial eugenics, craniometry and ethnography in the late eighteenth and nineteenth centuries, which were used by some to argue for racial hierarchy and segregation. In the sixteenth century, costume was often closely tied to group identity, and the printed texts that circulated stressed how habits such as sexual practices and religious beliefs were identifiable through visible signs worn on the body.[74] Many Venetian merchants lived in the Levant, and in the fifteenth century Venetians were even allowed to dress in 'the clothes of the Muslims, Mamluk and Bedouin on their journeys, so that there be no temptation to rob them'.[75] Gentile Bellini famously appeared in Ottoman dress when he returned from his sojourn in Constantinople. But by the sixteenth century there was some unease regarding the relationship between costume and identity, and fine distinctions were drawn between 'dressing as a Muslim (*da turco*), appearing as one (*far turco*), and turning into a Muslim (*farsi turco*)'.[76] A keen Venetian interest, even in times of conflict, in the habits, costumes and appearance of Muslims is not only evident in the popularity of costume books, but also in household inventories. These reveal that by the 1580s, portraits of 'Turks' could readily be found in domestic houses throughout Venice.

Conclusion

This chapter has reviewed some aspects of the social and cultural diversity of early modern Venice, and how it affected the art of the period. In particular, attention has been paid to Venice's relations with 'the East' in its several manifestations: the legacy of Orthodox Christian Byzantium, Venice's commercial and cultural ties to North Africa and the Levant, rivalry with the powerful contemporary Islamic societies of the Ottomans and Mamluks, and through its Mediterranean trading partners, a more diffuse acquaintance with Asia in general. The situation, however, was evolving rapidly. The great trading empire on which Venetian wealth was based came under increased pressure in the late fifteenth century from relentless Ottoman expansion. Soon, the Ottomans had even vanquished the Mamluks, taking Cairo in 1517. It was in response to this developing threat to their *Stato da Mar* that, at the end of the fifteenth century and with gathering pace in the early years of the sixteenth, Venice expanded into the north Italian mainland, the *terrafirma*. Despite a crushing defeat in 1509 by the forces of the League of Cambrai, in which the kings of France and Spain, the Holy Roman Emperor and the pope joined forces to curtail Venetian power, by 1516 Venice had recovered. This shift of power marked both a decline in Venice's orientation eastwards and a corresponding increase in engagement with the classical heritage associated with a more conventional sense of the Italian Renaissance. In art, these changed priorities are manifest in the work of the Venetian school of the sixteenth century: Giorgione, Titian, Tintoretto, Veronese, the 'great masters' who came to be ranked with Michelangelo, Raphael and others in the subsequent Academic construction of the Western canon that held sway until the advent of modernism in the nineteenth century. But that is another story. The story told here is drawn according to a different set of coordinates, before the age of empire when the lineaments of West and East hardened into cultural and racial stereotypes that have only recently begun to be widely questioned. The printing press and the Protestant Reformation would transform the spiritual world of Europe. And alongside that spiritual change came material change on an unforeseen scale. Since biblical times, indeed earlier, the eastern Mediterranean, spreading westwards into Europe and eastwards into Asia, had been the crossroads of the world. In 1488, however, the Portuguese navigator Bartholomeu Dias rounded the southern tip of Africa, and in 1498 Vasco da Gama reached India. In 1492, the Italian Christopher Columbus sailed west and stumbled across America. By 1522, a fleet under Ferdinand Magellan had sailed all the way round the globe. A new horizon was, with remarkable rapidity, being drawn around a new world.

One of the effects of contemporary globalisation, and the attendant meltdown of inherited Eurocentric assumptions, has been to lift historians' eyes to that great roof which has been built over European culture to protect it from the impure, the adulterous, the kitsch, the primitive and the hybrid. Known as the Western canon, it counts among its stoutest pillars 'antiquity' and 'the Renaissance'. As the wind from the future blows harder, more and more tiles are beginning to blow off the canonical roof and gradually a new past is being revealed. Renaissance Venice is one of those places where the light gets in.

Notes

[1] Bonami and Basualdo, 2003, p. 594.

[2] See Kristeller, 1965

[3] Greenblatt, 1980; Martin, 1997; Elmer, 2000; Brown, 2000.

[4] See Grube, 1989; Fortini Brown, 1997, pp. 23, 26, 37; Aikema and Brown, 1999; Howard, 2000, p. 111; Humfrey, 1995, p. 9.

[5] De Commynes and Sansovino, as quoted in Martin and Romano, 2000, pp. 20–1.

[6] Martin and Romano, 2000; Fortini Brown, 1996, p. 54.

[7] Rosand, 2001.

[8] Burke, 2000, p. 398; Wilson, 2005.

[9] Burke, 2000, pp. 403–4.

[10] Fortini Brown, 1996.

[11] Hocquet, 2007; Ashtor, 2014.

[12] Howard, 2000.

[13] Nelson, 1996.

[14] Born et al., 2015; Behrens-Abouseif, 2014; Aksan and Goffman, 2007; Goffman, 2002; Harper, 2011.

[15] Hills, 1999.

[16] Howard, 2000, p. 142.

[17] Howard, 2007, p. 82.

[18] Tafuri, 1995.

[19] Howard, 1999, pp. 37–8.

[20] Nicol, 1988.

[21] Mack, 2002; Contadini, 2006; Molà and Ajmar-Wollheim, 2011.

[22] Contadini, 2016, p. 290.

[23] Spallanzani, 2010, pp. 11–12; Contadini, 2016, p. 297.

[24] Auld, 2004; Auld, 2007, pp. 212–25; Mack, 2002, pp. 142–3; Behrens-Abouseif, 2005.

[25] McCray, 1999; Tait, 1999, Hess, 2004; Barovier Mentasti and Carboni, 2007; Carboni, 2007, cat. 159.

26 Cordez and Schmitz-Esser, forthcoming, 2018.

27 Mack, 2002, p. 123; Carboni, 2007, p. 344.

28 Molà, 2000; Schoeser, 2007.

29 Denny, 2007; Monnas, 2008; Jacoby, 2010.

30 Zrebiec, 1995–96; Watt, 2013.

31 Rosand, 1982, Ch. 1; Pedrocco, 2002, p. 56.

32 Rodini, 2011.

33 See Babinger, 1978.

34 Runciman, 1969.

35 Meserve, 2008.

36 Babinger, 1978, p. 431

37 Raby, 1980, p. 242.

38 Kritovoulos of Imbros, writing in 1467, cited in Brotton, 2002, p. 196. See also Raby, 1982a; Necipoğlu, 2012, p. 7.

39 Necipoğlu, 2012, pp. 7–9.

40 Rogers, 1991; Necipoğlu, 2012.

41 Necipoğlu, 2012.

42 Venetian reports, cited in Valensi, 1990, pp. 181, 182.

43 Raby, 1987; Spinale, 2003, pp. 164, 191, 251–4; Campbell and Chong, 2005, p. 107; Necipoğlu, 2012, pp. 27–30.

44 Campbell and Chong, 2005, pp. 106–19.

45 Gatward Cevizli, 2015; Roberts, 2016, pp. 19–38.

46 Campbell and Chong, 2005; Raby, 1991; Jardine and Brotton, 2000, p. 32.

47 See Vickers, 1978.

48 Mack, 2002, p. 149; Grabar, 2003, p. 190.

49 Madar, 2011.

50 Carboni, 2007, cat. 116–17.

51 Campbell and Chong, 2005, pp. 78–9; Monnas, 2008, p. 245.

52 Pixley, 2003, p. 9; Necipoğlu, 2012, p. 34.

53 Pedani Fabris, cited by Bagci, 2004.

54 Raby, 2000, pp. 72–3; Necipoğlu, 2005, p. 88; Necipoğlu, 2012, pp. 45–8; texts reproduced in Newall, 2017, pp. 59–62.

55 Pamuk, 2001.

56 Rogers, 1991; Necipoğlu, 2000, pp. 28–30.

57 Necipoğlu, 1989; Wilson, 2003; Necipoğlu, 2012, pp. 37–9; Born et al., 2015, pp. 182–3.

58 Howard, 2000, p. 36.

59 Fortini Brown, 1988, p. 146.

60 Frankopan, 2015, pp. 122–3.

61 Kaplan, 2010, pp. 93–101; Lowe, 2013.

62 Fortini Brown, 1988, pp. 87–97.

63 Raby, 1982b, p. 17.

64 Ilg, 2010.

65 Fortini Brown, 1988, p. 191, Bellini document quoted on p. 293.

66 Raby, 1982b.

67 Schmidt Arcangeli, 2007, pp. 128–9.

68 Howard, 2000, pp. 67–74.

69 Mack, 2002, p. 162. Campbell and Chong, 2005, p. 23.

70 Campbell, 2013; Carboni, 2007, cat. 29.

71 Campbell, 2013, p. 115; Howard, 2007, p. 84; Carboni, 2007, cat. 29.

72 Wilson, 2004; Wilson, 2005; Wilson, 2007.

73 Quoted in Wilson, 2004, p. 221.

74 Wilson, 2004; Wilson, 2007.

75 Howard, 2000, p. 38; Dursteler, 2006.

76 Wilson, 2003, p. 49.

Bibliography

Aikema, B. and Brown, B. (eds) (1999) *Renaissance Venice and the North: Crosscurrents in the Time of Dürer, Bellini, and Titian*, Milan, Bompiani.

Aksan, V. H. and Goffman, D. (eds) (2007) *The Early Modern Ottomans: Remapping the Empire*, Cambridge, Cambridge University Press.

Ashtor, E. (2014) *Levant Trade in the Middle Ages*, Princeton, NJ, Princeton University Press.

Auld, S. (2004) *Renaissance Venice, Islam and Mahmud the Kurd: A Metalworking Enigma*, London, Altajir World of Islam Trust.

Auld, S. (2007) 'Master Mahmud and inlaid metalwork in the 15th century', in Carboni, S. (ed.) *Venice and the Islamic World, 828–1797*, New York, The Metropolitan Museum of Art; New Haven, CT and London, Yale University Press, pp. 212–25.

Babinger, F. (1978 [1953]) *Mehmet the Conqueror and his Time* (trans. R. Mannheim), Princeton, NJ, Princeton University Press.

Bagci, S. (2004) catalogue entry no. 226, in Roxburgh, D. J. (ed.) *Turks: A Journey of a Thousand Years, 600–1600*, London, Royal Academy of Arts, p. 434.

Barovier Mentasti, R. and Carboni, S. (2007) 'Enameled glass between the eastern Mediterranean and Venice', in Carboni, S. (ed.) *Venice and the Islamic World, 828–1797*, New York, The Metropolitan Museum of Art; New Haven, CT and London, Yale University Press, pp. 252–75.

Behrens-Abouseif, D. (2005) 'Veneto–Saracenic metalware, a Mamluk art', *Mamluk Studies Review*, vol. 9, no. 2, pp. 147–72.

Behrens-Abouseif, D. (2014) *Practising Diplomacy in the Mamluk Sultanate: Gifts and Material Culture in the Medieval Islamic World*, London and New York, I.B. Tauris.

Bonami, F. and Basualdo, C. (eds) (2003) *Dreams and Conflicts: The Dictatorship of the Viewer*, Catalogue of the 50th Venice Biennale, Venice, Marsilio.

Born, R., Dziewulski, M., Messling, G., Beuing, R. and Carter, B. (eds) (2015) *The Sultan's World: The Ottoman Orient in Renaissance Art*, Brussels, Bozar Books and Hatje Cantz.

Brotton, J. (2002) *The Renaissance Bazaar: From the Silk Road to Michelangelo*, Oxford, Oxford University Press.

Brown, R. D. (2000) 'From Burckhardt to Greenblatt', in Whitlock, K. (ed.) *The Renaissance in Europe: A Reader*, New Haven, CT and London, Yale University Press in association with The Open University, pp. 4–11.

Burke, P. (2000) 'Early modern Venice as a center of information and communication', in Martin, J. and Romano, D. (eds) (2000) *Venice Reconsidered: The History and Civilization of an Italian City-State, 1297–1797*, Baltimore, MD and London, Johns Hopkins University Press, pp. 389–417.

Campbell, C. (2013) 'The "Reception of the Venetian ambassadors in Damascus": dating, meaning and attribution', in Norton, C. and Contadini, A. (eds) *The Renaissance and the Ottoman World*, Farnham and Burlington, VT, Ashgate Publishing, pp. 107–22.

Campbell, C. and Chong, A. (eds) (2005) *Bellini and the East*, London, National Gallery Company and Yale University Press.

Carboni, S. (ed.) (2007) *Venice and the Islamic World, 828–1797*, New York, The Metropolitan Museum of Art; New Haven, CT and London, Yale University Press.

Contadini, A. (2006) 'Middle-Eastern objects', in Ajmar-Wollheim, M. and Dennis, F. (eds) *At Home in Renaissance Italy*, London, Victoria and Albert Museum, pp. 308–21.

Contadini, A. (2016) 'Threads of ornament in the style world of the fifteenth and sixteenth centuries', in Necipoğlu, G. and Payne, A. (eds) *Histories of Ornament: From Global to Local*, Princeton, NJ, Princeton University Press, pp. 290–308.

Cordez, P. and Schmitz-Esser, R. (eds) (forthcoming, 2018) *Typical Venice? Venetian Commodities, 13th–16th Centuries*, Turnhout, Brepols Publishers.

Denny, W. B. (2007) 'Oriental carpets and textiles in Venice', in Carboni, S. (ed.) *Venice and the Islamic World, 828–1797*, New York, The Metropolitan Museum of Art; New Haven, CT and London, Yale University Press, pp. 175–91.

Dursteler, E. R. (2006) *Venetians in Constantinople: Nation, Identity, and Coexistence in the Early Modern Mediterreanan*, Baltimore, MD, Johns Hopkins University Press.

Elmer, P. (2000) 'Inventing the Renaissance: Burckhardt as historian', in Kekewich, L. (ed.) *The Impact of Humanism*, New Haven, CT and London, Yale University Press in association with The Open University, pp. 1–22.

Fortini Brown, P. (1988) *Venetian Narrative Painting in the Age of Carpaccio*, New Haven, CT and London, Yale University Press.

Fortini Brown, P. (1996) *Venice and Antiquity*, New Haven, CT and London, Yale University Press.

Fortini Brown, P. (1997) *Art and Life in Renaissance Venice*, Upper Saddle River, NJ, Pearson/Prentice Hall.

Frankopan, P. (2015) *The Silk Roads: A New History of the World*, London, Bloomsbury Publishing.

Gatward Cevizli, A. (2015) 'Mehmed II, Malatesta and Matteo De' Pasti: a match of mutual benefit between the "terrible Turk" and a "citizen of Hell"', *Renaissance Studies*, vol. 31, no. 1, pp. 43–65.

Goffman, D. (2002) *The Ottoman Empire and Early Modern Europe*, Cambridge, Cambridge University Press.

Grabar, O. (2003) 'Review', *The Art Bulletin,* vol. 85, no. 1, pp. 189–92.

Greenblatt, S. (1980) *Renaissance Self-Fashioning: From More to Shakespeare*, Chicago, IL, University of Chicago Press.

Grube, E. J. (ed.) (1989) *Arte veneziana e arte islamica*, Venice, l'Altra riva.

Harper, J. G. (ed.) (2011) *The Turk and Islam in the Western Eye, 1450–1750*, Farnham and Burlington, VT, Ashgate Publishing.

Hess, C. (ed.) (2004) *The Arts of Fire: Islamic Influences on Glass and Ceramics of the Italian Renaissance*, Los Angeles, CA, J. Paul Getty Museum.

Hills, P. (1999) *Venetian Colour: Marble, Mosaic, Painting and Glass, 1250–1550*, New Haven, CT, Yale University Press.

Hocquet, J.-C. (2007) 'Venice and the Turks', in Carboni, S. (ed.) *Venice and the Islamic World, 828–1797*, New York, The Metropolitan Museum of Art; New Haven, CT and London, Yale University Press, pp. 37–51.

Howard, D. (1999) 'Ruskin and the East', *Architectural Heritage*, vol. 10, no. 1, pp. 37–53.

Howard, D. (2000) *Venice and the East: The Impact of the Islamic World on Venetian Architecture, 1100–1500*, New Haven, CT and London, Yale University Press.

Howard, D. (2007) 'Venice and the Mamluks', in Carboni, S. (ed.) *Venice and the Islamic World, 828–1797*, New York, The Metropolitan Museum of Art; New Haven, CT and London, Yale University Press, pp. 72–89.

Humfrey, P. (1995) *Painting in Renaissance Venice*, New Haven, CT and London, Yale University Press.

Ilg, U. (2010) 'On the difficulties of depicting a "real" Turk: reflections on ethnographic orientalism in European art (14th to the 16th centuries)', in Schmidt Arcangeli, C. and Wolf, G. (eds) *Islamic Artefacts in the Mediterranean World: Trade, Gift Exchange and Artistic Transfer*, Venice, Marsilio, pp. 231–44.

Jacoby, D. (2010) 'Oriental silks go West: a declining trade in the later Middle Ages', in Schmidt Arcangeli, C. and Wolf, G. (eds) *Islamic Artefacts in the Mediterranean World: Trade, Gift Exchange and Artistic Transfer*, Venice, Marsilio, pp. 71–88.

Jardine, L. and Brotton, J. (2000) *Global Interests: Renaissance Art between East and West*, London, Reaktion.

Kaplan, P. H. (2010) 'Italy, 1490–1700', in Bindman, D. and Gates, H. L. (eds) *Image of the Black in Western Art, Volume III, From the 'Age of Discovery' to the Age of Abolition, Part I, Europe and the World Beyond*, Cambridge, MA and London, Belknap Press of Harvard University Press, pp. 92–189.

Kristeller, P.O. (1965 [1951]) 'The modern system of the arts', in *Renaissance Thought II: Papers on Humanism and the Arts*, New York, Harper & Row, pp. 163–227.

Lowe, K. (2013) 'Visible lives: black gondoliers and other black Africans in Renaissance Venice', *Renaissance Quarterly*, no. 66, pp. 412–52.

Mack, R. E. (2002) *Bazaar to Piazza: Islamic Trade and Italian Art, 1300–1600*, Berkeley, CA, Los Angeles, CA, and London, University of California Press.

McCray, P. (1999) *Glassmaking in Renaissance Venice: The Fragile Craft*, Aldershot, Ashgate Publishing.

Madar, H. (2011) 'Dürer's depictions of the Ottoman Turks: a case of early modern Orientalism?', in Harper, J. G. (ed.) *The Turk and Islam in the Western Eye, 1450–1750*, Burlington, VT, Ashgate Publishing, pp. 155–83.

Martin, J. (1997) 'Inventing sincerity, refashioning prudence: the discovery of the individual in Renaissance Europe', *American Historical Review*, no. 102, vol. 5, pp. 1309–42.

Martin, J. and Romano, D. (eds) (2000) *Venice Reconsidered: The History and Civilization of an Italian City-State, 1297–1797*, Baltimore, MD, Johns Hopkins University Press.

Meserve, M. (2008) *Empires of Islam in Renaissance Historical Thought*, Cambridge, MA, Harvard University Press.

Molà, L. (2000) *The Silk Industry of Renaissance Venice*, Baltimore, MD and London, Johns Hopkins University Press.

Molà, L. and Ajmar-Wollheim, M. (2011) 'The global Renaissance: cross-cultural objects in the early modern period', in Adamson, G., Riello, G. and Teasley, S. (eds) *Global Design History*, New York and London, Routledge, pp. 11–20.

Monnas, L. (2008) *Merchants, Princes and Painters: Silk Fabrics in Italian and Northern Paintings 1300–1550*, New Haven, CT and London, Yale University Press.

Necipoğlu, G. (1989) 'Süleyman the Magnificent and the representation of power in the context of Ottoman-Hapsburg-papal rivalry', *The Art Bulletin*, vol. 71, no. 3, pp. 401–27.

Necipoğlu, G. (2000) 'Word and image: the serial portraits of Ottoman sultans in comparative perspective', in Kangal, S. (ed.) *The Sultan's Portrait: Picturing the House of Osman*, Istanbul, Isbank, pp. 22–61.

Necipoğlu, G. (2005) *The Age of Sinan: Architectural Culture in the Ottoman Empire*, Princeton, NJ, Princeton University Press.

Necipoğlu, G. (2012) 'Virtual cosmopolitanism and creative translation: artistic conversations with Renaissance Italy in Mehmed II's Constantinople', *Muqarnas*, vol. 29, pp. 1–83.

Nelson, R. S. (1996) 'Living on the Byzantine borders of Western art', *Gesta*, vol. 35, no. 1, pp. 3–11.

Newall, D. (ed.) (2017) *Art and its Global Histories: A Reader*, Manchester and Milton Keynes, Manchester University Press in association with The Open University.

Nicol, D. M. (1988) *Byzantium and Venice: A Study in Diplomatic and Cultural Relations*, Cambridge, Cambridge University Press.

Pamuk, O. (2001) *My Name Is Red* (trans. E. M. Göknar), London, Faber & Faber. (Originally published as *Benim adim kirmizi*, Istanbul, Iletisim, 1998.)

Pedrocco, F. (2002) *The Art of Venice: From its Origins to 1797*, Florence, Scala; New York, Riverside.

Pixley, M. L. (2003) 'Islamic artefacts and cultural currents in the art of Carpaccio', *Apollo*, vol. 158, November, pp. 9–18.

Raby, J. (1980) 'Cyriacus of Ancona and the Ottoman Sultan Mehmet II', *Journal of the Warburg and Courtauld Institutes*, no. 43, pp. 242–6.

Raby, J. (1982a) 'A sultan of paradox: Mehmed the Conqueror as patron of the arts', *Oxford Art Journal*, vol. 5, no. 1, pp. 3–8.

Raby, J. (1982b) *Venice, Dürer and the Oriental Mode*, London, Sotheby Islamic Art Publications.

Raby, J. (1987) 'Pride and prejudice: Mehmed the Conqueror and the Italian portrait medal', *Studies in the History of Art*, vol. 21, pp. 171–94.

Raby, J. (1991) catalogue entry 107, Portrait Medal of Mehmed II, in Levenson, J.A. (ed.) *Circa 1492: Art in the Age of Exploration*, Washington, DC, National Gallery of Art; New Haven, CT, Yale University Press, p. 211.

Raby, J. (2000) 'Opening gambits: from Europe to Istanbul', in Kangal, S., Orbay, A. and Işin, P. M. (eds) *The Sultan's Portrait: Picturing the House of Osman*, Istanbul, Topkapı Palace Museum, pp. 64–91.

Roberts, S. (2016) 'The lost map of Matteo de' Pasti: cartography, diplomacy, and espionage in the Renaissance Adriatic', *Journal of Early Modern History,* vol. 20, pp. 19–38.

Rodini, E. (2011) 'The sultan's true face? Gentile Bellini, Mehmet II, and the value of verisimilitude', in Harper, J. G. (ed.) *The Turk and Islam in the Western Eye, 1450–1750*, Burlington, VT, Ashgate Publishing, pp. 21–40.

Rogers, J. M. (1991) '"The gorgeous East": trade and tribute in the Islamic empires', in Levenson, J. A. (ed.) *Circa 1492: Art in the Age of Exploration*, Washington, DC, National Gallery of Art; New Haven, CT, Yale University Press, pp. 69–74.

Rosand, D. (1982) *Painting in Cinquecento Venice*, New Haven, CT and London, Yale University Press.

Rosand, D. (2001) *Myths of Venice: The Figuration of a State,* Chapel Hill, NC and London, University of North Carolina Press.

Runciman, S. (1969) 'Constantinople-Istanbul', *Revue des études sud-est européens*, vol. 7, pp. 205–8.

Schmidt Arcangeli, C. (2007) '"Orientalist" painting in Venice, 15th–17th centuries', in Carboni, S. (ed.) *Venice and the Islamic World, 828–1797*, New York, The Metropolitan Museum of Art; New Haven, CT and London, Yale University Press, pp. 120–39.

Schoeser, M. (2007) *Silk*, New Haven, CT and London, Yale University Press.

Spallanzani, M. (2010) *Metalli islamici a Firenze nel Rinascimento*, Florence, SPES.

Spinale, S. (2003) *The Portrait Medals of Ottoman Sultan Mehmed II (r.1451–81)*, PhD thesis, Harvard University.

Tafuri, M. (1995 [1985]) *Venice and the Renaissance*, Cambridge, MA and London, MIT Press.

Tait, H. (1999) 'Venice: heir to the glassmakers of Islam or of Byzantium?' in Burnett, C. and Contadini, A. (eds) *Islam and the Italian Renaissance*, London, The Warburg Institute, University of London, pp. 77–97.

Valensi, L. (1990) 'The making of a political paradigm: the Ottoman state and Oriental despotism', in Grafton, A. and Blair, A. (eds) *The Transmission of Culture in Early Modern Europe*, Philadelphia, PA, Pennsylvania State University Press, pp. 173–204.

Vickers, M. (1978) 'Some preparatory drawings for Pisanello's medallion of John VIII Palaeologus', *The Art Bulletin*, vol. 60, no. 3, pp. 417–24.

Watt, M. (2013) 'Length of velvet', in Peck, A. (ed.) *Interwoven Globe: The Worldwide Textile Trade, 1500–1800*, London, Thames & Hudson, pp. 143–4.

Wilson, B. (2003) 'Reflecting on the Turk in late sixteenth-century Venetian portrait books', *Word and Image*, vol. 19, pp. 38–58.

Wilson, B. (2004) 'Reproducing the contours of Venetian identity in sixteenth-century costume books', *Studies in Iconography*, vol. 25, pp. 221–71.

Wilson, B. (2005) *The World in Venice: Print, the City, and Early Modern Identity*, Toronto and London, University of Toronto Press.

Wilson, B. (2007) 'Foggie diverse di vestire de' Turchi: Turkish costume illustration and cultural translation', *Journal of Medieval & Early Modern Studies*, vol. 37, pp. 97–139.

Zrebiec, A. (1995–96) 'Length of Velvet', *Textiles in The Metropolitan Museum of Art: The Metropolitan Museum of Art Bulletin*, vol. 53, no. 3, winter, p. 45.

Conclusion

Leah R. Clark and Kathleen Christian

This book has looked closely at select works of art, architecture and material culture to highlight their entangled and connected nature. The conclusion will reflect on the importance of looking at European art through this lens and tie together themes encountered throughout. The four chapters have considered a diversity of objects across varied geographies: sacred altarpieces in Christian settings; 'hybrid' buildings and objects in Spain that fused Islamic and Christian traditions; the kaleidoscope of objects in the collections of merchants and princes; and finally the metalwork, silk and history paintings of Venice. Many of the objects considered were not stationary, and some travelled great distances. Their journeys across the globe brought knowledge of new materials, techniques and visual forms that was a significant source of inspiration for European artists and craftsmen. These journeys also inspired the imaginary voyages of Renaissance viewers who greatly desired textiles, pigments, works of art and domestic furnishings that referenced distant places. Knowledge about the world in this era was limited and often only mediated through material objects or representations that could both clarify and distort understandings of cultures other than one's own.

The four chapters have underlined how the Renaissance was a time when age-old global networks were expanding, bringing about new consumption habits and technological innovations, and fusing old and new conceptions about the world. Images and objects were a means of cultural communication, exchange and differentiation. This book has been about looking again – looking again at works of art that are well-known, as well as at works of art and material culture that have been neglected. It has challenged the notion that the transformations associated with the Renaissance were part of an internal, European revival, or are symptoms of the West's advance towards modernity and global dominance. It has been about rereading a period that has been understood inside and outside academic scholarship as a paradigm of Western civilisation, yet the examples chosen for discussion have broken down simplistic categories such as 'West' and 'East'.

Places and geographies, and the innumerable variety of concepts they could evoke, have played a central role in understanding objects and works of art, as well as the perceptions of their makers, consumers and viewers. Some particular categories of objects were discussed across chapters to elucidate the theme of trade and travel: for example, ceramics and featherwork have reappeared often in the discussion of different cultural contexts. Examining the production and consumption of these two types of objects has opened up a wide range of questions which are worth reviewing here: what significance did ceramics and featherwork assume in different settings? How were they connected to their places of origin or their destinations of travel? In what ways were their materials and techniques imitated across cultures, or represented in painting and print? How can the concepts of cultural transfer, translation and hybridity be applied to these examples?

Considering the discussion of ceramics across the book, it is clear these were key in transmitting motifs across geographic and religious boundaries and can thus be linked to the notion of cultural transfer or translation. A devotional image by Mantegna discussed in Chapters 1 and 3 depicts Chinese porcelain as a gift from the eldest magus to the Christ child (Chapter 3, Plate 3.4). In this context, porcelain channels the symbolic, aesthetic and religious aspects of the theme of the 'three magi', bound up with imaginary concepts of the East. It also recalls the objects given as gifts by Mamluk sultans to European sovereigns, as it was a key marker of trade and diplomatic partnerships. In Chapter 2, ceramics were explored as hybrid productions that reflect the close interaction between Islamic and Christian cultures in Spain. Both Chapters 2 and 3 discussed the importance of Islamic innovations in ceramic production in terms of lustreware. In this process, glazes and firing techniques gave ceramics a brilliant sheen, a quality closely associated with imports from Asia, which formed part of cultural understandings of magnificence and splendour in Europe. Ceramics were functional as well as symbolic, transferring motifs and materials into new surroundings – from apothecary shops to domestic interiors – where they evoked the allure of the foreign. As ceramic production around the globe became increasingly imitative and cross-cultural, motifs converged and became hybridised. As was underlined by the discussion of Veneto-Saracenic metalwork in Chapters 3 and 4, uncertainty surrounding the provenance of particular objects can be regarded as an indicator of close artistic contact and exchange across the eastern Mediterranean and beyond.

Featherwork was an indigenous Meso-American art form that fascinated and delighted Europeans. It first arrived as a curiosity from discoveries in the Americas, but, unlike the products of Eastern encounters that had been sustained over centuries, featherwork formed part of a visual and material culture which was, from the European perspective, entirely novel. It could

never be duplicated outside of the Americas, and Chapter 3 considered how featherwork was prized and collected in Europe as a unique art form. In accordance with European collecting practices, it operated as a symbol of the wider world (the macrocosm) and the owner's knowledge and even power over that world. In representations of the peoples of the Americas discussed in Chapters 1 and 3, feathers worn on the body were signs of difference and exoticism, becoming a stereotype that conflated the diverse cultures of the Americas. However, as Chapter 2 explored, featherwork also played a role in conversion, when featherwork artists were taught to depict religious subject matter and their dexterity in this craft became a way to gauge their 'humanity'. Featherwork depicting Christian subject matter offers a particularly interesting case study of artistic and cultural hybridity, as well as the ethical, moral and political complexities of hybrid art.

Ceramics and featherwork were mobile, light and easy to transport; they possessed a sense of technical virtuosity, making use of methods or materials that were unknown in Europe. All of these elements made them highly prized, admirable and adaptable: they were thus subject to 'cultural transfer' into European contexts, as religious objects, collectables or decor for domestic settings.

This book has demonstrated that at the beginning of the timespan under consideration, *c.* 1350–1550, Europe was still at the periphery of the most profitable and desirable global trade routes. The New World and the sea routes to Asia were not yet known; the East was still highly mysterious, though had become more accessible during the Pax Mongolica, or by improved trading partnerships with the wealthy Islamic courts in western Asia and North Africa. Still, encounters between Europe and the wider world were largely ad hoc rather than sustained or continuous, and trade or diplomatic networks could frequently shift and change, for example as commercial enterprises such as merchant-banking families established outposts outside Europe. By the middle of the sixteenth century, however, Europe's relationships in the wider world were expansive and transformative – Spain had begun its conquest of a New World and the Habsburgs' rise to power was directly linked to their growing empire and the trade in goods from the Americas. The

Portuguese had established a 'pepper empire' and set up colonies in India and elsewhere. Venice, while not a leader in overseas navigation and colonisation like Portugal or Spain, had learned to master many new technologies by importing global goods and became highly competitive in the production of textiles, glass, ceramics and other commodities; a similar pattern is seen in other centres of manufacturing across Europe.

In addition to global trade, another major theme of this book has been the representation of the Other, manifested in the ways that objects imported from other cultures were collected or represented by artists, or in the depictions of non-Christians and foreign peoples of the world. In the framework of a Renaissance fascination with 'mimesis' – the art of representing and imitating nature – objects of distant origins travelling into Europe were studied, observed and often evoked in paintings and other art forms as symbolic markers. They could have religious connotations, or conjure up imagined notions about the East, as evidenced in altarpieces as well as *scuola* paintings in Venice. Venice's direct and sustained contact with the Ottoman Empire and Mamluk Sultanate resulted in relatively accurate depictions of Mamluk dress, but these representations were framed by artistic fantasy, as well as stories of conversion and Christian triumph. People of the wider world were rarely observed directly by European artists, who rather relied upon stereotypes and cultural perceptions that were often derogatory, with notable exceptions such as the portrait that Mehmed II ordered from Gentile Bellini at the Ottoman court. The Renaissance fascination with the East as a source for luxury goods and knowledge coupled with a general intolerance for the 'infidel' is exemplified in many of the altarpieces discussed in Chapter 1. Here, attention to the dress and accessories of the magi and their attendants, or the exotic animals and luxury gifts they brought with them, evoked a sense of wonder and signalled for viewers themes of conversion and crusade. Modes of representation thus had profound effects on the ways that other cultures were to be imagined, and art should be understood as a vital part of European encounters in this era and their very real consequences: conversion, colonisation and the radical transformation of entire civilisations.

Looking again at Renaissance art has meant a close observation of not only *how* imported novelties and curiosities – from Oriental carpets to giraffes – are represented using European techniques (close observation of nature, modelling of form, classical proportions and perspective), but also why, where, and for what purpose. It has meant a consideration of how and why artists adapted particular motifs, materials or ideas at a time of expanding and accelerating cultural transfer. It has also meant a close examination of the so-called 'decorative arts' and examples of material culture, since travelling objects offer unique insight into global encounters. Looking again also means opening up new lines of inquiry to break down boundaries and 'national' borders and provide innovative models for understanding European art of this period.

Index